THE ASHGATE RESEARCH COMPANION
TO MULTICULTURALISM

ASHGATE
RESEARCH
COMPANION

The *Ashgate Research Companions* are designed to offer scholars and graduate students a comprehensive and authoritative state-of-the-art review of current research in a particular area. The companion's editors bring together a team of respected and experienced experts to write chapters on the key issues in their speciality, providing a comprehensive reference to the field.

The Ashgate Research Companion to Multiculturalism

Edited by

DUNCAN IVISON

University of Sydney, Australia

ASHGATE

Published by
Ashgate Publishing Limited
Wey Court East
Union Road
Farnham
Surrey GU9 7PT
England

Ashgate Publishing Company
Suite 420
101 Cherry Street
Burlington,
VT 05401-4405
USA

www.ashgate.com

British Library Cataloguing in Publication Data
The Ashgate research companion to multiculturalism.
   1. Multiculturalism.
   I. Research companion to multiculturalism II. Ivison,
   Duncan.
   305.8-dc22

Library of Congress Cataloging-in-Publication Data
The Ashgate research companion to multiculturalism / [edited by] Duncan Ivison.
      p. cm.
   Includes bibliographical references and index.
   ISBN 978-0-7546-7136-7 (hardback) 1. Multiculturalism. I. Ivison, Duncan, 1965-
   HM1271.A747 2010
   305.8--dc22
                                                                    2010007123

ISBN 9780754671367 (hbk)
ISBN 9780754689676 (ebk)

Mixed Sources
Product group from well-managed
forests and other controlled sources
www.fsc.org Cert no. SA-COC-1565
© 1996 Forest Stewardship Council

FSC

Printed and bound in Great Britain by
MPG Books Group, UK

Contents

List of Contributors

Barbara Arneil, Department of Political Science, University of British Columbia, Canada.

Thomas M. Besch, Department of Philosophy, University of Sydney, Australia.

James Bohman, Department of Philosophy, Saint Louis University, USA.

Rita Kaur Dhamoon, Department of Political Science, University of the Fraser Valley, Canada.

Avigail Eisenberg, Department of Political Science, University of Victoria, Canada.

Ghassan Hage, Department of Anthropology, University of Melbourne, Australia.

Michael Humphrey, Department of Sociology and Social Policy, University of Sydney, Australia.

Duncan Ivison, Department of Philosophy, University of Sydney, Australia.

Charles Jones, Department of Political Science, University of Western Ontario, Canada.

Geoffrey Brahm Levey, Department of Politics and International Relations, University of New South Wales, Australia.

Fiona MacDonald, Department of Political Studies, University of Manitoba, Canada.

Jocelyn Maclure, Department of Philosophy, Université Laval, Canada.

Monica Mookherjee, School of Politics, International Relations and Philosophy, Keele University, UK.

Paul Patton, Department of Philosophy, University of New South Wales, Australia.

Jeffrey Riegel, School of Languages and Cultures, University of Sydney, Australia.

Nicholas H. Smith, Department of Philosophy, Macquarie University, Australia.

Introduction:
Multiculturalism as a Public Ideal

Duncan Ivison

Introduction

Multiculturalism is an awkward term. Some suggest it merely restates the very problem it is meant to resolve; others that it should be abandoned altogether. But what would it mean to abandon multiculturalism? And not just the phrase or concept, but the attitudes, beliefs and practices associated with it?

However inelegant a word, the concept of multiculturalism now occupies a central place in the public culture of Western liberal democracies and increasingly in global political discourse too. Some of the fundamental ideas associated with multiculturalism underlie a remarkable shift in approaches to minority rights that have occurred over the past 25 years in domestic and international law. Multiculturalism has also become a central topos in modern social and political theory, as well in the contemporary social sciences more generally. There is no question that there has been a fundamental shift in our thinking about the nature of ethnic and cultural diversity.

One thing the 'multicultural turn' in political theory has done is put cultural and ethnic diversity at the centre of contemporary debates. It broke up the explicit (and often implicit) monoculturalism at the heart of many of the dominant ways of conceiving of modern statehood and citizenship. It brought to the fore various occluded aspects of the way nation-building often presumed a cultural uniformity that legitimated harmful modes of assimilation, or was indifferent to the aspirations of minorities. Even more recently, multicultural ideas have spread to debates over the nature of global justice and the search for global norms of human rights and redistributive justice.

This volume seeks to bring together some of the leading and emergent scholars working on multiculturalism from a range of different disciplines and approaches – including philosophy, political science, sociology and anthropology. One general background against which the book is set is the rise of multiculturalism as an increasingly global political ideal, and yet also a sense of unease about many of its consequences. The book is divided into three thematic sections: 'foundations', 'challenges' and 'alternatives'. Each author was asked to provide a distinctive angle and response to the question they were posing, but also to provide enough background so that someone coming to these issues for the first time would be able to situate the argument in a broader context. What I want to do in this chapter is introduce some of the main themes of the book. But I also want to identify some of the key ideas and questions at the heart of multiculturalism understood as distinctively *public* ideal.

Three Logics of Multiculturalism

First of all, what do we mean by multiculturalism? Even here there is argument, as we might expect. But for the general purposes of this book, multiculturalism refers to a broad array of theories, attitudes, beliefs, norms, practices and policies that seek to provide public recognition of and support for accommodation of non-dominant ethnocultural groups. The nature of these non-dominant groups will vary: some may be immigrant minorities (including refugees), others will be 'historically settled' minorities such as national minorities (e.g. the Quebecois) or indigenous peoples. These differences are important, as we shall see. However, what is distinctive about multicultural approaches to social and cultural diversity – and especially *liberal* multiculturalism – is the aim is to go beyond the protection of basic civil and political liberties associated with liberal citizenship to forms of *differentiated citizenship* that allows groups to express their distinct identities and practices (Kymlikca 1995b; 2001; 2007b; and Chapters 2, 3 and 4 of this volume). Some of these measures include the recognition and support of minority languages, exemptions from generally applicable laws and the recognition of 'inherent rights of self-government' (for indigenous peoples). This means debates about multiculturalism inevitably involve deeper claims about not only the vexed question of culture, but also the nature of freedom, equality, democracy and justice.

It is important to acknowledge an immediate problem with this broad conception of multiculturalism. As this book makes clear, the prospects for multiculturalism, as well as what it means (in theory and practice), can vary from place to place. This is particularly true when comparing attitudes towards multiculturalism in many parts of Western and Eastern Europe, in North, Central and South America, in Australasia, and also increasingly in Africa and Asia. Some of this is to do with different facts on the ground (e.g. different patterns of immigration), and some to do with different histories of settlement and forms of nation-building. So context is crucial; although we can pick out certain broad elements that most forms of (liberal) multiculturalism share, there will also always be important differences. In Canada and Australasia, for example, 'multiculturalism' is not generally used to refer to the situation of indigenous peoples and many indigenous groups resist the extension of the concept multiculturalism to cover their claims. This is because there is a prior question about the legitimacy of the state that remains to be addressed for indigenous peoples (Turner 2006; Ivison 2002). Their situation is clearly not akin to recent migrants. Elsewhere, however, such as in Latin America, 'multiculturalism' *is* often used to refer to the claims of indigenous peoples as opposed to immigrant groups.

I want to identify three broad 'logics' of multiculturalism that will serve as a general framework for the discussion in this chapter, as well as in the book as a whole. They don't define any particular doctrine, but rather represent three general modes of understanding the nature of multiculturalism.

The first logic is *protective* or communitarian multiculturalism. Here the basic idea is that the central point of any form of public recognition or accommodation of an ethnocultural group is to preserve the cultural integrity and authenticity of its way of life. This is often accompanied by a reified sense of culture, which is reduced to a discrete set of 'traditional' practices said to be at the heart of the group's identity. Thus in order to protect the individuals you must preserve the group and that means protecting the culture. The right to preserve one's cultural authenticity is assumed then to preclude others from making judgments about the practices involved, including appealing to universal standards of justice or human rights. The legitimacy of the exercise of authority within these groups, along with the consequences of various internal practices for the well-being of its members, are matters for the group to decide and no one else. This links multiculturalism closely to forms of communitarian political thought (e.g. Van Dyke 1982; see also Kymlicka 2001).

The next logic is *liberal* multiculturalism, which has been far and away the most prominent in recent political theory. There are many variations of this form of multiculturalism, which will be explored in the chapters below. However, the basic idea is this: multiculturalism is justified as an approach to accommodating and protecting diversity on the grounds that it promotes liberal values such as equality, autonomy, toleration or equal respect. Thus, although it may well allow a degree of cultural preservation or protectionism, that isn't the central aim or *telos* of this approach. Cultural preservation will be a function of the degree to which it helps promotes liberal ends.

Liberal multiculturalism is also universalist in orientation: the value of autonomy or equality is said to be valuable for everyone, whatever their cultural background. Thus, those practices that undermine a person's autonomy, or basic human rights, are not supposed to be entitled to protection or accommodation. Moreover, liberal multiculturalism aims explicitly at *transforming* current social and political arrangements, and especially the cultural dimensions of these arrangements. It seeks to transform the way dominant majorities have treated minorities within their boundaries, as well as the way minority groups have conceived of their claims. It seeks to transform the identities and practices of both minority and majority groups in line with liberal-democratic norms of anti-discrimination, equality and basic human rights. It aims to do so through the distribution of targeted rights and resources for minorities. This includes ensuring minorities enjoy the fair value of their basic civil and political liberties, but also providing differentiated rights tailored to the specific circumstances of the groups in question. Of course, the liberal multiculturalist accepts that simply imposing liberal democratic practices on certain groups is often unjustified and also impractical. But ultimately, illiberal practices (whether embraced by minorities or majorities) – defined in relation to certain key liberal principles – ought be transformed. More controversially, some cultural practices (those which are more 'liberal') are clearly seen to be better than others. Liberal multiculturalism is superior to any form of monoculturalism (liberal or otherwise) because – so the argument goes – it increases the range of choices and options available to individuals.[1] This means diversity isn't valuable in itself, as it might be for the biologist, but because it is correlative with liberty and is crucial for the development of autonomy.

The third logic of multiculturalism is neither protective nor liberal but what we might call *imperial*. Imperial multiculturalism is essentially a new version of the hierarchical and/or racialized modes of political order that it was supposed to have displaced. As a framing device, it provides a critical lens through which the various relations of power that operate via forms of liberal government can be analysed (Foucault 1991, 2007). Critics of multiculturalism are often concerned with the limits of multicultural toleration and accommodation, and especially the practical consequences of 'really existing liberal multiculturalism'. In particular, they point to the ways in which liberal accommodation is essentially *conditional*: cultures that qualify for rights are assumed to be homogenous and bounded (even as the liberal state is pluralized), and minorities are not expected to challenge the basic legitimacy of the state as well as live up to preconceived notions of what a 'good migrant' or 'indigenous person' is supposed to be like. Liberal legal pluralism, on this reading, is basically a means of re-subordinating marginal groups within a legal system that leaves their substantive disadvantage intact. Liberal pluralism might be subtle and less heavy-handed than earlier forms of colonialism, but liberal multicultural government (understood in the broadest sense of the term) is basically continuous with it (Day 2000; Povinelli 2002; see also Chapters 11, 13 and 14 this volume). Even more broadly, insofar as imperial multiculturalism puts *power* at the heart the analysis, it raises questions about the way in which 'minorities' and 'majorities' are defined and produced in the first place. Who is the 'we' that tolerates 'them' and what are the underlying assumptions about who or what can be accommodated and why? What are the ontological presuppositions of multicultural theory today? (See Chapter 4 this volume.)

Each of these logics picks out a distinctive strand of both the academic and public discourse surrounding multiculturalism. I think we can identify different clusters and interweavings of these strands in various contexts. There can be harder and softer versions of all three. For example, one can find forms of *protective liberal* multiculturalism amongst scholars for whom cultural difference is the crucial variable in identifying and addressing disadvantage. Within this quadrant there are then any number of variations: some modes of protective liberalism license greater

---

1   Liberalism then divide between those who think a diversity of potentially mono-cultural groups satisfied liberal multiculturalism, as long as people have the right to exit, and those who think the value of diversity goes all the way down.

intervention in cultural practices to promote liberal ends; others almost none, save for the right to exit. Some liberals base their arguments on the value of autonomy, others on toleration. An analysis of *imperial liberal* multiculturalism, on the other hand, might focus on the conditions surrounding multicultural citizenship. Or it might question the very ontology of liberal conceptions of 'minorities' and 'majorities' in general.

A crucial question for the study of multiculturalism in the humanities and social sciences is this: what or who is the proper *subject* of multiculturalism – individuals, groups, cultures, peoples? Are we seeking to protect various cultural, linguistic or ethnic groups and their practices just because human beings value them? Or are we seeking to promote a greater diversity of cultures, languages and ethnic groups in order to provide a richer set of choices and experiences for individuals? Both perspectives presuppose that protecting cultures is often valuable, but for different reasons. One could easily believe in the former without embracing the latter. I might grudgingly accept that there are different minority groups that deserve minority rights without thinking the world is a better place because they exist. For example, I might think an extant societal culture in some given place should be accommodated, even if it doesn't have all that much internal diversity and doesn't add much to my choice set either. This is very different from thinking that multiculturalism is valuable because it provides a much richer set of options for individuals to choose and learn from.[2] Taking up one or the other of these perspectives will have important consequences for what you think the possibilities and limits of multiculturalism are.

The Rise of Liberal Multiculturalism

As I mentioned above, liberal multiculturalism has been one of most influential forms of multiculturalism over the last twenty years. The history of the emergence of this cluster of ideas is complex and can't be told in any detail here (see Kymlicka 1989a, 1995b, 2001, 2007b). It's clear that the rise of multiculturalism is connected in various ways to the emergence of the discourse of human rights after World War II, and of a heightened 'rights consciousness' in general. What is striking about the period immediately following the enactment of the *Universal Declaration of Human Rights* in 1948, however, is that minority rights were generally frowned upon as a device for protecting vulnerable individuals and groups. Part of this was driven by straightforward realpolitik, and the desire of powerful nation-states to ensure they wouldn't be threatened by secessionist claims, or be forced to recognize minorities within their own borders. But it also stemmed from a principled argument that suggested that the best way to realize individual freedom and equality was through the protection of *individual* rights, not group rights.

---

2   This paragraph touches on an important debate between Kymlicka (1995b) and Waldron (1995, 2000). See also Goodin (2006).

5

Going back even further, liberalism's approach to diversity has it roots in the seventeenth century and the response to the chaos and strife of the wars of religion in northern Europe (Rawls 1993). In this context, ideas of toleration, the separation of church and state and the idea of the state being 'neutral' between different faiths, emerged as ways of dealing with deep social and political diversity (see Chapter 5 this volume). Allowing individuals the right to freedom of conscience in the private sphere, the right to associate with whom they pleased, all the while remaining subject to the judgment of the magistrate in matters of public concern, seemed to provide a framework for mitigating the consequences of deep disagreement over religion and morality. Note that this meant the justification of religious liberty (and religious toleration) was based, ultimately, on the value it has for *individuals*,[3] and as something that should be extended to all (or at least all Christians, in the first instance) as a matter of mutual respect.

Another aspect of the liberal approach to diversity is a link between the protection of basic civil and political liberties and equality. If everyone is fundamentally equal and owed equal respect, then the best way of realizing equality is to ensure people's basic rights are respected and they are able to live their lives by their own lights (consistent with the rights of others to do likewise). Diversity is best promoted and protected by allowing individuals to exercise their freedom as they see fit, regulated by a liberal theory of justice. Recognizing 'special rights' or 'group rights', according to this line of argument, would either break with equality – properly understood – or be redundant. If immigrants or national minorities have been badly treated then this has more to do with a failure to live up to liberal principles than it is evidence for the introduction of cultural rights (Barry 2001; Scheffler 2007; see the discussion in Chapter 3).

The standard liberal response to religious diversity emphasized the neutrality of the state, equal treatment in terms of non-discrimination and the privatization of religious belief as a matter of individual conscience. Multicultural political thought did not reject these ideas outright so much as subject them to critique and reconstruction from the point of view of very different kinds of groups and claims. Although religious diversity remains an important issue, the scope of diversity has been radically extended. It is not only claims by religious minorities that need to be addressed, but also those by cultural and ethnic groups, racial groups, national groups, linguistic minorities, as well as those based on gender, sexuality and disability. The suggestion that liberal democratic states like the United States or Canada were somehow ethnoculturally neutral was taken to be patently false: The history of the way boundaries were drawn, the way symbols were chosen and used in the public culture, the dominance of English as a national language (at least in the US), among other things, all pointed beyond neutrality (Kymlicka 2007a: 33–34).

One way to see these developments goes like this: If the struggle for equal citizenship throughout the nineteenth and twentieth centuries involved extending the rights of citizenship to encompass a greater number of people, as well as across

---

3   Though it also generates a very important collective good (i.e. social peace).

a broader range of entitlements (civil, political, social and economic), then the demand for multicultural citizenship was simply the next step along this path. It does not entail a break with liberal citizenship, so the argument goes, but rather the logical extension of it in modern conditions of deep diversity.

In considering the range of claims for recognition, it should be immediately clear that what might be appropriate in one case might not be in another. Religion, for example, entails a commitment to various practices, creeds and institutions, whilst gender and sexuality are often experienced and practiced in very different ways. Indigenous peoples consider themselves self-governing and lay claim to territories from which they were forcibly removed, whilst minority migrant groups often seek forms of recognition that enable them to integrate fairly into mainstream society. Although there are attempts to draw analogies between different groups – between the situation of the disabled and certain racial or national groups, for example – the differences are also significant. There is no standard multicultural formula for minority rights that can be applied to each and every situation, regardless of context.

However, the basic claim at the heart of liberal multiculturalism is that certain social and cultural identities deserve to be recognized because, without them, individuals lack what they need for living decent lives. If human beings are also culturally embedded beings then equal respect for individuals means equal respect for the cultural forms they inhabit and help sustain. There are two important moves here that we need to evaluate. The first has to do with the appeal to equality. The second has to do with the relation between individuals and groups.

Equality and Culture

The first move is the suggestion that 'recognition', or the accommodation of cultural, national, religious or ethnic difference, is connected to a rich sense of *equality*. Recall that on the liberal neutralist view, we treat someone equally when we respect and protect their basic rights. Lying behind this idea is an appeal to the relation between equality and treating people similarly. Of course, equality is always a matter of treating like cases alike and that means deciding what are the relevant cases to consider. But on the richer view, influenced by the work of John Rawls (1971, 1993), we treat someone equally when they have the resources to genuinely enjoy the fair value of their basic rights as well as genuine equality of opportunity. In a culturally diverse society, members of both majority and minority groups may well have very different capacities and needs that are relevant to judging whether someone enjoys genuine equality of opportunity. A disabled person, for example, will need to be treated differently than an able-bodied person to receive 'equal respect' in many cases. Both are entitled to equal civic liberties, but a disabled person may require more resources in order to realize the equal value of their freedom. The interesting cases are when this analogy is extended to cultural and national groups. Are there forms of accommodation or protection for minority groups that can be justified on the grounds of promoting equality (whether of persons or of groups?). This cuts to the heart of recent debates in multicultural political theory and is discussed in many of the chapters here.

There is a related question about different kinds of disadvantage an individual or group might suffer from, and therefore what forms of compensation or public policy might be justified in addressing them. Some argue that another problem with the neutralist model is that it leaves many forms of inequality that are the product of certain *structural* features of society unaddressed. Interestingly, the same argument is applied to multicultural models too. Iris Marion Young, for example, has distinguished between two forms of what she calls 'the politics of difference' (Young 1990, 2007). The first involves 'positional difference' and the second 'cultural difference'. Positional difference refers to the way individuals are structured by various kinds of norms, practices and institutions. That is, it refers to the way norms and practices are reproduced in society through, for example, the division of labour or various decision-making processes that systematically disadvantage certain groups by inhibiting the development of their capacities. These structural inequalities persist despite people enjoying the same (formal) civil and political liberties. Recall the example above to do with the disabled. The claim here is that it isn't simply a case of the physically or mentally handicapped lacking certain capacities required to lead fulfilling lives, but rather that there is a problem with the practices and norms of the *rest of society* that prevent them from exercising their capacities to the fullest extent. What constitutes the 'normal range' of valuable human functioning, for example, includes facts about the built environment, social expectations and attitudes, aesthetic standards and so on, that have real consequences for the handicapped to be able to lead decent lives. Similar claims could be made about the persistence of institutional racism and the gendered division of labour. The argument is that even with the extension of basic civil and political liberties to the handicapped (or to racial minorities and women) certain structural features of society prevent genuine equality being realized for these citizens.

To address positional difference, therefore, requires going well beyond 'difference-blind' or neutralist liberalism. But it's also a *structural* difference as opposed to a cultural one and so focusing on cultural difference might well leave structural disadvantage inadequately addressed. Cultural differences present another set of challenges. Here inequality can exist in virtue of the relation between the dominant 'societal culture' and minority cultural groups with their own cultures. These minority cultures become difficult to sustain and if it is mainly as a result of the circumstances members find themselves in, as opposed to the choices they've made, the situation is potentially unfair. The dominant group can limit the opportunities of other groups to realize their ends, whether through explicit domination or repression, but also merely by growing or allowing minority practices to wither away. Of course, cultural change is not in itself something that can or should be prevented; the case for sustaining a minority culture will depend on the connection between its survival and the well-being of its members.

Now these two approaches to the kinds of disadvantage that emerge in modern pluralist societies are clearly not mutually exclusive, despite what some of the literature suggests.[4] Members of a minority cultural group might well suffer from various structural forms of inequality too. Feminist analyses of the situation of women within minority cultural groups, for example, bring this out very clearly, as do analyses of racism (see Chapters 6 and 7). However, it is true that depending on the nature of the disadvantage with which you are concerned, different solutions and approaches may be called for and tensions between these approaches can occur. A move to provide more autonomy for national minorities, for example, will require finding ways of ensuring vulnerable members *within* those groups are treated equally and can exercise their freedom or autonomy in meaningful ways. As we will see, focusing on disadvantage through the lens of structural disadvantage tends to shift discussion towards ideals of democratic citizenship that cut across cultural and national differences (see Chapter 8). Focusing on the accommodation of cultural differences, on the other hand, tends to shift discussion towards forms of autonomy and freedom, especially of groups. Needless to say, any adequate analysis of the challenge of diversity will require a subtle interweaving of the two.

Up until now we have been moving between ideas of what is owed to individuals and groups, as if this relation was relatively unproblematic. Remember that one of the crucial moves we identified above was equal respect for *persons* being extended to equal respect for *cultures* or *groups*. But we need an argument to link these two claims; one does not follow automatically from the other. The tension is neatly demonstrated in the frequent slippage between talking about the 'rights of minority cultures' and the 'rights of cultural minorities'. Are cultures the kind of things that can have rights? Or are we instead concerned mainly with the rights of the individual members of those groups?

From Persons to Groups and Back Again

One of the most influential arguments linking the well-being of individuals with the public recognition of minority groups has been provided by Will Kymlicka. For Kymlicka, access to a secure cultural structure provides a 'context for choice' for individuals (1989a, 1995b). Culture, in other words, or at least what he calls a 'societal culture', helps people realize their autonomy – their freedom. This is a universalist claim about the value of autonomy for persons in general. A societal culture is basically a territorially concentrated culture, centred on a shared language used in a wide range of societal institutions in both public and private life (schools, media, law, economy, government etc.) (Kymlicka 2007a: 34–5). So a societal culture is different from a set of religious beliefs or personal lifestyles; skateboarders may well share a common subculture, but they don't share a societal culture. Societal

---

4   See especially the so-called 'recognition vs redistribution' debate, discussed in Chapters 7, 9 and 10.

cultures are, however, inevitably pluralistic; they may contain different religious faiths, sexual orientations and class differences. But that pluralism is balanced by a certain amount of linguistic and institutional cohesion, often created through deliberate state policies.

Many have criticized Kymlicka for this seemingly overly homogenous and bounded conception of culture, however much he has used it to try and pluralize the singularity of the nation-state (e.g. Carens 2000). However, for our purposes, it's important to see how he thinks access to a societal culture and freedom are connected. Providing some groups with support for the preservation of their societal culture is something that not only extends a privilege larger groups enjoy, but helps promote important liberal goods. What is being protected through self-government rights or language rights isn't the particular *content* of any culture, but rather the *structure* within which people can exercise their freedom and through which they can make sense of the world. This content/structure distinction is supposed to track the idea that what some cultural groups may therefore be entitled to are certain *external* protections that enable them to sustain their cultural structures, as opposed to *internal* restrictions on the rights and liberties of their members. The closer we get to considering the actual cultural structures and practices at issue, however, the harder it gets to keep these distinctions apart. Protecting cultural structures in practice seems inevitably to have consequences for the choice-sets of members of the group. We'll return to this issue below, especially in relation to questions of gender.

Kymlicka's argument is not the only one to link cultural membership with liberal values, and indeed many have criticized it for appealing to a value that might not be as universal as he thinks (i.e. autonomy). There are at least two other ways of linking cultural membership to liberal ends. For Charles Taylor, 'recognition' is a crucial human good, given the way it is linked to forms of personal and collective identity that enable common deliberation about the good in the first place. Because our sense of self is shaped by the recognition (and indeed *mis*recognition) of others, the way the group I identify with is recognized matters too. For Taylor, our identities are fundamentally intersubjective, and this has important consequences for thinking about how we should manage the deep diversity of modern societies (see Chapters 3, 9 and 10). Joseph Raz (1998), on the other hand, appeals to the values of equal concern and dignity: if we take the equal worth of persons seriously then we need to be concerned about the well-being of the cultural groups to which they belong and help sustain.

So the most important forms of group membership are those that provide people with access to valuable human goods. For many people, these forms of identity are not easily shed, but nor are they so constraining as to be necessarily incompatible with a conception of liberal freedom. For Kymlicka and other defenders of liberal multiculturalism, the main task then is to distinguish between ways of accommodating diversity that are compatible with liberal ends and those which are not (as well as thinking of ways of 'liberalizing' currently illiberal practices). And this is a difficult task, as many of the chapters in this book make clear.

For Kymlicka, groups that violate their members' basic liberties, or prevent them from exercising their autonomy, are not entitled to multicultural accommodation or protection (although how we handle these situations in practice is a separate issue). For Raz, similarly, the value of the equal worth and dignity of each individual constrains what cultures can do to their members. In each case, individuals must be free to exercise their right to exit – however difficult that can be – and it must be a genuine right, not merely a formal one. The right to freedom of association is only really valuable if it also includes the freedom *not* to associate.[5]

At this point, for many critics, liberal multiculturalism begins to look less multicultural and more about a particular liberal way of life. As we've seen, for some liberal multiculturalists, this is hardly a contradiction: the whole point of liberal multiculturalism, in their view, is to transform the way states engage with minority groups and the way minorities understand the nature of their practices. But the deeper critique of the liberal neutralist perspective we explored above also points to a deeper critique of liberalism itself. Recall that for Iris Marion Young, the positional or structural disadvantage suffered by some individuals in society was, in part, a product of how they were treated as a group or class.[6] This is another reason why groups matter. But it also implies going beyond not only the liberal paradigm of ensuring non-discrimination and equal rights, but also the almost exclusive focus on the activities of the state. A more thoroughly critical approach to liberal multiculturalism would question this assumption as well, and focus equally on the way that non-state processes and institutions help reinforce and reproduce structural inequalities that cut across cultural and positional differences (Young 2000).

Multiculturalism and its Discontents

Multiculturalism is not only an awkward word; it is a demanding and risky ideal to realize in practice. Adopting a multicultural perspective and implementing multicultural policies has real costs. It asks people to change not only the way they think about the world, but also how they interact with others, and especially the shape and look of their public institutions. It asks states to change the way they engage in nation-building, and it changes the distribution of economic and political power.

There are clearly social, economic and political conditions required for multiculturalism – and especially liberal multiculturalism – to succeed as a public ideal. In many ways, research into exactly what these conditions are and how they can best be promoted is still patchy. Kymlicka lists five crucial conditions that enabled

---

5   A rich literature has grown up around the meaning of the right to exit. For helpful discussions see Okin (1999), Shachar (2001), Gutmann (2003) and Kukathas (2003).

6   This can also generate reactive modes of collective identification, driven in part by the harms people feel they are suffering from. See Brown (1995).

liberal multiculturalism to emerge in the West: (i) increasing rights consciousness; (ii) demographic change; (iii) multiple access points for non-dominant groups to press their claims; (iv) the de-securitization of ethnic relations; and (v) consensus on human rights (Kymlicka 2007b: 122ff.). Where one or more of these elements is missing, we can expect trouble for certain forms of multiculturalism, whether in the West or elsewhere.

In fact, the success or failure of multiculturalism is highly context-sensitive. The presence or absence of crucial variables will shape how multiculturalism develops (or not) in particular ways. The general prospect for multiculturalism in the former Communist countries of Eastern Europe will be very different then in Africa, which will be different again from Asia and Latin America. The variations within these regions will be significant too. The intellectual sources may be different (see Chapters 12 and 15), the 'subject' of multicultural rights may vary, and the power relations and histories will be different.

For example, in some contexts there may be no dominant cultural group, but rather a mix of roughly equal groups in terms of influence or size. This will shape the range of multicultural rights deemed necessary. In some contexts, a minority group may be both economically and politically weak, but in others, a group might be politically marginalized but economically powerful. Once again, this will shape how receptive a society might be towards accommodating minority rights. Granting self-government rights to national minorities might seem politically impossible for various historical and practical reasons. Where there are still deep security fears about the stability of the state or region, and where minority groups within one set of borders are linked to groups in neighbouring states, multicultural accommodation might seem incredibly difficult. These complexities are reflected at the international level too. Although there has been an internationalization of multicultural norms and a global diffusion of various policy models over the past 25 years, they are also running into a 'veritable minefield of conceptual confusions, moral dilemmas, unintended consequences, legal inconsistencies and political manipulation' (Kymlicka 2007b: 8).

At the same time, the public ideal of multiculturalism has come under sustained criticism in the West. After the bombings of the World Trade Center and Pentagon in 2001, and the subsequent bombings in Bali, Madrid and London, along with the wars launched in Iraq and Afghanistan, some commentators have questioned the value of multiculturalism and indeed linked it to the rise of extremism itself. Many critics associate multiculturalism with three worrying claims: (i) that it entails moral relativism or nihilism (Finkielkraut 1988); (ii) that it undermines social cohesion and 'social capital', and especially the trust required for cooperative and productive social relations (Barry 2001; Putnam 2007[7]); and (iii) that it encourages

---

7 Note that Putnam is not a critic of multiculturalism per se. In fact, he thinks something like a liberal approach to cultural and ethnic diversity is necessary, given the unavoidable increase in ethnic diversity. However, he claims that his research on diversity and social capital points to some worrying short- to medium-term trends. For more discussion of his thesis see Chapter 6.

separatism and conservatism that threatens the rights and well-being of the most vulnerable members of minority groups, especially young girls and women (Okin 1999). Perhaps the most extreme version of anti-multiculturalism has been associated with a deep anxiety over Muslim migration in Europe in particular. The title of a recent book epitomizes this kind of reaction: *Surrender: Appeasing Islam, Sacrificing Freedom* (Bawer 2009). The author considers multiculturalism to involve nothing less than the evisceration of Western civilization.

This is nonsense, to be sure, but these kinds of arguments tap into a general unease about multiculturalism that has permeated Western democracies in recent years. Having said that, it's important to identify exactly what is at issue. Although one can find arguments justifying multiculturalism as a means of protecting and promoting cultural or ethnic separatism, or as grounded in a form of cultural relativism, the overwhelming focus of attention has been on justifying and implementing *liberal* multiculturalism. That is, a form of multiculturalism that is an *expression* of liberal democratic values, not a repudiation of them. Liberal multiculturalism, as we've seen, is a concept that is closely tied to the principles of individual freedom and equality. If you turn to any of the major international documents concerning minority rights, or national legislation embedding multiculturalism in law and public policy, what you find are references to the protection of basic human rights, to fundamental equality, or to the promotion of equal citizenship.[8] Of course, that doesn't mean there aren't lively debates about the nature of those values, but the choice is not between nihilism and liberal democracy. That is a false dichotomy. So the first worry about multiculturalism entailing relativism or nihilism is either wildly overstated or simply false.

The second worry is one about multiculturalism undermining social cohesion, and especially support for the kind of redistributive policies associated with liberal democratic welfare states. Once again this requires careful consideration. Part of the answer will be a straightforward empirical matter: it will involve examining the levels of support present in a country for various kinds of welfare programs and correlating this to attitudes towards immigration etc. It will also involve studying the extent of the various redistributive policies of different states and comparing that with the degree to which each has embraced 'strong', 'weak' or no multicultural policies at all. (Preliminary research suggests there is no significant correlation between strong multiculturalism and weak redistributive policies; see Banting and Kymlicka 2006.[9])

---

8   See for example the *UN Declaration on Minority Rights* 8(2); *European Framework Convention on the Rights of National Minorities* Article 21; Canada's Multiculturalism Act (1988). The latter declares in its preamble that just *because* everyone is equal before the law and has the right to protection under the law without discrimination, and because everyone has the right to freedom of conscience, religion, thought, belief, opinion, expression etc., it is adopting an official policy of multiculturalism.

9   However, in some cases (especially Latin America) multiculturalism has been used in tandem with neo-liberal privatization policies. See the chapter by Van Cott in Banting and Kymlicka (2006).

A related concern is more abstract. This is the claim that minority rights, although not inherently unjust, make it more difficult to generate and sustain social cohesion. This forms part of a more general concern about the decline of public spiritedness and engagement in Western liberal democracies today (Putnam 2000, 2007). It also raises larger questions about the nature of democratic stability. This is an important issue. Multicultural citizenship is undoubtedly demanding (Ivison 2008). It requires citizens not only to act in such a way that promotes justice through a fair distribution of resources, and participate in a political process that holds their leaders accountable, it also requires living and working closely with others who have very different worldviews and cultural practices. It asks minority groups to remain committed to a political system in which they will always struggle to match the influence larger groups are able to exert on the broader public culture. However, there isn't any actual evidence that countries which have pursued liberal multiculturalist policies experience greater political instability or alienation among migrant groups than others. In fact, research suggests quite the opposite (see Kymlicka 1998; Adams 2007). Even where there have been serious problems, such as in parts of Europe, this has had more to do with the lack of properly inclusive forms of multicultural integration, as opposed to multiculturalism per se.

As I mentioned, the current anxiety over multiculturalism is actually a very specific kind of worry (or set of worries). The concern is essentially to do with Muslim migration, especially in countries that have experienced large inflows of 'illegal' migrants (e.g. Italy), or where migrants have struggled to integrate (e.g. in the Netherlands, and in parts of the UK). Concerns about Muslim migration are often linked – however clumsily – with fears about international terrorism (see Chapters 11, 13 and 14). This links multiculturalism with domestic and regional security issues. As Kymlicka points out, Canada's (and Australia's) original multiculturalism policy was developed in the context of large inflows of mainly white ethnic groups, whereas the largest group of non-European immigrants in Western Europe has been Muslim (Kymlicka 2007b: 55). This accounts for the close association between 'multiculturalism' and Muslim immigration in public discourse in Europe.[10] There are clearly extremists at work in some Muslim minority communities in Europe and this is a problem that needs to be addressed, but this is hardly the *result* of multiculturalism as many critics in the UK and the Netherlands have suggested. Where policies have been implemented that have enabled extremists to gain a foothold in a community, or unjust practices to go unchallenged, they should be stopped and the consequences carefully considered. Where reasonable and fair integration has failed to occur, more work on identifying the obstacles needs to be done. But any long-term solution will inevitably require developing new ways of accommodating and engaging with diversity, not suppressing it (see Chapters 2 and 13).

---

10   Some of this has spilled over into other parts of the world, including Australia and the US. Muslim migration, however, represents a much smaller proportion of total immigrants in those countries. See the discussion by Hage (Chapter 13).

Anxieties about Muslim migration touch on the second but also the third worry about multiculturalism; that multicultural policies provide cover for illiberal practices within minority cultures. Sometimes these fears are based on misunderstanding and misinformation, as much as anything else (see Bouchard and Taylor 2008 and Chapter 13 this volume). In other cases there are genuine concerns for the rights and interests of the most vulnerable members of minority groups, especially young girls and women.[11] Gender is clearly becoming one of the litmus tests of multicultural toleration, both in the West and elsewhere (see Chapter 7), but it also raises complex issues about gender inequality in general, which cuts across cultural lines. As we have already seen, this challenge requires a more sophisticated approach then simply posing a stark dichotomy between 'culture' and 'reason', or the assumption that women face a choice between 'their culture or their rights' (Shachar 2001; Gatens 2008; cf. Phillips 2007b).

Take, for example, the issue of recognizing supplementary or alternative forms of jurisdiction based in religious and cultural practices. This has proven to be an explosive issue in relation to both indigenous customary law and Islamic sharia. First, there is the issue of whether a liberal state should allow any exemptions at all from generally applicable laws (Barry 2001). Assuming there are plausible grounds for some exemptions, the next question is whether these particular kinds of exemptions are eligible and how they ought to be coordinated with other legal norms and practices. If women, for example, are taken to be severely disadvantaged by customary rules concerning marriage, conflict resolution and property (however true it might be that they assent to the alternative jurisdiction), then how can this be accommodated within a wider system of law based on respect for human rights and the equal treatment of men and women? As I mentioned above, this raises a general issue about gender equity, and it isn't clear liberals have a monopoly of virtue on this front. However, these are still genuine concerns. The most interesting and innovative approaches have attempted to ensure that any accommodation of alternate jurisdictions is coordinated in such a way that individuals' basic rights are respected and that they have genuine options within those frameworks for informed and effective choices (see Shachar 2001; Deveaux 2006; Gatens 2008). The aim is for mutual accommodation – or as Shachar aptly puts it – *transformative* multicultural accommodation (2001). Still, defending and implementing these kinds of ideas has not proven easy, as recent experience in the UK, Canada and Australia has shown (Phillips 2007b; Eisenberg 2007).

Having said all this, the contested nature of multiculturalism – at least within liberal democracies – should not be overstated. Despite many concerns, most liberal democratic states have not abandoned multiculturalism as such. And international norms that recognize and protect minority rights remain in place, as weak and imperfect as those processes often are. There is, however, a need to find new ways of articulating and defending multiculturalism as a distinctly public ideal in light

---

11   The issue of so-called 'honour killings' in the UK in some migrant communities presents a striking example of the complexity of the challenges here; see the discussion in Brandon and Hafez (2008).

of new circumstances and in ways that can be endorsed by the citizens in whose name it is proclaimed. This is difficult when the rhetoric of multiculturalism can be deployed in so many different ways. Subtle distinctions between internal and external protections, protective and integrative models and between autonomy and diversity etc. can get lost in the cacophony of public debate driven by fear, and the short-term agendas of politicians and the media. The challenges of defending pluralism in newly democratizing states and those emerging from civil war or authoritarian rule are even greater.

At the heart of multiculturalism as a public ideal is the notion that we are all members of a range of overlapping (and sometimes conflicting) communities. Our membership in these communities can be liberating but also constraining. These forms of belonging can help define who we are and what ends are worth pursuing and yet also shrink our moral world and thus the scope of moral concern. The challenge is to find political forms that manifest this diversity and yet at the same time keep these different identities and commitments engaged in an expansive and civil conversation. This book is a modest contribution to that task.[12]

---

12 I am grateful to Kyla Reid for her research and editorial assistance.

PART I
FOUNDATIONS

Liberal Multiculturalism

Geoffrey Brahm Levey

Multiculturalism as a public policy began its career in liberal democracies. At its most general, it represented a new way of thinking about cultural difference and the integration of cultural minorities. Until the last third of the twentieth century, the standard liberal responses to cultural diversity had variously emphasized *assimilation*, or the insistence that all citizens integrate by conforming to the dominant culture, and *toleration*, where citizens may live as they please as long as they respect the law and established institutions and do not interfere with the dominant culture. Instead, in places such as Canada, Australia, The Netherlands, and Britain, multiculturalism proclaimed that integration would be better served if it involved some mutual adjustment between minorities and the dominant culture and governing institutions, such that minority members would be better able to participate in the common life of the country and feel they genuinely belong. Many factors contributed to this rethinking, as noted in the Introduction. For our purposes, what is crucial is that multiculturalism not only emerged *in* liberal democracies, it also emerged *from* liberal democracy. That is, for the countries that adopted it, the aim was to better realize liberal values and democratic citizenship (Modood 2007: 7–8).

Much of the debate over multiculturalism, not surprisingly, is a family argument among liberals over what liberalism or liberal values entail. Many liberals who defend multiculturalism nevertheless disagree about how it relates to liberal principles, and what kinds of cultural accommodation follow from them. Some liberals hold that multiculturalism exceeds, if not violates, liberal notions of equality and justice or that it undermines national identity and social cohesion. Another branch of the family – the democrats – tends to think that liberal multiculturalism doesn't go far enough, that it is too narrow and prescriptive, and that what is needed is rather a more open-ended and democratic response to cultural diversity. Such criticism is pushed even further by avowedly *anti-* or *non*-liberal multiculturalists, who contend that genuine multiculturalism requires first according respect to people's culture or identity.

In this chapter, my task is to canvass specifically liberal accounts of multiculturalism. I will also discuss some of the main criticisms of liberal multiculturalism, since these help to differentiate it from other approaches, and allow us to consider what might be said in its defense. And liberal multiculturalism – or, at least, a certain version of it – *is* worth defending, or so I shall argue. First, however, we need a working definition of liberal multiculturalism.

What is Liberal Multiculturalism?

Categorizing political positions is always a tricky exercise. In the case of multiculturalism, positions might be categorized according to their key principles or how they end up treating cases – and especially 'hard cases' – in practice. As we shall see, some arguments that start out from liberal principles seem to abandon them in particular contexts, while some avowedly non-liberal approaches to multiculturalism seem implicitly to appeal to liberal values at crucial junctures. Here, I shall define liberal multiculturalism according to its key assumptions or what it primarily values *in principle*. On this basis, liberal approaches to multiculturalism are those that seek to accommodate cultural difference by placing paramount importance, in some way, on the individual. The rider 'in some way' is important because, as we shall see, there are vying liberal approaches to valuing and protecting the individual. However, it is fair to say that valorizing the fundamental interests and rights of the individual is – or has become – essential to a liberal position in politics.

A good example of liberal multiculturalism at work in this sense is the approach taken on cultural rights in various international protocols and legal instruments, all of which carefully privilege the individual person. For example, the 1948 Universal Declaration of Human Rights states that '[e]veryone, as a member of society' is entitled to 'cultural rights indispensable for his dignity and the free development of his personality' (Article 22). Article 27 of the International Covenant on Civil and Political Rights (1966) asserts the right of 'persons belonging' to 'ethnic, religious, or linguistic minorities' to 'enjoy their own culture, to profess and practice their own religion, or to use their own language'. The Declaration on the Rights of Persons Belonging to National or Ethnic, Religious and Linguistic Minorities (1992) stipulates further that such persons have the right to enjoy their own culture 'in private and in public', and that states 'shall take measures to create favourable conditions to enable' individuals to exercise their cultural rights (Articles 2 and 4). Although not binding, a major United Nations research report, *The Human Development Report 2004: Cultural Liberty in Today's Diverse World*, similarly views cultural liberty as the province of the individual member of cultural groups.

This emphasis on the individual is, of course, deliberate. It expresses a commitment to the liberal idea that the ultimate unit of moral worth is the individual, and it avoids one of the traditional liberal concerns about cultural and group-differentiated rights, namely, that the interests and rights of the individual may be jeopardized in the interests of the group. Nevertheless, legal or quasi-legal protocols such as UN declarations tend to be stipulative and exhortatory rather than explanatory; they assert rights rather than justify them or explain their basis. They also tend to contain contradictory or politically expedient provisions. For example, in the Declaration on the Rights of Persons Belonging to National or Ethnic, Religious and Linguistic Minorities, the right to participate in national or regional decision making as it affects one's own minority applies insofar as it is 'not incompatible with national legislation' (Article 2), which rather begs the question of what is left of the asserted right if it can be so readily overridden. Similarly, the duty of states to create favourable conditions for individuals to enjoy their own cultures applies 'except where specific practices are in violation of national law and contrary to international standards' (Article 4). We are left to wonder what the relevant international standards are, and, even more importantly, what they should be. By what they do and do not say, then, international legal provisions and even national multicultural policy regimes tend to raise rather than answer the fundamental questions about multiculturalism within liberalism. For a clearer sense of the possible answers, we must turn to political theory and the analysis of what liberal principles exactly betoken for the status of cultural minorities and their members in liberal societies.

The Range of Liberal Multiculturalism

Various liberal arguments have been advanced in support of some conception of multiculturalism. Among the more important are those that emphasize, respectively, autonomy, toleration, minimizing harm, and diversity – with a principle of equality sometimes playing a supportive role.

Autonomy

For many liberals, the value of individual autonomy is the foundation of liberal political morality; it underwrites individuals' rights and liberties, marks the limits of liberal toleration, and sets the terms by which a liberal society can also be a multicultural society (Gaus 2005). Autonomy itself has been variously understood, but most advocates (and critics) take it to capture the general idea that individuals have a basic interest in being able to form, revise, and rationally pursue their own plans in life. Liberals traditionally have taken respecting autonomy to mean that religion and ethnicity are private matters to be pursued or not by individuals in voluntary associations without express help or hindrance by government (Rawls 1971, 1993; Dworkin 1978). Judged by these standards, cultural minorities seeking special state accommodation, recognition or support are at odds with liberal notions of justice and common citizenship, and should be ruled out of court. But oddly, so too, then, should many of the special privileges and immunities liberal states have seen fit to grant to cultural minorities, not only in the name of multiculturalism in recent decades, but also long before anyone had heard of multiculturalism.

Just as problematic for the orthodox liberal assumption that cultural identity is a private matter and not the business of the state is the typical privileging of the *majority* culture. A common point of departure for liberal multiculturalists (as, indeed, for many anti-liberals) is the recognition that the ethnocultural neutrality of liberal democracies is a fiction. All liberal democracies, including the standard exemplar of state neutrality, the United States, privilege particular cultural practices and traditions. They insist on a particular language or languages as the lingua franca of state business and societal intercourse, organize their year in terms of a particular calendar, recognize certain public holidays; prescribe what narratives are taught as history; and draw on particular cultural motifs and stories for the official symbols, insignia, flags, and anthems of the state. Some have gone – and do go – much farther than this in mandating particular cultures.

These discrepancies between orthodox liberal theory and liberal practice prompted several theorists, in recent years, to rethink the implications of autonomy as a core liberal value. According to these 'new autonomists', respect for individual autonomy, far from implying that the state should be 'culture-blind', actually entitles cultural minorities and their members to a plethora of cultural rights. Among these entitlements are – depending on the author – political autonomy, minority jurisdiction over land and language, the public subsidization of ethnic festivals and other activities, the symbolic recognition of ethnic and religious groups, exemptions from standing law, and even a right to national self-determination.

One way of connecting cultural rights such as these to the value on autonomy is to view culture as the background context that enables individuals to exercise their autonomous agency. This is the approach taken by the Canadian political philosopher, Will Kymlicka, who came to these issues particularly concerned about the situation of indigenous communities in Canada. In *Liberalism, Community and Culture* (1989a), Kymlicka argued that a secure cultural structure provides the background 'context of choice' which individuals need to exercise their autonomy and affirm their self-respect, and therefore should be considered a distinct liberal good. Where members of cultural minorities are disadvantaged through no fault of their own in relation to this good of cultural membership, they are entitled, he said, to special powers and immunities to redress the inequality. A difficulty with the initial theory was that it seemed to apply to many more cultural minorities besides indigenous communities (Danley 1991: 176).

In *Multicultural Citizenship* (1995b), Kymlicka distinguishes between national minorities, including indigenous groups, which were forcibly incorporated into liberal states, and ethnic or immigrant minorities, which, in general, voluntarily left their societies to join another. Different kinds of cultural disadvantage obtain in these two cases, and so different kinds of cultural rights should apply to each case. The key is that the kind of cultural community that provides a context of choice and which people are entitled to enjoy as a primary good is what Kymlicka (1995b: 76) now called a 'societal culture', one that provides its members with 'meaningful ways of life across the full range of human activities, including social, educational, religious, recreational, and economic life, encompassing both public and private spheres'. Liberal societies and most national minorities are said to constitute societal cultures, and so are entitled to self-government rights (including political autonomy, land and language rights). In contrast, ethnic minorities left their own societal culture to join another, and so are entitled at most to 'polyethnic rights' – measures that offset the disadvantages ethnic minorities might experience in accessing the liberal societal culture they have joined (such as exemptions from standing law and public subsidies). Finally, Kymlicka stressed that on his autonomy-based theory, national and ethnic minorities are only entitled to their respective kinds of cultural accommodation where these aim to 'externally protect' them from the deleterious impact of the decisions of the dominant societal culture. Excluded are measures that would allow them to 'internally restrict' the freedom and choices and thus autonomy of their own members.

Kymlicka's theory of minority rights has considerable appeal from a liberal point of view. For one thing, it treated cultural rights on the familiar model of socio-economic justice. In particular, the theory conformed to the structure of John Rawls's (1971) famous liberal theory of justice, according to which people who are disadvantaged, for morally arbitrary reasons, in realizing primary goods (such as wealth and income) are entitled to state assistance. Kymlicka simply extended Rawls list of 'primary goods' to include cultural membership, and drew attention to how self-respect – which Rawls (1971: 440) called the most important primary good – was tied to one's cultural membership. He suggested that Rawls overlooked the importance of culture because he seemed to operate on the assumption shared by many post-war political theorists that liberal democracies were simplified nation-states, 'where the political community is co-terminous with one and only one cultural community' (Kymlicka 1989a: 177). Kymlicka's theory also resonated because it addressed a common intuition among people that the situation of national and especially indigenous minorities is fundamentally different from that of ethnic and immigrant minorities.

As a practical matter, however, Kymlicka's theory seems specifically attuned to Canadian conditions. There, the challenge has been accommodating the special cultural interests of indigenous groups and French Canadians, as well as the claims of long-established and more recent immigrant minorities. The theory is not so neatly applicable to other immigrant democracies, such as Britain, where multicultural policies have largely sought to respond to migrants from its former colonies, or even Australia, where there is no issue of bilingualism and where multiculturalism mainly has been about the incorporation of immigrants rather than Aborigines. Nor does it easily apply to many Continental European democracies, a large proportion of whose migrants – or de facto migrants in the form of erstwhile guest workers – are Muslim, and whose claims for public recognition tend to be religious in nature (Modood 2007).

Kymlicka's argument for cultural rights also harbours theoretical difficulties. One problem is that by valuing cultures as a background context, one is inclined to protect the cultural context even over the liberal values it is meant to support. This is exactly what happened in *Multicultural Citizenship*, where Kymlicka ends up arguing that the attempt to impose liberal principles on national minorities violates their right to self-government. As many have noted, this makes his liberal theory of national minority rights seem redundant (Levey 1997: 227; Gill 2001: 87; Kukathas 2003: 185). Another problem concerns ethnic minorities. Their access to the liberal societal culture is clearly compromised where individuals are deliberately discriminated against – in seeking employment, housing, and other opportunities – on the basis of their ethnicity. However, a denial of access is harder to sustain in cases where ethnic minority traditions simply conflict with the societal culture, since on Kymlicka's own account, what ethnic minorities have a right to is just that societal culture, and not their original cultures, which they chose to leave.

Perhaps the most fundamental question that Kymlicka's approach to multiculturalism raises is whether cultural inequality can or should be treated on the model of socio-economic inequality.[1] Part of the problem is that liberal multiculturalists themselves accept that the cultural privileging of the dominant culture is both unavoidable and legitimate, so much so that many of them call their position 'liberal nationalism' (Tamir 1993; Miller 1995; Kymlicka 2001: 39–41). The other side of the problem is that, especially in the case of ethnic minorities, it is practically impossible to rectify cultural disadvantages and honour equality even if one wanted to. For example, state support of the dominant culture is often intimately bound up with institutions of symbolic recognition, be it official insignia and letterheads, mottos, flags, anthems, and public holidays. As a practical matter, it would be difficult to include the images, stories, languages, and festivals of all or even most minority groups in the official paraphernalia of multicultural states. In some cases, doing so is plainly unfeasible: there are only so many languages that can be included in a letterhead before the page disappears. India offers a possible model in recognizing the festivals of all the major religions (Hindu, Muslim, Sikh, Christian, Jains, and Buddhist) as official public holidays. As a proportion of the Indian population, the range in size of these faith communities is vast: from 82 percent in the case of Hindus to 0.4 percent in the case of Jains (National Commission for Minorities (India) n. d.). Yet, it is not clear if such an approach is feasible where there is need to recognize considerably more than a handful of communities. Nor is it clear what consolation should be offered to those communities that do not meet the arbitrary numerical threshold for recognition. To include a few is tokenism, while to include some but not all is scarcely the fulfilment of equality, and may actually magnify the felt disadvantage. These problems have led some liberal theorists to propose 'even-handedness' instead of equality as the appropriate yardstick of multicultural fairness, a concept that tends to be much more context- and case-specific (Carens 2000; Bader 2007).

The aforementioned difficulties with Kymlicka's approach all flow from the pivotal assumption that cultural rights depend on cultures or societal cultures being valued as the context for autonomy's exercise. A different autonomy-based argument for cultural rights sees cultural attachments rather as *following* from the exercise of individual autonomy (Tamir 1993; Habermas 1994; Spinner-

---

1   A non-liberal criticism of modeling cultural recognition on liberal egalitarian app-
     roaches to socio-economic disadvantage is that it fails to come to grips with a minority's
     interest in its culture's survival for future generations (Taylor 1992: 40–41).

Halev 2000; Levey 1997, 2001, 2006; Gill 2001; Crowder 2002; Reich 2002; Bader 2007; Phillips 2007b). Where Kymlicka stresses the generally unchosen nature of cultural membership, this school of thought tends not to put much store on whether cultural membership is or is not chosen; that is, even though people do not choose which culture they are born into, and even though this culture may shape one's identity in all sorts of ways, many people do come to affirm, modify, or reject their cultural inheritance. What is important, on this account, is that people have strongly held cultural attachments that they wish to express, however they may have come to hold them. Accordingly, proponents of this approach tend to defend cultural rights as universal entitlements rather than remedial rights that are contingent on conditions of cultural disadvantage.[2]

Another important issue dividing the new autonomists concerns the *scope* of autonomy. So-called 'comprehensive liberals' such as Kymlicka and Joseph Raz (1986, 1994) hold that the conditions of autonomy should apply consistently throughout liberal society, in the private as well as public spheres, such that illiberal and restrictive practices should be disallowed (although Kymlicka, as noted, has expressed reservations about actually coercing illiberal minorities in practice). Other liberals contend that the conditions of autonomy need not be uniformly observed in liberal societies. Respecting individuals as the authors of their own lives, they say, means we should respect their choices even if they are illiberal (Tamir 1995; Spinner-Halev 2000). This way of putting the point is a bit misleading since even these liberals tend to baulk at certain chosen practices, such as clitoridectomy (e.g. Tamir 1996: 21). The point rather is that not every group in society has to duplicate the same range of options in order for people to have an adequate range of options. As Jeff Spinner-Halev (2000: 51) argues in relation to 'closed' religious communities, as long as individuals are aware they have options in their lives, are not coerced by others to live a certain kind of life, and have enough education to survive if they chose to leave their community, then those 'who merely understand they have a choice about their lives meet the standard of autonomy minimally, but that is still meeting the standard'.

What the minimal standards of autonomy may be in contemporary liberal societies remains, however, a contested issue (Reich 2002; Bader 2007; Crowder 2007). The question arises with particular cogency in the area of education. Schools are central to the transmission of values and the reproduction of cultures. They also inculcate the virtues of good citizenship, and equip young people with the skills and talents to survive and, hopefully, flourish in society. Pressing questions thus arise regarding the kind and degree of education young citizens should have. The much-discussed case of *Mozert v. Hawkins* (1987), for example, raised the question of whether a public school should exempt a student from a course that teaches equality and mutual respect. Many liberals argue against exemptions of this kind on the grounds that all young people, including those belonging to cultural minorities, need to be equipped for citizenship and an autonomous life (Gutmann

---

2   A notable exception is Phillips (2007), who seeks to limit cultural recognition to redressing discrimination. I discuss Phillips' position below.

1995; Macedo 1995; Callan 1997). Some defend the exemptions by suggesting that parental choice also realizes the value of autonomy, and that presenting alternate ways of life to young children can actually deny them meaningful choice later in life (Burtt 1994). Yet others defend such exemptions on pragmatic grounds, noting that excluding children whose parents insist on shielding them from these aspects of a liberal education will likely see them entering religious schools, where they will have even less exposure to different perspectives (Spinner-Halev 2000). Cases such as this demonstrate that even where there is agreement on the importance of autonomy as a core value, there is often wide disagreement over how this value is best honoured in practice.

Toleration

The new autonomists, as I have called them, defend cultural rights for minorities on the basis of respecting individual autonomy. Not all liberals, however, are enamoured of autonomy and the post-Enlightenment emphasis on challenging religious authority and the application of reason. Another liberal tradition harks back to the origins of liberal thinking in the changing attitudes to heresy and heretics – chiefly, the acceptance of religious coexistence over persecution – that took hold in the wake of the religious conflicts and Protestant Reformation in the sixteenth century (Zagorin 2003). This tradition emphasizes toleration as a pragmatic way of securing the peaceful coexistence of groups. Where autonomy is said to be a very demanding value that supports at most a 'thin multiculturalism' limited to individual forms of diversity, the classical liberal approach of toleration is said to accommodate a thicker diversity among groups (Tamir 1995; Galston 2002: 21–23).

In recent years, Chandran Kukathas (1997, 2003, 2008) has been perhaps the most systematic defender of the classical liberal approach to diversity.[3] His is a distinctive liberal position in the contemporary debate over multiculturalism: rejecting the idea of cultural rights, but granting great authority to cultural communities to live as they please. In *The Liberal Archipelago,* Kukathas (2003: 4) poses a straightforward question: 'what is the principled basis of a free society marked by cultural diversity and group loyalties?' His answer is that it is one that respects individuals' freedom of conscience to live according to their moral beliefs, upholds their freedom to associate and dissociate, and instantiates toleration as the first virtue of political life, where what is tolerated is dissent or different beliefs or social norms. A free society built on such principles is one in which political society has no special or overriding authority and unifying role. Rather, this free society would amount to an 'association of associations' – an 'archipelago of competing and overlapping jurisdictions . . . operating in a sea of mutual toleration', much like international society (Kukathas 2003: 4, 22).

---

3 See also Gray (2000). For two very different defenses of toleration and freedom of conscience in the context of cultural-cum-religious pluralism, see Williams (2005) and Swaine (2006).

The Liberal Archipelago self-consciously cuts against the grain of most contemporary liberal theory. Instead of the standard concern with establishing what values, if any, state authority should pursue, Kukathas asks: who should have authority in the first place? Instead of the idea, revived by John Rawls, that justice is the primary concern of politics, Kukathas assigns this status to toleration. Instead of the deep assumption that the good or free society requires social unity and a closed or bounded society (such as a nation-state), Kukathas avers that such boundedness scarcely describes actual societies and, in any case, assigns political society a privileged authority it does not deserve. And instead of the assumption – shared by many 'liberal neutralists' and liberal nationalists alike – that liberal principles and institutions depend for their justification on respect for individual autonomy, Kukathas places centre stage the unqualified importance of freedom of conscience. So, for example, while the right to exit associations is crucial, there is no need for individuals to be informed that they have such a right.

To contemporary liberals accustomed to a regime of individual rights and at least the semblance of an informed citizenry, the liberal archipelago is likely to be suggestive of the illiberal gulag. Much critical attention, for example, has focused on the specified exit rights and whether they are meaningful given group pressures and the possible lack of information and education among group members (e.g. Barry 2001; Okin 2002; Spinner-Halev 2005; Phillips 2007b). Kukathas forthrightly acknowledges the latitude that his conception of liberalism grants to illiberal practices by and within communities, but he insists that this 'tyranny in a sea of indifference' is preferable to a liberal state that authoritatively seeks to impose a moral code on its citizens and constituent groups. Moreover, pointing to the murder of the Jews by the Nazis and the one-time policy of Australian governments to take Aboriginal children away from their families, he argues that 'the threat of oppression is as likely to come from outside the minority community as it is from within' (Kukathas 2003: 135–37). This is a curious argument, not least because the cited examples of state oppression represent rather vivid *violations* of respect for the autonomy and rights of individuals. The answer to these kinds of abuses would seem to be more respect for autonomy, not less. There is also the question of how, in the absence of social unity, overarching political authority, and shared institutions and values, and in the likely presence of myriad group tyrannies, the liberal archipelago transmits and reproduces the value on toleration.

Nevertheless, there is no question that Kukathas has identified in toleration an important dimension of the 'liberal inheritance'. Checking the politics of unity and suppression by allowing the possibility to dissent is a vital part of the history of liberal ideas and practice. In the end, Kukathas (2008) himself identifies the main problem with 'pure toleration' when he suggests that it is what multiculturalism looks like when pursued to its logical extension. As he recognizes, liberal societies today pursue and balance a range of values that check any such logic of purity.[4] This also is why the oft-heard criticism today that liberal multicultural policies promote cultural relativism is little more than polemical. The value set and social pressures

---

4   For a more detailed discussion of the limits of toleration see Chapter 5 in this volume.

in contemporary democracies are such that cultural relativism is implausible in practice. Or as Kukathas (2003: 269) puts it, the liberal archipelago is to 'imagin[e] a world that can never be'.

Minimizing Harm

In complete contrast to pure toleration is a liberal approach to multiculturalism that emphasizes the minimization of harm. Following Judith Shklar's (1989) 'liberalism of fear' and the 'negative' political concerns of Montesquieu, this approach to multicultural accommodation is alert to the often contradictory dangers of both recognizing and failing to recognize cultural identity in politics. This 'multiculturalism of fear', as Jacob Levy (2000) calls his approach, neither valorizes cultural communities and identity per se (as do many contemporary multiculturalists), nor dismisses their relevance for liberal principles and policy (as do many traditional liberals). Rather, what is crucial, on this account, is the mitigation of cruelty, conflict and humiliation, whether waged by a state upon an ethnic community, between ethnic communities, or by an ethnic community upon its own members. The 'multiculturalism of fear' is a pragmatic approach concerned with the worst abuses or the most prudent course, always grounded in contingency.

Levy applies this approach to a range of cases, including land rights, customary law, and symbolic recognition. For example, he argues that '[s]tate symbols that celebrate a history of violence and cruelty against a particular group – say, the Confederate battle flag – are legitimately taken to be humiliating', and should be disallowed (Levy 2000: 234). Or to take a case that needn't involve humiliation: whereas some might argue that children in public schools have some kind of moral right to wear religious garments, Levy (2000: 61) suggests that allowing such practices might still be warranted on prudential grounds alone: better to have them participate in public schools and a liberal education, than effectively banish them to private religious schools where they will only be further shielded from liberal ideas. Nevertheless, the 'multiculturalism of fear' is often a difficult notion to pin down. Sometimes it seems to be parasitic on more fundamental moral principles; for example, arranged marriages are considered illegitimate where they do not garner the consent – and thus seemingly the autonomy – of the two parties to the marriage (Levy 2000: 59). Otherwise, as Levy notes, what constitutes humiliation is itself highly debatable. For some groups, non-recognition or misrecognition by the state constitutes the most terrible slur, even where there was no wish to offend, and even where no rights or resources have been denied them. Indeed, as he openly acknowledges, a multiculturalism of fear is likely to encourage moral blackmail – 'We will cause havoc unless our group demands are met' – and claims of victimization. Such difficulties may be no more challenging than the ambiguous meaning of core values and the clamour for cultural rights faced by other liberal defences of multiculturalism. Levy's own sensible response is that claims must always be substantiated and gratuitous claims must be resisted.

The multiculturalism of fear's strong suit is that there is, of course, much to be said for mitigating cruelty, conflict, and humiliation. But this still leaves unanswered the question of the appropriate response to the many cultural claims that do not seriously involve any of these things. Like the liberalism of fear on which it is based, the 'multiculturalism of fear' does not so much supplant other moral defences of multiculturalism than operate at a different and, perhaps, more urgent level.

Diversity

A fourth liberal justification for multiculturalism – rounding out our survey of the range of liberal multiculturalism – stresses the value of diversity. Often diversity is promoted in order to serve some other value or interest, such as economic prosperity for all (OMA 1989), the lifestyle benefits to members of the dominant culture that come with exotic restaurants and cuisine (Goodin 2006), or, as we saw earlier, the importance of having an adequate range of options for living autonomously. But diversity also has been defended as a value in its own right.

William Galston (2002: 23), for example, has argued that '[p]roperly understood, liberalism is about the protection of legitimate diversity'. A state that backs individual autonomy undermines diversity, he says, because, while it may allow a multitude of variations of personal choice, it squeezes out communities and social practices that respect something other than personal choice. While the autonomous life is a legitimate mode of existence, it is, he argues, only one mode among others in a liberal state committed to diversity, and it should not define liberal principles.

Accordingly, the challenge is to show how an account of liberal democracy that respects group diversity may preserve the imperative of 'liberal social unity'. While Galston subscribes to the view that the internal life of cultural minorities need not conform to the values of the broader liberal society, he thinks that the 'liberal pluralist state has a legitimate and compelling interest in ensuring that the convictions, competencies, and virtues required for liberal citizenship are widely shared' (Galston 2002: 23, 127). Galston's citizen virtues include the capacities to discern and respect the rights of others, to discern the talent and character of candidates vying for office, to engage in public discourse, and to narrow the gap between principles and practices in liberal society (Galston 1991: 224–7). These are not inconsiderable intellectual and moral capacities and, indeed, some liberals cite exactly these kinds of responsibilities to show how liberal citizenship presupposes the critical capacities of autonomy (e.g. Gutmann 1987: 50–2, 282–91). Galston also cites three 'intrinsic virtues' that are legitimately promoted by a liberal polity, including Lockean rational self-direction; the Kantian capacity to act in accordance with duty over the sway of passion and interest; and Millian individuality (Galston 1991: 229–31). Just how different Galston's diversity-based liberalism is from autonomy-based liberalism is thus not altogether clear.

Key Challenges and Responses

Liberal multiculturalism has been criticized both from within and outside of liberalism. In a spirited defence of liberal neutrality, Brian Barry (2001) condemns multiculturalism on both practical and principled grounds. As a matter of practice, multiculturalism is alleged to make for bad politics, since politicizing cultural identity has the effect of heightening intergroup conflict and undermining political community as it encourages groups or their elites to make sectional demands on political authority. Multiculturalist arguments also reify the cultural aspects of people's identities and mistakenly view culture as an encompassing value. Finally, the concern with cultural recognition and rights perniciously diverts attention away from genuine cases of social injustice concerning welfare needs and inequalities of opportunity. In this, says Barry, multiculturalists often end up hurting the people most in need of assistance.

Multiculturalism obviously highlights cultural membership and attachments. However, it does not follow that politically ignoring these cultural realities makes them any less pressing or potent. Allowing institutional or societal discriminations to persist and disadvantage minorities can also incite political conflict. As Tariq Modood (2007: 39–40) observes, multiculturalism is largely about groups reacting to negative or limiting or oppressive categorizations emanating in the wider society and seeking to transform them into positive forms of appreciation and recognition. It is not clear why such agitation should be viewed as 'sectional' rather than as demanding the same sorts of liberties and opportunities as other citizens. But even where specific cultural claims may be sectional – funding for a community centre, say – it is hard to see why cultural minorities should be debarred from pursuing their particular interests when interest group politics is the stuff of contemporary liberal democratic politics. It is true that some arguments for multiculturalism reify the cultural aspects of people's identities and view cultures as encompassing; however, many do not, as we saw with those who defend cultural rights as the expression of liberal autonomy. And the suggestion that multiculturalism diverts attention and resources away from welfare needs now has been systematically studied cross-nationally and found not to be so (Banting and Kymlicka 2006).

Barry also argues that liberal multiculturalists misunderstand liberal principles such as equality. In insisting on state neutrality and common citizenship rights, liberalism does not pretend to be equally neutral toward all group traditions; rather, the point is to deny those groups that want to enlist state authority to impose their values on others. From an egalitarian perspective, cultural groups are not entitled to special treatment because 'all groups are free to deploy their energies and resources in pursuit of culturally derived objectives on the same terms' (Barry 2001: 318). However, as noted earlier, multiculturalists – liberal and non-liberal alike – notice how state institutions already embody and impose cultural values, and thus that not all groups *are* free to pursue their cultural objectives on the same terms. While Barry is right that every state needs a lingua franca and so privileging one or two languages can't be helped, language is not the only way majority cultures are typically privileged. Laws and regulations governing dress, food consumption, how we treat our bodies, and even the rhythms of our days and weeks are strongly inflected by norms that suit the majority culture. To be sure, as I suggested above regarding symbolic recognition, such cultural privileging does not necessarily constitute an injustice in every instance. Nevertheless, the proposition that all groups are free to pursue their cultural objectives on the same terms remains ill founded. And in many cases – such as public subsidization of ethnic festivals or exemptions from dress codes – the cultural objectives in question do not involve the state imposing minority cultural values on anybody.

Another liberal concern over multiculturalism is that the accommodation of many minority practices jeopardizes the interests of the most vulnerable members of the minority, typically women and children. This obviously applies to a position like Kukathas's cultural toleration (cf. Kukathas 2001), but the criticism is also pressed against Kymlicka's autonomy-based arguments for multiculturalism. As Susan Moller Okin observed, whereas the 'special rights that women claim qua women do not give more powerful women the right to control less powerful women ... cultural group rights do often (in not-so-obvious ways) reinforce existing hierarchies'. What is needed, she suggested, 'is a form of multiculturalism that gives the issues of gender and other intra group inequalities their due – that is to say, a multiculturalism that effectively treats all persons as each other's moral equals' (Okin 1999: 131). In fact, there are versions of multiculturalism that do seek to protect women's rights as a condition of cultural accommodation.

In arguing for a 'multiculturalism without culture' that respects individual autonomy, Anne Phillips (2007b), for example, suggests treating culture much as gender and class are treated, that is, its relevance to people should be acknowledged without assuming it to be a determinant of their action or identity. In practice, this means that courts and governments should adopt nuanced and more targeted responses to minority cultural practices instead of blanket judgments and bans. So, for example, governments should intervene only where they have evidence that Muslim girls are being coerced into wearing their headscarves, and otherwise not violate girls' right to dress as they please, even if socialization lies behind their choices. Phillips also suggests securing multicultural equality through our established legal framework of indirect discrimination, where there is no need to make any assumptions about identity or the impossibility of acting otherwise given one's gender, class or cultural background. One only has to 'demonstrate that it is harder – though not impossible – for people of one cultural group to meet [a particular] requirement' (Phillips 2007b: 113). Recognizing cultural claims on the model of indirect discrimination rights does, however, have a notable limitation: as the French ban on the wearing of conspicuous religious signs in state schools shows, one way of avoiding indirect discrimination and differential adverse impact is to restrict the liberty of *all* relevant groups. This suggests that equality concerns based on indirect discrimination need to be supplemented with an independent right to cultural liberty.

Phillips is leery of according powers and resources to cultural groups. While funding for ethnocultural associations and efforts to increase the political representation of minority group members are fine, granting 'regulatory authority' to cultural groups and recognizing customary or religious law are not, since this immediately subordinates the interests of some group members, women not least among them, to those who hold authority in the group (Phillips 2007b: 169). However, there are ways of granting of regulatory authority to cultural groups that need not compromise women's rights and interests. Ayelet Shachar (2001), for example, defends a 'joint governance' approach in which the legal authority over different jurisdictional areas, such as family law, is divided between the state and cultural groups. So, for example, in family law, the cultural group might be granted authority over 'demarcation' issues of who is recognized as a member, while the state retains authority over distributive matters such as property rights. Members of cultural minorities are then granted clearly delineated choice options regarding which authority will govern them on the particular jurisdictional area. Such choice is crucial because the prospect of group members opting for state authority ensures that minority group authorities will check their worst impulses out of fear of losing their members. Whatever the specific merits or deficiencies of Phillips' and Shachar's approaches, the point is that there are models of cultural accommodation available, in theory and in practice, that take women's vulnerability within cultural minorities very seriously indeed (Deveaux 2006; Arneil et al. 2007; Chapter 7 this volume).

Liberal multiculturalism is also criticized from the opposite direction – for being too *limited* by its commitments to individual autonomy and choice. In an influential essay much cited in these critiques, Charles Taylor (1992), distinguishes between 'equal dignity' or the kind of equality that addresses the common humanity or common citizenship status of individuals, and 'equal respect' that addresses the particular group identities and collective interests individuals may have. Failing to recognize or misrecognizing an individual's group-based difference can be, on this view, deeply damaging to their sense of self and a form of oppression (Young 1990; Margalit and Halbertal 1994; Honneth 2002; Galeotti 2002; Modood 2007). Taylor (1992) framed his argument for equal respect in relation to 'distinct societies' and bounded cultures – Quebec being his paradigm case – where the interest is a culture's survival. Yet, what is often overlooked is that Taylor understood 'equal respect' still to be an iteration of liberalism; even in its most 'hospitable' (to difference) version, it insisted on some fundamental individual rights.

Many putatively non-liberal defences of multiculturalism similarly pay homage to liberal values at some level. This, of course, is not surprising given that these arguments are typically intended to comport with existing liberal societies. What is surprising is how these accounts often overlook their own liberal commitments. Stressing the importance of 'culture' to human well-being, Bhikhu Parekh (2000: 265), for example, dismisses universalistic moral principles such as personal autonomy as either too vague or too contentious to be politically and morally feasible as guiding principles of liberal toleration. What is required, he argues, is instead an open-minded 'intercultural dialogue' governed by a society's 'operative public values', as found in a society's constitution, laws and civic relations (Parekh 2000: 267–8). The catch is that the operative values of contemporary liberal societies tend to include personal autonomy, uncoerced choice, and capacity for independent and critical thinking. Though these may now be considered local or contextual instead of universal values, how different is their impact? Many of the considerations Parekh (2000: 73–92) brings to bear in deciding whether minority practices such as arranged marriages, clitoridectomy, and polygamy should be tolerated revolve around whether the individual is freely choosing the practice or subject to too much social pressure, and whether the practice is harmful to them or limits their future capacities. To be sure, Parekh strives also to take into account the minority's viewpoint and values, which is to be commended. But liberal values are hardly being sidelined in this exercise. Similarly, although Tariq Modood (2007) stresses the importance of equality in relation to groups, and says little about the place of individual rights in a defensible multiculturalism, he clearly accepts such rights as limiting conditions. He would outlaw practices that 'would be unacceptable to just about everybody' (child sacrifice, sati, cannibalism) or even 'for many' (clitoridectomy), because '[r]ecognition should not infringe the fundamental rights of individuals or cause harm to others' (Modood 2007: 67).

This is not to suggest that there are no meaningful differences between these putatively non-liberal and liberal arguments for multiculturalism. They clearly do have different points of departure and emphases. However, as above, the difference between the respective approaches regarding where they end up on actual cases and the degree of latitude they allow is often far less dramatic than their theoretical points of departure might suggest. Perhaps the most significant practical difference is that these versions of non-liberal multiculturalism tend to grant much greater authority to groups or their elites than do avowedly liberal multiculturalists, who tend to be much more concerned about the welfare and common citizenship rights of the individual members of cultural minorities. Still, as we have seen with Kukathas's theory of cultural toleration and Shachar's theory of joint governance, some liberal defences of multiculturalism do grant considerable authority to cultural minorities.

Another claimed point of difference of these non-liberal approaches to multiculturalism – their openness to dialogue and contestation of the issues among all the parties concerned, minorities as well as majorities – is scarcely incompatible with liberal multiculturalism. It is true that liberal approaches to multiculturalism have tended to stipulate what this or that liberal principle allows by way of cultural accommodation, as illustrated by Kymlicka's autonomy-based theory, which prescribes certain cultural rights for certain kinds of cultural groups in advance. However, as we saw with the case of autonomy in education, the meaning of liberal values like autonomy, how they might apply in particular cases, and even their relative importance in the scale of values, all require interpretation and argument, and thus there is considerable latitude for vigorous contestation and dialogue by the parties concerned on any given issue. Indeed, Parekh's own proposal of intercultural dialogue seems less a rejection of liberal values than a model procedure for bringing non-liberal minorities to appreciate public values like autonomy, and the wider liberal society to rethink what its public values, including autonomy, might mean in any given case or conflict. Ultimately, the real dispute is less over the appropriateness of dialogue and contestation than who should engage in it – group elites vs. the rank and file; which institutions should conduct it; and what rules should apply in the case of continued deadlock (Bohman 2000; Deveaux 2000a; Benhabib 2002; Weinstock 2006; Bader 2007; Ivison 2008).

There is, however, a more radical critique of liberal multiculturalism. This is the criticism that liberal multiculturalism fails to come to grips with its own colonialist origins and imperialist ambitions. The criticism tends to be made at two levels. One is specifically in relation to indigenous peoples (Patton 1995; Tomasi 1995; Tully 1995; Povinelli 1998, 2002; Ivison, Patton and Saunders 2000), where the claim is that liberal multiculturalism is incapable of doing them and their situation justice. At this level, the point is difficult to refute. Kukathas's liberal archipelago aside, and notwithstanding Kymlicka's valiant efforts, most of what passes for liberal multiculturalism *is* ill equipped to respond to the claims and the specific circumstances of indigenous peoples. It is no accident that the Quebecois, and many indigenous leaders in Canada and in Australia, have resisted their inclusion in the multicultural policies of their respective countries, believing that this ignores their distinctive historical experience and special status and claims. In fact, Australian multicultural policy, to its credit, itself recognizes that the 'distinct needs and rights' of Aboriginal and Torres Strait Islander peoples should 'be reaffirmed and accorded separate consideration' (OMA 1989: 5) – although, unfortunately, this commitment has not been matched by efficacious policy to date.

For the most part, liberal multiculturalism in practice has been a political response to *post-immigrant* or, as in the situation of guest workers in Germany and other places, de facto immigrant minorities and their integration into their new societies. Though the rubric of 'multiculturalism' is often deployed to cover indigenous and national communities that predate the establishment of the governing liberal constitutions, these cases need to be considered on their own terms. Original title, prior self-government, standing treaties, and historical wrongs all variously figure in the special historical experience of indigenous groups. Of course, the post-colonial critique means to challenge liberalism as much as multiculturalism, and it is a large and involved question whether liberalism has the resources to respond adequately to the special situation of indigenous peoples (Tully 1995; Ivison 2002; Gatens 2008; Shaw 2008). Certainly, liberal governments have struggled to do so.

The radical critique of liberal multiculturalism is also made more generally. Here, the contention is that liberal multiculturalism is not serious about accommodating diversity at all, even in relation to immigrant minorities; rather, it is open only to those who share or are willing to abide its own presumptions and values. Indeed, calling it 'multiculturalism' is a kind of fraud, since its main purpose and modality is to preserve Western or 'white' dominance (e.g. Hage 1998; Hesse 2000). The radical critique – which is outlined more fully elsewhere in this book – identifies some genuine limitations in the theory and practice of liberal multiculturalism. However, it tends to run together three points that need to be disentangled.

First, there is no question that liberal multiculturalists often have fallen into the trap of reifying cultures and even liberal principles, simply presuming the unacceptability of certain minority practices in advance of their examination or explanation. However, it is important to recognize that liberal multiculturalism need not valorize or even worry much about defining culture, since it may be directed towards responding to the choices or identity of individuals, as they, themselves, define these things. Similarly, while liberal values *are* often wielded like blunt instruments, the fact that their meaning, order of priority, and application to particular cases require interpretation and argument means that dialogue and debate among and between liberals and minority members are actually needed, and should be encouraged. A good example of how certain interpretations of liberal principles can ossify unhelpfully, and yet be challenged on their own terms, is the popular understanding of church–state separation as meaning the absence of all religion in the public sphere. Such a view is often invoked today, for example, by those claiming that Islam and Muslims are ill-suited to life in liberal democracies. Yes, it is not difficult to show that church–state separation in the West originated as an attempt publicly to *accommodate* contending faiths, and was not about banishing them to a private sphere (Hunter 2008). Nor is it difficult to show that most liberal democracies today continue to *practice* church–state separation in much the same accommodationist spirit, notwithstanding the rhetoric of 'privatization' (Levey 2008, Modood 2008).

Second, there is undoubtedly a tendency among members of the dominant culture to identify liberal democratic values with their own cultural norms. Core liberal values of autonomy, equality, and justice are inflected with the sentiment: 'This is how we do things here'. Thus, various forms of modest headwear worn by some Muslim girls and women such as the *hijab*, *niqab*, and *burka* often raise hackles in Western democracies simply because they are seen as 'a visible statement of separation and of difference', as former British Foreign Secretary Jack Straw put it (BBC News 2006). Of course, that this prejudice occurs is hardly surprising given the subliminal force of culture. But this is precisely why the commitment to liberal values ought to be affirmed rather than spurned, since they offer a powerful check on the inevitable cultural biases of a dominant majority. Liberty and equality, after all, can't just be about 'taking it off' or stripping down; these values also entitle people to 'put it on' or cover up where there is no coercion or harm involved.

Third, and finally, some radical multiculturalists also want to challenge the reigning authority of liberal principles themselves. Why, they ask, should the autonomy and equality of individuals be privileged as the governing values? Why should the individual be valued over the group or its traditions? Is not universalizing its own values the ultimate Western conceit? Needless to say, radical critics aren't much impressed here by sophisticated contemporary theories of liberal neutrality, which seek, for example, to distinguish between 'neutrality of aim' (claimed), on the one hand, and 'neutrality of procedure' and 'neutrality of effect' (denied), on the other (Rawls 1993: 193). Nor should they be. Were liberalism to be all-accommodating it would stand for nothing, and not be worth defending. Whatever their universal pretensions, clearly liberal democratic values and institutions are not culturally neutral and might well be thought of as a kind of culture in its own right, albeit it with local and contextual variations, as is typical of cultures. In this respect, 'liberal democratic culture' is squeezed from both sides of the radical critique. Part of the post-colonial complaint is that indigenous lands and peoples were colonized and made unjustly subject to Western norms and institutions. Yet, for some radical critics, established Western societies are expected to forsake *their* core values when faced with newcomers who wish to observe illiberal traditions. In the final analysis, no amount of argument can resolve clashes between fundamental values. Yet, it is perhaps worth noting that the radical critics of liberalism tend themselves to live – and to want to remain – in liberal democracies. Compared with political arrangements that may allow 'deep diversity' and equality of cultures but little liberty and equality of their individual members, or with regimes that impose a comprehensive religious or cultural way of life, the limits prescribed by liberal values seem, to a great swathe of humanity, rather capacious and appealing. Liberal multiculturalism, broadly conceived, seeks to make them even more so.

Conclusion

Opposition to multiculturalism has been steadily gathering force among scholars, policy-makers, governments, and mass publics over the past decade or so (Barry 2001; Brubaker 2001; Entzinger 2003; Joppke 2004). It has, however, become especially strident since the 2001 World Trade Center attacks and the rise internationally of militant Islam, coupled with the increasing presence, through immigration, of Muslims in Western democracies. Suddenly, with Islam and Muslims, the boundaries of the acceptable are deemed to have been stretched too far. The fear and negative stereotypes provoked by the violent actions of a small minority of (militant) Muslims partly explain this sentiment. So does simple prejudice towards the new and unfamiliar, and a (mis)perception that the publicness of Islam and Muslim is *fundamentally* at odds with the liberal settlement of the (privatized) place of religion, as discussed above. But the current reaction against multiculturalism also has been inflamed by some real – though not necessarily intractable – clashes between Islamic precepts or Muslim sensibilities and liberal democratic norms, especially regarding matters of free speech and gender relations (Parekh 2006).

Yet, what is curious, on its face, is why moderate, liberal multicultural policies should be thought to be implicated in these affairs and unfaithful to liberal democratic norms. Doubtless a certain climate of license, as against liberty, does seem to have been allowed to take hold in places like Britain and the Netherlands out of mistaken sensitivity to being labelled a bigot, and so on. The obvious answer to such lapses and laxity, however, is *tightening* adherence to liberal multicultural limits, not letting go of them. The deeper explanation, I think, has to do with the word 'multiculturalism' rather than with specific multicultural programs and measures. The concern seems to be that talk of 'multiculturalism' has sent the wrong signals to individuals and groups, that it has encouraged 'separatism' and the idea that 'anything goes', and thus undermined national cohesion. The hope is that the language of 'citizenship' and 'integration' and a renewed emphasis on 'core liberal democratic values' will arrest these perceived trends.

To be sure, the term multiculturalism has always harboured an ambiguity. On the one hand, the 'ism' was simply meant to designate a broad commitment to the idea of cultural recognition, accommodation, and state support. On the other hand, the 'culturalism' in the word could be read – and often has been read – as signifying distinct and homogeneous cultures to which all else should defer. This is why the term 'interculturalism', which is more common in continental Europe than in the Anglophone democracies, and preferred in a place like Quebec, is not much help. The perceived trouble with multiculturalism is not – or not only – that communities do not adequately interact with each other; it is that they exist and interact as if they were monolithic, self-absorbed, and independent units. Having different cultural fiefdoms interrelate with each other as suggested by 'interculturalism' repeats rather than solves the problem.

The term 'multiculturalism' will continue, then, to grate on publics and governments. And it may well be that 'integration' and 'citizenship' better suit the times as overarching rubrics. But none of this semantic or semiotic concern should be allowed to obscure the fact that liberal multiculturalism, in general, and autonomy-based versions of it, in particular, are and always have been about integration. The question is not whether citizens of diverse backgrounds should integrate into the general society, but rather what are the fair and prudent terms on which they should do so? (Kymlicka 2001: 36). National chauvinism and exclusivity can spawn minority separatism no less than unbridled multiculturalism.

The political reality is that demanding cultural accommodation in the name of cultural authenticity or cultural relativism or preserving cultural integrity is unlikely to get far anymore in democracies today, if it ever did. In contrast, respecting core liberal democratic values itself gives rise to multiculturalism. Liberty must include some cultural liberty, equality must include people of diverse backgrounds and with different interests, and democracy must include all citizens and allow different voices to be heard. The challenge, as always, is in sorting out what are the justifiable limits – an impeccably liberal and democratic question.

Multiculturalism and Political Morality[1]

Jocelyn Maclure

There is a way of looking at the evolution of liberal democracies that suggests that societies seen as open to the recognition and accommodation of cultural diversity turned their backs on multiculturalism as public philosophy and public policy (Joppke 2004; Brubaker 2001). Significant portions of the citizenry of countries such as Canada, the United States, Australia, the United Kingdom and the Netherlands have expressed scepticism, if not downright hostility, towards multiculturalism as an integration model. Think, for instance, of how fingers were pointed at multiculturalism in the United Kingdom and the Netherlands after, respectively, the 2005 London bombings and the murder of Theo Van Gogh in Amsterdam in 2004 (Modood 2007; Buruma 2006). Think also of the reaction against the possible creation of Sharia-based arbitration mechanisms in matters of family law in Canada in 2004 (Boyd 2004; Chapters 2 and 7 in this volume), and of the heated debate over religious accommodations in Quebec from to 2006 to 2008 (CCAPRCD 2008). Multiculturalism has also been under pressure within academia. Scholars of very different bents, drawing from a wide gamut of perspectives (liberal egalitarianism, feminism, republicanism, conservatism, critical theory, postcolonialism, etc.), have raised more or less serious and damaging criticisms of multiculturalism as a public philosophy or orientation to public policy. The case against multiculturalism can be descriptive, normative or both. In the first section of this chapter, I'll discuss the more empirical 'decline of multiculturalism' thesis. In the second part, I'll defend a version of the argument according to which multiculturalism is a valid normative ideal and principle of political morality. The overall objective of this chapter will thus be to show that multiculturalism remains, both from a descriptive and normative perspective, a relevant analytical category.

---

1   I wish to thank Duncan Ivison for his insightful comments and Julien Delangie for his very effective research assistance.

Communitarian Multiculturalism vs. Civic Multiculturalism

I believe that the so-called backlash against multiculturalism witnessed in many countries is in fact a critique of a certain *type* of multiculturalism that we might call '*communitarian* multiculturalism'. From a communitarian multicultural perspective, a society is a mosaic of cultural communities that relate with one another through institutions and representatives. Citizens largely live their lives within the parameters set forth by their cultural group and have limited interaction with members of the other groups. Although this is not a matter of logical necessity, communitarian multiculturalism is highly compatible with a form of moral relativism and legal pluralism according to which cultural communities are seen as discrete and self-regulating normative orders based on their own set of moral principles and legal rules. The state coordinates the interactions between the cultural groups constitutive of the political community.

It's probably safe to say that that no existing liberal democracy matches the communitarian multicultural ideal-typical model. Models of multicultural integration can be more or less communitarian, but we can easily understand why communitarian multiculturalism is an unlikely candidate as an appealing normative ideal. Communitarian multiculturalism fragments the political space along cultural and religious lines; it encourages isolation rather than interaction and it makes, as a result, the creation of civic bonds across cultural differences difficult. The republican dimension of political life – the unending pursuit of the common good through processes of public participation and deliberation – almost completely vanishes from the picture. In addition, the *laissez-faire* aspect of communitarian multiculturalism implies that citizens will potentially have to tolerate practices that they find morally repugnant. This is not an attractive picture of a multicultural society. It is, I think, when multiculturalism is (rightly or wrongly) perceived as a form of communitarianism that it draws its most sustained and stringent criticism.[2]

Multiculturalism, however, need not be communitarian; it can also be liberal and civic. Multiculturalism is *liberal* when it is seen as an extension and deepening of the basic human rights traditionally championed by the liberal tradition (Taylor 1992; Kymlicka 1995b; Chapter 2 in this volume). From a liberal multicultural point of view, showing equal respect to citizens implies recognizing and accommodating their cultural differences, insofar as it doesn't impact adversely on the rights and freedoms of others. Multiculturalism is *civic* when the respect for cultural diversity is thought in interactionist rather than isolationist terms. Civic multiculturalism starts from the hypothesis that cross-cultural interaction and deliberation guided by the norm of respect for reasonable cultural diversity is the most promising route to the creation of new forms of belonging and solidarity in multicultural societies.[3]

---

2   It is, for instance, clearly communitarian variants of multiculturalism that are the object of Joppke's (2004) criticism.

3   See Tully (2009a, b), Modood (2007), Parekh (2000).

Take, for instance, the so-called 'reasonable accommodation' debate in Quebec. From, roughly speaking, 2006 to 2008, Quebec society intensely questioned itself on the appropriate place of religion in the public sphere, on the integration of immigrants and, *eo ipso*, on the character of Quebec identity. Although I cannot broach all the interrelated factors that triggered the debate here, it is safe to say that deep concerns about the compatibility between religious accommodations and common civic values and principles such as fairness, gender equality, secularism and interculturalism lay at its roots. Many commentators agree that the 2006 Supreme Court Multani decision that allowed, under certain conditions, a Sikh schoolboy to carry his ceremonial dagger (*kirpan*) at a Montreal public school sparked off an uproar in public opinion. The decision was widely seen as yet another example of Canadian-style (communitarian and relativistic) multiculturalism imposed upon Quebec at the cost of public safety, secularism, fairness and Quebec's own model of integration, i.e. interculturalism. Other cases of religious accommodations were reported (and sometimes distorted) by the media and many Quebecers felt that either some essential civic values or Quebec identity itself were threatened by the alleged proliferation of 'unreasonable' religious accommodations.[4] It is in this explosive context that the Consultation Commission on Accommodation Practices Related to Cultural Differences (CCAPRCD) was put together by the Quebec government.[5]

Interestingly enough, the critique of multiculturalism around which many Quebecers rallied *did not* coincide with the revival of republican assimilationism or strict liberal neutrality as integration models. On the opposite, many took advantage of the CCPARDC to reassert the importance of further developing 'interculturalism' as a (allegedly) distinct integration model, the main virtue of which being its capacity to achieve an appropriate balance between social cohesion and the respect for cultural diversity. The three pillars of the intercultural model were laid down in a policy statement in which Quebec is presented to immigrants as:

- a society in which French is the common language of public life;
- a democratic society where everyone is expected and encouraged to participate and contribute;
- a pluralist society that is open to multiple influences, within the limits imposed by the need to respect fundamental values and the need of intergroup exchanges (Government of Quebec 1990: 15).

Immigrants are thus expected to learn French (if they don't already speak it), through the language courses freely provided to them, to abide by liberal and

---

4 For a reconstruction of the reasonable accommodation debate, see CCAPRCD (2008, Chapter 2).

5 My take on the reasonable accommodation debate and on the CCPAPRCD is not that of an external observer. I served as an expert-analyst for the Commission and contributed to the drafting of its final report.

democratic principles and seek to participate in political and economic life. In turn, Quebec's duty is to reach out to immigrants, provide them with the means for a successful socio-economic integration and valorize and accommodate immigrants' distinct cultural heritage and commitments, within the limits of a liberal-democratic regime. Newcomers are free to 'choose their own lifestyles, opinions, values and allegiances to interest groups within the limits defined by the legal framework' and, if they wish, to 'maintain and develop their own cultural interests with the other members of their group' (Government of Quebec 1990: 17). Immigrants will not be asked, the policy document states, to repudiate or privatize their cultural heritage. These are the basic terms of the so-called 'moral contract' between immigrants and the host society.[6]

Rather than rejecting pluralism altogether, most participants to the public hearings set forth by the CCAPRCD invited the Quebec government to 'walk the walk' and do more in terms of implementing interculturalism as a public policy. The opposition to religious accommodations was grounded, for many, on the (often false) assumption that those claiming accommodation measures to practice their religion with their fellow observers were performatively refusing to integrate and to partake in the project of the perpetual recreation of a civic identity hospitable to cultural diversity.[7]

If Quebec's predicament as the only predominantly francophone society in North America made it plainly clear that a politics of recognition of difference needed to be seen as an element of a broader politics of *integration* that ought to include dispositions promoting language acquisition and intercultural interactions, it doesn't seem too much of a leap to think that a similar movement has been taking place elsewhere. Many were troubled in the Netherlands by the fact that a substantial number of Muslim immigrants – especially women – did not speak Dutch and had little contact with non-Muslim Netherlanders. This reaction arguably amounts more to a rejection of *communitarian* multiculturalism than to multiculturalism per se. Many more assimilationist or exclusionary initiatives taken by the former conservative-liberal government (VVD) were repudiated with the election of the Socialist Party in 2006, but the conclusion that the former *laissez-faire* model had to give way to a more integrative approach remained.[8] The same could be said the about the alleged 'backlash' against multiculturalism in Great Britain. Take, for instance, the former Prime Minister Tony Blair's important speech

---

6   For a normative assessment of Quebec's model of integration, see Carens (2000: 107–39).

7   The Quebec debate, then, was much more about secularism and the place of religion in the public sphere than about multiculturalism or cultural diversity per se. Many secular immigrants (including Muslims) were against religious accommodations, and many accommodation claims came from non-immigrants, such as long established Hassidic Jews and members of the majority who became Jehovah's Witnesses or Adventists, and so on. See Maclure and Taylor (2010) for a reflection on the challenges of the secular state under conditions of deep ethical diversity.

8   See Bader (2005).

in the wake of 7/7, 2005, that is often taken, falsely, as a proof of a move away from multiculturalism:

> *The reason I say that this is grounds for optimism, is that what the above proves, is that integrating people whilst preserving their distinctive cultures, is not impossible. It is the norm. The failure of one part of one community to do so, **is not a function of a flawed theory of a multicultural society**. It is a function of a particular ideology that arises within one religion at this one time … So it is not that we need to dispense with multicultural Britain. On the contrary we should continue celebrating it. But we need – in the face of the challenge to our values – to re-assert also the duty to integrate, to stress what we hold in common and to say : these are the shared boundaries within which we all are obliged to live, precisely in order to preserve our right to our own different faiths, races and creeds (Blair 2006, **my emphasis**).*

The idea is thus not to 'dispense with multicultural Britain', but to strike a balance between the respect of difference and the 'duty to integrate'.

This movement towards non-assimilative integration have also been taking place in Canada – a country that is seen by many Europeans (and Quebecers!) as one of the most advanced examples of communitarian multiculturalism. Yet, as Will Kymlicka showed, Canadian multiculturalism, designed by the liberal Prime Minister Pierre Trudeau in the late 1960s, was, from its inception, liberal and individualistic in character (Kymlicka 1998). The goal was to value and celebrate the diverse cultural fabric in the country within a framework that allows each individual to decide whether they wanted to identify with, or detach from, their cultural origins.[9] Moreover, social science research has shown that Canada took the integrationist turn early in the 1990s. Reacting to variety of potentially fragmenting forces – globalisation, the intensification and diversification of immigration, Quebec and indigenous peoples' struggles for recognition, etc. – the federal government decided to make of the promotion of social cohesion a priority. The policy of multiculturalism had to be reconceived as a tool for forging national unity and increasing social cohesion (Mc Andrew 2008). As the latest Annual Report on the Operation of the *Canadian Multiculturalism Act* testifies, this re-orientation of Canadian multiculturalism remains to this day the dominant policy orientation in Ottawa (CIC 2009). Although this goes against a widely shared belief in Quebec, Canadian multiculturalism and Quebec interculturalism have been converging for some time, and the image of Canada as a 'mosaic' distinct from the American 'melting-pot' has long been buried.

Although this is a matter for the empirical social sciences, I do not see much evidence that we are currently witnessing a 'return of assimilation'. Interestingly,

---

9   If multiculturalism as a vision of the country and as a public policy was well received by long established, mainly European, immigrants (like the Ukrainians), the proposal that it could be extended to Quebecers and indigenous peoples was promptly rejected by both constituencies.

the point of Roger Brubaker's oft-cited article 'The return of assimilation?' is not that assimilationist models are making a comeback, but rather that *some* forms of integration, such as language acquisition, economic integration and civic participation, are seen as desirable by host societies. As he puts it:

> The 'return of assimilation': It does not imply the desirability of complete acculturation. Analytically, this has involved a shift from an overwhelming focus on persisting difference – and on the mechanisms through which such cultural maintenance occurs – to a broader focus that encompasses emerging commonalities as well. Normatively, it has involved a shift from the automatic valorization of cultural differences to a renewed concern with civic integration (Brubaker 2001: 542).

What Brubaker is debunking in his article are the communitarian forms of multiculturalism, as well as postmodern celebration of difference and alterity; there is nothing in his analysis that suggests a move away from civic multiculturalism as a public philosophy and public policy: quite the opposite.

Even French republicanism, according to some analysts, is currently quietly moving towards civic multiculturalism. Sociologist and former Stasi Commission member Jean Baubérot, pointing out that France's model of laïcité and integration cannot be reduced to the law prohibiting visible religious signs at public schools, argues that several policy initiatives, such as selective religious accommodations, affirmative action measures for making public and private institutions more diverse and representative and, most importantly, the creation, in 2005, of the *Haute autorité de lutte contre les discriminations et pour l'égalité* (HALDE), are in fact consistent with civic multiculturalism. These initiatives have yet to alter the dominant theoretical self-understanding of French republicanism, but they are, according to Baubérot (2009), changing French society.

Multiculturalism and Justice

It thus seems that there is no overwhelming empirical evidence suggesting that liberal and civic multiculturalism has been shovelled into the dustbin of history. This, of course, is an empirical claim that can be falsified by careful empirical and comparative research. It doesn't tell us, however, whether contemporary liberal democracies ought to endorse multiculturalism as a public philosophy or, more accurately, as a principle of political morality. As I alluded to, the normative case in favour of a 'politics of recognition' or of 'the rights of minority cultures' has been challenged by many political philosophers and social/political theorists coming from a wide variety of perspectives (liberal egalitarianism, feminism, critical theory, postcolonialism, etc.) (Benhabib 2002; Barry 2001; Okin 1999; and Chapters 10, 13 and 14 in this volume). Even theorists largely or moderately sympathetic to the recognition and accommodation of cultural and religious differences warn us against the dangers of recognition politics (Appiah 2005; Sen 2006; Freeman 2002).[10]

Samuel Scheffler's paper 'Immigration and the significance of culture' is in my view one of the most cogent and helpful contributions to the normative debate on multiculturalism and justice in recent years (Scheffler 2007). Although not at all unsympathetic to the claims of justice made by immigrants, it offers what I take to be one of the soundest arguments against the case for 'multicultural' theories of justice. As I myself think that we should recognize that multiculturalism or, perhaps better, a principle of respect of reasonable cultural diversity, should play a role within our political morality, I want in the remainder of this chapter to question and amend his conclusion that we ought to 'forswear any appeal to cultural rights or to the language of multiculturalism' in thinking about justice in culturally diverse societies (Scheffler 2007: 117).[11]

The position that I wish to defend is that a principle of respect of reasonable cultural diversity ought to (and actually often does) act as an interpretive principle within our political conception of justice – an interpretive principle that modifies our understanding of the normative implications of the basic principles of justice. Although I agree with Scheffler that the descriptive and normative language used by many multiculturalists need to be revised and often deflated, as talk of 'cultural rights', 'group/collective rights' and 'cultural protection/preservation' often mischaracterizes what is really at stake, I also believe that positions such as Scheffler's fail to grasp the actual role and impact of the principle of respect for reasonable cultural diversity. I will argue, perhaps in contradistinction to other multiculturalists, that Scheffler's position's main shortcoming is conceptual rather than normative.

Here is how Scheffler sums up what he calls the 'Heraclitean' pluralist position he favours:

> I believe that the Heraclitean position is correct to forswear any appeal to cultural rights or to the language of multiculturalism in thinking about these questions. The constituents of political morality that are most relevant in thinking about the mutual responsibilities of immigrants and host societies are the principles of justice, which define a fair framework of social cooperation among equals (and which are understood to exclude special cultural rights); the basic liberties, including especially the liberties of speech, association, and conscience; and the important idea of informal mutual accommodation within the bounds of justice. Talk of cultural rights and of multiculturalism adds little that is useful to this, and it provides an invitation to mischief both by encouraging us to think in unsustainable, strong-preservationist terms and by promoting a distorted and potentially oppressive conception of the

---

10   See Smith's chapter in this volume (Chapter 9) for an alternative account of the relationship between recognition politics and multiculturalism.

11   I also discussed Scheffler's paper in Maclure (2010).

relations between individuals and cultures (Scheffler 2007: 117–18, see also
110).

Many of the points made by Scheffler in the course of his argumentation are
valid and, with the exception of the aforementioned conclusion, should, I think, be
accepted by multiculturalists. I think it's fair to say that Scheffler mainly opposes
two ideas that he sees as wedded to multiculturalism. First, he picks apart the
belief that either immigrants or host societies are entitled to a right to insulate
their 'culture' from alteration (Scheffler 2007: 105). Second, he challenges the
idea defended by multiculturalists that the establishment of fair terms of social
cooperation under conditions of cultural diversity requires that standard liberal
egalitarian conceptions of justice incorporate 'group-specific' or 'minority' rights
(Scheffler 2007: 110) I will first briefly review his first point and then expose what
is perhaps a blind spot in the argumentation that leads to his second point. Finally,
I will challenge Scheffler's conclusion that we should forswear the language of
multiculturalism altogether when we think about the fair terms of social cooperation
under conditions of cultural diversity.

Multiculturalism and the Preservationist Ethic

Scheffler begins by debunking the claim that either host societies or immigrants
have a right to 'preserve' their respective cultures. Although this critique is in no
way new or particularly controversial, at least in the philosophical literature,[12]
Scheffler's version of it is compelling. He inter alia makes the now commonplace
argument that the very ideal of cultural preservation can hardly be squared with
the evolving nature of cultures, and with the plurality and mutability of the
identifications and affiliations of most agents. A preservationist ethic, as Anthony
Appiah calls it, logically presupposes that we can delineate a fixed and stable
culture, defined by a set of immutable and cognisable properties, which can be
protected and preserved with the help of cultural rights and policies. Yet for reasons
that need not be rehearsed here, cultures are to varying degrees always changing
and, as Scheffler rightly points out, 'survive only by changing' (Scheffler 2007:
104). Cultural 'survival', as he puts it, 'is successful change' (Scheffler 2007: 107).
Moreover, as agents normally belong to a plurality of communities, draw on several
sources of meaning and orientation and take up a plurality of roles or practical
identities, it is misleading to assign each of them to a single culture standing in
need of protection (Scheffler 2007: 99).[13] As Scheffler eloquently observes, '[a]ll of
these identifications and passions and affiliations, and countless others, are aspects

---

12   See, for instance, Appiah (2005).
13   Amartya Sen tries to spell out the implications of the plural and mutable nature of
     identity in Sen (2006).

of human culture, and to live a human life is to trace a particular path through the space of possibilities they define' (Scheffler 2007: 101).

These points against the reification of culture and identity are, as I said, widely accepted. I know of no serious theorist of multiculturalism or of the politics of recognition – think of Will Kymlicka, Charles Taylor, James Tully or Bhikhu Parekh, for instance – that does not accept them (Kymlicka 1995b, Taylor 1992, Tully 1995, Parekh 2000). We might disagree with one or another of their arguments, but it is simply not true that they are working with an essentialized conception of culture or with a monistic notion of individual identity. It seems true to me, however, that both (1) a clear *conceptual* reflection on the meaning of cultural preservation in the light of the inevitability of cultural change and (2) a cogent *normative* reflection on the role and status of the ideal of cultural preservation within the justification of multiculturalism, are scarce in the literature. I, in line with Scheffler, believe that the language of cultural preservation, protection or survival is of no use in the normative justification of multiculturalism, and that it is not employed with sufficient care by multiculturalists, which in turn makes their position more vulnerable to criticism. I have argued elsewhere that multiculturalists should forgo the preservationist ethic altogether and replace it with arguments based on the right to self-determination (for national minorities) and on the illegitimacy of policies aiming (overtly or covertly) at full cultural assimilation of immigrants to the majority culture, i.e. arguments drawn from, or compatible with, the constituents of liberal-democratic political morality (Maclure 2007). I think, like Scheffler, that cultural minorities can pursue reasonable cultural reproduction projects, but that the ideal of cultural preservation does not *in itself* justify specific rights or resources for members of cultural minorities.[14] But contrary to what has widely been assumed by critiques of multiculturalism – including moderate ones like Scheffler's – I don't think that the ideal of cultural preservation is either the foundation or the telos of multiculturalism.[15] We can find, to be sure, countless examples of political entrepreneurs who seek to strengthen their political claims by grounding it in essentialized notions of self and other, but the cases of minority nations such as Quebec, Catalonia, and most indigenous peoples de facto demonstrate that a minority can, in practice, advance a vigorous struggle for recognition while at the same time intensely debating the substance and desired political expression of its common identity.

In fact, the more interesting and difficult question, from a conceptual point of view, raised by the politics of identity is this: how do cultures that are themselves differentiated and in constant transformation come to struggle for different forms of recognition? How can a minority recognize its own internal diversity while remaining capable of contesting the structures of recognition, redistribution, and governance that it deems unfair? Both the preservationist ethic *and* the view that

---

14   Compare to Scheffler (2007: 11): 'What they cannot do is demand additional rights or resources, beyond those they are owed as a matter of justice, in the name of cultural preservation specifically.'

15   See, among others, Habermas (1994), Waldron (1992), Barry (2001).

multiculturalism is logically predicated upon essentialism fail to provide us with enlightening answers to these questions.

Multiculturalism as a Principle of Political Morality

The second more general point made by Scheffler is that liberal egalitarian conceptions of justice need not be amended in order to do justice to immigrants:

> Some people interpret the legitimate grievances of immigrant communities in existing liberal democracies as evidence that the familiar conceptions of justice are inadequate and should be modified to incorporate a regime of cultural rights. The alternative conclusion that seems to me more plausible in many of these cases is that the societies in question have failed to meet the requirement of liberal justice, and that the remedy for the grievances of immigrants is not to modify those requirements but rather to ensure that they are satisfied (Scheffler 2007: 112).

Scheffler does not deny that actually existing liberal democracies often fail to treat immigrants fairly. His point is rather that this failure is due to a shortcoming of liberal democratic *institutions* rather than to a limit of liberal egalitarian *political morality*. The fulfilment of the demands of liberal egalitarianism gives, according to him, 'ample scope for immigrants (and others) to pursue reasonable preservationist projects' (Scheffler 2007: 110–11).

Although I agree that meeting the moral requirements of liberal egalitarianism would take us much closer to fair terms of social cooperation in multicultural societies, I want to take issue with the claim that liberal egalitarian theories of justice such as John Rawls' 'justice as fairness' already possess all the ethical resources necessary to address the contemporary challenges of a multicultural society. The proposition, quoted above, that '[t]he constituents of political morality that are most relevant in thinking about the mutual responsibilities of immigrants and host societies are the principles of [standard liberal egalitarian] justice' (Scheffler 2007: 117) omits an important part of the story.

My dissatisfaction with Scheffler's position perhaps lies in what I take to be his incomplete account of liberal political morality. Although there is a kernel of truth in the idea that the satisfaction of the demands of standard liberal egalitarianism – if seen, as Scheffler rightly argues, as including the reasonable legal accommodation of minority practices (I will come back to this below) – is all that is needed with regards to the immigrant–host society relationship, I believe that his justification, as presently stated, fails to grasp the mutation in the political morality of most liberal democracies that took place in the past few decades.

The phenomenon that I have mind and that stands in need of explanation is the fact that most liberal democracies now recognize, in many different ways, the normative authority of a principle of 'respect,' or maybe 'hospitality,' for cultural diversity. For example, integration models seeking the full assimilation (or acculturation) of newcomers, which were pretty much the norm in most liberal democracies up at least until the 1960s, now appear to many as morally suspect. As we saw in the first part of this chapter, most liberal democracies are currently trying to design and implement incorporation models that seek to bring about integration in some spheres (language acquisition, economic integration, education, civic participation, etc.) while simultaneously letting immigrants engage in the reasonable cultural preservation and reproduction projects of their choice. The aim of such incorporation models is 'integration' rather than 'assimilation' (Glazer 1997).

Take, for instance, the norm of legal accommodation discussed by Scheffler. Both American and Canadian jurisprudences now stipulate that public and private institutions have a legal duty to accommodate reasonable minority practices when it is proven that legitimate and prima facie neutral laws, norms or rules indirectly discriminate, in their application, against the members of a vulnerable group (Greenawalt 2006). As Scheffler rightly puts it:

> *the principles of justice may themselves require, by virtue of their guarantees of liberty of conscience and association, that certain limited exemptions from otherwise just laws should be provided to people for whom compliance would conflict with deeply held conscientious convictions, whether religious or nonreligious in character. Justice may also require other forms of legal accommodation for conscientious convictions in some circumstances (Scheffler 2007: 114–15).*

As a legal doctrine contributing to the better realization of equality rights or of the freedom of conscience and religion, the norm of reasonable accommodation is now seen in many countries as a legal obligation. But it is only recently in the history of liberal democracy that the accommodation of cultural and religious minorities is construed as such. As far as religious accommodation is concerned, it was seen as sufficient, from John Locke's 'Letter concerning toleration' to late in the twentieth century, to recognize and protect the agent's sovereignty over their own conscience and to tolerate minority religious beliefs and practices in the *private* sphere.[16] Even though we are still greatly indebted today to Locke's *Letter*, he didn't think a duty to accommodate minority beliefs and practises had to be derived from freedom of conscience and religious toleration. When a valid law conflicts with a deeply held belief, one should, according to Locke, follow the dictates of one's conscience *and* accept the ensuing sanction:

> *But some may ask 'What if the magistrate should enjoin any thing by his authority, that appears unlawful to the conscience of a private person?' I*

16　Some exceptional figures, of course, such as Roger Williams in the states of Massachusetts and Rhode Island, were in favour of religious accommodations all along. See Martha Nussbaum's interpretation of Williams' thought in Nussbaum (2008).

answer, that if government be faithfully administered, and the counsels of the magistrate be indeed directed to the public good, this will seldom happen. But if perhaps it do so fall out, I say, that such a private person is to abstain from the actions that he judges unlawful; and he is to undergo the punishment, which is not unlawful for him to bear; for the private judgment of any person concerning a law enacted in political matters, for the public good, does not take away the obligation of that law, nor deserve a dispensation (Locke 1963: 43).

Although many oppose the idea that reasonable accommodation is a moral and legal obligation – ranging from Brian Barry to arch-conservative Justice Antonin Scalia of the US Supreme Court – it is nonetheless recognized as such by most human rights tribunals and constitutional courts in the West.[17] How did that happen?

In another direction, think of how the idea of fair treatment of national minorities and aboriginal peoples has changed in the past half-century.[18] It is now widely recognized, including in international law, that minority peoples or nations are entitled to some form of political and cultural autonomy. To illustrate this point, consider, for instance, the case of the former liberal Canadian Prime Minister Pierre Elliot Trudeau. Trudeau thought in 1969 that the best liberal egalitarian solution to the deplorable life conditions of aboriginal people in Canada was to encourage their assimilation to mainstream society by making sure that they could exercise the *exact same rights* as non-aboriginal Canadians. This involved both refusing the special status and collective rights claimed by aboriginal leaders and fighting vigorously against the discrimination that aboriginal people still had to put up with (Indian and Northern Affairs Canada 1969). The intent – securing the equal protection of the laws for aboriginal people – was clearly liberal. The Liberal Party's policy with regards to aboriginal people was a part of the 'Just Society' envisioned and championed by Trudeau.

Interestingly, Trudeau and the Liberal Party were back in power in 1982 when the Canadian constitution was patriated from Great Britain and a Canadian charter of rights and freedoms was enshrined in the Constitution Act, 1982. A clause 'recognizing' and 'affirming' 'the existing aboriginal (i.e. ancestral) and treaty rights of the aboriginal peoples of Canada' was included in the new constitution

---

17 Note, however, that Barry's position on religious accommodations is less crystal clear than he was ready to admit. If he starts off saying that a proper theory of justice rules out religious accommodations, he ends up admitting that such accommodations are often either wise or acceptable on prudential grounds, and thus not incompatible with appropriate standards of justice. See Barry (2001: Chapter 2).

18 Scheffler explicitly excludes national minorities from his analysis and focuses only on immigrants. I do however need to reintroduce them in the picture in order to make my point about the evolution of political morality. It would be interesting to see what Scheffler thinks is a fair treatment of national minorities and aboriginal peoples, and whether the integration of this different form of cultural diversity would lead him to amend his general position.

(Department of Justice Canada 1982). The egalitarian but overtly assimilative policy of 1969 was dead and no serious political party has tried to unearth it since then. The Canadian Crown has since resumed with treaty negotiations (or is, more often, paying lip service to nation to nation negotiations).[19] Although there are many reasons – some of them no doubt purely instrumental – why a political leader might change their views in such a drastic way, this example nicely illustrates I think the ethical mutation I alluded to above. As Scheffler (1994) convincingly argued elsewhere, instrumental and ethical reasons sometimes converge.

Now, underneath the significant differences between immigrants and national minorities, the requirement or expectation of full cultural assimilation is in both cases seen as unduly demanding from a moral point of view. The illegitimacy of active and even passive policies seeking the assimilation of members of cultural minorities has arguably become, in Rawls' terms, a 'well considered judgement'. Individual members of minority groups can of course decide to assimilate, but a new norm of respect for cultural diversity now sets limits to the types of policies that can be implemented in the name of integration. It is this new sensitivity to cultural difference – call it 'multiculturalism' or 'the politics of recognition' – that multiculturalists have tried to track and to incorporate into a wider conception of justice. As both the examples of religious accommodations and aboriginal rights reveal, standard liberal principles of justice are not, left to themselves, incompatible with at least passive or indirect assimilation policies, such as the 'benign neglect' approach.

The shift just described within the structure of our considered moral judgements is invisible in Scheffler's analysis. But perhaps one could argue that the 'respect for reasonable cultural diversity' principle I alluded to is better understood in terms of an interpretive clause or axiological filter that modifies our understanding of the principles of justice constitutive of standard liberal conceptions of justice. Basic liberal rights would henceforth need to be interpreted and applied in a culturally sensitive rather than blind manner. Insofar as we are concerned with the immigrant–host society relationship, a 'multicultural' theory of justice, contrary to what Kymlicka opines, would not be needed, at least if such a theory entails incorporating 'cultural' or 'group specific' rights into our system of rights. This position has some plausibility. As we saw, the legal obligation to accommodate is derived from more general rights and freedoms (such as equality rights and the associated antidiscrimination laws, and freedom of conscience and religion). Along the same line, affirmative action programs, often construed as multicultural policies, can be derived from a more general principle of equal opportunity. In both cases, one can plausibly argue that standard liberal conceptions of justice need not be revised or augmented. Our institutions, as Scheffler writes, need to live up to, and better realize, basic liberal principles.[20]

---

19   See Indian and Northern Affairs Canada (1996).

20   Can all measures associated with multiculturalism be straightforwardly derived from basic individual rights? What about language rights? Are immigrants entitled to some public services in their native language or is this just a matter of public policy not

A standard liberal conception of justice read through the lens of the norm of respect for cultural diversity would thus be capable of setting out fair terms of cooperation among the citizens of a multicultural society. But then, does Scheffler's position, according to which the only relevant constituents of political morality are the standard liberal principles of justice, survive even the minimal interpretation of the norm of respect for reasonable cultural diversity as an interpretive principle? What is the respect for reasonable cultural diversity if not a principle of political morality? It does seem to have a nature and function similar to a principle of political morality, as it impacts upon constitutional interpretation, institutional design and policy making, although we perhaps need a more textured notion of political morality, i.e. one that allows us to distinguish between interpretive principles and principles of justice, as interpretive clauses and fundamental rights are distinguished in constitutional law.

Does Political Morality Evolve?

Scheffler's position is, as I said, persuasive. I do think, however, that it occludes the ethical transformation that I have sketched out here. Although this would require a separate chapter, the very way Scheffler frames his position raises some questions about the possible metaethical position implicit in his argumentation. As far as I can tell, Scheffler nowhere makes it explicit that he believes that what it means to treat cultural and religious minorities fairly has changed in the past few decades. In his article, Scheffler comes across either as a moral realist for whom principles of justice are atemporal properties that societies can grasp and actualize (or fail to do so), or as a Kantian constructivist for whom practical reason yields unvarying moral truths. One gets that perhaps false impression not only from the fact that he does not acknowledge the ethical transformation I referred to, but also from his rendition of his grandfather's experience as a Galician Jew immigrating to New York in 1914. Telling the story and predicament of his grandfather allows him to demonstrate that it makes little sense to think that immigrants come with a 'single fixed and determinate "culture" to which they could be assigned and that they would want to preserve from change' (Scheffler 2007: 95–9). However, the tale's perhaps undesired consequence is that it also seems to entail that what it means for a host society to treat immigrants fairly is the same today as it was in the 1910s. To be sure, this is not the lesson that Scheffler wishes to draw from the narrative. He rather takes it to mean that 'even for people whose lives may seem, superficially, to be assimilable within some fixed cultural framework, the appearance of cultural fixity and determinacy is often illusory or at least misleading' (Scheffler 2007: 100).

---

regulated by the political conception of justice? The derivation seems looser here, although I am not prepared to address this question here. See Kymlicka and Patten (2003).

This point is well taken. Yet passages such as the following make us think that political morality is pretty much fixed and stable:

> *If someone had asked him whether it was important to him to have his culture recognized by his new country, or whether he thought the national identity of the United States should be replaced by a new, multicultural identity in order to accommodate him and other immigrants, I doubt he would have known what to say (Scheffler 2007: 96).*

I do not want to make too much out the narrative and caricature Scheffler as a naïve Platonist or Kantian. My point is rather that the fact that he does not specify that we do not live in the exact same moral context that his grandfather did, combined with the fact that he does not at all ponder the normative implications of the new ethical sensitivity with regard to cultural difference, could be taken to mean that he believes that normative expectations and political morality do not change through time, an assumption that pragmatists and political constructivists, such as Rawls, would rightly want to challenge.[21] This silence or blind spot in Scheffler's argument might help explaining why he finds no use for the idea that liberal theories of justice need to be reworked in the light of a normative concept of multiculturalism.

Leaving this metaethical issue aside, Scheffler could perhaps reply that the ethical mutation within our well-considered judgements that I described did indeed take place and that there was an explicative blind spot in his argument, but that it doesn't alter the basic position he defends in the paper: standard liberal egalitarian conceptions of justice have the normative resources to set out fair terms of social cooperation in multicultural societies, and talk of multiculturalism and recognition only creates unnecessary conceptual and normative problems.[22] Although I am prepared to grant him that multiculturalists do not always have a clear view of the meaning and normative status of the goal of cultural preservation, it seems more accurate to think that a principle of respect of reasonable cultural diversity has gradually weaved its way into the fabric of our political morality and modified

---

21 I cannot address here the difficult question of how moral contexts and structures of well-considered practical judgements evolve through time, but I'm confident that such an investigation would have to include the struggles for recognition of excluded or marginalized minorities.

22 Perhaps Scheffler could say that standard liberal egalitarianism is not incompatible with our ensemble of well-considered judgements pertaining to the respect of cultural diversity. The reflective equilibrium method, as is well known, tells us to revise abstract theoretical principles if they fail to match with the moral practical judgements that we have no good reason to abandon or revise. There would thus be no need to amend standard liberal egalitarianism along the lines suggested here. Yet, as I argued earlier, basic liberal principles need to interact with a principle of respect for cultural diversity in order to steer clear of cultural assimilationism. Reflective equilibrium also tells us that changes in our structure of well-considered judgments normally have an impact on our theoretical conception of justice.

what we see as the requirements of social justice in culturally diverse societies. As I argued earlier, basic liberal principles need to interact with a principle of respect for cultural diversity in order to steer clear of cultural assimilationism.

It might thus be that we need to have a more textured conception of political morality; a conception that would allow us to distinguish between interpretive principles and more straightforwardly normative ones. It could well be, although I am not prepared to take a definitive stand on this yet, that multiculturalism does most of its normative work at the level of the interpretation of more basic liberal and democratic principles (equality, freedom of conscience and religion, freedom of expression, popular sovereignty and the right to self-determination). If so, this would constitute another reason why 'multicultural' theories of justice, that generally zero in on group-specific or cultural rights, are ripe for a new round of conceptual revision and clarification.

Conclusion

Political philosophers defending multiculturalism as an element of a sound public philosophy and as an orientation to public policy have been hard pressed in recent years, both by citizens and theorists, to explain how it relates to basic individual rights and to the demands of civic integration and social cooperation. These challenges forced multiculturalists to make their commitments to a liberal and civic form of multiculturalism explicit and to think hard about how principles of recognition and accommodation fit within a broader political conception of justice. However, evidence suggests that liberal democracies are not turning their back on reasonable forms of recognition and accommodation of minority claims, and the normative case in favour of liberal and civic multiculturalism appears to be strong.

Now, I focussed here on the standard liberal egalitarian criticism of multiculturalism because it seems to me the most cogent and serious one both in theoretical discussions and public debates.[23] Standard liberal egalitarianism has the merit of articulating an alternative political philosophy according to which fairness requires the identical treatment of all citizens regardless of their religious beliefs or ethnocultural origins. All citizens should enjoy the same set of rights and opportunities; a principle that is thought to rule out religious accommodations, linguistic rights or self-government rights for national minorities, which are seen as unwarranted privileges. I think the difference-blind liberal egalitarian position

---

23 The most serious challenges to principle of accommodation during the Quebec debate discussed in the first part of this chapter came from citizens who argued that religious accommodations were incompatible with shared public values such as fairness between religious and non-religious persons, gender equality or the secular character of public norms and institutions.

is less attractive than its multicultural counterpart, but I appreciate the fact that it offers a conception of social justice that can be openly discussed and criticized.

But liberal multiculturalism can also be criticized on other grounds, such as that it doesn't challenge the foundations of liberal-democratic regimes and thus leaves deep-seated and systemic asymmetrical relations of power between groups intact. Not digging deep enough, liberal egalitarian multiculturalism would divert us from the more troublesome inequalities that undermine the moral legitimacy of contemporary liberal democracies. Such criticisms are often made by theorists inspired by critical theory, poststructuralism or postcolonialism. But according to which normative standards can these persistent inequalities be assessed and criticized? What would look like a just multicultural and/or multinational political community? Answering these questions logically requires referring to a normative conception of justice that (at least loosely) defines and articulates the moral ends that our institutions should seek to achieve.[24] This is what liberal-egalitarian multiculturalism attempt to do. Critics of liberalism in general, and of liberal multiculturalism in particular, often seem to lose sight of the fact that the critique of prevailing norms and institutions and the attempt to formulate appropriate moral standards are the two sides of the same coin.

---

24   See Ivison (2002) for a rare (and stimulating) attempt to reshape normative liberal theory in light of what he calls the 'postcolonial challenge'.

Multiculturalism and Political Ontology

Paul Patton

Introduction

Much of the debate over multiculturalism has been, as Geoffrey Levey rightly observes, 'a family argument among liberals over what liberalism or liberal values entail' (Chapter 2, p. 19). It has involved disagreements over the extent to which liberal concepts of freedom, individual autonomy and equality sustain the public recognition of different ethnic, national and linguistic identities. There are good reasons why French poststructuralist political philosophers for the most part did not join in this argument. In the first place, the public policy context was different. As a liberal and democratic country with a strong republican tradition, France has long remained reluctant to embrace multicultural policies. The issues that attracted attention tended to involve the denial of basic citizenship rights to migrant workers, or the lack of hospitality towards illegal immigrants. Cultural difference and cultural rights did not play an important role in such campaigns. More recent debates, such as that provoked by the insistence of young Muslim women on wearing the veil in French schools, have been no more friendly towards what was often described as 'Anglo-Saxon' multiculturalism. A second reason why the overtly political philosophy of poststructuralists such as Deleuze, Derrida and Foucault did not contribute to this debate was that, for the most part, they did not engage with liberalism or liberal values. It was only towards the end of their respective careers, after the normative turn in poststructuralist thought that occurred during the 1980s, that these philosophers engaged directly with liberalism and liberal values (Patton 2007a, b, 2010). Despite these differences of political and theoretical context, there are significant areas of convergence between elements of poststructuralist political ontology and the theoretical debates over multiculturalism. I propose to discuss two of these, namely the debates around the nature and identity of cultures, and the debates around power and its bearing on cultural identity.

Culture and Minority

In its contemporary forms, liberalism is often defined by reference to its commitments to individualism, to egalitarianism and, at least in some varieties, to universalism. These commitments imply a belief that individual persons are the ultimate units of moral worth, that they have equal moral status and that all human beings are persons in the relevant sense of the term. The challenge posed by multicultural public policy is to provide an acceptable justification for differential treatment of particular groups or communities that is compatible with these commitments, especially the first two. Beyond that challenge is a broader issue, namely whether and, if so, in what ways the cultural contexts of individual lives should be reflected in the political constitutions, laws and public policy of liberal democratic states. Some critics of the post-Second World War consensus around the idea of a colour-blind and culture-neutral state argued that a degree of bias towards a particular culture or cultures is both unavoidable and desirable. In a similar vein, Will Kymlicka and other so-called 'liberal culturalists' such as Joseph Raz responded to the multicultural challenge by arguing that a person's membership in a given culture should be included among the primary social goods to which they have a prima facie right. However, in doing so they not only broadened the ontology of liberalism to include cultures as well as persons, but also raised difficult questions about what it means to belong to a culture and what are the limits of the 'cultures' within which individuals acquired and modified their conceptions of the good.

Building upon the rights-based liberalism of Rawls and Dworkin, the liberal culturalists argued that the principle of equality with regard to access to primary social goods provides justification for measures to protect the cultural integrity of minority groups such as substate nations or colonised indigenous peoples. A key premise of this argument affirms the role of culture in providing a context of choice within which individuals exercise their freedom to live according to their own conception of the good. A further premise claims that the freedom that liberalism seeks to protect is the freedom to pursue a good life as this is understood by the individual concerned. No-one has the right to impose upon others their own particular vision of the good, or, as Kymlicka puts it, our lives ought to be led from the inside 'in accordance with our beliefs about what gives value to life' (Kymlicka 1989a: 13). He argues that we form beliefs about values and the good life from within a culture which provides us with different ways of life, a particular language and a history, all of which together provide us with a context of choice: 'Our language and history are the media through which we come to an awareness of the options available to us, and their significance' (Kymlicka 1989a: 165). Such contexts are the necessary preconditions of an individual's capacity to make informed choices, to critically examine these and to maintain a sense of their own worth and agency in doing so. For these reasons, cultural membership ought to be regarded as a primary good and consideration of equal access to it is something that ought to be a concern for the parties to Rawls' original position. In short, 'Liberal values require both individual freedom of choice and a secure cultural context from which individuals can make their choices. Thus liberalism requires that we can identify, protect and promote cultural membership as a primary good' (Kymlicka 1989a: 169).

Whereas the negative libertarian liberalism of Bentham or Berlin focussed upon the free pursuit of interests and satisfaction of desires, regardless of how these were formed, Kymlicka's liberalism pays attention to the social formation of our interests and desires. He draws upon liberals such as Mill and Rawls in order to stress the importance of the manner in which our 'affections and desires' are formed through social interaction, and the importance of a public sphere of liberal education and free expression for the examination of what we take to be worthwhile interests and desires. In other words, the 'essential interest' of every individual in leading a good life is not restricted to pursuing what we currently believe to be a good life but must also include the possibility of deliberation and revision of what we take to be good: 'Our essential interest is in living a good life, not the life we currently believe to be good' (Kymlicka 1989a: 11). It follows that individual freedom also includes the freedom to form, examine and revise beliefs about the good.[1]

Liberalism should not only protect the freedom of individuals to act on their present desires but also the freedom to question their desires along with the beliefs and values which enter into a particular conception of the good life.[2] Liberal political institutions ought to sustain this freedom along with the capacities that it presupposes. This implies the need for those traditional freedoms of liberal society that enable us to examine and question beliefs about the good, such as civil and personal liberties, freedom of expression, freedom of the press and so on, but also the need to protect those things that enable us to decide for ourselves what is valuable, such as access to a certain level of education or access to information about other cultures. Kymlicka is careful to specify that the important context for individual choice is not the particular character of the cultural community at any moment but rather the 'cultural structure' within which particular contents appear or disappear. What matters is not culture defined in terms of its current norms

---

1   Kymlicka quotes Rawls's 1974 view that individuals have 'a highest order interest in how all their other interests, including even their fundamental ones, are shaped and regulated by social institutions. They do not think of themselves as inevitably bound to, or identical with, the pursuit of any particular complex of fundamental interests that they may have at an given time ... Rather, free persons conceive of themselves as beings who can revise and alter their final ends and who give first priority to preserving their liberty in these matters' (Kymlicka 1989a: 33–4).

2   A further, related reason why culture is an important precondition of individuals' freedom to pursue their conception of the good concerns its role in relation to self-respect. One of the reasons that the freedom to examine our beliefs and confirm their value is important to Rawls is that doing so is a condition of self-respect (Kymlicka 1989a: 164). Kymlicka advances an even stronger claim about the importance of culture and 'a sense of belonging to a cultural structure', namely that this can affect 'our very sense of agency' (Kymlicka 1989a: 175). In other words, cultural structure is important not just to the formation and pursuit of ends of life, but also to 'the very sense that we are capable of pursuing them efficiently' (Kymlicka 1989a: 176).To the extent that this is true it provides another reason why secure cultural membership is a primary good.

but culture defined in terms of a viable community with a shared language and history. In this sense, a cultural structure persists even when the norms and values of that culture change. What is important is the persistence of a distinctive context of choice: 'It is the existence of a cultural community viewed as a context of choice that is a primary good, and a legitimate concern of liberals' (Kymlicka 1989a: 169).

The second key premise of the liberal culturalist argument is the principle that individuals should not suffer disadvantage in their access to primary social goods as a result of circumstances over which they have no control. In multicultural societies, the viability of minority cultural contexts of choice may be threatened by actions of the majority. Members of the majority culture do not face this problem. The liberal principle of equality implies that the good of cultural membership should be equally available to all, even if this involves differential treatment. Hence protection for national minorities is 'clearly justified ... within a liberal egalitarian theory, such as Rawls's and Dworkin's, which emphasizes the importance of rectifying unchosen inequalities' (Kymlicka 1995b: 109). Since it is clear that 'some groups are unfairly disadvantaged in the cultural market place' and that certain kinds of political recognition and support can rectify this disadvantage, there is a case for group-differentiated rights such as limited self-government, which may compensate for the unequal circumstances that place members of minority cultures at a disadvantage: 'This is one of the many areas in which true equality requires not identical treatment but rather differential treatment in order to accommodate differential needs' (Kymlicka 1995b: 113).

Kymlicka's argument justifies certain limited kinds of 'minority cultural rights', but only insofar as these are necessary to maintain equality of access to cultural membership. It only supports special rights if there actually is disadvantage with regard to cultural membership and if these rights will serve to rectify that disadvantage. As such, it may not justify the full extent of rights to land, resources or self-determination sometimes claimed by indigenous peoples. Since this argument ties the case for minority group rights to facts concerning the culture of the peoples concerned, it leads to empirical questions about whether or not their distinct cultures have survived, or whether in fact they do provide viable culturally distinct contexts of choice. Facts about the specificity and integrity of minority cultures are difficult to establish, especially in postcolonial contexts where decades of assimilation and the corrosive effects of removal from traditional lands, alcohol and religion have undermined the bases of many indigenous cultures. It is therefore a weakness of the liberal culturalist argument that it mortgages the case for distinctive rights to such difficult anthropological questions about the identification and viability of indigenous cultures now surrounded by liberal, democratic and capitalist societies.

Critics such as Jeremy Waldron have also argued that it relies upon an outdated vision of the social world as divided up into distinct, self-identical cultures. Waldron agrees with Kymlicka that choosing patterns of behaviour requires meaning and therefore relies upon the kinds of cultural framework within which activities acquire meaning, but denies that everyone needs access to 'a single, coherent culture' to give shape and meaning to their lives. Kymlicka's argument 'shows that people need cultural materials; it does not show that what people need is a rich and secure cultural structure'. It shows the importance of access to a variety of stories and roles, but it does not show the importance of something called *'membership* in a culture' nor the need for 'homogenous cultural frameworks' (Waldron 1995: 107–8). On the contrary, Waldron argues, in an increasingly (post)modern cosmopolitan world people draw the elements of their contexts of choice from a variety of cultural sources. These do not have to be coherent or even consistent. There is no basis for the view that individual freedom requires the preservation of any particular framework of individual choice, much less a single framework or 'cultural structure'. In the contemporary world, cultures are just fragments that 'happen to be available in a given place and time but which do not amount to the existence of a single culture in any socially or philosophically interesting sense of singularity' (Waldron 2000: 231). Waldron's image of a cosmopolitan world in which the very idea of distinct cultures is dissolved in a sea of superficial differences amounts to a spirited attack on efforts to justify the preservation of minority cultures by appealing to their role as contexts of individual choice. At the very least, it points to the need to justify differential treatment in ways that do not depend on identifying distinct and independent 'cultures'.

Culture and Difference

James Tully drew upon the work of anthropologists such as Clifford Geertz, James Clifford and Michael Carrithers to suggest that a conception of cultures as 'overlapping, interactive and internally negotiated' provides a more plausible ground on which to respond to contemporary demands for the constitutional recognition of cultural diversity (Tully 1995: 10). According to the 'billiard ball' conception of cultures as separate, bounded and internally uniform, otherness was associated with another culture and cultural difference was always external to one's own culture: 'one's own culture provided an identity in the form of a seamless background or horizon against which one determined where one stood on fundamental questions' (Tully 1995: 13). By contrast, on the contemporary view, the 'experience of otherness' is internal to one's own culture and indeed to one's identity (Tully 1995: 13). Tully takes this revised conception of cultures, according to which difference is as much internal as it is external to the cultures in which people live, to provide a basis for thinking that it is precisely the space in between the national conglomerates of differences that ensures the possibility of dialogue, negotiation and compromise between people from diverse cultural backgrounds. All citizens are:

> to some extent on a negotiated, intercultural and aspectival 'middle' or 'common' ground with some degree of experience of cross-cultural conversation and understanding … The politics of cultural recognition takes place on this intercultural 'common' ground (Tully 1995: 14).

Tully draws attention to the echoes of poststructuralist understandings of difference in this revised conception of culture by citing Jacques Derrida's non-identitarian conception:

> What is proper to a culture is to not be identical to itself. Not to not have an identity, but not to be able to identify itself, to be able to say 'me' or 'we'; to be able to take the form of a subject only in the non-identity to itself or, if you prefer, only in the difference with itself [avec soi]. There is no culture or cultural identity without this difference with itself (Derrida 1992: 9–10).

How do we affirm the identity of something like a national culture that is constantly changing over time and that is never strictly identical with itself? The issue here is the peculiar form of identity that cultures share with such things as meanings, intentions or languages. For Derrida, these are not stable, well-identified objects but rather differential and mobile entities whose identity is entirely parasitic on their internal as well as their external differences. In this respect, his understanding of cultures is consistent with the vision of the world he shared with other 'philosophers of difference' such as Gilles Deleuze. In *Difference and Repetition* Deleuze sought to outline an ontology in which difference 'in itself' was the fundamental principle so that the identity of things in general was to be understood as something produced from the differences of which they are composed. In these terms, identity was always something achieved or imposed upon a primary field of differences that he described as 'a pluralism of free, wild or untamed differences' (Deleuze 1994: 50).

There is considerable overlap between this poststructuralist vision of a world of differential entities or 'multiplicities' and the conception of cultural 'unities' produced out of differences that we find in the work of Geertz and his colleagues. In his Tanner Lecture on 'The Uses of Diversity,' he argued that cultural diversity begins at home:

> Foreignness does not start at the water's edge but at the skin's. The sort of idea that both anthropologists since Malinowski and philosophers since Wittgenstein are likely to entertain that, say, Shi'is, being other, present a problem but, say, soccer fans, being part of us, do not, or at least not of the same sort, is merely wrong. The social world does not divide at its joints into perspicuous we's with whom we can empathize, however much we differ with them, and enigmatical they's, with whom we cannot, however much we defend to the death their right to differ from us. The wogs begin long before Calais (Geertz 2000: 76).

In addition to the deep differences within a given national culture, of the kind that divide British soccer fans and Oxford dons, the kinds of differences that used to be attributed to different peoples in different parts of the world have become much more intermingled. As a result, it is less and less the case that different forms of human life are spatially and communicationally separated from one another, and more and more the case that these bump up against one another within the same national boundaries and the same cities and towns: 'we are living more and more in the midst of an enormous collage' (Geertz 2000: 85). Geertz takes this change in the spatial distribution of diversity to imply a need for a different conception of culture, built upon a more refined appreciation of the differences within a given society and the changes in the global interaction and intermingling of peoples from different ethnic, national and cultural backgrounds.

In 'The world in pieces: culture and politics at the end of the century,' he is explicit about the manner in which the geopolitical changes of the last decades of the twentieth century call upon us to revise our understanding of peoples and cultures. The old unities such as Europe or Russia or Vienna must be understood not as unities of spirit and value standing in marked contrast to other such unities. Rather, each of these must be understood as 'a conglomerate of differences, deep, radical, and resistant to summary' (Geertz 2000: 224). He describes his preferred way of understanding these conglomerates of cultural differences in a manner that echoes the poststructuralist philosophers of difference:

> First, difference must be recognized, explicitly and candidly, not obscured with offhand talk about the Confucian Ethic or the Western Tradition, the Latin Sensibility or the Muslim Mind Set ... Second, and more important, difference must be seen not as the negation of similarity, its opposite, its contrary, and its contradiction. It must be seen as comprising it: locating it, giving it form. The blocs being gone, and their hegemonies with them, we are facing an era of dispersed entanglement, each distinctive. What unity there is, and what identity, is going to have to be negotiated, produced out of difference (Geertz 2000: 226–7).

This conception of cultural unities as conglomerates of differences is apparent in Derrida's openly paradoxical description of European identity as that of a culture that has always defined itself by reference to an idea or 'heading', in the sense of an orientation, but which has now thoroughly internalized the idea of its internal and external differences. As a result, he argues, the idea of Europe today has become the idea of advancing towards what it is not, of heading towards its other:

> What if Europe were this: the opening onto a history for which the changing of the heading, the relation to the other heading or to the other of the heading, is always experienced as possible? An opening and a non-exclusion for which Europe would in some way be responsible? For which Europe would be, in a constitutive way, this very responsibility? (Derrida 1992: 17).

Derrida's relentless campaign against the propriety, properness, purity or essence of all things linguistic or cultural is clearly incompatible with attempts to ground normative claims by appealing to the identity of particular cultures or to the essential connection that particular subjects (we Europeans!) are supposed to have to their natal culture. In *Monolingualism of the Other or The Prosthesis of Origin* he argues that such identification with a culture or with a language is always phantasmatic. There is a constitutive but paradoxical alienation, without an originary subject that is alienated, in the relation of every individual to their culture or language of origin. For this reason, he argues that our culture or our language is always the culture or language of the other. This should not be taken to imply that there ought not to be rights for specific minorities, on the contrary. However, it does imply that these rights should be determined on the basis of the history, politics and power relations involved in their constitution as minorities: 'All culture is originarily colonial ... Every culture insinuates itself through the unilateral imposition of some "politics" of language' (Derrida 1998: 39).

David Scott's polemic against the ubiquity of appeals to culture in contemporary political theory points in a similar direction. He criticizes Tully and other liberal political theorists for their supposed uncritical acceptance of the conception of culture advocated by Geertz and other postwar anthropologists. His criticism ultimately amounts to the claim that this conception of culture as the set of constructed meanings within which individuals live their lives is an ideological conception of culture that answers a need for a new way to acknowledge difference between peoples in a 'post-ideological' world. It is the contemporary form in which the difference of the Other is expressed and recognized, in the same manner that the discourses of race, civilization and religion functioned during earlier periods of European colonial expansion. This is a conception of culture that, in 'a post-Cold War world now assumed to be safe for differences' may be supposed to answer to

> an ideological demand for a post-ideological conception of democratic pluralism, a cosmopolitan idiom in which the otherness of the West's Others, once a souce of defensive anxiety and the object of truth-determining investigations, could now be understood conversationally, antiessentially, ironically, as mere difference (Scott 2003: 111).

Scott's curiously uncritical criticism does not tell us what is wrong with this way of understanding culture, much less offer a revised conception. The objection rather is that Tully and others overlook the ideological history of conceptions of culture themselves. This is perhaps more a concern for politically engaged anthropologists than it is for political theorists. Scott poses a more interesting question for political theory when he suggests that critical attention to the history of concepts of culture might 'press us in the direction of more promising conceptions of the relation between historically constituted ways of life and organizations of political community' (Scott 2003: 97).

Cultural Practices and Societal Cultures

Kymlicka's response to criticisms of his liberal culturalist defence of minority rights arguably moves in precisely the direction recommended by Scott. In *Multicultural Citizenship*, he accepts some of Waldron's account of the nature of cultures as diffuse and open-ended phenomena and retreats from his earlier terminology of 'cultural structures,' which he now describes as 'potentially misleading': unlike structures, cultures 'do not have fixed centres or precise boundaries' (Kymlicka 1995b: 83). Instead of cultural structures he proposes the concept of 'societal culture' in order to highlight the fact that what matters is the shared institutions, languages and territorial location within which individuals acquire access to all forms of social life. By 'societal culture', he writes:

> *I mean a territorially concentrated culture, centred on a shared language which is used in a wide range of societal institutions, in both public and private life (schools, media, law, economy, government, etc.). I call it a societal culture to emphasize that it involves a common language and social institutions, rather than common religious beliefs, family customs, or personal lifestyles. Societal cultures within a modern liberal democracy are inevitably pluralistic, containing Christians as well as Muslims, Jews and atheists; heterosexuals as well as gays; urban professionals as well as rural farmers; conservatives as well as socialists (Kymlicka 2002: 346).*

The concept of societal culture does not so much solve the problem of individuating cultures as retreat from the thick conception of cultures as contexts of meaning and individual choice to a more 'thin' conception of culture. Kymlicka notes that this conception differs from the way in which culture is understood in most academic disciplines, 'where it is defined in a very thick, ethnographic sense, referring to the sharing of specific folk customs, habits and rituals' (Kymlicka 2002: 374 fn. 22). He agrees that citizens of modern liberal states do not share a common culture in this thick, ethnographic sense, but insists that modern liberal forms of governance depend upon citizens sharing a common culture in the different and thinner sense of a societal culture based upon a common language and institutions. The concept of societal culture allows him to reiterate his earlier distinction between the content and the identity of a culture at any given moment and to accept that 'it is natural and desirable, for cultures to change as a result of the choices of their members' (Kymlicka 1995b: 104). Such change affects the particular cultural practices which make up a culture at a given moment, but not its identity over time as the same culture. Secondly, the concept of societal culture enables him to differentiate between the situation of immigrant peoples and those 'national' cultural groups who were present on the territory at the time of its incorporation as a distinct nation-state. Whereas the latter have at the time of their incorporation an ongoing societal culture which they have struggled to preserve and to protect, the former have chosen to leave behind a societal culture and live in a new country.

The distinction between societal culture and thick cultural practices helps to distinguish the situation and entitlements of immigrants and originary national groups. It also helps to clarify the kinds of entitlements to which minority groups may have a legitimate claim. However, it does so at the cost of withdrawing from claims about the role of cultural contexts in providing contexts of choice and abandoning the earlier argument for minority cultural rights that relied on the principle of equality of access to such contexts. For it is thick cultural practices that provide us with options from which to choose and make those options meaningful to us. No doubt the viability of such cultural practices is not unrelated the existence of the relevant societal culture, especially the common language of the people concerned. But does the paradoxical identity of a societal culture over time ensure stable contexts of choice for individual citizens? In any case, the focus of Kymlicka's argument now shifts away from the contexts of meaningful individual choice to the consequences of the nation-building policies employed by liberal democratic states. Almost all liberal democracies have at one time or another sought to impose a uniform societal culture on their citizens in order to foster a shared national identity that would encourage mutual solidarity and underwrite the legitimacy of the state and its institutions. Switzerland is the sole exception to his assertion that 'historically, virtually all liberal democracies have, at one point or another, attempted to diffuse a single societal culture throughout all of its territory' (Kymlicka 2002: 347).

Taking account of the history of measures undertaken in order to integrate people into a common societal culture leads Kymlicka to question the idea that liberal democratic states have been or should be culture neutral. If, as he and other liberal nationalists have argued, such nation-building policies serve useful goals in encouraging solidarity, trust, deliberative democracy and so on, then there is no reason to object to them in principle. The question raised by the forms of resistance to such practices on the part of minority national groups or colonized indigenous peoples is whether, in a given case, the pursuit of nation-building has involved injustice towards particular minorities. Kymlicka argues that the burden of justification rests upon those who would deny to such minorities the same nation-building powers as those which the national majority takes for granted. In colonial countries such as Australia or Canada, indigenous peoples have fought long and hard against the loss of their traditional lands, the non-recognition of their laws and customs, and the loss of their languages. In European countries such as Belgium, Britain, France and Spain, there have been similar long-standing movements for autonomy on the part of minority national groups. In these and other cases of resistance, it is possible to see the claims to some form of multicultural state policy as 'a response to perceived injustices that arise our of nation-building policies' (Kymlicka 2002: 365).

In this manner, the focus on a thin conception of societal culture implies a retreat from the kind of argument that sustained the original liberal culturalist support for minority rights. It moves the argument away from liberal universalist conceptions of the relationship between individual freedom, autonomy and the conditions of their exercise and towards more historically sensitive conceptions of the relationship between ways of life and the organization of political community. Here too there is some convergence with the approach taken by poststructuralist philosophers for whom the question of minority is always considered in relation to power.

Minority and Power

Kymlicka's initial approach to the problem of minority cultural groups relied heavily on the claim that particular cultures were endangered by their minority status and that the rights of individuals were threatened as a result. The processual conception of culture put forward by anthropologists, along with the differential ontology advanced by Deleuze and Derrida, tends to undermine arguments that relied upon the identification of cultures. In the definitive statement of their political ontology, *A Thousand Plateaus* (1987), Deleuze and Guattari outline a 'minoritarian' politics that is concerned less with the political status or rights of minority groups than with the degree to which minorities embody a distinct power or capacity to transform majorities. Insofar as their concept of the minor or 'minoritarian' is defined in relation to power, their approach is convergent with Kymlicka's more recent focus on the injustices occasioned by nation-building practices. Insofar as they are not concerned with the justification of minority rights but with the general conditions that ensure the emergence of new forms and new systems of right, they are engaged in a different kind of political reflection and, as a result, a different concept of minority.

As Guillaume Sibertin-Blanc points out, their starting point it is not unrelated to the problem of minority cultural groups in the aftermath of the Austro-Hungarian empire (Sibertin-Blanc 2008). They introduce the concept of minority in the context of a discussion of Kafka's use of the German language. In this context, in which Czech was already a minor language in relation to German, while the German of Prague was a minor language in relation to the German of Vienna or Berlin, 'Kafka, a Czechoslovakian Jew writing in German, submits German to creative treatment as a minor language' (Deleuze and Guattari 1987: 104). Deleuze and Guattari are less concerned to characterize or to identify minority languages than to distinguish major and minor treatments of language. Major treatments of language include the processes of standardization of spelling and grammar that invariably accompany nation-building: 'The unity of language is fundamentally political. There is no mother tongue, only a power takeover by a dominant language ...' (Deleuze and Guattari 1987: 101). Minor treatments or uses of language involve processes of variation or deterritorialization of the grammatical, phonological or semantic rules of a language, such as we encounter in the creolization of colonial languages or the creativity of ghetto languages: 'The problem is not one of distinction between major and minor languages; it is one of becoming' (Deleuze and Guattari 1987: 104).

Moreover, their concept of minority is not confined to the context of language. It refers to the complex and abstract processes of becoming-minor that may be found in a variety of registers: linguistic, literary, musical but also affective, juridical and political. Majority and minority are not quantitative characteristics but refer to the relative position of the parties involved in relations of economic, political and institutional power. In this sense, they suggest that the non-white population of the underdeveloped and developing economies constitute an immense minority that outnumbers the predominantly white majority of the developed world. The difference between majority and minority supposes the existence of a constant or standard against which other contents are measured. In a national political regime, this implies the existence of a majoritarian subject against which the rights and duties of all citizens are measured:

> Let us suppose that the constant or standard is the average adult-white-heterosexual-European-male-speaking a standard language (Joyce's or Ezra Pound's Ulysses). It is obvious that 'man' holds the majority, even if he is less numerous than mosquitoes, children, women, blacks, peasants, homosexuals, etc. That is because he appears twice, once in the constant and again in the variable from which the constant is extracted. Majority assumes a state of power and domination, not the other way around. It assumes the standard of measure, not the other way around (Deleuze and Guattari 1987: 105).

Any individual or group that differs from this constant will be considered minoritarian, regardless of their number. Deleuze and Guattari include lifestyle, ethnic, economic and national groups among the minorities that challenge the majoritarian political order, but also groups defined by their distance from the norms of late twentieth century capitalist societies. 'Ours is becoming the age of minorities', they wrote in 1980, with reference to the struggles of national minorities such as the Basques and the Corsicans but also with reference to women, youth movements and 'irregular' workers (Deleuze and Guattari 1987: 469–70).

In the terminology of formal logic they employ in describing capitalism as an increasingly global axiomatic system, the variant economic, social and political formation of national economies is accounted for by the possibility of different axioms being used to reproduce formally isomorphic systems: 'there is isomorphy, but heterogeneity, between totalitarian and social democratic states wherever the mode of production is the same' (Deleuze and Guattari 1987: 464). The capitalist axiomatic encompasses and regulates only well-defined denumerable sets, which in turn correspond to majorities governed by the particular axioms of a given local system. By contrast, minorities constitute lines of flight that are defined as non-denumerable sets, characterized by the mode of connection that eludes both the majoritarian figures and the axioms that define them:

> The axiomatic manipulates only denumerable sets, even infinite ones, whereas the minorities constitute 'fuzzy,' nondenumerable or non-axiomatizable sets, in short 'masses,' or multiplicities of escape and flux (Deleuze and Guattari 1987: 470).

The struggles of particular minorities can sometimes lead to connections or compositions 'that do not pass by way of the capitalist economy any more than they do the State-form' (Deleuze and Guattari 1987: 470). States may well respond to the demands of particular national, cultural or economic groups by adding or subtracting particular axioms, but from Deleuze and Guattari's point of view this only amounts to translating these groups into elements of the majority or denumerable sets. What interests them is the status of such groups as nondenumerable sets or processes that

> *would receive no adequate expression by becoming elements of the majority ... What is proper to the minority is to assert a power of the nondenumerable, even if that minority is composed of a single member. That is the formula for multiplicities. Minority as a universal figure, or becoming-everybody (Deleuze and Guattari 1987: 470).*

The idea that there is a potential becoming-minoritarian in every individual or group has as its correlate the idea that majoritarian identity is always a fiction. The becoming-minoritarian of everyone is expressed in the many ways in which individuals or groups deviate from the standard. However, this deviation from the standard is also expressed in the ways that majoritarian political orders refuse to recognise or positively discriminate against certain thick social identities, often at great cost to those who bear them. Both of these forms of divergence from the standard are sources of change in the majoritarian social and political order and it is for this reason that Deleuze and Guattari are more interested in becoming-minoritarian than in the status of particular minority groups that have achieved recognition as sub-elements of a given majoritarian political order. Because individuals never entirely conform to the majoritarian standard, all societies exist in a process of continuous variation of greater or less frequency. With reference to the politics of autonomy practised by sections of the Italian left in the 1970s and 1980s, they suggest that there is a universal figure of minoritarian consciousness and that this figure is

> *continuous variation as an amplitude that continually oversteps the representative threshold of the majoritarian standard, by excess or default. In erecting the figure of a universal minoritarian consciousness one adresses powers (puissances) of becoming that belong to a different realm from that of Power (Pouvoir) and Domination. Continuous variation constitutes the becoming-minoritarian of everybody as opposed to the majoritarian fact of Nobody. Becoming-minoritarian as the universal figure of consciousness is called autonomy (Deleuze and Guattari 1987: 106).*

It is because this minoritarian consciousness implies an autonomous development of individual and collective capacities that it is not achieved by acquiring the majority. From the perspective of Deleuze and Guattari's minoritarian politics, 'the problem is never to acquire the majority' (Deleuze and Guattari 1987: 106). Philippe Mengue relies upon comments such as this to argue that Deleuze and Guattari's minoritarian politics is fundamentally hostile towards democracy. Since democracy is the realm of consensus and of the opinions of the majority, it follows that democracy is in essence majoritarian. If the task of minoritarian politics is never to acquire the majority then it appears that Deleuze and Guattari's interest in the potential of minorities and minoritarian becoming to bring about change implies no commitment to democracy. Indeed Mengue suggests that the position of majority is by nature opposed to the creativity of the minoritarian and that majoritarian and democratic politics inevitably 'crushes' creative becomings (Mengue 2003: 102).[3] Deleuze and Guattari indeed suggest that majorities do not determine the limits of the potential for transformation and that, for them, the interest of minoritarian struggles lies in their genuinely revolutionary potential. They argue that the power of minorities 'is not measured by their capacity to enter and make themselves felt within the majority system', but that it lies in their power to 'bring to bear the force of the nondenumerable sets, however small they may be, against the denumerable sets, even if they are infinite, reversed or changed, even if they imply new axioms or, beyond that, a new axiomatic' (Deleuze and Guattari 1987: 471).

It is clear that, despite their differences with Marxism, an orientation towards revolutionary political change persists in Deleuze and Guattari's minoritarian politics. However, their insistence on the transformative potential of minoritarian becomings does not imply a refusal of democratic political practice, since the reconfiguration of majoritarian political institutions is often achieved through democratic and legal means. Nor is their conception of political activity limited to electoral politics, since changes may also be brought about by extra-parliamentary forms of political struggle. At the same time, however, the aspiration that underpins their politics of minority is profoundly democratic. What interests them is the way in which minority struggles can function as vectors of pure becoming that open up possibilities for transforming majorities. They do not deny the importance of struggles for new rights, new forms of recognition and government: on the contrary, they insist upon the importance of such struggles at different levels of the political order: 'women's struggle for the vote, for abortion, for jobs; the struggle of the regions for autonomy; the struggle of the Third World; the struggle of the oppressed masses and minorities in the East or West' (Deleuze and Guattari 1987: 471). Even if they do not exhaust the political force and potential of minorities, such struggles are important for the conditions under which individuals and groups live. Deleuze and Guattari insist upon the importance of piecemeal changes to the form and content of a given majority: 'molecular escapes and movements would be nothing if they did not return to the molar organizations to reshuffle their segments, their binary distributions of sexes, classes and parties' (Deleuze and Guattari 1987: 216–17).

Western democracies have seen a range of legislative measures in recent years to broaden the standard to included non-whites, non-males and even to allow equal rights to homosexual partners. These measures suggest that, far from

---

3   For detailed discussion of Mengue's argument, see Patton (2005a, b).

'crushing novelty', democratic politics has its own forms of creativity. Mengue's suggestion that democratic politics is inimical to creative becomings is therefore unwarranted. In political terms, the difference between majoritarian change and minoritarian becoming amounts to the difference between the constitution or reconfiguration of the majoritarian standard and the ongoing process of non-coincidence with the standard. The irreducible character of the difference in kind between majority and minority aligns Deleuze and Guattari firmly with proponents of democratic pluralism such as William Connolly. The different forms of minority becoming provide the impulse for change, but this only occurs to the extent that there is adaptation and incorporation on the side of the majority. For this reason, Connolly insists on the importance for democratic politics of the 'productive tension' between, on the one hand, majoritarian governance, rights and recognition and, on the other, the forms of minoritarian becoming that periodically disrupt and eventually reshape the majority (Connolly 1999: 154). He argues that, in order to be responsive to new claims for the reconfiguration of the majoritarian standard, democratic political life needs to be infused with a public ethos of critical engagement (Connolly 1999, 51). Deleuze and Guattari are more concerned with the power of minoritarian becomings, whether borne by minorities excluded from the majority or by subjects of the majority who no longer coincide with its norms. For these carry the potential for new assemblages of affect, belief and opinion that imply the emergence of new peoples and thereby transform existing systems of governance, recognition and rights.

PART II
CHALLENGES

Diversity and the Limits of Liberal Toleration

Thomas M. Besch

Introduction

From the perspective of an account of toleration, the multicultural quest for the proper recognition of identities and cultural orientations can be seen to raise a important and familiar challenge: namely, the challenge to duly respect, and limit, diversity not just at the level of the application of principles of toleration, but also at the level of the justificatory foundations that a conception of toleration may appeal to. Toleration, of course, is difficult to come to terms with in its own right. Not only is it difficult to determine what toleration is, why we ought to tolerate, and what we ought to tolerate. It is also difficult to determine where we may draw the line between the tolerable and the intolerable. However, these difficulties are aggravated if we seek to tolerate on grounds that are equally justifiable to all affected others – including not only people who share our most important moral, ethical, or cultural commitments and concerns, but also people whose identities, practices, and cultures deeply differ from ours, and that might hence seem, say, mistaken, flawed, or even intolerable to us. Arguably, this desideratum is not easily met. For instance, some liberals appeal to an idea of individual autonomy in order to ground and delineate tolerability – thus, they argue that toleration is needed to protect individual autonomy, or at least a meaningful diversity of practices and ethical orientations that nourish individual autonomy, and that practices and orientations are tolerable only if they do not harm that autonomy (e.g. Kymlicka 1995b: 152–72; Raz 1986: 400–29). Yet, as has often been noted, the view that individual autonomy should be accorded such an important role might not be equally justifiable to all relevant others. After all, some people and groups could not coherently place suitably high priority on individual autonomy without first fundamentally changing their ethical outlooks. Thus, from their perspective, an autonomy-promoting practice of toleration would not duly respect their non-individualistic commitments, and would hence fail to be truly tolerant. Can there be a conception of liberal toleration that takes the cultural and doctrinal diversity characteristic of multicultural societies seriously both at the level of the application of its principles and at the level of its foundation?

Some philosophers take constructivist approaches in practical philosophy to be particularly suited to accommodate a deep and pervasive diversity of practices, lifestyles, doctrines, and identities. In one way or other, practical constructivists construe accessibility and acceptability, or some form of accessibility and acceptability, as something that can constitute the very correctness, validity, or epistemic-practical authority, of a conception of justice and its reasons. And some constructivists argue that a conception of justice can achieve suitably wide accessibility and acceptability only if it fundamentally and systematically respects reasonable disagreement – and, in their view, to respect reasonable disagreement is to tolerate. John Rawls and other political liberals have accordingly advanced what he calls a 'political' brand of constructivism as the best way to respect such disagreement, and to suitably respond to a 'fact of reasonable pluralism', and this not only at the level of the application of a conception of (political) justice, but also at the level of the justificatory foundations and resources such a conception draws on (e.g. Rawls 1993; Larmore 1990, 1994; Macedo 1991). What I want to examine here is an exemplary constructivist, broadly Rawlsian conception of toleration, namely, Rainer Forst's view. In much of his recent work, and in particular in his impressive book *Toleranz im Konflikt* (Forst 2003a) – a book which might be the most comprehensive and advanced philosophical study on the topic in the recent German discussion – Forst has advanced an ambitious account of the history and the structure of toleration that culminates in an attempt to overcome several 'paradoxes' of toleration, as Forst and others have referred to them, and, most crucially, what he calls the 'paradox of drawing the limits' (the German phrase is Pradoxie der Grenzziehung) (Forst 2003a: 38ff., 2003b: 70ff., 2004). Forst describes this paradox as follows. All toleration

> *necessarily implies intolerance toward those who are seen as intolerable and, quite often, as intolerant as defined by those limits [i.e., the limits between the accepted and the tolerated, and these two things and the intolerable]. The concept of tolerance makes no sense without certain limits, though as soon as these are substantively defined, tolerance seems to turn into nothing but intolerance. There is thus no 'true' tolerance. To resolve this paradox a conception of toleration must show how far its limits can be drawn in a mutually justifiable and non-arbitrary way (Forst 2003b: 72).*

Thus, the problem of the paradox of drawing the limits is the problem that even our best attempts to delineate tolerability might fail to be duly tolerant, so that there might not be any real, 'true', or not self-undermining conception (and practice) of toleration (see Forst 2003a: 38, 2003b: 72). For Forst, this problem is crucial: the concept of toleration must be abandoned as incoherent unless this paradox can be resolved (Forst 2003a: 40, 2004).

Forst suggests a 'reason-based' conception of toleration that aspires to overcome the paradox of drawing the limits. And, it would seem, if he succeeds, there might be a way to tolerate in ways that deeply accommodate diversity. In essence, he advances two claims. He argues (i) that this paradox can be resolved only if the criterion of toleration – i.e. the criterion by which we distinguish between the tolerable and the intolerable – is not the subject of reasonable disagreement: only then, he insists, can our conception (and practice) of toleration be tolerant itself. Moreover, he claims (ii) that the idea of reasonableness entails a criterion of toleration that indeed meets this threshold, namely, a constructivist requirement of public justifiability: as this requirement cannot reasonably be rejected, it can be used as a criterion of toleration that overcomes that paradox. Like Rawls, Forst sees toleration as a matter of respecting reasonable disagreement, and takes such respect to be part of reasonableness; and, like Rawls, he takes a constructivist requirement of public justifiability to not be the subject of reasonable disagreement. Unlike Rawls, however, he anchors his views in a notion of reasonableness that does not depend for its authority and appeal on a commitment to the values of a liberal public–political culture, but that aspires to have wider and more fundamental authority and appeal. If it is successful, then, Forst's account points the way toward a conception of toleration suitable for the culturally diverse conditions of contemporary liberal societies.

Even if we are sympathetic with these ideas and aspirations, however, we have reasons to be less optimistic than Forst is about the prospects of this type of approach: his constructivist, 'reason-based' attempt to resolve the paradox of drawing the limits, I shall argue, is bound to fail. On the one hand, the broadly Rawlsian criterion of toleration that Forst advocates and the idea of reasonableness that is intertwined with it is the subject of reasonable disagreement. Thus, by Forst's own lights, it fails to be tolerant itself. At the same time, there is reason to believe that it is self-defeating to advance a constructivist requirement of public justifiability as a criterion of toleration, while characterizing reasonableness in terms of this requirement. In conjunction, all this suggests that constructivist, broadly Rawlsian conceptions of toleration of the overall type advertized by Forst are fundamentally incoherent.

It is necessary to start from somewhere, but as Forst's account of the history of toleration is by far too rich and complex to be addressed here with any accuracy (see Forst 2003a: 53–58), I shall leave it aside and focus directly on his structural and normative views on the topic. To get things started, I shall survey aspects of his view of the structure and of forms of toleration. After that, I will sketch his view of the limits of toleration and place them in their systematic context. Once this reconstructive work is in place, I shall move on to criticism, and thus will address a range of problems at the heart of Forst's constructivist thinking about the criteria, role, and foundation of toleration.

Toleration: Concept and Conceptions

All forms of toleration involve an 'objection component' and an 'acceptance component' (Forst 2003b: 71–6). The object of toleration (e.g. some belief, doctrine, or practice) must in some respect be thought of as wrong, misguided, bad, deficient, or some such thing; without this objection component, there would not be toleration, but indifference or acceptance. However, toleration requires, too, that the object of toleration is at the same time approved of or accepted in some respect. This acceptance component, Forst insists, may not 'cancel out the negative judgment [i.e., the objection component] but gives certain positive reasons which trump the negative ones in the relevant context. The said practices and beliefs, then, are considered to be wrong, but not intolerably wrong' (Forst 2003b: 72).[1] Not least, toleration involves limits that mark 'the point where reasons for rejection become stronger than the acceptance reasons' (Forst 2003b: 72). More precisely, it involves two types of limits: one separating the things that are accepted from things that are rejected, but still tolerated, and one separating these two things from the things that are strictly rejected as intolerable. Only the latter limit is the limit of toleration 'properly speaking' (Forst 2003b: 72), and this is the limit that gives rise to the paradox of drawing the limits.

Next, Forst distinguishes between various conceptions of toleration; three of which should be mentioned now. First, there is a 'permission conception' of toleration. According to this conception (and practice) of toleration, the tolerator assumes a position of superiority, and grants toleration as a means to an end, e.g. the end of avoiding conflict, or of maximizing stability, or power. On a permission conception, toleration marks an instrumental and non-symmetrical relationship (Forst 2003b: 74, 2004: 42–8). Next, there is a 'co-existence' conception of toleration. According to this conception, toleration is an instrumental and symmetrical relationship; it is still instrumental in nature, but now each of the tolerating parties equally gives and receives the benefit of toleration. Toleration thus becomes a mutually endorsed, reciprocal (but potentially instable) modus vivendi (Forst 2003b: 74, 2004: 42–8). Many contemporary discussions construe of toleration along

---

1   As it is worth noting, in many discussions of the topic, the objection component of toleration is taken to be the dominating and thus characteristic component, and where it is taken to dominate, toleration is easily seen as something that fails to properly recognize or appreciate other people (to give just one example, see Brown 2001). Such views, it seems, in effect see cases where agents essentially *suffer* other agents without interfering with them as paradigm cases of toleration. It is important to note, however, that this at most marks one particular (even if often-encountered) way to tolerate, or one conception of toleration, rather than the nature of toleration. As we shall see shortly, there are others ways to tolerate – ways, that is, that amount to ways to respect the equal standing of other people, and that thereby in effect give essential, dominating importance to the *acceptance component* of toleration. From the outset taking the objection component to dominate thus conceals the substantive normative question of how we ought to tolerate, or how we ought to appreciate what we also have reasons to object to.

the lines of one of these two conceptions. A third conception, however, is crucial for Rawls and those who follow him, and it marks the form of toleration that is the focus of Forst's attempt to overcome the paradox of drawing the limits. According to the 'respect conception' of toleration, then, toleration is a non-instrumental and symmetrical relationship in which the tolerating parties respect each other as equals, while toleration is, or is seen as, something is demanded by, and expresses, this respect. In Forst's terms:

> [e]ven though [people] hold incompatible ethical beliefs about the good and right way of life, and differ greatly in their cultural practices, they respect each other as moral-political equals in the sense that their common framework of social life should – as far as fundamental questions of the recognition of rights and liberties and the distribution of resources are concerned – be guided by norms that all parties can equally accept and that do not favor one specific 'ethical community' (Forst 2003b: 74).

Forst focuses on a respect conception of toleration partly because he takes this form of toleration to be normatively superior to the other types just referred to. In his view, only respect-toleration duly reflects the freedom and equality of reasonable people, their reasonable disagreements, and, crucially, their discursive moral standing as beings that have a 'right to justification', or, as Forst sometimes also puts it, that are worthy of being given adequate, justifying reasons in matters that affect them. However, Forst's view of the superiority of respect-toleration is not our focus here, and it relies on ideas that are at the core of his view of the criterion of toleration – and the latter is our main concern. Let me therefore sidestep his view of the superiority of respect-toleration, and turn instead to some of the ideas just referred to.

Finally, not much depends here on the distinction between toleration as a virtue of persons, or tolerance, and toleration as a property of social arrangements.[2] Like Rawls, Forst takes toleration in the first sense to be part of reasonableness, and takes reasonableness to be the standpoint from which political principles must be acceptable to count as justified, or legitimate, or just.[3] On this view, authoritative political principles, and the social arrangements they prescribe, are consistent with toleration in the first sense, and so will be tolerant in the second sense. Toleration as a virtue of persons thus becomes (part of) what grounds toleration as a property of social arrangements. As I read Forst, his attempt to resolve the paradox of drawing the limits in the first instance focuses on toleration in the first sense, or tolerance proper, but it finds its point and upshot in a view of toleration as a property of social arrangements.

---

2   On this distinction, see, e.g. Murphy (1997).
3   See Rawls (1993); on reasonableness in Rawls, see Besch (1998).

A Constructivist Narrative

Forst's view of toleration is embedded in a constructivist narrative about the sort of justifiability that political principles (allegedly) need – a narrative that draws not only on Rawls's political constructivism, but also on the Kantian constructivist views of Habermas and O'Neill (see Forst 2003b: 80, 1994: 280–306, 2002: 182–200). The following are key ideas of this narrative that are particularly relevant for our purposes:

1. People are worthy of being given adequate, justifying reasons in matters that affect them: they have a right to justification (Forst 2003b: 76f., 81, 1999).
2. Political principles raise validity claims to the effect that their correctness requires them to be justifiable to all others to whom they apply. 'The realm of justification,' Forst insists, 'must be identical with the realm of the validity of a norm' (Forst 2003b: 76).
3. Given the right to justification and the validity claims that political principles raise, such principles need to be, or be based on what is, equally accessible and acceptable by all relevant others – or, as Forst often puts it, they need to be reciprocally and generally acceptable. In other words, they need to meet a requirement of public justifiability (Forst 2003b: 76).
4. Given Rawls-type burdens of judgment, there exists reasonable disagreement about a wide range of comprehensive, philosophical, ethical, religious, metaphysical and other matters.

Following Rawls, Forst takes the most important of the burdens of judgment to be 'that the way individuals assess and weigh moral and political values is shaped by their total experience and whole course of life, which will always differ between persons, especially in modern, diverse societies' (Forst 2003b: 80ff., see also Rawls 1993: 50ff.). For Forst, as for Rawls, these and similar factors do not distinguish between reasonable and unreasonable disagreements, but explain, or are part of what explains, how reasonable disagreement between reasonable persons can arise and persist without impugning their reasonableness. Correspondingly, Forst endorses a Rawls-type maxim of the avoidance of reasonable disagreement:

5. Given the requirement of public justifiability, political principles may not be based on grounds that are the subject of reasonable disagreement (Forst 2003b: 76).

For what comes later, three things should be highlighted now. First, the idea of public justification at the center of this broadly Rawlsian picture is constructivist in a sense that surfaced earlier on already, namely, it construes of the equal accessibility and acceptability – or the reciprocal and general acceptability – of political principles and their reasons as something that constitutes their correctness, validity, or their epistemic-practical authority. This, of course, marks a philosophically controversial doctrine. Anti-constructivists, such as Platonists, moral realists, or perfectionists,[4] reject the idea that equal accessibility and acceptability can in its own right justify, or constitute correctness – even though anti-constructivists might, and sometimes do, agree that equal accessibility and acceptability is a valuable by-product or desideratum of good reasons and justifications, and could even be an important constraint on the legitimacy of (independently justifiable) political principles.[5] Second, like Rawls, who sought to apply 'the principle of toleration to philosophy itself' (Rawls 1993: 10), and so applied it at many different levels of thought, Forst does not restrict the attempt to avoid reasonable disagreement to substantive, first-order normative, evaluative, or other considerations or reasons. For Forst, as for Rawls, we should avoid reasonable disagreement across a wide range of resources that a public justification of political principles may need to invoke.

Not least, third, for what comes later we should note now that it is not quite clear what systematic relationship obtains between some of the views at the center of Forst's constructivist narrative. In particular, it is not clear what relationship obtains between (1) and (2) on the one hand, and (3) on the other. Forst often emphasizes that the right to justification is 'basic' or 'fundamental', and more fundamental than other rights; and he suggests both that it is 'constructed' and that the attribution of this right to others implies a commitment to the requirement of public justifiability (or the criteria of reciprocity and generality). In conjunction with his other views, this means that his narrative in effect oscillates between at least three distinct views about the relationship between the right to justification and the constructivist requirement of public justifiability:

1. the right to justification is basic in the sense of being a key part of the justification of other rights; but it is still a constructed right in that it depends for its content or authority on its public justifiability;
2. if and where we recognize that others have a right to justification, we commit ourselves to the view that political principles must be publicly justifiable to them (in other words, the right to justification grounds the requirement of public justifiability);
3. the commitment to justifying things to others is motivated by, or is based on, recognition of their right to justification, or of the normative standing to which this right refers, while other, independent considerations suggest that public justification is the form of justification most suitable for the task.

Later on, we will have reasons to consider the justificatory dependencies that obtain between the right to justification, or the standing to which this right refers,

---

4   For more on the difference between constructivism and these brands of anti-constructivism, see O'Neill (1996: 54ff), O'Neill (1989, Chapter 11), O'Neill (2003).
5   At the same time, Platonists might require reasons to be the (possible) subject of what Nagel calls 'ideal unanimity' – i.e. an agreement that would occur if the relevant others grasped the epistemic merits of those reasons (where these merits are not seen as a function of the acceptability of these reasons) (Nagel 1991: 33f).

and the commitment to public justifiability, understood in constructivist terms. For now, it suffices to note that (1) and (2), but not (3), take the right to justification to entail or suppose or depend on a constructivist requirement of public justification. That is, according to (1), the right to justification supposes for its authority constructivism, while (2) takes the ascription of this right to others to commit us to a particular, constructivist way to respond to it, namely, the way of public justification. Consequently, if constructivism is reasonably controversial, then so would have to be the idea that people have a right to justification. By contrast, (3) does not bundle constructivism into the view that the people have a right to justification, or the normative standing to which this right refers. All that (3) entails is that if we accord this right to others, we commit us to justifying certain things to them, but (3) leaves open what requirements or criteria those justifications are to meet – thus, (3) does not entail, but is consistent with, a constructivist view of public justification. In short, then, by the light of (3), but not by the light of (1) and (2), we can accept that there is a right to justification, or that people have, or should be taken to have, the discursive moral standing of being worthy of being given adequate, justifying reasons, whether or not we are committed to constructivism. I shall come back to this in the section on the burdens of judgment, validity claims and the right to justification.

Toward a Criterion of Toleration

Against this background, Forst suggests the following as the criterion of toleration:

> Citizens are tolerant if they accept the boundary set by the criteria of reciprocity and generality as both delineating the justifiability of mutually binding norms and the limits of toleration. Tolerant citizens are 'reasonable' in accepting that ... they have a moral duty to tolerate all those ethical beliefs and practices that they disagree with but that do not violate the threshold of reciprocity and generality (trying to force their views on others). Such a violation of the basic right to justification is a form of intolerance that cannot be tolerated (Forst 2003b: 78).

Persons are tolerant to the extent that, even though they disagree with others about the nature of the good and true life, they tolerate all other views within the bounds of reciprocity and generality. That is why toleration is a virtue of justice and a demand of reason (Forst 2003b: 78).

On this view, the requirement of public justifiability – referred to in these passages in terms of the criteria of reciprocity and generality – is the criterion of toleration. Practices and beliefs are tolerable only if they are consistent with that requirement (and therefore with treating others in accordance with their right to justification). It is not entirely clear what, for Forst, it actually takes to interact with others within 'the bounds of reciprocity and generality', and what range of practices and beliefs can justifiably be claimed to be ruled out as intolerable by that standard. But at its core it involves a commitment to the idea that political principles, or, more generally, ideas of the good and the right, may not be treated or enforced as binding for other people unless these principles are publicly justifiable to, and hence equally accessible and acceptable by, these others – that is, despite, and in avoidance of, their reasonable disagreements.[6]

Yet why should we draw the limits of toleration in these terms? Forst's 'reason-based' case for his criterion of toleration amounts to this. A criterion of toleration (and the practice of toleration that is prescribed by it) can be duly tolerant itself only if it meets the threshold of reciprocity and generality – that is, only if it is equally accessible and acceptable by, or publicly justifiable to, the relevant others. However, a criterion of toleration cannot achieve this form of acceptability if it is the subject of reasonable disagreement. Thus, it must not be based on any reasonably controversial conception of the good and the right (widely conceived so as to include religious, metaphysical, 'ethical', and other doctrines) – and if a conception draws the boundary between the tolerable and the intolerable on the basis of reasonably controversial content, the resulting criterion and practice of toleration will be intolerant by unduly, unfairly, arbitrarily, or dogmatically, privileging one conception of the good and the right over others. Now, for Forst, a commitment to the criteria of reciprocity and generality – that is, to the requirement of equal accessibility and acceptability, or of public justifiability – is part of what it means to be reasonable in the first place. Consequently, the criteria of reciprocity and generality cannot reasonably be rejected. But if they are not the possible subject of reasonable disagreement, then these criteria, if anything, can provide a criterion of toleration that is itself tolerant (see Forst 2003a: 649ff., 2003b: 80). If we sum this up, this yields:

1. A criterion of toleration, to be tolerant itself, must be equally accessible and acceptable by, or be publicly justifiable to, the relevant others.

---

6   For attempts to apply his criterion to actual political conflicts, see Forst (2003a: 675–748, 2004: 320ff). As far as I can see, it remains unclear how the application of this criterion can steer clear of the invocation of content that can be rejected reasonably and that, in being the subject of reasonable disagreement, ought to be the object of toleration *by the light of this criterion*. As the (purported) standing of the criterion does not necessarily infuse the content required to meaningfully apply it with similar standing, the application of the criterion can fail to pass the test posed by it. Waldron and McKinnon have in effect argued that the attempt to avoid reasonable disagreement is insufficient to determine where the line between the tolerable and the intolerable is to be drawn, and Forst, it seems, is faced with problems of the sort they discuss. See Waldron (2003: 21ff.) and McKinnon (2006: 76ff.). While these applicative problems have the potential to be damaging, the concerns I shall address later target more fundamental problems – problems, that is, that remain even if a Forst-type, Rawlsian conception of toleration has considerable applicative yield.

2. A criterion of toleration can meet the condition expressed in (1) only if it is not the subject of reasonable disagreement.
3. The requirement of public justifiability cannot reasonably be rejected: a commitment to public justification is part of what it means to be reasonable in the first place.
4. Therefore, the requirement of public justifiability (or of equal accessibility and acceptability, or of reciprocal and general acceptability) is a tolerant criterion of toleration.

As illustrated by the central role of (1), Forst anchors his criterion of toleration in a conception of reasonableness – or, as he puts it, in 'elements' of reasonableness. For Forst, reasonableness involves insight in the burdens of judgment and recognition of the existence of reasonable disagreement (as part of a more general insight in the finitude of both theoretical and practical reason), and two main commitments, one 'epistemological', one 'normative':

> The epistemological element of being reasonable consists in an insight into the finitude of both theoretical and practical reason … The finitude of reason … [implies] the task of finding and defending justifiable reasons, because this is what reasonable and finite persons … owe to each other … Thus the normative element of being reasonable implies this form of respect for others as reasonable and worthy of being given adequate reasons; that is respect for their basic right to justification. Both elements in combination … are the basis for the acceptance and the recognition of the threshold of reciprocity and generality. They provide the essential reasons for being tolerant. Being tolerant thus means seeking reasonable agreement within the limits of reciprocity and generality, and being aware of the different contexts of justification that persons are part of (Forst 2003b: 80f.).

Given its context, this passage suggests that reasonableness involves at least three things, namely,

1. insight in the finitude of reason and recognition of the burdens of judgments and of the existence of reasonable disagreement;
2. a commitment to providing adequate, justifying reasons – reasons, that is, that, where appropriate, pass the threshold of reciprocity and generality – that is, reasons that are equally accessible and acceptable by the relevant others, or that publicly justify;
3. a commitment to respecting others as worthy of being given adequate reasons, or respecting their right to justification.

Note that Forst is committed to the view that the conception of reasonableness that is characterized by (1), (2) and (3) is suitably accessible and acceptable by the relevant others. If it fails to be suitably acceptable, e.g., by being the subject to reasonable disagreement, then it would not be reasonable by its own lights – in which case, it would seem, it could not coherently ground a tolerant criterion of toleration. (I shall come back to this point later, especially in the discussion of the problem of incoherence.)

In short, then, for Forst, the paradox of drawing the limits can be resolved only by a criterion of toleration that is not the subject of reasonable disagreement, while the requirement of public justifiability – or of reciprocity and generality – as it reflects elements of reasonableness, is not the subject of such disagreement, and therefore provides a criterion of toleration that resolves the paradox of drawing the limits. Writes Forst:

> *The [paradox of drawing the limits] says that toleration, as soon as its limits are defined by a certain content, becomes intolerant toward those 'outside' [i.e., those deemed intolerable]. As an answer to this, ... we cannot call any form of moral critique 'intolerance', because then we lose the concept of toleration completely. Instead, by drawing the 'limits of toleration' with the help of the criteria of reciprocity and generality, we draw them ... in the widest possible way given the existence of a large diversity of world-views, without sacrificing one for the sake of the unjustifiable claims of the other. Thus there is no arbitrary substantive content that defines the tolerable (Forst 2003b: 81).*

That is, to retain the concept of toleration, we need to concede that not all rejections of conceptions of the good and the right are intolerant, but only those rejections that are not based on adequate, publicly justifiable reasons – and a commitment to public justifiability is part of what it means to be reasonable. Where rejections are based on the criteria of reciprocity and generality, then, they are not intolerant.

Reasonableness, Public Justifiability and Reasonable Disagreement

So much as a reconstruction of this constructivist conception of toleration. At its core, we have seen, are two ideas: the idea that a criterion of toleration, to be tolerant itself, may not be the subject of reasonable disagreement, and so needs to be compelling from the standpoint of reasonableness, and the idea that a requirement of public justifiability can play the role of such a criterion. These ideas, in turn, are embedded in a view to the effect that the requirement of public justifiability answers to the validity claims of political principles and duly reflects the discursive moral standing of people as beings that have, as Forst often puts it, a 'right to justification'. It is not entirely clear what relation obtains between the requirement of public justifiability and Forst's right to justification; what is clear, however, is that this conception of toleration takes reasonableness to entail, amongst other things, a commitment to public justification and a commitment to according to others the sort of discursive moral standing just referred to.

In the remainder of my discussion, I shall call into question the plausibility and coherence of this conception of toleration. If a criterion of toleration, to overcome the paradox of drawing the limits, may not be the subject of reasonable disagreement, then Forst's criterion does not seem to be suitable for the task. For, it is plausible to believe, both the requirement of public justifiability and Forst's conception of reasonableness are, or can be, the subject of disagreement that is, or can be, reasonable. At the same time, there are reasons to believe that a Forst-type approach cannot coherently characterize reasonableness in terms of a constructivist requirement of public justifiability. I shall turn to the issue of incoherence later on, and shall now address concerns that relate to the first issue.

To begin with, Forst's criterion of toleration, i.e. the requirement of public justifiability, is a constructivist requirement, and constructivism is a philosophically disputed doctrine. As we have seen above already, anti-constructivists, such as Platonists, moral realists and perfectionists reject the view that accessibility and acceptability justifies in its own right, or constitutes correctness. Thus, Forst's criterion of toleration is the subject of disagreement, and some of this disagreement reflects long-standing, intelligent, conscientious, informed and systematic controversies about the criteria and the foundations of practical reasoning and justification. Now, it is plausible to claim that intelligent, conscientious, informed and systematic disagreement about constructivism is, or can be, reasonable disagreement, if anything is. If that is right, though, then we would have to conclude that Forst's criterion of toleration is, or can be, the subject of reasonable disagreement, and so fails to be tolerant itself. By implication, his criterion of toleration does not overcome the paradox of drawing the limits.

Of course, this line of thought, while plausible, might beg the question. After all, it simply takes it that it is not, or at least not necessarily, unreasonable to reject the requirement of public justifiability. Nevertheless, disagreement, or at least intelligent, conscientious, informed, and systematic disagreement, gives rise to a simple dialectic that undermines the aspirations of a Forst-type, 'reason-based' constructivist conception of toleration. That is, suitably sophisticated disagreement about a constructivist criterion of toleration either is reasonable, or it is unreasonable. If it is seen as reasonable, the conclusion drawn in the last paragraph follows. If it is seen as unreasonable, however, another problem ensues. For the view that suitably sophisticated disagreement about a constructivist requirement of public justifiability fails to be reasonable will amount to little more than a mere stretch of dogmatism unless it is made the subject of justification itself. Thus, constructivists like Forst would need to (publicly) justify to others who disagree with them that we cannot reasonably reject the constructivist requirement of public justifiability. Now, it seems that this justification cannot without vicious circularity, or, again, dogmatism, presuppose that reasonableness involves a commitment to a constructivist requirement of public justification. Instead, such a justification would have to establish the link between reasonableness and that requirement in the first place. But this entails that the 'reason-based' conception of toleration at hand would in effect cease to be reason-based: rather than being reason based, that is, it would have to be based on whatever it is that justifies the claim that reasonableness involves a commitment to a constructivist requirement of public justifiability.

All this assumes that reasonableness can coherently be thought of in terms that are thin or abstract enough in content to not entail constructivism. And of course this is possible. Consider, for instance, Moore's view of the meaning of the word 'reasonable':

> *The idea of being reasonable, at least in ordinary discourse, involves the idea of offering reasons for one's actions and being prepared to listen to and be persuaded by the reasons of others. This practice of reason-giving, which defines the reasonable person, presupposes that others are worthy of reason-giving and some minimum consideration, but it is also compatible with highly partial reasons. Indeed, many of the reasons that people offer to justify their actions are inextricably linked to the things that they deem important from the personal perspective, such as their own desires, aims and ends (Moore 1996: 1712).*

This seems to get things approximately right. On this picture, reasonableness, at least as far as the meaning of the term is concerned, involves a commitment to a practice of reason-giving, or justification, but not necessarily to a constructivist practice of reason-giving, or justification. And reasonable people take it that others are, as Moore puts it here, worthy of reason-giving and some minimum consideration: but being worthy of reason-giving and some minimum consideration marks a discursive moral standing that may or may not amount or entail to a right to (public) justification. That is, that reasonable people should pursue their willingness to engage in reason-giving and to accord to others a certain discursive moral standing by adhering to a constructivist requirement of public justification is a substantive claim – a claim, that is, that might have much in its favor, but that is nevertheless disputed by reasonable people who reject constructivism. And even if we go beyond Moore's view of reasonableness, and add that reasonable people attach positive value to reasoned agreement (or, say, reasoned convergence in judgment, or unanimity), constructivism would still not follow – this is so at least so long as it remains open what justificatory role, if any, reasonable people accord, or should accord, to reasoned agreement, and by what standards they take, or should take, such agreement to be reasoned in the first place. As far as the meaning of the term 'reasonable' is concerned, then, reasonable people can coherently reject a constructivist requirement of public justifiability and with it a Forst-type criterion of toleration.

Another remark is in place. Especially if we follow constructivists like Forst and place considerable importance on inclusive reasoned agreement, or wide accessibility and acceptability (whether or not we also accord a genuinely justificatory role to agreement or acceptability), do we have reasons not to presuppose in our justifications a view of reasonableness that some relevant others are committed to reject. To apply O'Neill's terms to the case at hand, we should select starting points for our justifications that abstract from, or 'bracket', (purported) elements of reasonableness that some relevant others intelligently dispute, and we should do so not only to ensure that our starting points and the conclusions that we seek to build on them are suitably acceptable by all relevant others, but also in order to avoid dogmatism.[7] As there is intelligent, conscientious, informed and systematic disagreement about constructivism, then, we have reasons to base an account of toleration (or indeed of anything else), if it is to be 'reason-based', on a notion of reasonableness that is abstract or thin enough in content to allow such disagreement about constructivism to qualify as reasonable disagreement. (In fact, as we shall see in the discussion below, there might be reasons to endorse a much stronger version of this claim.)

The Burdens of Judgment, Validity Claims and the Right to Justification

Let us observe next that a rejection of the requirement of public justifiability does not commit us to reject the view that there are burdens of judgment, or that political principles raise special validity claims, or, not least, that people have a right to justification, all understood in suitable terms. Thus, these things neither entail that requirement, nor do they suffice to establish that reasonable people should understand their commitment to a practice of reason-giving, or justification, in constructivist terms.

Take the issue of the burdens of judgment first. We do not need to deny that there are burdens of judgment if we reject a constructivist requirement of public justification. Rawls-type burdens of judgment explain how disagreement that is characterized as reasonable on other, independent grounds can come about. Thus, where we reject a constructivist requirement of public justifiability, or, say, concede that this requirement, too, is the subject of reasonable disagreement, we simply (and plausibly) add to the list of reasonable disagreements the emergence of which would need to be explained by a true account of the burdens of judgment. That is, rejecting the requirement of public justifiability might enrich or deepen the explanatory agenda of an account of the burdens of judgment, but it does not entail that there are no such burdens.

Next, consider the validity claims of political principles. Much depends on how we conceptualize validity claims in the first place. If we seek to construe of validity claims in terms that do not depend on or suppose the resolution of long-standing epistemological, ontological and normative disagreements about the nature of practical, political justification, then, evidently, we have reasons to construe of them in terms that neither entail constructivism nor anti-constructivism. And, quite on

---

7   O'Neill elaborates on abstraction in O'Neill (1996: 38ff). See also O'Neill (1988).

the lines of the point made at the end of the previous section, it would seem that we have such reasons anyway. On the one hand, if we positively value inclusive reasoned agreement about the foundations of toleration, or, more narrowly, of practical justification, then we have reasons to construe of validity claims in terms that abstract enough from constructivist assumptions to be accessible and acceptable to all relevant others, including, as it were, anti-constructivists, such as Platonists, moral realists, or perfectionists. Thus, constructivists have reasons to conceptualize validity claims in terms that do not require constructivist public justification. On the other hand, that we claim our political principles to be correct (or true, valid, or reasonable) does not by itself entail any particular conception of the standards of the correctness of such principles. The practice of raising validity claims might give us reasons to search for some such conception, but it does not single out any particular conception as the right one. After all, the search for the best account of the nature of correctness in political principles is shared by proponents and opponents of constructivism alike.

Not least, does a rejection of the constructivist requirement of public justifiability entail a rejection of the idea that people have a right to justification? Again, the issue turns on how we construe this right in the first place. As we have already seen, it is not entirely clear how Forst's narrative relates the right to justification to the requirement (and the practice) of public justifiability. Now, if we are to assume that this right is a constructed or attributed right in the sense that it depends for its authority on constructivist public justification, then this right is as controversial as constructivism itself. If, by contrast, the right to justification does not depend on the resolution of long-standing disagreements about the nature of practical justification, then it cannot entail or suppose constructivism. It would seem that the latter marks a more plausible way to construe of this right anyway. Forst's label 'right to justification' refers to the discursive moral standing of being, or being seen to be, worthy of being given adequate, justifying reasons – or, to use Moore's terms, of being 'worthy of reason-giving and some minimum consideration'. And construing of others as having discursive moral standing does not by itself, or conceptually, commit us to any particular conception of the goodness of reasons or of the requirements of justification. More specifically, there are at least two distinct types of discursive moral standing that one can accord to others: one justification-constitutive type and one justification-consequential type. If we take it that other people have constitutive discursive moral standing, then we not only believe that we should interact with them on the basis of reasons that they could accept – as a way to treat them as being worthy of reason-giving and at least minimal consideration – but also take it that the goodness of good reasons at least in part is a function of what these others could accept. This, it seems, is the kind of discursive moral standing that constructivists like Forst have in mind; and if the right to justification refers to this sort of discursive moral standing, then attributing that right to others comes with a commitment to constructivism, while anti-constructivists will have reasons to reject that others have a right to justification.[8] Things are different, of course, if we accord to other people consequential discursive moral standing. In that case, we seek to interact with them on the basis of reasons they could accept, but we do not take the acceptability of those reasons as something that (in part) constitutes the goodness of good reasons, but, rather, see it as something that flows from, or is a consequence of, a proper appreciation of their goodness.[9] This is a kind of discursive moral standing that anti-constructivists can accord to other people, as it does not commit us to constructivist criteria of good reasons or justification. However, once we consider that there are distinct types of discursive moral standing, it emerges that a right to justification that actually does entail constructivism would at best amount to a reasonably controversial, constructivist conception of the right of justification, or, say, a substantive ideal of discursive moral standing, rather than something that truly reflects what a right to justification necessarily entails, or that unpacks what it necessarily means to regard others as worthy of reason-giving and some minimal consideration. Accordingly, a constructivist requirement of public justification cannot be grounded in a right to justification unless it is already established on independent grounds why one should endorse a constitutive conception of discursive moral standing. By implication, especially if we follow constructivists like Forst and value reasoned agreement about the foundations of an account of toleration (or indeed of anything else) do we have reasons not to premise such an account on a right to justification that is understood in the constructivist terms of constitutive discursive moral standing. Instead, prior to further argument we should try to interpret our commitment to the discursive

---

8   It is not always clear what kind of moral standing constructivists take others to have. Discursive standing, of course, is not the only kind of moral standing that we can accord to other beings. For example, if we take sentience to be the morally relevant feature of a being, some non-human animals will merit moral standing, or, as we might also say, will be appropriate beneficiaries of moral concern, even though they will be unable to have discursive moral standing (in their own right). However, even where discursive standing is attributed, it is often unclear whether it is of the constitutive or the consequential type. Philosophers who are influenced by contractualist and Kantian ideas tend to construe of moral standing in terms of discursive standing, while interpreting the latter in constitutive terms – which often comes to the fore not so much by what they explicitly say, but by how they use the idea of discursive standing in substantive argument. For example, political liberals often suggest that respect for other people requires us to interact with them on the basis of reasons that they could accept, and therefore commits us to constructivist public justification. Exemplary here is Larmore (1990, 1994). Yet as much as there is no direct inference from moral standing to discursive standing is there no direct inference from discursive standing to constitutive discursive standing: in each case, we need substantive argument to show why beings that merit the more general type of standing should also be accorded the more specific type of standing.

9   By implication, according to others consequential discursive moral standing would give us reasons to seek Nagel-type ideal unanimity (Nagel 1991: 33f).

moral standing of other people in a way that allows it to be, as it certainly already is, shared by constructivists and non-constructivists alike.

To sum up, at least as far as the meaning of the word 'reasonable' is concerned, reasonable people embrace a practice of reason-giving, or justification, and accord to others discursive moral standing; and they can accept that there are burdens of judgment, that political principles raise special validity claims, and that people have a right to justification, while rejecting a constructivist requirement of public justification. And, again, there are reasons not to draw a distinct conclusion especially if we place positive value on reasoned agreement. All this suggests not only that Forst's criterion of toleration is the subject of reasonable disagreement – so that, by his own lights, it fails to be suitably tolerant, and so cannot overcome the paradox of drawing the limits. It also suggests that constructivists, insofar as they seek reasoned agreement, have reasons to premise an account of toleration, if it is to be reason-based, on an idea of reasonableness that is thin or abstract enough not to entail a constructivist requirement of public justifiability.

The Problem of Incoherence

Perhaps we can strengthen this conclusion – a conclusion, however, that looks quite plausible in its own right. There is something self-defeating about the constructivist assumptions at the heart of the approach to toleration that we are considering. To conclude this discussion, let me now outline the nature of this problem.

To begin with, then, even if we build a constructivist requirement of public justifiability into the idea of reasonableness, we can still ask whether it is reasonable to accept that requirement. In fact, especially if we build such a requirement into the idea of reasonableness will we have reasons to ask that question, given the importance that equal accessibility and acceptability – or reciprocal and general acceptability – thereby acquires, and given, too, that the resulting, constructivist conception of reasonableness will be the subject of intelligent, conscientious, informed and systematic disagreement. Let us note, as well, that the question of the reasonableness of the requirement of public justifiability is consonant with the very point of the search for a tolerant criterion of toleration. At least by Forst's light, this search is a search for a criterion of toleration that cannot be rejected reasonably, and that hence is not the subject of reasonable disagreement. The search for a tolerant criterion of toleration, therefore, is the search for a criterion of toleration that is reasonable in a particularly strong sense. Now, if we characterize reasonableness in terms of a constructivist requirement of public justifiability, then if we ask whether it is reasonable in that sense to accept that requirement, what we in effect ask is the question of whether that requirement passes its own test.[10] If it does not pass its own

---

10   As it is worth adding, on a Kantian constructivist view of reason, a requirement can adequately define reason as such only if it passes its own test. See O'Neill (1989, Chapter 2).

test, then it would not be reasonable in the relevant sense to accept it – it would, in other words, be self-defeating, or incoherent, to characterize reasonableness accordingly. However, it seems that the requirement of public justifiability does not pass its own test. Given the existence of sophisticated forms of anti-constructivism, the constructivist claim that equal accessibility and acceptability – or, in Forst's terms, reciprocal and general acceptability – constitutes the correctness (or the reasonableness, validity, or truth) of views, or, more generally, of stretches of thought, is not equally accessible and acceptable by all relevant others, and so is self-defeating.

To elaborate, consider the following claim (for some view or stretch of thought, S):

1. S is correct (or has epistemic-practical authority) only if S is equally accessible and acceptable by all relevant others.

This claim simply expresses a generic version of a constructivist requirement of public justifiability. Now, anti-constructivists, such as Platonists, moral realists, and perfectionists, cannot coherently accept that it is the equal accessibility and acceptability of S that constitutes the correctness (or epistemic-practical authority) of S – even though they might concede that equal accessibility and acceptability is an important desideratum or by-product of good reasons, justifications, or stretches of thought. Thus, anti-constructivists are committed to reject (1). However, if Betty cannot coherently accept S without first abandoning major, defining elements of her current anti-constructivist outlook on matters relating to the acceptability of S, but Paul can coherently accept S without any such changes to his outlook, then, it seems, S is not 'equally accessible and acceptable' by Betty and Paul. But if that is so and if anti-constructivists count as 'relevant others' at the level of discourse about the nature of reasonableness, the requirements of toleration, and the nature of correctness – which, it seems, most constructivists would concede – then two things seem to follow:

2. It is not the case that (1) is equally accessible and acceptable by all relevant others.
3. Given (2) and the condition expressed by (1), (1) is not correct (or does not have epistemic-practical authority).

If (3) indeed follows, then a constructivist requirement of public justifiability is self-defeating if and when it needs to pass its own test. Taking the equal accessibility and acceptability of stretches of thought to be something that constitutes the correctness of stretches of thought fails to be equally accessible and acceptable by all relevant others.[11]

If we translate this back into the language of reasonableness, the following is suggested. If we understand reasonableness in terms of a constructivist requirement of public justifiability, then it is unreasonable to accept stretches of thought that need to meet, but fail to meet, that requirement. However, if the requirement of public justifiability needs to meet that requirement, or needs to pass its own test, then it would be unreasonable to accept it: as I have just suggested, that requirement does not pass its own test. Consequently, it would be unreasonable to be reasonable. And this looks very much like a *reductio ad absurdum* of the attempt to define, explain or characterize reasonableness in terms of a constructivist requirement of public justifiability.

As it is worth emphasizing, though, the lesson here is not that we must reject a constructivist requirement of public justifiability, or that it could never be coherent to endorse that requirement as a criterion of toleration. The lesson is more complex. Strictly speaking, all that follows is that it is incoherent to require a criterion of toleration not to be the subject of reasonable disagreement, while both (i) construing reasonableness in terms of that requirement and (ii) advancing this requirement as a criterion of toleration. If a criterion of toleration can overcome the paradox of drawing the limits only if it is not the subject of reasonable disagreement (that is, if we endorse one of Forst's key intuitions about the coherence of the very idea of toleration), then we have at least two options. Either we abandon claim (i) by conceding that it is not, or not necessarily, unreasonable to reject the constructivist requirement of public justifiability; or we abandon claim (ii) by accepting that this requirement is not a suitable criterion of toleration. It has been the drift of my argument to suggest that abandoning (i) is a good thing in its own right, given the meaning of the word 'reasonable' and the fact that discursive moral standing is not necessarily of the constitutive type, and considering, as well, the implications of

---

11   For a detailed discussion of this problem, see Besch (2008). To mention just two possible strategies to overcome it, constructivists could tweak the requirement of public justifiability in such a way that it can be claimed to be accessible and acceptable by all relevant others despite the fact that some people intelligently and conscientiously reject it. For example, they might argue that these people could accept this requirement in the conditional sense that they would accept it, or could coherently accept it, if they did not endorse the views, interests or preferences that actually keep them from accepting it. Another move might be to impose restrictions on the membership in the group of the 'relevant others'. For example, constructivists might insist that a criterion of toleration needs to be equally accessible and acceptable only by those people who do not reject that political principles can be correct (or valid or reasonable) only if they are equally accessible and acceptable by all relevant others. Either way, however, it is hard to see how the attempt to save the requirement of public justifiability can draw its rationale from its equal accessibility and acceptability. It would be more plausible to argue that the importance or value of this requirement does not depend on its equal accessibility and acceptability, and to attempt to defend constructivism on non-constructivist grounds. I elaborate on this in the paper just referred to.

placing positive value on wide accessibility and acceptability. Once this is supposed, though, it would follow that a constructivist requirement of public justifiability can be a criterion of toleration only if such a criterion may be the subject of reasonable disagreement. This implication would call for either of two things: constructivists would have to show that a criterion of toleration does not need to overcome the paradox of drawing the limits, or that such a criterion, to overcome that paradox, does not need to avoid reasonable disagreement. But this would seem to give away the very essence of a respect conception of toleration and the search for a tolerant conception of toleration. Consequently, if we abandon (i), but adhere to a respect conception of toleration and seek a tolerant criterion of toleration, we have reasons to also abandon (ii) by concluding that a constructivist requirement of public justifiability cannot be the criterion of toleration.[12]

---

12   For helpful feedback I am indebted to Sabine I. Jentsch, Duncan Ivison, Andreas Muth, Paul Redding, J. L. Sands, W. Todd Davidson, as well as the attendants of a presentation of an earlier version of this chapter at Bogazici University, Istanbul, in early 2008.

Multiculturalism and the Social Sphere

Barbara Arneil and Fiona MacDonald

Over the last five years there has been a growing body of literature in western political theory analyzing the nature of the relationship between diversity, multiculturalism, social capital and the welfare state, particularly in Europe and North America. This literature has largely focused on the question of whether the politics of diversity undermine certain long-standing liberal or social democratic principles. The degree of the challenge has been such that some scholars have suggested there is now a 'retreat of multiculturalism' in both political theory and practice (Joppke 2004). The challenges to multiculturalism have come from several different directions: liberal scholars have argued that recognizing cultural 'group rights' undermines individual freedoms; feminists have argued that cultural protections may undercut sexual equality and politicians of various stripes have claimed that multiculturalism undermines a shared national identity or set of values. But some of the strongest critics have been scholars on the 'progressive left' who have argued that multiculturalism fundamentally undermines the 'social' sphere, expressed as social cohesion, solidarity, capital and/or justice. It is these critiques of diversity politics that we address most directly in this chapter, but we draw on the other critiques as well.

We hope to demonstrate three things through the following analysis: first, despite the considerable literature to the contrary, respect for diversity and support for social justice can work together to mutually support each other in democratic societies; second, the debate over ethno-cultural diversity versus social justice has left underanalyzed important limitations of liberal multiculturalism in addressing other kinds of 'difference' politics (three specific problems that we discuss are gender, 'race' and indigeneity, and faith); third, that the focus on the 'social' or civic sphere has meant not enough attention is paid to the state and its role in multiculturalism, most particularly the role of the *neoliberal* state. We will begin with an overview of the debate over multiculturalism versus the social sphere in the US, UK and Europe before turning to consider an alternative perspective of some leading Canadian scholars. Although multiculturalism has been challenged in a number of different ways at both the academic and political levels in the 'West', the exact emphasis of each critique differs depending on the theoretical and geographical context within which scholars approach the question, as we shall see. Overall, we hope to defend multiculturalism from further backlash while at the same time we hope to show that – at least in its current conception – multiculturalism does not fully address issues of diversity and inequality.

The Challenge to Multiculturalism: Social Capital, Cohesion and Justice

In the United States, scholars have argued that ethnic diversity can be correlated to a decline in solidarity amongst citizens, community participation and levels of generalized trust. Robert Putnam in his much discussed theory of social capital (2000) argues that Americans in the last generation have become less inclined to join organizations and participate in civic society then previous generations. More recently, he claims that this 'pulling apart' or 'collapse of community' can be correlated to the degree of ethnic diversity in a community – the more diverse a community is the less likely its members will be to either trust each other or engage in associational activity (2007). Over the same period, theorists like Richard Rorty (1999) and Todd Gitlin (1995), who describe themselves as part of the 'progressive' left, have critiqued the rise of the so-called 'cultural left' with its emphasis on multiculturalism and difference as shifting the focus away from the issues of inequality and poverty and undermining the solidarity necessary to challenge economic and social injustices. Nancy Fraser (1997) has tried to address these twin concerns of economic and cultural injustice through her analysis of the politics of 'redistribution' and 'recognition' and Iris Young (1996, 2002) has likewise attempted to reconcile these two dimensions of contemporary political thought. Other American scholars have argued that the emphasis on diversity in the context of the cultural wars needs to be reversed with a shift towards the political center in American politics and society (Wolfe 1998; Skocpol 2000).

In the United Kingdom, there has been a parallel although somewhat different debate at both the academic and broader societal level. While Brian Barry (2001) challenges multiculturalism's tendency to undermine both liberal rights and social solidarity, other scholars and politicians have focused on the degree to which multiculturalism, particularly with regard to new immigrants from Asia and the Middle East, undermines a unifying idea of 'Britishness' (understood as a shared set of political values) and/or the social solidarity necessary to undergird the social welfare state and equality (Pearce 2004). Scholars like David Miller (2004) have explored whether multiculturalism is reconcilable with national unity while critics like Trevor Phillips (2004) and David Goodhart (2004a, b) have concluded that multiculturalism undermines claims to racial equality, social justice and national solidarity.

The debate in the UK has been attenuated by the debate over 'faith-based communities', particularly British Muslims, with critics arguing that is necessary to create greater social and national cohesion and integration than is possible under a multicultural rubric. Under the auspices of Tony Blair's New Labour government, there has been a considerable backlash against multiculturalism and the promotion of a shared set of British values, ideas that are sometimes defended in terms of building 'social capital'. Indeed Blair himself, in the Labour journal *Renewal* (2002), uses the idea of 'social capital' as the theoretical framework through which he defended the principle of British values. Then Prime Minister Gordon Brown likewise gave a speech in 2004 defending the idea of 'Britishness', including a rethinking of the positive dimensions of British imperialism (Brown 2004).

In Europe, the debate has involved analysis, at both the theoretical and policy levels, of the relationship between immigration, cultural difference, social cohesion and economic solidarity. Some scholars have examined multiculturalism from the perspective of European integration either in terms of linguistic diversity or immigration while others have described what they see as a 'retreat of multiculturalism' (Joppke 2004); or a 'skeptical turn' (Vertovec and Wessendorf 2005) against cultural diversity; or an 'excess of alterity' (Sartori 2002). In 2004, German Chancellor Angela Merkel famously suggested that 'the notion of multiculturalism has fallen apart' (Furlong 2004). While *social capital* is the term often used in recent years in both the US and UK, the more common terms in Europe are *'social cohesion' or solidarity* which are deemed to be under threat. Thus, in 2003, Phillipe van Parijs organized a conference that brought together various individuals in Brussels to specifically discuss the proposition: 'Other things being equal, the more cultural ... homogeneity within the population of a defined territory, the better the prospects in terms of economic solidarity' (2004: 8).

The Canadian Response: A False Dilemma

While skepticism over multiculturalism has been growing in the US, Europe and the UK because of its perceived impact on the 'social' realm as described above, a different perspective has developed amongst the leading scholars of political science and theory in Canada, where claims of an inverse correlation between cultural diversity or multiculturalism and social solidarity, social capital or a strong welfare state are challenged through both normative and empirical analysis.

Barbara Arneil (2006b) has challenged Robert Putnam's social capital thesis arguing that participation in civil society has changed rather than declined largely as the result of claims for justice on the part of cultural minorities and women. She concludes that such change involves a shift from traditional service-oriented organizations towards new kinds of political groups that advocate for inclusion and equality with respect to gender, culture, sexual orientation and disability – while divisive and damaging to solidarity in the short term, such a shift is nevertheless a net gain to civil society as a whole if a more inclusive and diverse society is the result. She also argues, with respect to 'trust', that while generalized trust *has* declined over the last 40 years as Putnam argues, such a decline has to be understood within the context of the divisive nature of the debates over civil rights, women's equality and changing societal norms as citizens became less certain of the world around them and the people in it – the changes happened too quickly for some and too slowly for others. Moreover, any *decline* in trust over time is dwarfed by the persistent *gap* in trust between privileged and marginalized groups in American society (Wuthnow 2002). This gap is racialized as Orlando Patterson has demonstrated, concluding that the average percentage of African Americans who say they trust others between 1972 and 1994 is 17 per cent compared to 45 per cent of white Americans (1999: 190). This *gap*, Arneil argues, is not only statistically much larger than the decline but also suggests there are larger historical and social causal factors for distrust beyond those proposed by Putnam that need to be explored.

Within the defense of the 'social' in much of the literature on social capital in the UK and US, Arneil sees a deep nostalgia for a time when the world was more homogenous and connected but also far more exclusionary and unjust (2006b, 2006c). Arneil concludes *Diverse Communities* by arguing that if liberal democratic societies and the diverse communities that constitute them are to move forward and become more just, discord must be accepted as inevitable as previously excluded groups are included and express their views. In other words it is not diversity that leads to a decline in trust or changes in civil society participation but the *politics* of diversity, as groups over the last 40 years, such as women, racialized and sexual minorities, and people with disabilities have challenged the norms by which civil society is governed. The key issue therefore is not to reduce diversity or divisiveness, but to figure out the principles and procedures by which such differences are to be renegotiated in the name of justice. Thus, diversity and multiculturalism are not inherently at odds with social justice but *necessary* ingredients to its full expression. Canada provides an important empirical case study for how building on both simultaneously can work in practice.

Keith Banting and Will Kymlicka (2004, 2006) provide empirical evidence that the 'progressive's dilemma' between redistribution and recognition is a false one showing that in Canada not only is there no trade-off between the two but an emphasis on cultural politics and multiculturalism can actually increase the attention and resources spent on redistributive policies. This finding is corroborated with respect to diversity through immigration and social capital by Canadian scholar Irene Bloemraad (2006) who concludes that Canada's multicultural immigration policies (where immigrants are provided with a wide variety of services in their own languages and encouraged to preserve their own cultural ways even as they become Canadian citizens) is the main reason why the naturalization rate in Canada is twice that of the United States. Like the previous study, Bloemraad suggests that much depends upon government policies with respect to cultural minorities to explain the degree to which new immigrants feel that they belong to a new country, in this case Canada, and therefore trust their fellow citizens and engage in society. There is not, therefore, a negative correlation between cultural diversity through immigration and national solidarity; rather one can strengthen the other if the appropriate policies are in place to support new immigrants and respect their cultures of origin.

This argument is further reinforced by John Helliwell, a Canadian economist who concludes that social capital and diversity are not necessarily incommensurable with respect to new immigrants as long as governments engage in an 'integrationist' and multicultural rather than 'assimilationist' immigration policy (2003). Helliwell argues that Canada's emphasis on multiculturalism rather than a 'melting pot' approach has led to higher levels of trust amongst Canadian immigrants than American immigrants as well as doubled the likelihood that immigrants to Canada will naturalize (and join the national community). The conclusion that could be drawn from this analysis is that the relationship between social capital or solidarity and multiculturalism may be more a product of 'governmental policy … than natural law' as some of the previous analysis might suggest. Immigration policies, if they are to reconcile redistribution and recognition, must have a dual focus on economic integration and the protection of cultural heritage.

Perhaps more importantly, studies suggest that this positive correlation between multiculturalism and social solidarity is not unique to Canada but can be found in other countries as well. Based on comparative analysis of sixteen OECD countries, Banting and colleagues (2006) provide evidence that there is no statistical relationship between the strength of multicultural policies in any country and a decrease in welfare spending. They reject Van Parijs's suggestion (2004), therefore, that the effects of multiculturalism policy have yet to be seen – there is enough evidence, they argue, to conclude that the trade-off between the two is simply not present. With respect to social capital, Banting, Courchene and Seidle (2007) have also argued, using research mainly from North America, that contrary to the fears raised in both the UK and US, no negative correlation exists between diversity and generalized trust; rather it is more of a contingent relationship than scholarship like Putnam's and others suggests. One key factor in determining levels of trust in Europe according to Marc Hooghe and colleagues (2007) is whether non-EU citizens residing within European countries are granted early voting rights – a more inclusive political approach to immigrants is the key to reducing distrust in ethnically diverse societies.

It should be noted, however, that Will Kymlicka (2008) has questioned the extent to which specific multicultural policies adopted by the Canadian state from Pierre Trudeau in 1971 through to the present can be extrapolated to other jurisdictions – his argument is that 'multiculturalism' in Canada had a unique history that may not be easily replicated in other countries. Kymlicka's point is well taken (particularly the degree to which multiculturalism in Canada as a response to a Royal Commission on 'bilingualism' and 'biculturalism' has had from its inception a different set of majority political dynamics behind it, as well as the degree to which it was initially proposed by *'white'* ethnic minority *citizen* groups, namely Ukrainians and other Eastern European critics of biculturalism, which created a different kind of racialized politics around its implementation than is the case in Europe where multiculturalism tends to be focused on *racialized* minorities who are often *not citizens*).

It may also be the case, however, that these very aspects of Canada's policies and theories could provide important lessons as to how to construct multicultural policies in other jurisdictions, most particularly the recognition that multiculturalism should be embedded in the idea of 'citizenship' rather than directed at non-citizens (usually new immigrants) as well as specifically addressing the issue of 'racialization' separate from the question of multiculturalism, a point to which we will return in the next section. Ultimately, the importance of the Canadian literature is to demonstrate that there is no inherent conflict, as many scholars have argued, between social solidarity and justice on the one hand and the recognition of cultural difference on the other, but this depends on creating the right conditions for these concerns to be woven together in society rather than sacrificing one for the other.

Going Beyond Multiculturalism: Social Justice and New Challenges

The debate over the impact of multiculturalism and its implicit focus on ethno-cultural differences on the social sphere has left little room for other dimensions of social justice. The challenge for multiculturalism in the future is not so much the question of redistribution, trust or solidarity, but rather whether liberal multiculturalism can address *other* social differences beyond that of ethno-cultural diversity and if it can accommodate both issues of inequality and the fluid nature of intersectional identity politics. Thus, in the next section we will move beyond this debate over social justice and ethno-cultural diversity to examine four critical challenges to a fully developed theory and practice of social justice in diverse societies. The key to the first three of the challenges we describe below is the need to go beyond ethno-cultural differences and examine the vexed but understudied problems of gender, faith and indigeneity/race, none of which can be fully addressed within a liberal multicultural model (indeed in some cases are somewhat obfuscated by it).[1] It is also necessary to move beyond an almost exclusive focus on civil society (which

---

1   Liberal multiculturalism focused on ethno-cultural differences would claim to deal with these other concerns as well. In the case of minority faiths, the principle of individual religious rights combined with some polyethnic rights or recognition would serve to protect religious adherents from the majority culture (as we shall see however there are profound differences between the exercise of religious and cultural rights that move some dimensions of faith beyond the scope of multicultural theory). In the case of indigeneity, multicultural theorists would claim that self-government rights addresses these problems (but reduces 'peoples' to 'national minorities' or cultural groups). In the case of gender (women/men or sexual orientation), multicultural theory would claim that these could be protected as individual rights. As we hope to demonstrate neither of the broad principles of liberal multicultural theory (individual rights or cultural group rights are enough to address the full range of issues posed by faith, race/indigeneity or gender.

animates so much of the debate described above) and refocus on the state itself, most particularly the *neoliberal state*, and problematize how it is able to deploy both multiculturalism and group autonomy to serve its own ends.

Gender and Multiculturalism

One of the most important early critiques of multiculturalism was the liberal feminist challenge, represented in the works of Susan Okin (1999) and Martha Nussbaum (1999). Okin famously wrote an essay entitled 'Is multiculturalism bad for women?'- a question she answers in the affirmative. Her argument presents the problem as a dilemma between the right to sexual equality on the one hand and the right to cultural or religious accommodation on the other. According to Okin's analysis, there have been many instances where the protection of cultural group rights comes at the expense of the women within that minority group. Thus, she reasserts not only the need to protect and preserve the 'rights' of women, particularly in the case of cultural minorities, but equally the universal principle of 'equality'.

Martha Nussbaum's analysis is more global but, like Okin, she expresses her fears over the 'relativist' and 'anti-universalist' commitments in multiculturalism and difference feminism. Moreover she argues that the only 'universalism that has a chance to be persuasive in the modern world must … be a form of political liberalism' (1999: 9). Nussbaum sees cultural traditions as often 'obstacles ... to women's flourishing' and emphasizes instead the need to universalize all women's experiences in terms of fundamental capabilities (rather than rights).

As important as this feminist critique was for bringing needed attention to the gender/sexual dimensions of the multiculturalism argument, it became apparent very quickly that there were serious flaws in the manner in which the debate has been framed. First, both Okin and Nussbaum seem to attach 'culture' and 'cultural traditions' largely to minority cultures, leaving the majority culture as the background against which those with 'culture' should be examined. Secondly, in both cases, culture was seen almost entirely as negative, as an obstacle to women's self-realization rather than an important source of identity and meaning for women. Okin's argument forces women to choose between 'your culture and your rights'. Thirdly, there was an underlying assumption that ethnic minority women lacked agency and needed in some sense to be 'saved' from themselves by the more 'universalist' western white feminists. Finally, Okin and Nussbaum shared with the multiculturalists a definition of culture, particularly within minority cultures, of a bounded and unchanging set of values and traditions rather than an ever-evolving, contested, hybrid set of processes.

In response to these critiques, there has been a new generation of scholars sympathetic to both feminism and multiculturalism including Arneil et al. (2007), Ayelet Shachar (2001), Avigail Eisenberg (2003 and Chapter 7 this volume), Monique Deveaux (2000b, 2006), Rita Dhamoon (2006) Melissa Williams (1995, 1998), Iris Young (2002), Seyla Benhabib (2002), Chandra Mohanty (2003), bell hooks (1981,

2000), Bonnie Honig (2003), Anne Phillips (2007), and Sarah Song (2007) who have sought in different ways and through different mechanisms to recast the terms of the debate and/or develop theories regarding how such conflicts are to be resolved without seeing 'gender' and 'culture' as an either/or choice. Thus, feminist multiculturalism has tried to move the debate away from a dichotomous world-view in which 'culture' is set in opposition to 'sexual equality' (bifurcated static wholes) and towards a vision of politics constructed by overlapping and constantly evolving multiplicities. The central question then becomes how to negotiate these multiple identities based on several key principles.

The first and perhaps most important principle is that feminist multiculturalists, unlike earlier feminist critics, argue that multiculturalism is to be defended (for *women* as well as men), although whether that takes a liberal, discursive or radical form remains contested. This is particularly true in the last five years or so as multiculturalism finds itself in retreat or on the defensive. Feminist multiculturalists argue, however, that the meaning of 'culture' needs to be rethought and expanded. Liberal multiculturalism tends to see culture as a discrete and bounded identity inherently in conflict with and therefore as something to be preserved and protected from the forces of assimilation or integration. There is a certain kind of bounded and conservative aspect to seeing culture in this way, which is partly what feminists are reacting to in their critiques in the first place. Some feminist multiculturalists (Arneil 2006a; Dhamoon 2006) have argued that it is necessary to look outside political theory to other disciplines to find insights into a more pluralized, contested and fluid concept of 'culture'. Anthropologists David Scott (2003), Clifford Geertz (1973) and political theorist James Tully (1995) have raised questions about a so called 'billiard balls' notion of culture – arguing that cultural identity must be seen as fluid, hybrid and contested terrain. As Geertz comments 'The concept of culture I espouse is essentially a semiotic one.' 'Culture' in Rita Dhamoon's analysis is thus more a 'process' of meaning-making than a 'thing' that is given to us and intersects with other kinds of 'difference' (2005, 2006).

Cultural studies, post/colonialism also provides an expanded definition of 'culture' that may be useful to feminist multiculturalists for incorporating various cultural markers (colour, sexual orientation, disability) as well as colonialism into an understanding of 'national culture' and politics. At the heart of these theories is not only the idea that 'culture' is multiple but most importantly, it is constructed by historical power relations. Stuart Hall (1996), Edward Said (1979) and Homi Bhabha (1994) all centre their analyses of culture in 'power' both in the state and beyond into the cultural realms. Stuart Hall comments: 'A national culture has never been simply a point of allegiance, bonding or symbolic identification. It is also a structure of cultural power.'

Feminist multiculturalists such as Anne Phillips (2007b), Sarah Song (2007) and Arneil (2006a) use these insights from cultural studies and anthropology to argue that culture is not as 'solid' or deterministic as it appears in multicultural theory and practice but rather a process of meaning-making in which identities are constructed through a variety of intersecting cultural elements – gender is a critical element within this construction of identity. Thus the goal of multicultural theory, to preserve and protect cultural minorities, needs to be complemented by a new conception of culture that is unbounded, fluid and constantly evolving within a renegotiated set of power relations.

At the same time that feminist multiculturalists have argued for the need to rethink culture, some have also made the case for rethinking feminism and more specifically the goal of sexual or gender *equality*. While it has been assumed in much of second-wave feminism that equality is the goal of 'women' and more specifically feminists, this term (like culture) has been problematized and the issue of whether it is indeed the goal of *all* women has been challenged. While the 1995 Beijing Conference on Women made 'gender equality' the central plank of the international agreement and 'plan of action', it was clear during negotiations that various women's groups took very different views on whether or not 'equality' was the goal particularly if it meant 'same treatment'. Two issues are worth highlighting in this context.

First is the important scholarly literature that highlights differences between 'men' and 'women' rather than assuming equality as 'same treatment' – this argument has been made by 'difference feminists' like Carol Gilligan (1993) who suggest that the goal should not be to see women the same as 'men' – which tends to push women towards a dominant paradigm of masculinity but rather to recognize the 'different voice' of women. An extraordinarily important theoretical insight developed out of Gilligan's work – the body of work known collectively under the rubric of an 'ethic of care' was created in contradistinction to an abstract liberal theory of universal 'rights'. The ethic of care's approach to cultural pluralism would suggest that one should not apply abstract or universal principles such as 'rights' or 'autonomy' to diverse moral or political problems, but rather develop theoretical and practical solutions by paying attention to the particular relations between individuals as well as the contextual and historical dimensions within which issues emerge and the conflicting voices or narratives at stake in these debates.

Second, the words 'women' and 'equality' (understood as same treatment) tend to erase the differences *between* women as well as the possibility that for some groups of women 'equality', particularly gender equality, may not be their first priority. This has been the central focus of much third-wave feminist criticism of the second wave (Walker 1995). A specific Canadian example that highlights this problem would be the 1999 Aboriginal Roundtable on Gender Equality organized by Status of Women Canada. When indigenous women were asked to comment on the degree to which Canada had fulfilled its obligations under the Beijing Plan of Action to implement 'gender equality', they said that the term gender equality did not have much meaning for them, as their main concern was the issue of colonialism and racism, as *indigenous women*. Thus, broadly, multicultural feminism has argued that the recognition of the differences *between* women is important and given the degree to which equality tends to erase these differences, it may not serve the interests of all women, particularly those who are culturally or racially marginalized.

In conclusion, as Susan Okin originally argued, multiculturalism must take 'gender' more seriously. However, unlike Okin, we need to think in terms of 'gender justice' rather than sexual equality – as Arneil et al. (2007) have argued, this term broadens out the meaning of what it is women and/or sexual minorities are seeking, takes seriously the *differences* between women and allows different groups of women to define their own goals. Gender, like culture, is fluid, hybrid and contested in various ways. If indigenous women seek to address the issue of colonialism as more critical to their lives than 'inequality' with indigenous (or other) men, this expanded vocabulary allows them to do so. 'Same treatment' or even 'equal rights' may be powerful tools but carry with them considerable western cultural baggage and therefore cannot be the single universal goal of feminism. At the same time, interrogating the construction of gender and its relation to power must remain central to political theory and practice.

Finally, if gender and culture are both multifaceted, in constant flux and at times in conflict with each other, feminist multiculturalism ultimately pushes political theory and analysis away from the emphasis on rights in liberal multiculturalism and towards some kind of communicative or discursive democratic processes. The recent and award winning additions to feminist multiculturalism by Sarah Song (2007) and Monique Deveaux (2006) point to democratic practices as the mechanism by which to address concerns over both sexual and cultural justice. These scholars stress the political and strategic dimension of culture with a complexity that is lacking in earlier multiculturalism scholarship. In so doing, they shift the theoretical focus away from accommodating *cultures* and towards the assessment of individual cultural *practices*. While rights are an essential part of multiculturalism these scholars illustrate the need to include aspects of democratic deliberation. Democracy may be key to fully realizing the contested and politicized nature of cultures and offers the best strategy for overcoming the culture/gender impasse. As Deveaux argues:

> If cultural groups want to retain as much say as possible over the evaluation and reform of their practices then democratizing their internal processes and agreeing to hold their own practices to a test of democratic legitimacy may actually hold the best options available to them (2006: 222).

The key point is not to transcend difference or conflict but to facilitate the capacity for all to have a voice. Other scholars, such as Anne Phillips (2007b) while broadly sympathetic to Song and Deveaux's accounts, are concerned that the deliberative approach may exaggerate the scale of value conflict while leaving underdeveloped a notion of where to go next in substantive terms (2007b: 41).

Multiculturalism and Faith

Faith is perhaps the hardest case for multiculturalism and in many ways the most contradictory. We separate it out from other cultural claims not only because it is unique but because in the last decade or two it has taken on increasing importance in political debates. The key question to address is whether within the social sphere, multicultural theory and practice as currently understood can encompass faith claims? Will Kymlicka has recently argued (2008) that liberal multiculturalism can accommodate faith groups in the same way that it has accommodated both national minorities and polyethnic minorities (the latter in particular overlapping in many important ways with faith groups). We argue, however, that while liberal multiculturalism works extremely well for certain kinds of faith claims, it *cannot* fully accommodate all claims made on the basis of religious belief because of the profound differences between other 'cultural' claims to group rights and recognition and those claimed by faith communities. We will thus outline these differences in detail, showing where liberal multiculturalism seems to fit and where it does not.

The first critical difference between faith claims and those of ethnic-cultural communities is the appeal to the 'sacred' or an authority that exists outside of human relations, creating a difference in kind rather than degree from those claimed on the basis of ethnic or cultural identity. The sacred is important not only in terms of the kinds of claims made by adherents of religion but also because the 'sacred' has given rise to some of the key principles of liberal political thought, for example 'human dignity'. Jurgen Habermas has described this as 'the linguistification of the sacred' in his *Theory of Communicative Action* (1984). Faith thus provides an important alternative way of thinking about ethical and political issues in relation to either 'scientific' approaches or the materialist approaches of economic capitalism championed by many modern thinkers. With respect to people with disabilities for example, religious perspectives on the sacred nature of life in all of its diverse forms are seen as a much better normative foundation than the science of genetic selection and engineering.

Liberal multiculturalism, to the extent that it respects religious differences in public institutions, is more respectful of the sacred nature of religion and its symbols to its adherents then either classical liberals or republicans are, but is this enough? The question of course is how far should liberal democratic secular states go in recognizing the special nature of faith and how does it change the nature of the claim being made? Habermas has recently argued that John Rawls's notion of public reason does not allow enough room for religious citizens to make their faith claims and proposes instead an 'institutional translation proviso', by which citizens of faith would 'be allowed to express and justify their convictions in a religious language if they cannot find secular 'translations' for them' but must also approach 'faith reflexively from the outside and to relate it to secular views' (2006: 9–10). In essence, Habermas is attempting to level the playing field between religious and non-religious citizens and build in a greater degree of respect for the sacred nature of the former's expressed views.

A second difference between faith groups and cultural groups is that unlike 'cultural' group rights which are, by definition, claims by *minority* cultures seeking justice or recognition from majority cultures, faith is not necessarily rooted in a 'minority' claim – indeed it can be a 'majority' claim, such as Christianity in the United States. The issue with respect to majority religions, particularly Christianity, is very different and the century old appeal to separate religion and the state becomes particularly important to protect minority religious groups but also, in some cases, the rights of sexual minorities and women.

George Bush's faith-based initiatives in the United States (Arneil 2006b), in which public services are delivered by churches rather than government agencies, have been critiqued by Jewish groups who have deep and legitimate concerns about churches being financed through federal dollars to deliver drug-dependency counseling or child care programs. The exceptionalism of the US (meaning its deep religiosity in the form of majority Christianity) is critically important to the question of whether liberal multiculturalism can be used to protect faith communities because it directly contradicts the idea that cultural claims are protecting a 'minority' concern. Moreover, within the United States, the exceptional growth of the Christian church and its adherents has been largely within evangelical denominations, even as the traditional churches have declined in numbers (Ladd 1999: 46–7).

This dimension of religiosity in the United States heightens concerns with respect to multiculturalism, for as Wald et al. have concluded evangelical religion 'is a major predictor of attitudinal cohesion' and intolerance (1990: 210). Thus, studies on attitudes towards certain cultural minorities (most particularly atheists and gay or lesbian Americans) demonstrate that evangelical Christians are more intolerant than other Americans (Wald 1997, Jelen 1982, Wilcox and Jelen 1990). Wald also finds that evangelical Christians are more likely than any other religious group to be opposed to women's rights and abortion and to have 'a more traditional understanding of women's roles' (1997: 185–6). If the fastest-growing religious group in the United States is intolerant of sexual minorities and seems to undermine sexual justice for women, than it is clear that the multicultural model advocated by Kymlicka and others should not apply – rather the continuing hard separation of faith and state, first articulated by Jefferson, makes much more sense.

The third difference is that state support for minority faith groups and faith-based initiatives (under a broad multicultural rubric), particularly in the UK but also in other countries intersect in troubling ways with concerns over national 'security'. While multiculturalism tends to begin with the goal of national unity or integration, such a goal with respect to religious minorities can result in double-edged initiatives on the part of the state. Since 9/11 in America, and 7/7 in the UK, this is particularly true with respect to Muslim minorities. In the United States, in the immediate aftermath of the terrorist attacks, George Bush proposed the establishment of a Terrorist Information and Prevention System (TIPS) – a nationwide mechanism that would enlist American utility workers, letter carriers, transportation workers and neighbours in a joint effort to 'prevent' terrorism in their local neighbourhoods – it was clear who the targets of such local surveillance were meant to be. The program was challenged in Senate and ultimately shelved when Congress passed the Homeland Security Act that explicitly prohibited such programs.

Faith-based initiatives in the UK are located in the Home Office (which is also responsible for domestic security). Having multiculturalism initiatives and inter-faith 'dialogue' housed under the same minister as homeland security creates significant issues as Lowndes and Chapman (2006) have shown. The question in the case of the UK is whether the state is seeking 'dialogue' with Muslim communities to create better understanding between different faith communities or to keep tabs on a particular group for security reasons. Kymlicka admits that liberal multiculturalism, most particularly the key principle of national unity, means that fostering such 'intercultural dialogue' from above in order to 'know more about' the Muslim community in Canada is problematic given the mixed motivations for fostering such dialogue – does it matter if 'national unity' is deeply interlinked to 'national security'? The case of Maher Arar and others in Canada suggests that such 'knowledge', at an official level, can be put to extremely nefarious uses.

The fourth difference is the manner in which faith can cut across the public goal of providing universal delivery of social or educational services. In response to the perceived drawbacks of what has been called by Richard Neuhaus (1984), the 'naked' public square (in which liberal or republican secularism has been critiqued for marginalizing faith-based claims and communities in the name of the secular state), both minority and majority faith groups have demanded a larger role within the public or social realm. While there are many good reasons, as articulated by liberal pluralists like William Galston (2002), for recognizing the right of various groups to educate their children in ways that respect community values or to use community groups (including faith-based organizations) to provide social services rather than relying on the welfare state, it is critical that theorists analyzing these faith-based initiatives take into consideration the very different dimensions they entail. There are cases where multiculturalism or pluralism is the right response with respect to faith claims in the public/social realm, in other cases it is not. We want to address the issue of faith and the 'public square' or social sphere through four specific lenses: schools, social services, dress, and the law.

Faith and Schools

State funding of faith schools became a central concern in the last provincial Ontario elections in Canada and is debated in many different liberal democratic jurisdictions. Partial funding for faith-based schools is already in place in other parts of Canada and there are conditions on such funding. In the province of British Columbia, for example, any public funding requires the school to teach the provincial curriculum and thus material on multiculturalism, religious tolerance and gender equality. However, while it is true that such funding helps to protect and preserve faith communities consistent with multicultural policy and theory, faith-based schools can also undermine public education (in large part because it provides subsidized spaces for children in 'private' schools whose parents want to leave the public system for many reasons beyond religious ones but cannot afford the fees of an independent private school). Thus, the analysis of faith-based schools must go beyond the issue of protecting or preserving minority cultures to also address the broader implications for the public school system as a whole, including the degree to which public funding drains resources away from the public system.

The impact on the public education system can also be analyzed in relation to multiculturalism in a different way. It could be argued that the increasing numbers of students enrolling in single faith schools undermines a critically important dimension of the public provision of education, namely the opportunity for students to meet and develop relationships and learn with others from a wide variety of religious and cultural backgrounds. Public schools provide daily lessons on multiculturalism through the student body itself – this is a different dimension to the debate that is very rarely addressed in the multicultural literature, and more specifically in the debate over the impact of religious schools on the social sphere.

Faith and Social Services

The delivery of social services through faith groups has grown in liberal democracies. Faith groups are seen as less punitive, closer to the local community and more connected than state welfare offices and their staff might be. However, there are some real concerns with social service delivery, particularly when it is majority faith groups involved. Under George Bush's 'Faith-based initiatives', first in Texas and then in the White House, delivering social services through churches, including various kinds of counseling including for substance abuse, child care services, housing has raised very troubling questions about how minority faith or sexual minority members have been treated when they seek state aid for a particular social need (Arneil 2006b). In Texas in particular, the state legislature raised issues over the lack of oversight and regulation of faith groups. Thus, multiculturalism may apply when the faith-based group is a minority culture (but even then it raises issues for sexual minorities) but it certainly does not apply particularly well when it replaces the pluralist state with a majority faith group as the social service provider because this tends to reinforce the dominant cultural values and practices and potentially threaten rather than protect and preserve minority ones.

Faith and Dress

The issue of wearing particular apparel because of one's faith has raised issues with respect to both gender and culture.[2] In Canada, multiculturalism policy applies very well to this particular expression of faith in the public square. Unlike France and other jurisdictions that rigidly ban religious apparel in the name of a policy of republican secularism in public institutions like schools, multiculturalism argues that respect of difference means individuals have the right to wear turbans, veils, yarmulkes as their religion requires. As many of the examples provided by Kymlicka and Taylor suggest, cultural protection in dress is often deeply connected to religious belief. Feminist multiculturalists have also made clear that the notion that the 'veil' should necessarily imply gender inequality or submission to men is to misunderstand the degree to which such symbols can have multiple meanings.

---

2   See Chapter 7 this volume.

Faith and the Law

The extent to which multiculturalism is applicable to the incorporation of faith-based adjudication in liberal secular states is unclear. The debate over religious tribunals in Canada, as an alternative to judicial court mediation over family law, has been an extended one. While Ayelet Schachar has argued that religious arbitration may be appropriate in areas like family law, some scholars and commentators both outside and within the religious group suggest that the issue of gender justice/injustice raises important challenges. Other scholars (Eisenberg 2007) have argued that religious arbitration should not be seen as a case of multiculturalism at all. The issue of faith-based arbitration has a long history that predates multicultural policies and like other issues related to faith should be separated out from multicultural theory and practise and debated on its own merits.

This brings us to our fifth and final point with respect to faith, namely how extraordinarily important it is to examine faith claims with particular attention to gender. Faith is double-sided for both women and sexual minorities (lesbian, gay, bisexual, transgendered [LGBT]/queer communities). Many feminist scholars argue that religious institutions often operate in opposition to the interests of women and sexual minorities emphasizing how large traditional religions (Christianity, Judaism and Islam in particular) have fought women's equality, reproductive freedoms and sexual autonomy and the demands for inclusion and equality by queer citizens. Some discrimination is obvious – women cannot hold certain senior offices in many religious organizations; traditional religious tenets in many faiths call on women to be submissive to their husbands; gay men and lesbians are seen as 'sinful' and required to repress their sexuality. The key problem is that when claims are made against women or sexual minorities rooted in 'faith' or religion, it pulls these claims out of the various political claims and makes them, by definition, a prior claim, a 'sacred' claim on the part of religious adherents. This is the negative side of religion and its sacred nature, as discussed above with respect to women and sexual minorities. While we have argued for the necessity of a fluid conception of culture to guard against its employment in perpetuating injustice, this idea does not translate well to certain kinds of religious claims.

The other side of the faith issue, which feminists often ignore, are the studies that have shown how religion is generally more important for women than for men. Verba et al. (1995), Smidt (2003) and O'Neill (2005) have all demonstrated the importance of religion in women's lives. Thus, there is a deep *positive* relationship between women and faith that needs to be recognized in thinking through the protection and preservation of faith communities and practices. If the diversity of women's experiences, including religious women, is to be taken seriously, religion cannot be seen as wholly negative with respect to gender. This overlaps considerably with the analysis of feminist multiculturalists who in opposition to Okin and Nussbaum, make the case that 'culture' is not wholly negative for women but is an important part of their identity and life. Within this general rubric, the particular role that religion plays in the lives of many cultural minority women as enormously positive must also be recognized. One obvious example would be African American women, many of whom see faith not only as an important resource for themselves as individuals but critical to their ongoing struggles as African Americans, beginning in the civil rights era through to today where the black church is both a refuge from an unjust world and the centre of political resistance and change for *women* more than men. As Smidt comments: 'Black women represent an overwhelming majority of congregants in black churches' (2003: 128).

Thus, the response to the challenge of faith communities cannot be a simple knee-jerk assertion of secularism if the importance of faith to many citizens is to be fully recognized. At the same time, faith claims cannot be wholly protected under the rubric of multiculturalism if this means state-sponsored majority faith-based initiatives that potentially violate the rights of minority religions are protected. Bush's faith-based initiatives suggest that a firm separation of state/religion should be reasserted in many instances. The growth of the evangelical churches and their tendency to be intolerant of homosexuality and women's rights is a critical test in developing a political theory that differentiates faith from culture – these attitudes are not to be protected in the name of faith or culture but challenged in the name of justice. While multiculturalism may work for some aspects of faith in the public square (faith and dress), it cannot fully encompass other dimensions (faith and schools, faith and social services) since it potentially undercuts some very important principles with respect to both minority religions and a publicly funded quality education system and inclusive delivery of social programs. Finally, one needs to be skeptical of state support for faith communities and 'inter-faith' dialogue to the extent that it can and has been used to further the state's security agenda, as has been the case in both the US and UK. For all these reasons, faith cannot be wholly subsumed within a liberal multicultural perspective as something associated with a minority group that is to be preserved and protected, rather, it needs to be interrogated in all of its different dimensions.

Multiculturalism, Race and Indigeneity

Multiculturalism may provide a useful framework for the protection and preservation of certain cultural practices and beliefs against dominant ethno-cultural norms as described earlier, but can it encompass 'race' and 'racialized minorities' and/or indigenous peoples through either the politics of recognition or groups rights for polyethnic and national minorities? Like 'culture' the idea of bounded groups defined by 'race' has been undermined by critical race theory which has fundamentally challenged the idea that race can be either bounded or even determined (through genetics, ancestry, or physiology), arguing instead that race is a social construction. This shift, while important, has resulted in a tendency on the part of some scholars to see race as equivalent to or a parallel category to that of ethnicity or culture – leading some to argue that it can be subsumed within a multicultural analysis.

The history of race or more specifically racialization is distinct and it is important to retain conceptual differences for a number of historical and contemporary reasons, as Joel Olson notes:

> *Race is … a constructed but socially significant category,* **distinct from ethnicity***, whose meaning and function vary across time and nation … race is not static, universal or derivative of some other more fundamental category. It is dynamic, historical and relatively autonomous from other social structures. It is a form of power that shapes the public sphere and is in turn shaped by it. It is therefore necessary to … look at how race is reproduced within the political realm' (2004: 9–10,* **emphasis added***).*

'Race' is different from the idea of 'culture' as it is articulated in liberal multiculturalism because it is not a static category to be protected and preserved in relation to a majority 'culture' but rather a relationship of privilege between socially constructed racialized groups based and defined by power relations, discrimination and colonialism. Or as Charles Mills puts it: 'Whiteness is not really a colour at all, but a set of power relations' (1997: 127).

Thus liberal multiculturalism's tendency to protect and preserve cultural difference can, in the context of unequal power relations, tend towards the obfuscation and even preservation of racialized inequality, if such 'diversity' is always viewed through a multicultural lens of 'difference' rather than 'power'. Trevor Phillips in the UK uses the lack of attention to racial equality in multiculturalism to argue that it should be replaced with a classical form of liberalism and individual rights, but such a solution obscures as much as liberal multiculturalism does the historical power relations *within* liberalism that give rise to racialized discrimination in the first place (Tully 1995, Arneil 1996). What is required of 'Western' political theory and practice, as Olson and others have suggested, is an analysis of 'white' privilege through contemporary forms of racialization rather than relying solely on either individual rights alone and/or the protection and preservation of cultural group rights as the solution to racialized injustice. While liberalism's emphasis on color blindness and multiculturalism's emphasis on recognition of difference may appear to be competing ideals, ultimately they both fundamentally seek stability before justice. 'What the two ideals share is more significant than their differences. The purpose of both is to secure political stability in an increasingly global and rapidly changing economy' (Olson 2008: 17).

Within the broad area of race and racism, the issue of 'indigeneity' and indigenous peoples are particularly problematic with respect to multiculturalism. Indigenous scholars, like Glen Coulthard (2007), have challenged the multicultural theories of Charles Taylor, arguing that the politics of recognition are flawed both because it reduces indigenous 'peoples' who existed prior to Confederation in the case of Canada to 'minorities' or 'cultures' and because it places power in the hands of the dominant majority (non-indigenous peoples) to 'recognize' the 'minority' culture. For Coulthard, this continues the colonial relationship, the negative politics of 'self-image' described by both Franz Fanon and Taylor, in a different more subtle form. Similarly Richard Day and Tonio Sadik conclude that Kymlicka's form of liberal multiculturalism is fundamentally just a *'redistribution of traditional inequalities* within the established categories of colonizer, colonized and immigrant' (2002: 22). Indigenous scholars have also challenged the *liberal* dimension of liberal multiculturalism, most particularly the singular reliance of individualism and individual rights as largely anathema to indigenous self-conceptions. Mary Ellen Turpel-Lafond states: 'the collective or communal base of Aboriginal life does not really, to my knowledge, have a parallel to individual rights: the two conceptions of law are simply incommensurable' (1997: 67).

While the questions at stake in this debate go well beyond the scope of this chapter, the single most important point to be taken from the literature described above is that for many indigenous and postcolonial critics, the analysis must go beyond multiculturalism and recognize the historical power relations between indigenous and non-indigenous peoples. Some, like James Tully (1995) and Dale Turner (2006) argue for the fundamental renegotiation of the existing constitutional arrangements while others, Taiaikae Alfred (1999) and Patricia Monture Angus (1995) suggest that indigenous peoples separate from the various land claims and treaty processes, to disengage from a neocolonial context and develop their own politics and understandings of sovereignty. What is clear is that from the perspective of many indigenous scholars, liberal multiculturalism is an inadequate model. As Olson argued with respect to race relations more broadly, multiculturalism can become a tool used by the liberal state to stabilize and preserve existing power relations. We turn, in the next section, to look in detail at how the neoliberal state can use multiculturalism to serve its own ends with respect to both a shrinking welfare state and indigenous peoples.

The Neoliberal State and Multiculturalism

Conventional wisdom assumes that the concurrent trends of neoliberalism, characterized by processes of privatization, and multiculturalism, characterized by processes of cultural accommodation and/or recognition through group rights, have emerged from different starting points and result in distinct ends. We argue, however, that neoliberalism can actually foster certain forms of group rights, particularly those centered on the discourse of 'group autonomy'. The result is practices of 'neoliberal multiculturalism' – that is, specific policies touted by the state as enhancing group autonomy, that appear to respond to group demands, but which create negative policy effects left unexplored in the dominant multiculturalism literature. Neoliberal multiculturalism involves a kind of 'privatization'. It involves the appearance of state distance from a given policy area through devolution while the state actually remains the ultimate authority over the jurisdiction in question. This practice problematizes the traceability of power and decision-making while at the same time it co-opts and, in many ways, neutralizes demands from critics of the state by giving the appearance of state concessions to these demands. These policies serve a neoliberal welfare state agenda and, most troublingly, their effects often run in opposition to meaningful autonomy for group members. Neoliberal multiculturalism presents a serious new challenge for defenders of multiculturalism because it brings with it powerful processes of co-optation made possible through a shared emphasis on the notion of autonomy.

To date, scholars on both sides of the social capital–multiculturalism debate have failed to consider the possibility that the shrinking welfare state context, under the impact of neoliberalism, may shape the kinds of multiculturalism and forms of 'accommodation' that have emerged in recent years. This omission can be explained firstly by the fact that groups, particularly what Will Kymlicka has termed 'national minorities', have themselves demanded differentiated rights that grant group autonomy over various policy areas. Thus, prima facie the policy changes appear to be direct and progressive responses to group demands as opposed to state-crafted responses based on the social and economic objectives of the state. Second, this dynamic is likely unexplored due to the fact that the complexities and inconsistencies of neoliberalism are often overlooked. The dominant perception of neoliberalism is of a viewpoint fundamentally at odds with multiculturalism (Giddens 1998: 12).

This characterization, however, overlooks two important realities. First, neoliberalism features different streams to which alternative kinds of multiculturalism can make different appeals. While the main one, the origin of the term 'new right', is socially conservative and is committed to 'traditional' notions of the state and the family, there is an important second stream associated with the free market that, in contrast to the conservative stream, is often libertarian on moral as well as economic issues. Unlike social conservatives, libertarians favour the idea of individual 'autonomy'[3] (Giddens 1998: 6) and are open to claims made in the language of group autonomy. Put simply, multicultural citizenship rooted in notions of autonomy can fit well with the values of a more libertarian stream, particularly if it is framed as Kymlicka does in terms of liberalism and personal freedom and involves divestment of responsibility by the state in areas of social policy. Even within the conservative stream, limited room exists for claims to multicultural accommodation and recognition as articulated by Charles Taylor, especially where it calls on the preservation of traditional values of community and cohesion that underpin socially conservative thought and where an appeal can be made to such communitarian sensibilities.

A second reality often overlooked regarding the diversities of neoliberalism is the practical benefits to neoliberal governments of shrinking the scope of state activities by co-opting and conceding certain forms of cultural accommodation. We argued earlier in our discussion of social capital that multiculturalism does

---

3   The term autonomy is being used here in a very broad sense – not to mean simply 'self-rule' or individual autonomy but rather it also includes the idea of 'self-determination' by either individuals, peoples or nations and self-government. In other words, autonomy can be applied to both individuals and groups – indeed that is exactly the issue at stake in the overlap between neoliberal and multicultural theory and practise.

not necessarily undermine the welfare state. This does not mean, however, that there is no relationship between the two. By analyzing both the actual practices of neoliberal states (i.e. neoliberal governance) as well as the abstract neoliberal values (i.e. neoliberal ideology) we are better prepared to see the discursive overlap between the demands of multiculturalism and the language of the neoliberal state, as well as the differences in terms of motivations and/or expected outcomes.

While the discourse of autonomy is central to neoliberal ideology and practice, it is also found in various forms in the multiculturalism literature and in the political demands made by various groups within multinational states, most particularly from those groups seeking either greater independence within the state, self-government or self-determination. It is critically important, however, to recognize that this overlap in discourses around the principle of autonomy does not automatically indicate an overlap in values and/or objectives. This kind of overlap in language can, however, obfuscate significant differences in policy goals and can give the appearance of shared or common ground when in fact, the situation is much more complex and potentially oppositional.

The motivations behind state accommodation must be interrogated as we hope to show how, despite the similar use of language in relation to autonomy, they actually run counter to the objectives of so-called 'accommodated groups' within liberal multiculturalism and/or the presupposed benefits of multiculturalism as articulated by its advocates. At its worst, neoliberal multiculturalism can result in vulnerable populations facing further domination and exclusion, but in newer and less obvious forms as the traceability of government policy and state accountability are altered in troublesome ways under the 'progressive' auspices of accommodation and recognition.[4]

The most worrying dimension of this overlap between the neoliberal state and multiculturalism is probably in relation to indigenous peoples and social policies (from health care to welfare). While defenders of multiculturalism like Kymlicka (2002) argue that the politics of multiculturalism is about 'inclusion', equality and 'accommodation' of 'national minorities' rather than exclusion or inequality, MacDonald's (2009) analysis of indigenous child welfare devolution in Manitoba shows that the concrete practices of multiculturalism in Canada have created new forms of material exclusion, inequality and domination unexplored in the standard multiculturalism literature.[5]

---

4   For further insights into the ways in which 'recognition' have been used by the state to undermine indigenous communities see Coulthard (2007).

5   While most Indigenous scholars and activists do not identify with, indeed they reject the multiculturalism rubric because they view themselves as 'peoples' who precede the formation of settler nations and not as cultural or national minority groups within those nations, prominent scholars of multicultural citizenship have made the experiences of Indigenous peoples a central part of their scholarship, particularly Will Kymlicka. The prescriptive force of the work put forth by these scholars should not be underestimated. Recent court decisions in Canada on Aboriginal rights for example have increasingly moved away from justifying these rights on the principle of first occupancy that characterized the Calder decision of 1973 and has remained the

Neoliberal multiculturalism works because it is broadly consistent with practices of neoliberal governance more generally. The main identifier of neoliberal politics is a 'politics of privatization'. While in its original use the concept of privatization referred to the sale of government assets to the private sector, it is now invoked to reference an overall shift in public policy and political orientation that involves both the contraction and re-regulation of the public as well as the expansion of the private (Cossman and Fudge 2002, Kline 1997, Brodie 1995). The majority of critical work on neoliberalism has highlighted 'the market' and 'the family' as key areas that are currently being (re)defined by the neoliberal context. We argue, however, that traditionally understood bounded 'cultures' (particularly, though by no means exclusively, 'national cultures' with strong claims to self-determination/ group autonomy) are also (re)defined by the state in relation to neoliberal attitudes and practices. This trend is evident by the politics of privatization, namely: re-regulation, re-privatization, co-optation, and de-politicization which emerges in the state's negotiations with indigenous peoples.

MacDonald shows in detail in her analysis (2008) how each of these processes works to create a discursive overlap leaving the politics of multiculturalism vulnerable to the politics of state privatization, and the various trends within it which can result in negative outcomes. While on the surface, policies of 'accommodation' and 'recognition' by the state appear to meet the demands of indigenous peoples and other groups for progressive change, through the processes described above, they tend to foster a group–state dynamic that, in many ways, is regressive. Overall, these practices of state privatization shift social policy away from a holistic, transformative, capacity-building approach to one that makes it more difficult to obtain any kind of radical change as both the political and discursive terrain within which change can happen is narrowed (i.e. autonomy is already granted).

A similar analysis in Guatemala by Charles Hale (2002) argues that state bodies that seek a neoliberal restructuring have also adopted groups rights and multiculturalism as a means by which the state can defuse the claims of indigenous movements while retaining a form of colonial rule. Hale points to the policies of the World Bank which seek to protect 'indigenous rights' but fall short of supporting traditional communal land ownership. Like MacDonald's analysis in Canada, Hale concludes that state bodies can use this language of group autonomy to advance a neoliberal economic agenda and essentially undermine the more radical democratic demands of indigenous groups. Alongside the third-wave feminist multiculturalists discussed earlier, analyses of neoliberalism and multiculturalism

---

central argument of many Indigenous peoples; and towards a much more restrictive notion of Aboriginal rights based on 'culture', a fact demonstrated by the 1996 Van der Peet decision. Thus, while the majority of indigenous scholars and activists do not see themselves as part of 'multiculturalism', this fact has not led to the rejection of this framework by many dominant and politically powerful voices. There is, therefore, significant reason to analyze Indigenous politics alongside the prevailing, influential multiculturalist perspective. In so doing however we do not wish to contest the fact that indigenous peoples identify as, and should be recognized as, peoples or nations.

suggest that focusing on the democratic requirements of multicultural citizenship may be the best way to guard against the dangers of neoliberal multiculturalism. If neoliberal co-optation of group autonomy obscures decision-making and accountability then our models of multiculturalism must suggest new forms of holding the state accountable. Given the long colonial history at stake here, it may be that the democratic nature of politics for the foreseeable future will be agonistic rather than discursive.

Conclusion

We have analyzed the debate between multiculturalism and politics of diversity and the 'social' sphere, articulated by various scholars in terms of the potential threat of the former to social capital, justice, solidarity or cohesion. In the first section we provided an overview of the main contours of this debate and how the emphasis shifts between different countries and regions but how many leading scholars on the left see multiculturalism as undermining 'progressive' ends with respect to social justice. Using some recent Canadian scholarship, we demonstrated in the second section how such a trade-off is not inherent within political theory or practice but depends upon the particular ways in which multicultural policy, immigration policy and the welfare state are constructed. We even suggested that respect for cultural diversity and support for social justice can work together to mutually support each other in democratic societies. To the extent that there are divisions within multicultural societies, this should not be seen as negative since it is often the result of societal processes by which new and more diverse groups are included in political and civil society and begin to articulate their voices in ways that may be at odds with long-standing values of the dominant culture and/or gender. Divisions are, in other words, often a necessary by-product of a fully developed conception of justice.

We argued that we need to move beyond this debate over the welfare state and social solidarity/capital to address other kinds of 'identity' politics in liberal democratic societies that deserve more attention/analysis in addressing the broad demands of social justice. Thus in the third section of this chapter we examined in detail three broad categories of difference politics and how they provide new kinds of challenges to multiculturalism. We began with gender, not as an opposing force to multiculturalism as early liberal feminists argued but rather how the second wave of feminist multiculturalist analysis has broken down both 'sexual equality' and the meaning of culture to suggest that the former is too limiting to advance the ends of the full diversity of women in any multicultural society and the latter is too static, conservative and protectionist to capture the ever-changing, multiple and conflicting nature of identity politics. Thus, we pointed to the emerging promotion of communicative or discursive democracy as a possible means by which to negotiate the different claims, rooted in either culture broadly understood or gender justice.

We also examined faith and the important ways it differs from 'culture' as understood in multiculturalism (including the role of the 'sacred', the reality of 'majority' faiths, the degree of intolerance in some of the fastest-growing religions including evangelical and fundamentalist faiths and the worrying intersection between minority faith and state security concerns). We then examined, through the four lenses of education, social services, religious dress and the law, the degree to which faith can be incorporated into the delivery of public social, legal and educational services through a multicultural frame. Of these four kinds of public services, only religious dress seemed to fit wholly within the multicultural framework; the other three could not wholly be encompassed within the multicultural principles of either 'group rights' or recognition for various reasons as outlined. Finally we examined the issue of race and indigeneity, demonstrating again, the degree to which multiculturalism is limited in its analysis with respect to either racialization or the aspirations of indigenous peoples.

In the final section, we examined the role of the neoliberal state in relation to group autonomy, something that has been strangely underanalyzed – that is how the state can use multiculturalism to further its own privatization ends. While much has been written about the impact that multiculturalism has on the welfare state, much less has been written on the impact of the shrinking welfare state on multiculturalism, through the vehicle of neoliberalism. As we argued above, the neoliberal state has used the language of group autonomy, particularly in relation to indigenous peoples, to divest itself of political accountability. Consistent with a long history of colonization the state remains in various ways as an ultimate political authority in their negotiations of various kinds of 'self-government' agreements. Examples from Canada and Guatemala provide evidence for how this has worked in practice in relation to child welfare and land ownership.

Ultimately, we hope this chapter helps those of us who are engaged in this scholarship with respect to justice and difference to rethink the terms of the debate as we move into the future, to re-examine in a more critical fashion the relationship between diversity and the welfare state, broaden terms like gender and culture and recognize that multiculturalism may work to further the interests of cultural minorities in some cases of identity politics, but hinder other kinds of justice and hence to look beyond the ethno-cultural differences of multiculturalism to the various claims made on behalf of historically disadvantaged groups and how these might be reconciled.

Multiculturalism, Gender and Justice

Avigail Eisenberg

Over the last ten years, practices such as veiling, arranged marriages, genital cutting, polygamy, sexist membership rules and divorce practices have raised public outcries against multiculturalism. The fate of multiculturalism in North America and Europe seems to depend on public perceptions about how women are treated within minority communities. Yet, at the same time, the effects of trenchant criticisms of these practices have not been entirely beneficial for women. To criticize minority communities for adhering to sexist practices sometimes contributes to backlash against vulnerable minorities. In part, this is because exposing sexist practices tends to heighten the cultural insecurity of targeted groups, causing them to close ranks. This leads some people to worry that feminist criticisms of minority practices have had the unintended consequence of strengthening the position of traditional minority elites and the traditional practices they defend. Others have pointed out that these critics draw on examples of minority sexism to illustrate a more general problem of sexism, they risk reaffirming stereotypes about minorities and thereby playing into the racism that minorities already experience.

With these concerns in mind, this chapter examines two paths feminist political theorists have taken to address concerns regarding the relation between gender equality and multiculturalism. One path raises questions about the interpretation of autonomy which lies at the heart of liberal multiculturalism. The second path raises questions about inequality in political power within communities and utilizes the values of democratic legitimacy, inclusion and participation to ask whether sexism within minority groups can be eliminated through democratic reform. This chapter examines several arguments along each of these paths and then sets out three challenges that multiculturalism and feminism face together in the future.

Autonomy and Feminist Multiculturalism

The relation between individual autonomy and cultural community is at the heart of the liberal multicultural project. According to leading interpretations of liberal multiculturalism, liberalism values the capacity of individuals to examine their own ends or lead their lives 'from the inside' (Kymlicka 1989b). This capacity receives some protection through individual rights, especially rights which ensure that individuals can dissent from their communities. The question for liberal defenders of multiculturalism is how to protect individual autonomy in light of the fact that individuals are deeply tied to particular communities. These attachments constitute people's identities while, at the same time, constraining their autonomy by making it difficult for them to choose freely how to lead their lives. The mark of a culturally sensitive liberalism is that it protects the capacity of individuals to reflect on their cultural identity while at the same time protecting the conditions under which their cultures can thrive.[1]

On this understanding of individual autonomy, the liberal state's obligations go beyond protecting only individuals and require that cultural groups also be protected in some ways. This is because meaningful individual autonomy always exists in a context of choice amongst various options (Kymlicka 1995b: 83). A context of choice is furnished by 'societal cultures' which are cultural communities that are large and dynamic enough to provide practices and institutions that allow people choice over a 'full range of human activities, including social, educational, religious, recreational and economic life, encompassing both public and private spheres' (Kymlicka 1995b: 76). Respect for individual autonomy thereby requires both ensuring that individuals have the capacity to make autonomous choices, such as whether or not to adhere to a particular community practice, and ensuring that the conditions are in place to help communities thrive and reproduce themselves so that they are able to continue to provide individuals with a decent range of options from which to choose. In other words, individual autonomy sometimes requires that states accommodate the key practices of communities to which people belong. As Kymlicka puts it, 'considerations of identity provide a way of concretizing our autonomy-based interest in culture' (Kymlicka 1997: 87 fn. 6). What people actually identify with is a concrete expression of their context of choice, or at least one component of it. Therefore, in order to protect individual autonomy, the liberal

---

1   Rawls's view is in fact common within the liberal tradition ... The freedom that liberals demand for individuals is not primarily the freedom to go beyond one's language and history, but rather the freedom to move around within one's societal culture, to distance oneself from particular cultural roles, to choose which features of the culture are most worth developing, and which are without value' (1995b: 90–1). Kymlicka's insistence on the individual's capacity to revise their attachments is highlighted in his criticisms of the position taken by Rawls in 'Justice as fairness: political, not metaphysical' (1985), that some religious commitments are neither revisable nor autonomously affirmed. See Kymlicka (1995b: 158–63).

state must sometimes also protect practices and institutions which sustain contexts of choice.

From a feminist perspective, there are several potential problems with this liberal multicultural understanding of autonomy, all of which stem from a general scepticism that cultural communities ever offer gender-neutral contexts of choice. The range of meaningful options available to women within any actual societal culture is often different from the range available to men. Many examples readily come to mind of important cultural institutions and practices (e.g. those related to sexual conduct, marriage, and child rearing) that restrict the capacities of women by offering them fewer meaningful choices than men, that impose different expectations on them, and that attribute to their choices disadvantageous meanings.[2] Feminist theorists have questioned whether some minority practices and institutions can be protected without compromising gender equality. Moreover, they question the criteria that can be used reliably to distinguish between practices which are crucial to sustaining a cultural context of choice and those which sustain and deepen gender inequality. Amongst feminists who focus on the value of autonomy, three general approaches are usually taken to address these questions.

The Rights-based Approach

The first of these is the 'rights-based' approach[3] which holds that, from a feminist perspective, the only palatable version of multiculturalism is one in which basic individual rights are always considered foundational so that when a conflict occurs between a cultural practice and an individual right, the individual right takes priority over accommodating the cultural practice. On this view, cultural practices should not be protected if they conflict with a woman's freedom of choice, sexual equality, or if they pose a threat of harm against her. The rights-based approach asks that minority practices are regulated in the same way as majority practices are, by using the norms of liberal individualism as a guide to ensuring that all women, regardless of culture or religion, have basic rights to, e.g., education, to marry who they choose, to choose what they wear, and to be protected from practices, like genital mutilation, which are physically harmful while amplifying the subordinate status of women and girls within their families and communities.

The most famous (or infamous) rendition of this approach was defended by Susan Okin (1998 and in Cohen et al. 1999), who argued that multiculturalism may be bad for women because many cultural communities adhere to practices

---

2   For instance, see Nancy Hirschmann's (1992) study of the problem of consent and obligation in liberal approaches to autonomy. Hirschmann argues that the responsibilities of parents for children and specifically the obligation of mothers to their children fails to fit the liberal ideal of consent and obligation even though this relation is central to human experience.

3   See Eisenberg (2003) for a fuller description of the rights-based approach and the problems it raises.

which subordinate and oppress women. Okin pointed to numerous sexist and exploitative practices from a broad range of religious and cultural groups and concluded that some women '*may* be much better off, from a liberal point of view, if the culture into which they were born were either gradually to become extinct … or, preferably, to be encouraged and supported to substantially alter itself' (1998: 680). This way of reasoning through conflicts involving gender and culture gave rise to a heated debate amongst feminists, many of whom criticized Okin's argument for advancing a culturally exclusive understanding of rights and one that strengthened false dichotomies between either protecting sexual equality or accommodating cultural autonomy. The rights-based approach seems to ask that we interpret conflicts between sexual equality and cultural autonomy as dilemmas between different kinds of putative rights.[4] The dilemma is resolved by choosing the right which seems to be more important or foundational – in other words, the one that seems to be more solidly a *right*. Okin resolves the dilemma by outlining compelling reasons why the right to sexual equality is more important to women's well-being than cultural autonomy. But posing the choice as a dilemma in the first place is where the rights-based approach goes wrong, because it suggests that women have to choose between their culture and their rights (Shachar 2001: 5).

More specifically, framing the choice as a dilemma mistakenly suggests that individual rights can be substantively interpreted independently of cultural context. Okin's position was criticized in this respect for being insensitive to the implications it holds for vulnerable women within minorities.[5] One implication is that if minority women followed Okin's argument and chose their rights over their culture, they wouldn't become culture-free. Rather, they would become assimilated into the Anglo-American mainstream culture. Unsurprisingly then, a second implication is that the rights-based approach has the potential to backfire in practice, because if women from vulnerable minorities *really* think that their choice is between their culture and their rights, many will understandably put their faith in their cultural community rather than assimilating into the mainstream culture. They may even be persuaded by the misleading message of the rights-based approach, namely that the protection of their community's well-being exists in tension with protecting rights like sexual equality. Contrary to the intentions of those advocating the rights-based approach, the approach could encourage women to resolve the tension between sexual equality and cultural autonomy by abandoning efforts to change their communities in ways that enhance women's equality.[6]

---

4   The tension between sexual equality and cultural autonomy is described as a dilemma in many early discussions of the problem. Besides Okin's work, also see Nussbaum (1999: 38–9). Kukathas (2001) also poses the tension in terms of a dilemma but then, in contrast to Okin and Nussbaum, resolves the problem in favour of cultural autonomy.

5   See several of the responses to Okin's position published in Cohen et al. (1999), especially those by Al-Hibri, Tamir, An-Na'im, Sassen and Nussbaum.

6   Some examples of this problem are discussed by Deveaux (2000b: 533) and Narayan (1997).

A third implication of framing the tension between sexual equality and cultural protection as a dilemma is that this framework makes it difficult to understand how women within minorities can be both autonomous and faithful to their cultural traditions. Women who remain faithful to their communities appear, from this rights-based perspective, to be rejecting individual rights related to their sexual equality and personal autonomy, and hence to be either dupes to their cultural context or victims of coercion from their families and communities. By highlighting the choices confronting women in terms of dilemmas, the rights-based perspective lends credibility to the view that a sure sign that minority women lack autonomy is that they adhere to cultural traditions which appear to be sexist. The perspective may also, in effect, encourage governments to interfere in the activities of religious minorities because of an over-inflated concern that women are not *really* choosing their religious practices. This appears to have happened in the conflict over Muslim headscarves in France. The main reason to have a law which bans headscarves in public schools, according to Patrick Weil, one of the influential participants on the Stasi commission which investigated the conflict, is to prevent Muslim girls from being pressured by their families into wearing the scarves (see Bowen 2007: 244). Many Muslim girls denied being coerced, yet their denials did not sway those in France who favoured the ban from believing that these girls were being pressured to wear them.[7] In addition, many people involved in this debate seem to have been blind to the irony of the state forcing girls not to wear headscarves in order to protect them from being forced by their communities to wear them. This blindness partly arises as a result of the simplistic dichotomy, which informs the rights-based approach, between protecting individual autonomy through rights and protecting cultural traditions. Even though values like sexual equality and individual autonomy are foundationally important to all human beings, the discourse that usually accompanies rights sometimes positions these values dichotomously and as dilemmas between seemingly incompatible rights-based claims, and then asks that we choose between the values as though they are mutually exclusive.

The Relational Autonomy Approach

A second feminist response to multiculturalism is the 'relational autonomy' approach. Relational autonomy refers to a range of arguments developed in the context of feminist theory which holds that people are socially embedded, and therefore what counts as autonomy is inevitably influenced by social circumstance including class, gender and ethnicity (Mackenzie and Stoljar 2000). Like liberal multiculturalists, relational autonomists argue that individual autonomy has to be understood in relation to a context supplied, in part, by a person's culture. But relational autonomists go further in raising difficult questions about what it

---

7   As Bowen (2007) reports, many people in France rejected the testimony of the girls who claimed it was their choice to wear headscarves (272 n3).

means to take context seriously in assessing autonomy, and argue that contexts informed by class and gender as well as culture or ethnicity should be included in any credible assessments. In the context of multicultural debates, for instance, the approach raises questions about how autonomy ought to be understood in light of the fact that women often choose to adhere to seemingly sexist and oppressive cultural practices.[8] Are women who choose to cut their genitals dupes to their cultures while those who resist such traditions autonomous? What is the relation between autonomy and socialization? And if one cannot identify autonomy or the lack of it simply by looking at the practices people choose or resist, then how should autonomy be understood (Meyers 2000: 470)?

The relational autonomy approach has been especially effective at showing that cultural stereotypes, rather than deep value differences, often influence perceptions about who has agency and who does not, and that these stereotypes are often driving forces in cultural conflicts. For instance, in the headscarf debates in France, many non-Muslims were quick to conclude that headscarves were a means to control Muslim girls by requiring them to dress modestly. In response, vocal (and seemingly autonomous) Muslim girls and women throughout Europe and North America countered that the modest clothing prescribed by Islam is liberating because it allows them to interact in the public sphere without being treated as sexual objects by men. What looks like non-autonomous behaviour to an outsider is actually robust and healthy autonomy on closer inspection, once we appreciate the meaning of choices and opportunities within a particular cultural context. Similarly, behaviour which is assumed to be autonomous can be drawn into question upon closer scrutiny. All sorts of practices which are harmful to women in western societies are conventionally viewed as practices that women freely choose. Few westerners think that liposuction or collagen breast implants should be prohibited, despite the fact that these practices are chosen under cultural pressure exerted on western women by their communities and the consumer market which are in many ways similar to the pressures exerted on minority women who decide they 'want' their genitals mutilated to please their husbands.[9]

Despite the apparent influence of stereotypes on how cultural differences are understood, the question remains how best to respond to harmful practices regardless of whether they are chosen by seemingly autonomous people in mainstream or minority groups.[10] Perhaps the best course of action requires imposing more restrictions on all sorts of harmful practices, whether of majorities or minorities, and regardless of whether or not they are chosen. Clare Chambers

---

8   See Friedman (2003), Hirschmann (1998), Meyers (2000) and Saharso (2000, 2003) for arguments that develop the relational autonomy perspective in light of challenges associated with cultural accommodation.

9   For an insightful and provocative discussion of choice and culture from a feminist perspective, see Chambers (2008).

10   This is related to a broader question of whether communities with illiberal practices ought to be tolerated. Levy (2005) explores this question in relation to minorities who refuse to tolerate homosexuality.

argues, for instance, that the value of liberal autonomy should not be used to protect the choices women make to harm themselves under pressure from social norms. Whether the norms in question are related to female beauty or chastity, western or non-western, inspired by the market or the Koran, should not determine whether or not they are restricted. What makes a moral difference in decisions to regulate harmful choices, Chambers argues, is whether people are encouraged to harm or disadvantage themselves under social pressure, whether that comes from their cultural groups or from mainstream society (2008: 265).

This doesn't resolve the matter as much as it raises a further question, namely, how do we distinguish between acceptable and unacceptable social pressure? To take into account the importance of particular relations – e.g. relations to our children, families, and communities – as the relational autonomy approach suggests, is not especially helpful as a way of distinguishing between circumstances where legitimate concerns exist that women are being oppressed and coerced and those where no such concerns arise. For example, Sawitri Saharso (2003) points out that sex-selective abortion, though emblematic of sexual inequality and the devaluation of female children, is often freely chosen by women when the range of options available to them offers no better alternative. Within some communities, a woman who has four daughters may be at risk of endangering herself and her children by giving birth to a fifth female child. As a measure to improve women's autonomous choice, Saharso worries that public policies which restrict sex-selective abortions can actually worsen the position of women from cultures that value male children. The problem is not that women lack agency but rather that they lack good choices and good choices sometimes require cultural transformation. In communities where harmful sexist practices exist, it is unclear whether autonomy understood as free choice is at all helpful in advancing the sort of cultural transformation most likely to improve the lives of women.

The need for cultural transformation returns us to some of the difficulties feminists have with Okin's argument. Despite the broad criticisms of Okin's position, most feminists agree with her that some cultural practices offer women impoverished choices and that some practices have to be changed. Where the differences between the approaches are clearest is with respect to how to affect change. Whereas the rights-based approach suggests that cultural practices which violate basic rights ought to be prohibited, relational autonomists insist that cultural change which is autonomy-sensitive should not and probably will not occur by alienating women from their communities. Women's status is best improved by honing skills that enable women to function well within their cultural communities. 'Functioning well' means that women should have the capacity to use the repertoire of concepts and interpretative schemas available within their cultures to affect cultural change (Meyers 2000: 485). Equality-enhancing cultural transformation, according to Diana Tietjens Meyers (2000), occurs when women are free to imagine different ways of living, to reflect on their way of life, and engage empathetically with the concerns of others. Autonomy is stifled when social pressures are used to impair autonomy skills like reimagining, empathy, and introspection. Meyers argues, with respect to debates about female genital cutting, that meaningful choices about this practice can only be made by women who have autonomy skills. Autonomy skills are developed through educational programs which strengthen women's introspection, empathy and imagination, and thereby better equip them to 'lead their lives from the inside'. To improve women's autonomy is no guarantee that women will abandon seemingly harmful practices. But that should not be the aim. Autonomy skills, along with a relational approach to autonomy, provide a more effective means to transforming community than does prohibiting practices which outsiders judge to be harmful. Feminist approaches to cultural transformation which employ the resources of relational autonomy aim at helping women to become leaders of effective cultural change without being alienated from their communities either for importing foreign ideas, or still worse, for appearing to side with the enemy.

The Jurisdictional Multicultural Approach

A third autonomy-based feminist response to multiculturalism is 'jurisdictional multiculturalism' which advocates dividing jurisdictional authority over areas of public and community life between the state and minority communities, in order to generate a system of checks and balances, which has the net effect of improving the bargaining power of women and other vulnerable members. The jurisdictional autonomy approach maximizes the 'autonomy' of minority communities by recognizing their jurisdiction over specific areas of life which are crucial to maintaining their distinctiveness as a community. For most minorities, this means recognizing minority jurisdiction over membership rules because membership rules define and control the boundary between the minority and the dominant group, and thereby provide some measure of protection from assimilation. To control membership rules is one important means to protecting a distinctive way of life governed by collective rules. For cohesive minority communities, jurisdiction over who counts as a member of their community is essential to maintaining their collective existence.[11]

Membership rules, like other cultural norms and practices, can be sexist. According to jurisdictional multiculturalists, the tension that sometimes arises between protecting sexual equality and respecting the rules and practices of minorities is not best resolved by requiring that minorities conform to the values of outsiders in their internal dealings with each other. To require minorities to conform denies these communities control over what they most care about, namely the opportunity to live by their own rules and values. In some contexts, imposed conformity is a form of imperialism such as in cases involving indigenous peoples where the group demanding conformity has a history of colonial relations with the minority group. In addition, attempts to impose conformity can strengthen the power of conservative elites within minority groups who will sometimes react

---

11   See Spinner's (1994) seminal study of the relation between membership rules and other practices and retaining the boundary between insiders and outsiders.

to demands from outside the group for change by demanding of their members stronger loyalty, greater insularity, and more 'traditional' interpretations of community practices in order to protect their own power. Ayelet Shachar calls this 'reactive culturalism' (2001: 35–7) and cautions that, like the choice between 'your culture or your rights', the imposition of minimal rights-based conditions by the liberal state can easily worsen rather than improve the position of women within minority communities.

One way to protect the jurisdictional autonomy of minority groups while ensuring that groups do not coerce their members is to require that minorities provide resources to dissenting members who wish to exit their communities. Chandran Kukathas (2003), amongst others, suggests that minorities can legitimately adhere to practices within their communities which are oppressive or discriminatory as long as these communities guarantee their members the right to exit communities if they choose to. But one problem with this exit option[12] is that it puts the onus on the vulnerable and powerless to extract themselves from their oppressive situations. A second problem is that the kinds of costs typically borne by those who exit close communities – in particular, the loss of family and friends – are ones for which no adequate compensation exists.

For some jurisdictional multiculturalists a more basic problem with the exit option is that it presupposes an unrealistic understanding of people's identities as either entirely 'in' their community and thereby in harmony with community values, or entirely 'out of' or apart from their community and thereby at odds with an authentic view of its identity. A more realistic view recognizes that communities are internally pluralistic. Most people develop their identities through attachments to many different communities or have affinities to different roles that carry different interpretations of community values. They use the values they develop in one facet of their life to assess the values and practices in other facets of their life. When they disagree with some of the practices of their cultural or religious communities, they usually don't seek out the exit option. Instead, most of us try to change our communities. Instead, we contest the rules and practices that confine us. The exit option does not account for these internal struggles for change which are a conventional feature of most communities.

In fact, the exit option might impede healthy community change by diluting internal dissent. The more dissenting members exit their communities, the less communities are likely to experience the internal pressures that lead to change and renewal. Multicultural initiatives, such as those which require minorities to allow members to exit (and compensate those who exit), that recognize a particular ruling elite within the group as representative of the community to outsiders, or that accommodate particular rules, practices, or customs of the group, may interfere with healthy community transformation. Indeed all attempts to preserve the community's distinctiveness may have the unintended effect of encouraging the emergence of static and conservative communities.

---

12   See essays about the exit option by Levy, Spinner-Halev, Weinstock, and Reitmann in Eisenberg and Spinner-Halev (2005).

Jurisdictional multiculturalists address these concerns by advocating an approach which divides jurisdiction over different kinds of rules between minorities and the state. The aim is to encourage community transformation without imposing conformity on minorities to alter their most cherished practices. Advocates of this approach argue that jurisdictional authority over 'demarcation', or who counts as a member of the group is understandably crucial to minorities and therefore should remain within the jurisdictional authority of the minority. Jurisdiction over 'distribution', or how resources are distributed amongst members, is less important to minorities and more important to the state, therefore can be delegated to the state's jurisdictional authority.

Ayelet Shachar (2001) explains how a jurisdictional approach can transform sexist membership rules of religious communities that penalize women who marry outside their communities or who seek divorces from uncooperative spouses. Religious rules of divorce often place both the demarcation and distribution functions in the control of male spouses. For instance, if an observant Jewish or Muslim woman wants a divorce, religious law requires that she seek the permission of her estranged husband. Only if his permission is granted, which is required if she ever wants to remarry within the community, can the divorce go forward. Because it is up to husbands to decide whether or not the divorce is permitted, they also effectively control the terms by which property is distributed upon divorce and who gets custody of the children in the sense that unless they get the terms they prefer, they can refuse their wives a divorce. Women in these situations are faced with three choices: (1) agree to the terms set by their husbands and potentially leave the marriage without custody of their children or any resources; (2) reject these terms and therefore be alienated by community traditions which require a religious divorce in order for women to remarry according to the terms of their faith,[13] or (3) remain in marriages they want to leave. In effect, when both demarcation and distribution rest in the hands of husbands, women are highly vulnerable within their marriages and their communities. Communities remain conservative as a result of these rules which preserve stable patriarchal families in which children are socialized, and which force strong dissenters to leave usually without their children and without much by way of resources.

Shachar argues that multicultural states should not be in the business of condoning sexist practices, such as religious rules of divorce, which place all the costs of sustaining stable group membership on women. These costs can be redistributed by dividing jurisdictional authority so that the function of demarcation remains with the minority but the function of distributing property and apportioning custody is the responsibility of the state. When demarcation and distribution functions are divided in this way, minorities will be secure in having control over what is the most important function for the survival of their identity, which is to control membership rules. But minorities (or the male heads of households) should not have control over how resources are distributed upon divorce, which should

---

13   Often children of women who choose this second option are penalized as well by losing status as full community members and not being able to marry within the faith.

instead be in the hands of the state. When the liberal state takes on this responsibility, it enhances the bargaining power of women within religious communities because the community, not simply the woman of a divorcing couple, will have to share the costs of retaining sexist membership rules which place all power in the hands of men. Women are no longer as vulnerable in their marriages because they know they will not be destitute if they decide to leave their husbands. They may still be victimized by the rule that permits husbands alone to decide when a divorce is granted. But communities which stand by recalcitrant husbands risk alienating divorcing women from the community. In doing so, they risk witnessing the exit of not only a divorced woman, but also her children, and half the wealth of any couple who divorces. In the long term, Shachar argues, it makes sense for communities to alter their rules, and in the short term, women's power within marriage and within communities which adhere to such rules is enhanced when jurisdictional authority is divided.

In relation to autonomy, the jurisdictional approach is an extension of the liberal multiculturalist view of autonomy which holds that meaningful choices depend upon a 'context of choice'. Just as groups create contexts in which their members make meaningful choices, states create contexts in which sub-communities make meaningful choices. The question is how should such contexts be structured? States may not have effective control over minority traditions and practices, but they have some control over how the costs of these practices are distributed and they can structure the context so as to increase the costs that minorities must bear for making certain kinds of choices. On this view, multicultural states are partly responsible for the sexist membership rules of minority communities because states create a context in which minority communities can choose to have sexist rules of membership while bearing few if any costs for doing so. When women within religious minorities are systematically disempowered by these rules, states should not be viewed as innocent bystanders; they participate in shaping choices by distributing their costs one way rather than another.

Jurisdictional multiculturalism is committed to gender equality rights, but sensitive to the ways in which imposing rights on minority communities can backfire and leave women and other vulnerable members worse off. The jurisdictional approach takes seriously the relational and contextual features of autonomy, but also tries to take account of the multiple and overlapping contexts in which people live their lives. The position is sensitive both to the value of gender equality and women's agency without imposing on women an agenda from outside their communities which they do not or cannot support. In these ways, the approach seems to adopt the best features of the rights-based and relational autonomy approaches while tackling the question at the centre of liberal multiculturalism, namely how can multiculturalism co-exist with respect for women's rights.

Democracy and Feminist Multiculturalism

The central question which flows from the autonomy-based approaches to cultural and gender equality asks how can women's autonomy be protected from the sexist values of their cultural or religious communities. Few people would dispute the importance of this question, but some feminists argue that questions about women's autonomy and how it is best protected cannot be addressed without first asking what constitutes a democratically legitimate community capable of answering these questions. Who is appropriately considered a legitimate participant in this decision-making?

Feminists use the resources of democratic theory to situate conflicts about sexual equality and multiculturalism within a framework focused on addressing what constitutes democratically legitimate solutions. These feminists do not dispute the importance of autonomy or sexual equality, which are both values integral to any plausible conception of democracy, as long as these values are not imposed on minorities in a manner insensitive to the requirements of democratic legitimacy as they seem to be in other approaches. Liberal multiculturalism, in particular, is criticized in this regard because it asks that minority practices be assessed using values external to minority communities, and in the process of doing so, defines cultural groups in bounded terms so as to distinguish what counts as inside and outside the community in the first place. Even jurisdictional autonomists, who are especially sensitive to the drawbacks of imposed conformity, nonetheless impose on minorities costs should they decide not to change their practices in a way that conform to liberal notions of sexual equality.

In contrast, democratic approaches require that the values and priorities of cultural communities should arise democratically from processes of community engagement which include all of those affected. Fair resolutions to conflicts between women and their communities depend not on whether community practices are consistent with liberal values, but rather on whether the decision making and deliberative processes which communities use to resolve conflicts meet the standards of democratic legitimacy. From this starting point, the democratic approach highlights two issues which are at the heart of many conflicts involving minorities and the treatment of women. First, if most community boundaries are not clearly delineated, who then should count as a participant in legitimate processes of democratic decision making about community practices? Second, what counts as a legitimate process of decision making in light of the variety of decision-making practices adhered to by different communities?

Fair Terms of Inclusion

From a feminist perspective, the first issue raised by the democratic multicultural approach, namely who is a legitimate participant in the processes by which the practices of minorities are debated and reformed, is especially poignant given that many cultural and religious groups have customs which revoke membership status from women who marry outside their communities and from dissenters. One feminist response to this issue is found in the jurisdictional autonomy approach which holds that the state should raise the costs for minority communities of excluding dissenters. A second response is to challenge who counts as a legitimate participant in decision making about such questions. Cultural elites may claim that their communities are defined by strict jurisdictional boundaries between insiders and outsiders, but most communities are not easily delineated and viewing them as though they are contributes to the problem of exclusion and dissent. Some democratic multiculturalists argue that the democratic legitimacy of community practices depends on broadening our understanding of who counts as a member and thereby whose voice is included in deciding how conflicts are resolved within and between cultural communities. There are several different ways in which a broader perspective on cultural membership has been defended.

One way to broaden inclusion is to reframe what is meant by culture from a concept that refers to a group whose members are bound by a doctrine or body of rules to a concept that refers to a narrative construction.[14] According to Seyla Benhabib (2002), people use cultural narratives to tell a story about themselves, to justify their actions, and to evaluate the world around them. Cultural narratives constitute cultures in the sense that they offer complex ways of understanding evaluative terms like 'good' and 'bad' or 'just' and 'unjust' and thereby contribute to the view their members take of the world and how they interact with that world. Those who try to control cultural groups, such as elites of the group or state officials from other groups, do so by trying to control the way in which a cultural narrative is used and who can legitimately use it. Sometimes, the aim of controlling cultural narratives is to silence dissent and undermine plural views of what a cultural tradition involves. At other times, the point may be more benign – to understand some truth about a culture, in the way that anthropologists seek to understand groups. It is easier, in some sense, to understand and study a group when culture is defined statically and the lines demarcating who is within a group and who is outside it are clear.[15]

According to the narrative view, the problem with liberal multiculturalism is that it relies on clearly demarcated and bounded groups[16] and for this reason is also an attempt to control cultural narratives by defining minorities in bounded ways so that government policy can then 'accommodate' or 'recognize' specific cultural differences. Male elites within minorities end up gaining power in liberal multicultural societies as a direct consequence of this policy-driven need to define groups so as to accommodate them. From a perspective informed by the problems of democratic inclusion, liberal multiculturalism appears to offer a view of culture as something that embodies people rather than something people employ to make

---

14 For a narrative conception of culture, see Benhabib (2001). In contast, Shachar's (2001) approach emphasizes a group bound by similar rules or a 'nomos'.

15 Brubaker and Cooper (2001) explain that the scholarship on identity and identity politics can have the effect of delimiting group boundaries and thereby manufacturing the subject matter that research on identity politics then purports to study objectively.

16 See essays by Arneil, Dhamoon and Phillips in Arneil et al. (2007).

sense of their world. Some critics suggest that liberal multiculturalism creates a static idea of patriarchal culture and then uses western feminist ideals of sexual equality to justify regulating minorities and 'rescuing' minority women (Al-Hibri 1999: 41).

In contrast, a democratic approach to multiculturalism, in which culture is understood as constructed through narratives, recognizes culture to be more dynamic, contested, 'alive' and something that can be transmitted across generations through 'creative and lively engagement and resignification' (Benhabib 2002: 103). According to Seyla Benhabib, the 'collective practices in which we participate may be seen as the outcome of our legitimate processes of deliberation' (2002: 114). Therefore, any effort to alter these collective cultural practices or resolve culture conflicts that arise about these practices must put aside the static and bounded view of culture and build on a view of cultural dialogue and deliberation in which all people can develop their opinions and dispositions in democratic dialogue with others.

Benhabib specifies three normative conditions of inclusion which are required in order to facilitate fair dialogue in cases of cultural conflicts: (1) egalitarian reciprocity which requires that everyone affected enjoys the same degree of civil, political, economic, and cultural rights; (2) voluntary self-ascription which requires that people self-ascribe and self-identify rather than being assigned to a group by virtue of birth; and (3) freedom of exit and association which ensures that people can leave their communities and the state can regulate the costs of exit (Benhabib 2002: Chapter 5). Each condition refers to the terms by which people are included in cultural dialogue rather than the specific values or standards of sexual equality that minorities must embrace. According to Benhabib, community dialogue about contested practices ought to include a broader and more diverse set of voices than many community elites – whether of mainstream or minority communities – might otherwise recognize. Thus, Benhabib's view reflects one of the central aims of democratic multiculturalism, which is to establish legitimate norms and standards of democratic participation that then may be used to destabilize collective practices including those which are assessed by participants to be sexist, outdated, or a cover for oppressive power relations. At the same time, each normative condition specified by Benhabib underlines the importance of individual agency, rights, and sexual equality to fair dialogue. Autonomy and democracy are not mutually exclusive values in Benhabib's approach. Both are required for legitimate and fair dialogical assessment. Yet, in the end, the resolution to conflicts is supposed to arise from democratic engagement, not from the imposition of liberal values.

Fair Processes of Deliberation

The second issue that democratic multiculturalists consider important is how deliberation or decision making can be structured so as to ensure that everyone involved has a fair say and that decisions reached are implemented. Feminists are well aware that, in social settings, where power is skewed along gendered lines, women's voices may carry less authority than men's voices do. In deliberative settings, where discussion and persuasion are especially important to legitimate decision making, this risk is even greater. However, the problem with imposing on minorities normative conditions which must be respected in decision-making processes is that this appears to be just another way of imposing values on minorities from the outside. Methods of decision making have to be viewed as legitimate by group members, including those in power, because if they are not, communities may pay lip service to reforms but revert to traditional and sexist ways in their everyday lives. Reforms that require community transformation will be unsuccessful without community endorsement and specifically unsuccessful unless cultural communities are able to re-evaluate their customs through processes over which they have some control (Deveaux 2005: 341).

Monique Deveaux (2006) argues, in this regard, that community-endorsed, grassroots processes of deliberations are especially important in cases about conflicts between women's equality and community customs. Deveaux argues that community-endorsed deliberative processes of participation can be designed to be sensitive to the power relations that often exist within and between communities. Sometimes, community elites wish to cling to sexist customs because they see these customs as integral to maintaining elite power. Similarly, men from marginalized minority groups may support sexist traditional roles in the family through customary rules because they view their power over the household as the only kind of power left to them in a society that increasingly marginalizes them.

Although feminists are unlikely to sympathize with sexist practices – even ones that mollify the effects of racism on marginalized men – some democratic feminists, like Deveaux, argue that considerations such as these play a significant role in conflicts about sexual equality and culture traditions. If the objective is to improve the well-being of women in concrete and 'lived' terms, then processes of deliberation have to encourage participants to reveal their actual interests in a conflict, including their interest in retaining power and authority over certain matters, in order for deliberants to make effective compromises. The cases that Deveaux examines show that men and women within traditional cultural communities reach compromise solutions to conflicts about sexist cultural practices if they are able to engage in frank and open dialogue about their different interests. Sometimes these compromises don't perfectly reflect liberal values of individual autonomy or sexual equality, but they meet the standards of democratic legitimacy. They are considered legitimate by those who have agreed to them.

Democratic approaches to multiculturalism have both strengths and weaknesses worth noting from a feminist perspective. Probably their most important strength is the respect they show for communities with different and sometimes divergent values. Respecting diversity requires openness to the possibility of difference and requires an approach which is prepared to respect – not simply tolerate – differences in values, priorities and practices that arise when communities are democratically engaged on legitimate terms. Democratic feminists like Deveaux suggest that values like sexual equality can be interpreted, prioritized in relation to other values, and expressed in practice in many different ways, all of which are legitimate if they are freely endorsed by those who live by these values. How any group of people decides to interpret, prioritize and practice these values ought to be the subject of their legitimate deliberative processes rather than a matter that is imposed on them from outside, no matter how noble the intentions of outsiders are.

Yet, the question remains, what if minority communities adhere to deliberative processes which are not fully democratic? What if democratic legitimacy is not a priority for some minority communities? From a feminist perspective, one weakness of democratic approaches is that they present a 'chicken and egg' puzzle between the foundational importance of democratic decision making and the foundational importance of substantive values, like sexual equality or individual autonomy. Democratic approaches suggest that the best resolution to conflicts which involve cultural or religious practices that are sexist arises through democratic processes internal to communities with such practices. The best resolutions are the product of fair and democratic processes. But what counts as a fair and democratic process tends to be cashed out in terms of substantive values like equality and autonomy. In communities where practices reflect sexist values, the question remains how can processes be fair and legitimate when women are not treated as equals?

In practical contexts, this question is especially challenging. Many cases that involve conflicts between sexual equality and cultural autonomy also involve complaints that women lack equal political voice within their communities, that they don't have equal bargaining power, or that their voices don't carry equal authority due to their unequal political status. In other words, the challenge is precisely that women are not treated as equals within their communities and this prevents them from participating as equals in democratic decision making. An approach which requires that communities resolve their own conflicts through democratic processes which are inclusive seems to require that women within these communities be treated as equals in those processes. But the difference between ensuring that processes are democratic in this sense and ensuring that communities protect women's equal rights and women's autonomy may be slight. There is little difference between requiring that legitimate democratic processes respect the right to sexual equality and requiring that communities respect women's rights to sexual equality. Either way, to require that cultural conflicts be resolved using democratic processes will entail outside interference in the affairs of communities if their decision-making processes fail to meet fair and inclusive democratic standards, including the standard of sexual equality.

Feminism and Multiculturalism's Future

So far, two paths that feminist scholarship takes in critically assessing multiculturalism have been explored. The first path sheds light on the interplay between sexual equality and individual autonomy in relation to fulfilling multicultural principles. The second path develops democratically legitimate means to resolve cultural conflicts about sexual equality. Between them, these two paths raise and respond to most of the challenges that multiculturalism confronts today.[17] It is difficult to imagine a scholarship about multiculturalism which ignores concerns raised by feminists about autonomy and democratic legitimacy. Similarly, if we turn our attention to multiculturalism's future, the central role of questions related to gender remains.

In particular, feminism and multiculturalism together face three broad policy-based questions in the future. First, can cultural values play a reliable and fair role in developing public policy related to gender? Second, what role should western norms of sexual equality play in establishing the terms that immigrants must comply with in integrating into western societies? And third, what role should feminist non-governmental organizations play in the democratic processes by which policy towards minorities is formulated?

With respect to the first question – what role should 'culture' play in the development of public policy – political theory today is full of debates about the ambiguous nature of culture which question its suitability for the purpose of designing public policy (see Dhamoon 2006; Honig 1999; Phillips 2007b; Scott 2003). No one thinks that culture can be essentially defined or that policy makers should simply listen to cultural and religious elites in deciding how to accommodate minorities. But nor do they think that minority rights ought to be abandoned. So the challenge is to develop a satisfactory guide to how cultural accommodation policies can be formulated which addresses the potential risks that arise whenever we attempt to characterize a culture.

One hurdle to clear in this respect is what Sarah Song calls 'the congruence effect'. When dominant cultures have patriarchal norms, they tend to willingly accommodate patriarchal practices in minority cultures and thereby reinforce patriarchy all around (2007: 6). A good example of this occurs in majority–minority consultation processes where mainstream public institutions in western countries, which are often dominated by men – e.g. in legislatures, cabinet committees, judiciaries, upper levels of the bureaucracy – consult with minority organizations whose leadership is also dominated by men, in order to work out accommodation schemes.

The congruence effect is related to a second hurdle, namely that mainstream public decision makers may tend to rely on stereotypical representations of minority groups when they design accommodation policies. Often a central feature of these stereotypes will be sexist representations of women's roles.

---

17 One important set of challenges left out here is that related to national security in a post-9/11 world. The backlash against multiculturalism in Europe and North America has been driven by concerns specifically directed at Islamic minorities. As suggested here, most of these concerns involve the treatment and status of women within Islam. But their genesis is likely traceable to national security concerns about the radicalism and anti-western ideals of Islamic communities.

Some feminists argue that the best way to prevent mainstream public institutions from making decisions that reinforce cultural stereotypes about minorities, or that end up entrenching the power of minority elites, is to avoid distributing power to minority groups altogether. For example, they argue that the liberal state should not legally recognize culturally or religiously distinctive systems of law, such as religious laws over marriage and divorce. Instead, governments should guarantee similar kinds of protections for majority and minority communities using standards that reflect an awareness of cultural differences but also an awareness that, as Anne Phillips puts it, 'wherever there are groups, there is always the potential for coercion' (2007b: 176).

Phillips' proposal, which she calls 'multiculturalism without groups', responds to many of the questions raised by feminists about women's autonomy and political power in a multicultural context. She argues that multiculturalism requires public institutions capable of developing and implementing culturally sensitive policies and that these policies should include ones that allow minorities to set up community services, such as advocacy, counselling, and mediation services. Such services are important because they are the means by which minority express their interests or give advice to their members about marriage, divorce, fertility, the education and treatment of children, and so on. But, crucial to the success and fairness of these services, according to Phillips, is that they do not involve states in distributing legally recognized jurisdictional authority to groups, that they always involve procedures whose aim is to ensure that people are not being coerced into complying with community practices, and that, where relevant, the voices of dissenters within minority communities are heard.

It is worth reflecting on the kind of choice this position entails from a feminist perspective. Phillips' position relies on there being a commitment by mainstream public institutions to ensure that minority women's voices are heard in their communities' decision-making processes and that their participation in practices like arranged marriages, veiling, religious divorce proceedings, and sex-selective abortions is informed and consensual. In order for this proposal to be feasible, one must believe that mainstream public institutions are up to the task of safeguarding the interests of women within minority communities in these respects. But is this a safe assumption? Can Western public institutions, which are, after all, not themselves free of sexist practices and attitudes, and which are generally dominated by men, especially in decision-making roles, be trusted to ensure that minority women are consenting freely to engage in what appear to be sexist practices? The record of courts and policy makers in Canada, the United States, United Kingdom, France and probably most other Western countries is not especially good in this respect. Consent is one of the central and defining issues of Western feminism largely because of the dismal track record of mainstream courts and legislatures in assessing fairly when women are being coerced and when they are not in relation to domestic violence and sexual assault, in establishing no-fault terms of divorce, and in challenging the relation of choice to motherhood in the context of employment benefits. While public policy has changed for the better in each of these areas in response to feminist lobbying and activism, it should be unsurprising to find that feminist organizations today are sceptical that governments will be vigilant in establishing procedures to ensure that minority women are informed and consent to their cultural practices.

Phillips' response to these key challenges is that our best choice is often to listen to what women say they want, that the only way we can do this is to ensure that they can express themselves free of coercion, and that their voices must be heard. But, in the current climate of backlash and anxiety about minority rights, publics may refuse to take on the burdens associated with policies that establish and monitor safeguards to ensure cultural minorities don't coerce their female members. There are good reasons to suspect that Phillips' otherwise sensible solution is unlikely to command strong public support across a broad range of stakeholder groups in multicultural societies. Following from this, some challenging questions for research in this area include: what guidelines do public institutions use to assess the cultural practices of minorities? What role do minority elites play in representing their communities in the policy-making process? To what degree and in what ways do institutions or officials display awareness of the pitfalls they confront in interpreting cultural practices or consulting minority elites, especially where gender-related issues are concerned?

A second set of broad-based policy questions ask what are the reasonable and just terms of integration for minorities and can Western majorities legitimately require that immigrant minorities follow Western norms regarding the treatment of women? Anne Phillips and Sawitri Saharso (2008) point out that across many Scandinavian countries, 'degrees of integration are sometimes measured by degrees of assent to women's rights' (Phillips and Saharso 2008: 293). But are these trends morally justified? What role ought values related to sexual equality play in establishing reasonable and just terms of integration? The resources of democratic theory provide helpful insight here in that they suggest one way to answer this question is to design processes which use democratic participation and deliberation to decide on what democratically constituted publics view as fair terms of integration. Women's organizations, including minority women's NGOs, could play a central role in the public policy processes which establish these terms of integration. Moreover, democratic and inclusive processes could also be designed to include all of those affected, which could include immigrant communities or prospective immigrants who are not yet members of host countries.

Finally, a third question worth posing is how are women from minority communities affected by multicultural backlash? Insofar as Western democracies have grown sceptical about the wisdom of policies which aim to accommodate cultural and religious minority practices, has the status of women within minority groups improved? Evidence of what appears to be multicultural backlash is readily apparent today,[18] but very little if any scholarly research addresses the

---

18   The failings of democratic institutions to integrate British Muslims into British society were cited as a chief factor in the aftermath of the 2005 bombings of the London transport system. The Netherlands reversed its *laissez-faire* policies about

question of whether this backlash is benefiting or jeopardizing women within minority groups.

My guess is that multicultural backlash is not benefiting women. In many cases, governments have reacted against multicultural accommodation by prohibiting minority practices, like religious arbitration or veiling. Legal prohibition of this sort does little more than push into the private sphere oppressive means of implementing practices which might otherwise be publicly exposed and become matters of broader public debate and regulation.[19] The retreat from multiculturalism may be nothing more than a retreat of the state from albeit challenging areas of public policy. What replaces multicultural initiatives could be nothing better than policies that, in effect, erect a stronger public–private distinction and that leave vulnerable women more dependent on privatized notions of what counts as fair treatment.

Conclusion

Most political theory aims, in some way, at expanding human freedom and equality, yet only a small fraction of this theory has been designed to respond in particular to the unequal political, social and economic status of women. Multiculturalism is no exception to this historical trend. Multiculturalism was not designed, in the first instance, to improve the well-being of women, despite the fact that one of the leading explanations of women's subordinated status throughout the world are the sexist norms and practices of the religious and cultural communities into which they are born. Moreover, what has become abundantly clear in the last 20 years is that multicultural policy initiatives, which are intended to improve cultural equality by recognizing and protecting minority rights, sometimes have the unintended effect of increasing the vulnerability of women within minority communities.[20]

---

immigrant integration in favour of an aggressive integrationist agenda following the murder of Theo van Gogh in Amsterdam for his critical commentaries on women's subordinated status within Islam. In Canada, the Quebec government commissioned a public inquiry in response to growing concerns that minorities are not integrating adequately into Quebec society (see Bouchard and Taylor 2008). And in Ontario, the provincial government bowed to public pressure to rescind a law which legally recognized divorce settlements reached using religious arbitration, despite a public inquiry into the matter which urged the government to accommodate religious arbitration (see Boyd 2004).

19   This concern arose in light of the Ontario government's decision to 'ban' religious arbitration. See Eisenberg (2007).

20   Shachar calls this 'the paradox of multicultural vulnerability' which arises because many of the cultural and religious practices that control women also serve to protect communities, by reducing the chances that members will assimilate into the mainstream (Shachar 2001: 2–5).

Feminists have responded to these challenges by reinterpreting the values associated with autonomy and democracy which lie at the heart of the multicultural project. Autonomy-based and democracy-based feminist responses reflect broader debates in political theory between those who argue that moral values, like individual autonomy and sexual equality, ought to be enjoyed by all citizens equally even if this means prohibiting some minority practices, and those who argue that democratic inclusion and legitimacy demand a more wholesale rethinking of how the terms of integration and accommodation are established. These two different paths sometimes reflect strong disagreements amongst scholars. Yet neither path has a monopoly on offering solutions to many pressing questions related to multiculturalism. Women are at the forefront of multiculturalism's future both because the treatment of women within cultural and religious minorities has an impact on the public approval of multiculturalism and because feminist scholarship leads the way in developing innovative responses to the challenges of multiculturalism.

Multiculturalism, Pluralism and Democracy

James Bohman

As the citizenry of contemporary democracies becomes more and more heterogeneous along a number of dimensions, democratic theory must face the challenges of pluralism and diversity. Some have called for a 'differentiated' conception of citizenship that takes into account the presence of different cultural groups in modern polities. When linked with a multicultural democratic ideal, this approach focuses on accommodations that would rectify past injustices. The gradual expansion of demands of political inclusion to incorporate more and more groups has guided many of the fundamental reform movements of democratic societies, including movements of workers, gays, women and people of color. Others take the impact of diversity on democracy as more fundamental, as requiring that we rethink some important democratic ideals, such as the idea of the 'will of the People,' which has come to be capitalized whenever it is supposed to be constituted through democratic institutions and processes. We might associate differential inclusion through minority rights with the work of Will Kymlicka, while the latter approach to democratic justice has received its best formulation in the work of Iris Young. What unites these two approaches is their insistence that pluralism is a problem for democracy, an obstacle that potentially undermines its own conditions of possibility. But rather than an obstacle for democracy, pluralism is better thought to be integral to it and an opportunity to transform some of its fundamental conceptions. Moreover, it is misleading to say that pluralism has come about due to social circumstances beyond democratic control. Rather, democracy has been and continues to be the primary means by which pluralism has come about in the first place.

Pluralism may seem to be an obstacle to democracy because of long held understandings of citizenship and Peoplehood, both of which have been used to underwrite various forms of exclusion. Rawls, for example sees 'the fact of pluralism' primarily in terms of the presence of 'irreconcilable comprehensive doctrines' that have become a 'permanent feature of modern society' that 'profoundly affect the requirements of a workable conception of justice' (Rawls 1999b: 424).

Whatever the merits of this account, it assumes and does not explain how such pluralism becomes permanent in modern social and political institutions, some of which have historically inhibited its development. The fact of religious pluralism does not significantly alter the People practices of democracy until it is not thought of merely as a constraint on the will of the People. To put it in John Dewey's (1986) terms, the fact of pluralism is not merely an obstacle but also a resource.

Understood in this Deweyean rather than Rawlsian way, the fact of pluralism has to include much more than religion and culture, important as they are. Indeed, van Gusteren is correct when he argues that in a society such as ours, 'a definition of plurality only in terms of social groups will omit a great many phenomena for which we have not an established conceptual category' (van Gusteren 1998: 34). Pluralism remains open-ended in a democracy that claims to organize *a* People politically and democratically. If we do not see democracy as ongoingly transformed by pluralism, it is because the legitimacy of the People is either presupposed parametrically or simply assumed to be culturally determined. This understanding of pluralism and its remedy as incorporation into a People follows from the presuppositions of nation state democracy. If the goal of the democracy is to construct a People and thus a 'single perspective polity,' the exemplar of which is the modern nation state, it more often than not has emerged through the process by which linguistic and other forms of pluralism have been historically eliminated. But new political forms are emerging which may be better suited for the political task of constructing a democratic People or Peoples consistent with pluralism. Following Gerald Ruggie, I call these political forms 'multiperspectival' precisely because they seek to transform citizens' heterogeneity democratically into 'a multiperspectival polity' (Ruggie 2000: 186). Unlike a single perspective polity, such a polity will always be a People of Peoples. Such a People can take two forms. It can continually construct a plural People, as when political inclusion makes democracy more differentiated and complex. Or, it can see itself as a transnational entity, as a People of Peoples who join together to further their democratic ends. In both cases, I argue, the measure of success is the democratic criteria of self-rule without domination. The creation of many different unitary and sovereign Peoples out of one sovereign People is a form of pluralization, but very often simply leaves in place the problem it is supposed to solve: why is the People legitimate?

My argument for a democratic pluralism based on perspectives as the best way to think of the transformation of democracy under current circumstances has four steps. First, I consider the role of social facts in competing accounts of pluralism and the pluralisand. I mark a basic shift in the debate about pluralism towards such a conception of democracy in the work of Iris Young. Second, I consider the specific benefits of the democratic understanding of pluralism as emphasizing perspectives or doctrines. Third, I show why this particular account of pluralism is more genuinely transformative than the alternatives, precisely because it opens up the elided question of the legitimacy of the People as the basic unit of democracy. Finally, I consider the benefits of such a conception of plurality and diversity and how these are best realized institutionally when we see that nondomination is an internal requirement of democracy as such, but especially of increasingly decentered democracies.

The Fact of Pluralism: From Minority Rights to Transformative Democracy

How might cultural diversity be a problem for a democracy? Multiculturalism has developed an affirmative conception of cultural diversity, pointing out the ways in which culture is integral to identity and the fundamental context of choice in most circumstances. But the concept of culture here is not, however, the culture of groups as such, but rather the specific culture of national or intergenerational communities that have the distinctive societal characteristics of 'a People.' Will Kymlicka sees pluralism so understood as presenting a fundamental challenge to democracies, dependent as they are on shared national identities on the one hand and a universal conception of citizenship on the other. For Kymlicka, culture is understood in the sense of a 'societal culture,' so that 'a culture' is synonymous with 'a nation' or 'a People,' that is, as an intergenerational community, occupying a given territory or homeland, sharing a distinct language and history' (Kymlicka 1995b: 18). Much of the discussion of Kymlicka's work ignores the very specific, institutional, political and ultimately nationalistic conception of culture at work in his arguments. This can be seen most clearly in his discussion of 'multinational states,' an anomaly for modern states that depend on a shared sense of purpose, mutual solidarity, and a shared national vernacular language, to be stable. The problem then is the messiness of the world, in which some nations become national minorities within states, the solution to which is differentiated citizenship and minority rights, including cultural accommodation and, where necessary, some form of partial self-government. This accommodation can be accomplished through 'polyethnic rights,' which permit differentiation in the rights that various citizens enjoy. While polyethnic rights have the proper multiperspectival structure, they do so against the background of a single perspective nation that 'takes the authority of the larger polity for granted' (Kymlicka 1995b: 181).

Furthermore, it is not cultural diversity as such that is problematic, since cultural diversity brought about through voluntary immigration does not create the same set of broad claims of accommodation and self-government based on forced incorporation into a larger state. Because culture depends on a 'People' or a 'nation' that organizes it, this People or nation can be governed and constrained by the demands of liberal justice that accepts the fact of distinct Peoplehood as a source of legitimate claims. Self-governance rights go to the heart of democracy, since national minorities may claim that there is more than one 'People.' 'Self-government rights are, therefore, the most complete case of differentiated citizenship, since they divide the People into separate Peoples' (Kymlicka 1995b: 182). To the extent that a democracy depends on already existing and singular Peoplehood for legitimacy, it depends on a social fact. But why should multicultural democracies accept this kind of factual constraint? Kymlicka argues that multinational alternatives are unstable, and thus Peoplehood is the only way to attain important requirements of justice. But as Sofia Nasstrom (2007) has pointed out, this simply begs the question: what legitimates the claim to be 'a People'? How could the constraint of a shared societal culture be justified on democratic grounds? Democratic theory on the whole agrees with Kymlicka, but only by assuming that the People and its boundaries as simply given, and these boundaries are facts in the sense that they do not admit of democratic justification. Thus, for Kymlicka, once the legitimacy of the People is challenged, we no longer have a democracy, but a mere modus vivendi.

Social facts relevant to democracy can be both enabling and constraining. The willingness to accept voluntary constraints on action, such as commitments to basic rights and constitutional limits on political power, are both enabling as well as constraining. Social facts, on the other hand, are non-voluntary constraints, and, in this case, are constraints that condition the scope and application of democratic principles. Taken up in a practical social theory oriented to suggesting actions that might realize the ideal of democracy in modern society, social facts no longer operate simply as constraints. For Rawls, 'the fact of pluralism' (or the diversity of moral doctrines in modern societies) is just one such permanent feature of modern society, but its permanence is itself cast in terms of democracy. In a democracy, it is likely that there will be more rather than less pluralism (Rawls 1999b: 424). This fact of pluralism thus alters how we are to think of the *feasibility* of a political ideal, since whatever form democracy takes it will have greater pluralism as its result. In keeping with the perspectival nature of pluralism, not all actors and groups experience the constraints of pluralism in the same way. It may be experienced by some actors as a hurdle in their attempt to realize a democracy based on a social consensus of shared values and norms; while for others it may suggest that such a shared understanding is not the best available alternative and that we ought not to think of a common identity or shared societal culture as a requirement for democracy at all.

If this were the only role of facts in Rawls' political theory, it would have changed the terms of the discussion of pluralism that we have already seen in Kymlicka. It is unreasonable to think that democracies will depend on a shared national culture. Rather, Rawls' signal contribution is to show that social facts differ in kind, maintaining that social facts such as the fact of pluralism are permanent and not merely to be considered in narrow terms of functional stability. Social facts related to stability may indeed constrain feasibility without being limits on the possibility or realizability of an ideal as such; in the case of pluralism, for example, democratic political ideals other than liberalism might be possible. Without locating a necessary connection between its relations between feasibility under current conditions and mere logical possibility, describing a social fact as 'permanent' is not entirely accurate. It is better instead to think of such facts as 'institutional facts' that are *entrenched* in some historically contingent, specific social order rather than as universal normative constraints on democratic institutions. Thus, what Rawls calls 'permanent' facts about modern societies are rather those determinations that are embedded in relatively long-term social processes, whose consequences cannot be reversed in a short period of time – such as a generation – by political action. Practical theories thus have to consider the ways in which such facts become part of such a process which might be called 'generative entrenchment' (Wimsatt 1974). By 'generative entrenchment of social facts,' I mean a constructive process by which citizens act together in the relevant democratic institutions in order to promote those very conditions that make the institutional social fact possible in assuming those conditions for their own possibility. When the processes at work in the social fact then begin to outstrip particular institutional feedback mechanisms that maintain it within the institution, then the institution must be transformed if it is to stand in the appropriate relation to the facts that make it feasible and realizable. All institutions, including democratic ones, entrench some social facts in realizing their possibility and thus not all social facts should be regarded as already given because they are fixed conditions of possibility for democracy or some other ideal. We ought to see such conditions as themselves to be maintained and in being maintained ongoingly reconfigured and transformed.

When seen in light of the requirements of the generative entrenchment of facts and conditions by institutions, constructivists are right to emphasize how agents themselves produce and maintain social realities, even if not under conditions of their own making. In this context an important contribution of pragmatism is precisely its interpretation of the practical status of social facts. Thus, Dewey sees social facts always related to 'problematic situations,' even if these are more felt or suffered than fully recognized as such. The way to avoid turning problematic situations into empirical–normative dilemmas is, as Dewey suggests, seeing facts themselves a practical: 'facts are such in a logical sense only as they serve to delimit a problem in a way that affords indication and test of proposed solutions' (Dewey 1986: 499). In the context of discussions of the feasibility of a political ideal, they may serve this practical role only if they are seen in interaction with our understanding of the ideals that guide the practices in which such problems emerge, thus where neither fact nor ideal is fixed and neither is given justificatory or theoretical priority. In response to Lippmann's insistence on the preeminence of expertise, Dewey criticized the possibilities inherent in 'existing political practice, with its complete ignoring of occupational groups and the organized knowledge and purposes that are involved in the existence of such groups, manifests a dependence upon a summation of individuals quantitatively' (Dewey 1991: 50–51). In reply to Lippmann's elitist view of majority rule, Dewey held on to the possibility and feasibility of democratic participation by the well-informed citizen. However, he recognized that existing institutions were obstacles to the emergence of such a form of participatory democracy in an era when 'the machine age has enormously expanded, multiplied, intensified and complicated the scope of indirect consequences' of collective action and where the collectives – affected by actions of such a scope – are so large and diverse 'that the resultant public cannot identify and distinguish itself' (Dewey 1988: 255, 314). American democratic ideals that have been shaped by outdated local town meeting practices and ideals now must be appropriate to a 'continental nation state' whose political structures encourage the formation of 'a scattered, mobile and manifold public' (Dewey 1988: 280–1). Thus, Dewey saw the solution in a transformation both of what it is to be a public and of the institutions with which the public interacts. Such interaction will provide the basis for determining how the functions of the new form of political organisation will be limited and expanded, the scope of which is 'something to be critically and experimentally determined' in democracy itself, as a mode of practical inquiry about social facts as both obstacles and resources for realizing its ideals (Dewey 1988: 281).

The lesson learned from this debate about the status of culture is that even if pluralism is a social fact, indeed a permanent social fact, it does not suggest that democracy as such is possible only in one form or another. This is to commit a sophisticated version of the genetic fallacy in normative theory: it amounts to an instance of 'post hoc ergo propter hoc' reasoning. Consider Kymlicka's arguments against multinational democracy. According to Kymlicka, if democracy has historically organized around the idea of a People or a nation, then pluralism in democracy means a plurality of nations or Peoples. However, this is only one form of pluralism relevant to democracy, the form that takes as given 'culture' in Kymlicka's sense. Given that this form of plurality is a fact, Kymlicka sees the League of Nations national minority policy as a failure precisely because it attempts to solve this problem at the international level. It may well be a failure, but it is more likely to have failed because of its defects as an international institution. The methodological failure of this argument from empirical facts about pluralism is similar to the one that Gusteren pointed out: that if we see pluralism only or even primarily in terms of culture and cultural groups we will miss a great deal of phenomena that are relevant and possibly democracy-enhancing forms of pluralism that can be institutionally entrenched.

This conceptualization of pluralism necessarily sees it as an obstacle: the more pluralism, the weaker the democratic nation becomes as it is unable to act from common purposes, mutual solidarity or speak a common language. But this list of conditions are social facts over which democracy has no real influence; they are due to the contingencies of the existing societal culture that constrain democracy. This means the conditions for democracy are present only in such a culture, a fact which would fix certain eighteenth-century prejudices as canonical for democracy. Most of all, it provides a particular legitimation that takes the *demos* as given: it is the People that organize democracy (rather than democracy as organizing a People or Peoples). Rawls' fact of pluralism pushes us away from this idea. In the debate Iris Young's idea of various group perspectives takes us the full way beyond the People as legitimating pluralist democracy to the need for the explicit legitimation of the People in a more robust form of pluralism.

Pluralism about What? Decentering Democracy

Like Kymlicka, Young challenged the normative appropriateness of univocal categories of membership, calling for a 'differentiated' conception of citizenship that took into account the political role and experiences of social groups in modern polities. Young has set out to systematically generalize this theoretical project through rethinking the idea of inclusion that has guided many of the fundamental reform movements. Young challenges us to rethink the concept of inclusion when it is applied to complex and large-scale modern democracies, especially if we are to break the 'vicious circle' between democracy and injustice. Echoing Dewey's claim that the solution to the problems of democracy is more democracy, Young argues 'impediments to the ability of democracies to enact more just policies are best addressed by deepening democracy' (Young 2002: 35). Yet Young's overarching ambition appears more transformative. Borrowing a phrase used by Jürgen Habermas and Gerald Frug, her argument seeks to 'decenter' democracy in such a way that the negative dynamic between injustice and democracy ceases to apply. Many democratic norms and mechanisms are indeed 'decentered' in the arguments here in order to make them more inclusive: deliberation, representation, group membership and identity, the public sphere, the relations of the local to the regional and the global, and so on. Decentering suggests that no one level of democratic organization, such as the state, is to be favored, nor should democracy necessarily be organized by *a People* in the singular. Thus, Young challenges the central assumptions of democratic theory that are the basis for Kymlicka's arguments that plural Peoples lead inevitably to a modus vivendi.

How might democracy be decentered? As expressed by Habermas, the goal is to rid democratic theory of some of the metaphysical assumptions that it inherited from eighteenth-century voluntarism, about the collective will of 'the People' who control social processes (Habermas 1996).[1] In deliberative democracy, assumptions of the same sort are made in favoring face-to-face interaction in a single forum, so that such a deliberative body could take society as a whole as the object of a singular and orderly process of collective deliberation. Instead, Young argues that the motivation for the decentered view is that democratic politics is embedded in the 'context of large and complex social processes the whole of which cannot come into view, let alone under decision-making control' (Young 2002: 46). In this way, Young decenters democracy along two dimensions: the micro-dimension of the communicative processes that constitute decision making and at the macro-dimension of the scale of interlocking levels of governance from cities to regions to global society. The first involves for Young the recognition of the place of social perspectives in just and wise democratic decision making; the latter requires having smaller units embedded in larger units whenever the scope of People's actions and contexts of interaction constitute a common world. Understanding democracy in this way allows the genuine requirements of reasoning, communication and political unity under circumstances of pluralism to come into view.

---

1   See here especially Chapter 8. Also see Frug (1999), especially Chapter 4.

At the same time, Young fails to fulfill the promise of decentering democracy by appealing to the givenness of certain structures: first, a theory of objective social structure and the social distribution of perspectives and knowledge; and second, an orientation of its politics of inclusion to the 'unavoidable' functional capabilities of the institutions of the nation state. Given the kinds of social facts of pluralism and interdependence that are its premises, the task of decentering democracy today is much more a constructive one, requiring normative, conceptual and institutional innovation that goes beyond the dynamics of exclusion and inclusion typical of state-oriented democracy. The acceptance of the state form even after decentering democracy theoretically leaves the legitimation of the People once again an open question. Since arguments for decentering democracy are always explicitly or implicitly arguments about the relation between social facts and norms, their empirical basis is very important for their plausibility.

According to Habermas, the critical aim of 'decentering' is to rid democratic theory of some of the metaphysical assumptions that it inherited from eighteenth-century voluntarism that would have the collective will of the People control the society through the exercise of its public autonomy. Or, in Frug's more practical terms, it is no longer to assume the privileged locations for democracy in the inherited institutions of the past, which are often based precisely on eliminating pluralism by undermining intermediate entities such as cities for the sake of centralizing tendencies (Frug 1999: 73–91). In deliberative democracy, similar normative assumptions not only favor face-to-face interaction in a unified forum; they also see deliberation as a singular and orderly process that assures its own legitimacy. Such a concept of singular or unified deliberation finds little application in large-scale, complex and pluralistic societies. The democratic requirement for decentered democracies is that self-rule must be consistent with the nondomination. This is not an external requirement, but one which has to do with the democratic ideal itself. In a unitary democracy, the claim is that the People must rule themselves. But decentering adds the requirement that a People are legitimate only if it can rule itself without dominating others who also have justifiable claims to self-rule. Moreover, as recent security-minded democracies show, domination of those outside the polity leads to the undermining of democracy at home, as restrictions to the rights of others lessen the value of the rights of citizens. Nondomination thus suggests the need for a transnational justification for claims to self rule.[2]

According to the decentered view, democratic politics must surrender its ideal of full transparency and control over the social contexts in which it is embedded. Given a certain level of differentiation and complexity in state-organized societies, democracy has historically already been decentered institutionally along two dimensions: in the micro-dimension in the sheer variety of mechanisms and processes that constitute political decision making; and along the macro-dimension in a multiplicity of interlocking levels of governance from cities to federal states to regions and global society. Such decentering can be found in the lack of an adequate vocabulary in democratic theory to describe various emerging supranational

---

2   On this argument, see Bohman (2008).

polities such as the European Union (Schmitter 1998: 32). But the European Union is not a super-state with its Peoples comprising the People of Europe. It is rather a democracy of Peoples at various levels of aggregation depending upon whom is affected and how. Young differs from both Rawls and Habermas in that her account is not primarily concerned only with macrosociological facts as constraints but rather with locating democracy within an account of *social structure* that emerges in relations among groups, roughly 'the institutionalized background which conditions much of individual action and expression, but over which individuals by themselves have little control' (Young 2002: 92). Her social theory considers social structures to constitute a relational space of social positions, in which there are nonvoluntary and 'relatively permanent' structural groups, such as race, class and gender. Social structure as a 'field' suggests that structural groups will possess distinct perspectives, which in turn socially distributes the knowledge relevant to democratic communication.

If this account of social structure is correct, then the standard conceptions of citizenship, shared by Kymlicka's multiculturalism, as a kind of affiliation or identity can be decentered. Young calls for an alternative ideal of differentiated solidarity rather than citizenship, which 'does not presume mutual identification as an explicit or implicit condition for attitudes of respect and inclusion' (Young 2002: 221). This nonvoluntary character of structural groups creates a problem for democratic politics. If not from such identities, where does the sense of obligation come from in such solidarity, especially when a People are geographically and socially distant from each other? Here again Young has recourse to the facticity of social structure: the moral basis for such obligations are to be found from the sheer fact that People or Peoples live together, whether they like it or not. The ideal of differentiated solidarity then suggests that the greater the interdependence and mutual influence that can be established at the empirical level, the greater their mutual obligations, including the political obligation to include the interests of all those affected in political decision making in some way or another. Two problems plague this argument. The first is the absence of normative premises beyond mutual influence. Kant, for example, supplied the missing normative premise in his argument that the moral significance of such influence has to do with the way it impacts the freedom of agents. Second, causal and institutional interdependence does not require a common world. Less than a common space or a singular and uniform condition, the best empirical analyses of global interdependence suggest that it is highly stratified with 'differential interconnectedness in different domains' (Held et al. 2000: 27). Globalization is experienced in different ways by different Peoples or political communities, with markedly different impacts at different locations (Held et al. 2000: 213).[3]

As opposed to this convergent picture of living together, a decentered theory of democracy is better served, for example, by seeing how global activities, like many extended socially organized activities in modern societies, do not necessarily affect everyone or even the majority of persons in the same way. Rather, the sort

---

3   For various dimensions of this issue, see Hurrell and Woods (1999).

of social activities in question affect an *indefinite* number of People. Such activities are indefinite in the sense that they include spatially and temporally dispersed groups whom, as Onora O'Neill puts it, 'we cannot individuate but can specify' (O'Neill 1996: 119). Instead of dwelling together, indefinite social activities and the organizations that plan and carry them out create something more akin to the 'circumstances of politics.'[4] Interdependence *via* indefinite activity thus affects the scope of political obligation, precisely because the circumstance of global politics emerges through nonvoluntary inclusion in indefinite cooperative schemes. But not all forms of interdependence change political obligations, only those that bring about domination. Here it is tempting to make the issue one to be decided by juridical institutions, perhaps transnational character. The basis of such claims is, however, not against violations of some law or another, but of the very democratic self-rule that the violators claim for themselves. In such cases those affected have a right to justification as well as a legitimate democratic claim to have a say in those domains in which their freedom from domination is affected. These claims do not simply demand political inclusion in the dominating polity, but the establishment of democratic institutional space across them.

These circumstances of politics mean that in differentiated societies there is an increased potential for domination across social boundaries, so that the purpose of inclusion is now more like the struggle for civil rights: not necessarily to be included, but also to possess sufficient normative status of membership so as to resist domination and to avoid being included in the indefinite plans and activities of others. Like the mere fact of interdependence, the objectivity of social structure is not normatively fine-grained enough to pick out the sort of democratic obligations that we might have to others with whom we interact in a decentered polity. Next, we must see if the concept of perspectives can do further work in getting at the legitimacy of the People than it does on Young's overly structural and objective approach.

Deliberation and Plural Perspectives

Young's account goes some distance in recasting the legitimacy of group claims, which in most cases 'are not claims to the recognition of identity as such, but rather claims for fairness, equal opportunity, and political inclusion' (Young 2002: 107). Because of differences in experience among groups, such claims can be difficult to communicate and thus demand that we open up deliberative democracy to a wide range of communicative acts from greetings, narratives and rhetoric. Such forms of communication make it possible to experience, to some degree, the perspectives of others and to see how their situated social knowledge contributes to the outcome of democratic discussion. The central issue for democracy is the fundamental question of just what constitutes a perspective. In Young's account, perspectives

---

4   On the 'circumstances of politics' see Weale (1999: 8–13) and Waldron (1999: 114–17).

are structural and thus can be identified from a third-person, theoretical point of view, in terms of disadvantages in the relative position of a group within a system of relations that constitute a social structure. This leaves open a potential epistemic gap between one's perspective defined theoretically in terms of one's objective position as the member of a structural group on the one hand and one's practical perspective as a participant in democratic communication and deliberation on the other. Since perspectives are neither interests nor opinions, it remains unclear how the 'pre-reflective sensibility' that is attributed on the basis of objective social positions is translated into political claims or situated social knowledge. There is no democratic reason to restrict the axes of diversity in advance. Rather, the salience of various aspects of diversity is something to be discovered, as relevant to the issues at hand. This does not mean that the relevant aspects of diversity have already been discovered, since it may well be that deliberation is a process by which the diversity of the People is manifested.

The relevant aspects of diversity among citizens can be defined along cultural, social, and epistemic axes. Furthermore, each aspect of diversity can be measured along various deliberative dimensions: in terms of values, opinions and perspectives. These roughly correspond to the main *aspects* of diversity. Mill and others celebrate diversity of opinion as important to deliberation. This is certainly true so long as deliberators can isolate disagreements along this dimension, and difficulties arise when issues include not just basic beliefs, but also beliefs about the way in which beliefs are justified. Differences in values are perhaps the most discussed aspect of diversity in debates about culture or religion. Values in this sense include basic moral norms, various cultural conceptions of the good and important political norms (including conceptions of the common good). Values of this sort inform many different aspects of political life and thus often redound across many different contexts and issues in unexpected ways. Finally, there is also a diversity of perspectives in any complex and pluralistic society, afforded by different social positions primarily emerging from the range and type of experience.[5] Such experiences form the basis of a practical point of view shared by some but not all citizens, even if they do not explicitly regard themselves as members of a specific group. Perspectives are thus not reducible to any particular set of values and opinions, but are the experiential source of them. While it might be thought that the promoting diversity of all three kinds (of opinions, values and perspectives) is beneficial to the deliberative process, I argue that this role is achieved best by diversity of the right kind, the diversity of perspectives. Other kinds of diversity are not sufficient for achieving these benefits and promoting diversity *simpliciter* underestimates the difficulties of conflict for deliberation.

The epistemic motivation in selecting such a difference principle need not be to directly aim at better outcomes so much as at avoiding some bad ones. This is because the relevant aspect of diversity that is necessary for improving the process of deliberation is not the pool of *reasons* as such but the availability of the perspectives that inform these reasons and give them their cogency. The pool of

---

5   For a further development of this argument see Bohman (2003).

reasons can be increased even while still leaving out relevant perspectives. Before a reason can first be seen as a reason and then potentially as one that passes the critical scrutiny of all citizens, the perspectives of others and the experiences that inform them must be recognized as legitimate; in light of the inclusion of their perspective, groups are able to get uptake when they offer reasons and thus recognize for themselves that they are contributing to democratic decisions. One role for inclusion is epistemic, where multiple perspectives can contribute to the reduction of bias (Young 2002: 81–120). If all citizens fully deliberate together, each from their own perspective, they do not attempt to occupy the role of Adam Smith's 'impartial spectator,' who formulates reasons through the eyes of some neutral third person.[6] Mill's great achievement is to argue for the benefits of deliberation among citizens, who participate in discussion without having to renounce their concrete identities, interests and opinions.

Just as in arguments for the superiority of deliberation by a few, considerations of objectivity seem to suggest that certain perspectives are better than others, and the point of such deliberation would be to figure out which ones are somehow more likely to be the more correct or authentic voice of the People. The point of inclusion, however, is not to find the right perspective but to have such perspectives interact and inform each other, and in that way open up deliberation, as it is currently constituted, to correction. It could be argued that such correction occurred in the early days of the HIV epidemic when patients had no say about the regime for testing experimental drugs. From the perspective of patients, the highest possible standards of statistical significance in random controlled trials were simply unacceptable as a social policy. In deliberation that included the perspectives of patients (who also make up the pool of participants in tests and as such must restrict their use of other possible remedies), doctors, researchers and policy makers, standards of validity were balanced with other values such as quicker availability of drugs, safety and effectiveness. In a similar case, Bina Agarwal (2001a) has studied the effects of the exclusion of the perspective of women from deliberation on Community Forestry groups in India and Nepal. Because women had primary responsibility for wood gathering in their search for cooking fuel, they possessed greater knowledge of what sort of gathering was sustainable and about where trees were that needed protection. Mixed groups of guards thus would be a much more effective method of enforcement and epistemically inferior implementation.

As this example shows, perspectives are understood here in two main senses. First, perspectives are social, to the extent that they are practical stances towards the social world that are informed by experiences that agents have, often in

---

6   Adam Smith expresses this ideal in this way when considering two People with conflicting interests: 'Before we can make any proper comparison of opposite interests, we must change our position. We must view them, neither from our place nor from his, neither with our eyes nor with his, but from the place and with the eyes of a third person, who has particular connexion to either, and who judges impartially, between us' (cited in Daston 1992: 605). Mill, to the contrary, argues that the business of government 'is best left to those who are directly interested'.

common with others in their particular situation. Competent social agents are able to adopt and to employ a variety of social perspectives, often seeing some reason as convincing in deliberation precisely by taking up the perspective of others. Many accounts of deliberation are not so conceived, as is the case of proponents of impartiality who argue that deliberation succeeds when 'we the citizens' converge upon a reason that all can accept and constitute a common first person plural perspective. Gerald Ruggie's masterful analysis of the organizational shifts that produced the territorial state and new forms of organization beyond it shows that the modern sovereign state and the social empowerment of citizens emerged within the same epistemic self-understanding as single fixed-point perspective in painting, cartography, or optics. 'The concept of sovereignty then represented merely the doctrinal counterpart of the application of single point perspective to the organization of political space' (Ruggie 2000: 186).[7] If we are to embrace full diversity, then something like a 'multiperspectival polity' must emerge. Because democracies are more likely to be more pluralistic the more democratic they are, we should not expect that citizens can freely choose to constitute themselves as a singular People. Thus, multiculturalism and other attempts to pluralize democracy challenge those ideas of democracy that depend upon the idea of the legitimacy of a People cannot take for granted that all relevant perspectives are present. A multiperspectival polity organizes the People in such a way as to not only make such perspectives available, but also to also to see how decisions are democratically legitimate only if they are robust across perspectives. The point is not just to offer general or abstract reasons that 'all could accept'; rather, it is to determine in deliberation the multiperspectival cogency of various considerations, which in turn establishes a new basis for constituting a People or a People of Peoples. Even if democracy requites an inherently pluralistic ideal of deliberation, at any given time its practices may not be pluralist enough to solve problems or sufficiently test current solutions. These difficulties are not a matter of some inherent restriction of citizens' rationality, but rather related to the limitations of existing deliberative practices. In the case of a polity with several Peoples, it may be that its legitimacy may be the result of peace making as an inclusive deliberative process.

Pluralizing Democracy: Democratizing Practices of People Making

I have already noted that most theorists accept political legitimacy that existing Peoples and their boundaries are given prior to democracy: the boundaries of the

---

7   Besides its ultimate origins in George Herbert Mead, multiperspectival inquiry is common in feminist and democratic contexts, including multinational and transnational institutions. For a general account of multiperspectival inquiry as essential to practical and critical social science, see Bohman (2002).

People indeed taken to be a problem that is 'insoluble within democratic theory' (Whelen 1983: 16). Multiculturalism is but one challenge that makes such aspects of legitimacy no longer avoidable. When linked with liberal nationalism by Kymlicka and others, multiculturalism faces the same challenge at a different level when more than one People occupy the same political space. While Whelen argues that 'democracy presupposes the prior constitution of the group,' Habermas asserts 'the constitutional assembly cannot justify the legitimacy of the rules by which it is justified.' For others there can be no People without a constitution; but then, it is also true that the person does not give itself its constitution, and thus the constitution must be regarded as given (Richardson 2002: 57). The choice is then either an infinite regress or vicious circularity, between the People conferring legitimacy on the constitution or the constitution conferring legitimacy on the People. Thus, Habermas ultimately says that democracy must catch up with history, which only retrospectively transforms society into a legitimate and constitutional democracy. This view is still that it leaves the question of the legitimacy of the People entirely unresolved, as the legitimacy of the People is deferred in the perspective of the future for which it will simply become a fact. What all of these views share in common is that they place the legitimacy of the People outside of democracy itself, as something that is already given in the past or will be given in the future. But Peoples are made, not given, and no less social facts for it. However, debates about who are the People are endemic to democracy, and the legitimacy of the People is justified by no other way than practices of People making.

Once this presupposition of the givenness of the People is rejected, many important features of debates about multiculturalism can be recast. For example, discussions of aboriginal self-government are certainly questions about the composition of the People as well as about differentiated citizenship. For this reason, Kymlicka can discuss such rights as opening up the possibility of secession and the creation of a new People, particularly in cases in which a relatively large group remains outside the scope of the People. In discussing the example of the Supreme Court of Canada's recent decision to allow the admission of tribal stories as evidence for their land claims, for example, Seyla Benhabib argues that 'what lent legitimacy to the Canadian court's decision was precisely their recognition of a specific group's claims to be in the best interest of all Canadian citizens' (Benhabib 2002: 140–1). This is to argue that the decision was somehow neutral, impartial with respect to taking into account only 'our interests' as citizens. After the decision, however, Canada is a different, more multiperspectival polity, just as after *Brown* the United States became a multiracial polity that it was not before. In this case, the perspective of assessment, the attitude of the generalized other, now includes new points of view. In both cases, what counts as a reason and a justification has changed, precisely because the Courts exercised deliberative inclusion in considering new reasons and arguments, shifted the reflective equilibrium of the practical understanding of its complex democratic ideal, and expanded the scope of the Canadian 'People.' But notice also that the Canadian court permits pluralization via political inclusion and thus assumes the legitimacy of the properly expanded Canadian People. This assumption, too, can be put into question, in ways consistent with a differentiation not only within the People, but across Peoples. This requires broader democratic deliberation among the Peoples of Canada themselves, making possible a plural conception of a redistribution of self-rule. It is possible only in multiperspectival deliberation in which each takes the second person plural perspective distributively and thereby changes the nature of the community when new perspectives are introduced.

Similar arguments can be made about claims to 'special representation'. Such attempts to change a body of decision makers such as a parliament and a legislature are much like the Canadian Supreme Court decision. Demands for representation are not based so much on facts about demographic diversity of groups such as minorities and women. Rather, the primary claim is not based on such facts, but rather upon the consequences of being 'unrepresented' and thus excluded from the People as they exercise their legislative or other political powers. Once we no longer regard the population within a territory as a fact, the issue becomes a democratic question, the question of who the constituted People is and how they are to exercise effective rights of self-rule. Here we need to see that institutions are legitimate not only for constitutional reasons, but also because they could serve as the best collective means to represent the People. The issue here should not be decided simply in descriptive and demographic terms, since such an answer presupposes that there is some unbiased account of the legitimacy of a democratic People. Rather, it is a question of whether or not the People in all their diversity are represented, and that when unrepresented they are excluded from political life. The demands for inclusion in deliberative processes may be different than aggregative ones, and whether the issue is one that is resolvable only if statehood is on the table. Historically, it may well be that previously excluded members of the People need more representation in deliberative processes, in which their perspectives have previously not shaped the decision-making process (Warren 2007). Thus, the issue of representation is an issue concerning not merely groups, but perspectives, so that the aim of inclusion is to create a multiperspectival demos, not one that is defined in descriptive terms along ethnic or other preexisting ascriptive categories. Representation is a matter of legitimacy and thus of institutional People building. A theory of multiperspectival institutions at various levels from the local to the national to the global would then go a long way towards solving the problem of how it is that the variety of perspectives and situated forms of social knowledge get transformed into political decisions.

The pooling of knowledge or the practical testing of perspectives describes only part of the design of such institutions. The pooling of sovereignty that Young reserves for the state gives a fuller picture. It is possible that some institutional structures will not be organized as a People, as is the case for the European Union. In this sense, the EU is a highly differentiated, 'decentered' political structure that is both diverse and dispersed. It is diverse since there are at any location many different Peoples; and it is dispersed since political authority is exercised at many different sites and at many different levels. One crucial feature of multiperspectival institutions is that they would be precisely the location for innovations that would be required to bring about the practical decentering of democracy. Such a dispersed, diverse and differentiated structure neither resembles the unitary and sovereign national state, nor the network form of civil society.

So far, the main challenges to the legitimacy of a People have been internal to the borders of the state. For Rawls, since People enter their society at birth and exit at death, we cannot understand membership in a society as 'voluntary in any literal sense.' Given this methodological argument for closure, migration should be limited solely by functional considerations, such as the danger of undermining common societal culture as a basis of stability (Rawls 1999a: 34). Walzer sees the problem of legitimacy that such an argument poses for dealing with issues of migration, and argues that simply to assume 'an established group or fixed population: leads us to ignore 'the first and most important distributive question: how is that group constituted?' (Walzer 1984: 31).[8] Since Walzer does not concern himself with the historical origins of a People, he recognizes that migration concerns decisions that a constituted group makes in the present about its present and future populations. The problem's answer does not permit us to say who it is that can legitimately make such decisions. Legitimacy is not a question internal to the already constituted group, but the prior and persistent question of the democratic legitimacy of that constitution. To say that this is not itself a democratic question is simply to beg the question.

With regard to this most fundamental question of democratic theory, discussions of multiculturalism and diversity should be helpful. They show us that a democratic People building is an open and not a closed process, subject to certain constraints. Here we may think in terms proposed by Locke, who accepts that there is a burden of proof on those who would legitimately found a political community, since the burden of proof is to those who are excluded, that this new community 'injures not the freedom of the rest.' Of course, it may also not injure the freedom of others even after it is established, and this demand of nondomination is particularly important for preserving democracy. The burden of proof is at the very least to show that such membership will not be organized so as to lead to the domination of others, inside and outside the community, with other members. The issue is not simply granting consent. Rather, the task of People building depends on the further claim that freedom can be achieved on the basis of shared or common liberty. Constructive People building must pass the test of nondomination, that it 'injures not' the freedom of the rest. This requires an open and multicultural community at home and a cosmopolitan peaceful nondomination across communities. The abandonment of the assumption of the state of nature leaves Locke's proviso defeasible: it may very well be that a People who does not respect plurality in its political structure may very well fail to create the conditions outside of it that would justify it as a legitimate People.

---

8   As Nasstrom points out, Benhabib makes a similar assumption even for 'porous borders,' in conceiving of migration in terms of the possibility of a far process of naturalizing migrants into some existing People.

Conclusion

On one way of thinking about social facts, the existence of a People is a social fact; it is given prior to any consideration of democratic norms. Similarly, pluralism is a social fact, given as the result of an historical process that is ongoing. In the latter case, philosophers and theorists are more willing to say that this fact has transformative consequences for how we think of democracy and the circumstances of politics. For many years, anarchy was taken to be a fact of the international system, where anarchy is understood as the absence of centralized authority. Adapting a phrase of Alexander Wendt, democracy, like anarchy, 'is what states make of it,' and so too with pluralism. Pluralism is what citizens make of it, so that when citizens think that it undermines rather than enhances democracy they are making such a claim on the background of a particular conception of democracy and its requirements. For some, this argument suggests that the political community consists of 'a determinate group of persons, united by the decision to grant to each other precisely those rights that are necessary for the legitimate ordering of their collective existence by means of positive law' (Habermas 2001: 63).[9] The delimitation of political community is thus not a result of the de facto historical limits on current democracy, but rather a specific democratic ideal in the constitutional version that links it to the creation of positive law: a democratic ideal which normatively demands a social limitation of the relevant community that is then combined de facto with the centralized authority and the territorial limitations of the nation state. But if we think of the determinate set of persons who are the demos as a matter of historical contingency rather than as a necessary factual precondition for any democratic community, we then might maintain that its legitimacy depends on the ongoing construction of plurality, which is a permanent condition of free political institutions. Democracy enhancing aspects of pluralism involve seeing the importance of institutions and practices that make use of the wide diversity of perspectives, including a range of deliberative bodies, iterated forms of deliberation across sites and levels, as well as a plurality of publics and public spheres and new forms of citizen representatives that have been empowered to make proposals and set the agenda on various issues. Often democratizing processes embody just the sorts of interactions among publics and institutions that, as Dewey put it, 'break existing political forms.' Those forms to be broken are primarily the single perspective institutions of the nation state.

Does this call for a multiperspectival polity mean that multiculturalism has outlived its usefulness? I think not. The overemphasis on culture has led to freedom reducing forms of 'reactive culturalism,' which fail the Lockean test of

---

9   See also Benhabib (2004: 219). She says that there is 'no way to cut the Gordian knot linking territoriality, representation, and democratic voice' and thus to go beyond the current understanding of democratic community. This conceptual restriction is a consequence of accepting the demos as given. Kymlicka's assumptions lead him to a similar 'knot' concerning the inevitable instability of multinational states, or states of Peoples. In a democratic pluralism committed to nondomination, all levels of democracy are thus internally and externally transnational.

nondomination. This claim leaves undiagnosed the real harm of the violation of cultural rights and freedoms, the harm of domination that can be practiced by a People who constitute themselves as a demos. Whatever the basis for nondomination, that some in the political community have no status at all is a violation of the rule of law and basic conditions of justice. Republics need to heed Seneca's cosmopolitan injunction never to dominate others, if they are themselves to honor their constitutive and democratically grounded commitments to nondomination and are not themselves to become dominated at home through the very same institutional means by which they dominate others abroad. The true failure of the rule of law today is the prevalence of the status of 'illegal persons,' due primarily to the lack of status of many migrants, the destitute and other persons who are highly vulnerable to domination and violence. Thus, practices of pluralism that construct democratic spaces across which plural Peoples are able to make claims to nondomination do not necessarily end at the boundaries of the community. Rather, they show why pluralism is a resource rather than an obstacle for democracy and nondomination. Or, to put it another way, under the current circumstances of pluralization in politics, no one is free from domination unless all are free to engage each other on the terms of democratic self rule.

Multiculturalism and Recognition

Nicholas H. Smith

Introduction

It is hard to see how we can make sense of multiculturalism without invoking a concept of recognition. This becomes clear as soon as we reflect on the minimum conditions that must be in place for a practice, or a society generally, to count as multicultural. For a practice to count as multicultural, more is required than the matter of fact *co-existence* of many cultures (Parekh 2000: 6). Cultures existed alongside each other long before the concept of multiculturalism came along and before it became meaningful to talk about multiculturalism as such. The concept of multiculturalism only begins to have application when, in addition to the co-existence of many cultures, some *acknowledgement* of the 'many-culturedness' of a practice is sought or given. It is this acknowledgement or *recognition* of the fact of many cultures, and not just the fact itself, that provides a minimal condition of multiculturalism. The acknowledgement of matter of fact cultural multiplicity was one of the first demands of the multicultural movement, and it is likely that such 'demands for recognition' will continue to spring up wherever practices that are in fact 'many-cultured' do not *take themselves* to be. This is one reason why we need a concept of recognition to make sense of multiculturalism.

But the idea of multiculturalism is bound up with another sense of recognition. Acts of recognition sometimes involve not so much the acknowledgement of some fact as the *affirmation* of something's or someone's worth. Recognition in this sense implies a *positive estimation* or attitude, and not just an acknowledgement that something is the case. This concept of recognition feeds into a stronger, more controversial idea of multiculturalism than the one requiring recognition as acknowledgement, because it implies that cultural multiplicity, and the distinct cultures and identities that make up a many-cultured practice, be positively valued, endorsed and perhaps publicly supported. Acknowledgement of cultural multiplicity is necessary but not sufficient for multiculturalism, on this model, for what is also required is affirmation of the distinct cultures involved, and of the people whose identities are tied up with those cultures. The affirmation of the identities of distinct cultural groups, be it through law or public policy, through symbolic measures or the redistribution of resources, is another way in which 'demands for recognition' are made in the name of multiculturalism. And it is difficult to imagine what multiculturalism would amount to today without something like such demands for recognition.

For these two reasons at least – the close conceptual connection between multiculturalism and the acknowledgement of cultural multiplicity on the one hand and the affirmation of the worth of distinct cultural groups on the other – the concept of recognition seems to be indispensible for understanding multiculturalism. It is therefore no surprise that the emergence of multiculturalism as a practice and set of ideas over the past 25 years coincides with a resurgence of interest amongst philosophers in theories of recognition.

For convenience, we can think of the recent philosophical debate around recognition as falling into three phases. The first phase, which focused on the 'politics of recognition', took its terms of reference from Charles Taylor's controversial 1992 essay of that title. The essay was originally published as the centre piece of a volume entitled *Multiculturalism and the Politics of Recognition* (Gutmann 1992) but multiculturalism was not central to the argument of Taylor's essay – a circumstance that has occasioned much confusion, as we shall see. Amidst the plethora of critical responses to Taylor's model of the politics of recognition a second phase in the debate emerged. This endorsed the importance of recognition for contemporary politics as Taylor did, but it proposed a wider, more differentiated conception of what the politics of recognition rightfully involves, one that places struggles for recognition within a broader framework of oppression and emancipation. Jürgen Habermas's intervention took the debate a decisive step forward in this direction (Habermas 1993), but it was Nancy Fraser who systematically took up the challenge of mapping struggles for recognition onto new social movements, progressive politics and criticisms of contemporary modes of injustice (Fraser 1997). Fraser elaborated her model in response to rival positions advanced by theorists such as Seyla Benhabib and Iris Marion Young (Benhabib 2002; Young 2000), but it was above all her exchange with Axel Honneth on 'redistribution or recognition?' that defined this second phase of the debate (Fraser and Honneth 2003). As in Taylor's original model, multiculturalism plays a subordinate and ambivalent role in the unfolding of Fraser's theory of recognition. In the third phase of the debate, the focus can be seen as switching from recognition as one object of philosophical analysis and political contestation amongst others, to recognition as a kind of organising concept for a whole paradigm of critical reflection and social-theoretic research (Ricoeur 2005; Lazzeri and Caillé 2007; Schmidt-am-Busch and Zurn 2010). The key idea being explored here, which we owe above all to Honneth's writings (Honneth 1991, 1995a, 1995b, 2007), is that the very concept of the social is bound up with relations of mutual recognition and the struggles that must be entered into to realize them. For Honneth, mutual recognition provides a standard of 'intact' or 'undamaged' intersubjectivity in relation to which the 'pathologies of the social' characteristic of our times can be diagnosed (Honneth 2007). The theory of recognition thus assumes a paradigm-like status for Honneth not unlike the status the theory of value had for Marx (who considered the alienation and exploitation of labour as definitive of the capitalist epoch) or the status the theory of communicative action has for Habermas (who views the 'usurpation and distortion' of communicative action by strategic action – and so the colonization of the lifeworld by markets and bureaucracy – as the source of the defining conflicts of late modernity) (Habermas 1984, 1987). While Honneth is the most accomplished exponent of this ambitious conception of recognition theory, a younger generation of theorists has taken it up and is adapting it for the purposes of philosophically informed social criticism and the renewal of critical social theory in the Frankfurt School mould (Renault 2004, 2008; Deranty 2009; Petherbridge 2009).

So while the existence and challenge of multiculturalism forces us to think more carefully about recognition and the basis on which demands for it can legitimately be made, the main theories of recognition – Taylor's, Fraser's and especially Honneth's – are not addressed *first and foremost* to defenders or critics of multiculturalism as such. This is an important point to bear in mind when thinking about the relationship between multiculturalism and recognition. For the close conceptual relationship between multiculturalism and recognition has lead many theorists and commentators to interpret the main accounts of recognition as if they were, *ipso facto, multiculturalist* accounts – accounts that express a multiculturalist standpoint and more or less explicitly advocate for multiculturalism. This is a mistake, and much of what I have to say in this chapter is aimed at rectifying it. The widespread view that theories of recognition are direct expressions of a multicultural standpoint rests on a confusion that can be explained by the close association between recognition and multiculturalism just described. That is not to say, however, that the theories of recognition advanced by Taylor, Fraser and Honneth have nothing to do with multiculturalism, or have nothing interesting to say about it. The point is rather that we must be careful not to graft the multicultural problematic onto the theory from the start. If we resist that temptation, if we cautiously make our way into recognition theory free of preconceptions and wait to see show multiculturalism looks 'from the inside', so to speak, then much more plausible and interesting perspectives on multiculturalism come into view. To show this is the more constructive aim I have for the chapter.

I begin by looking back at Taylor's essay on the politics of recognition and the critical reception it received. I argue that at the core of Taylor's reflections is a claim about the multiplicity of legitimate manifestations of modern liberal ideals that has generally been overlooked by Taylor's many critics. My purpose here is not just to help set the record straight about the nature of Taylor's argument but to retrieve an insight that remains valid today about the kind of multiculturalism a politics of recognition can legitimately support. But the retrieval of this insight is by no means the end of the matter as far as the theory of recognition is concerned. Taking my departure from two of Habermas's criticisms of the limits of Taylor's approach, I turn in the second section to analyses that place struggles for recognition in a broader framework of morally grounded struggles against oppression, with particular reference to Fraser's account. After identifying certain problematic features of Fraser's approach to recognition and multiculturalism, I turn in the final section to Honneth's theory. The argument I make about Honneth has a similar shape to the one I make about Taylor: if we carefully reconstruct the motivation behind Honneth's theory, we see that it is not – as many critics have assumed – addressed in the first instance to the problems of multiculturalism, but that it nonetheless has an indirect relevance for multiculturalism that deserves further exploration. In the case of Honneth's theory, this has to do with the focus it provides on everyday contexts of moral experience and identity-formation in addition to the legal sphere of recognition targeted by the multicultural movement.

Taylor on the Politics of Recognition

Taylor's famous essay on the politics of recognition provides a framework for answering the following question: if the recognition of 'difference' is aimed at overcoming oppression, if it does possess a genuinely *emancipatory* character, what conception of freedom is operative within it, and does this conception come into conflict with the fundamental principles of liberalism? Taylor proposes that the politics of the recognition of difference is motivated by an *expressivist* understanding of freedom, tied more or less explicitly (and coherently) to a notion of *authenticity*, the historical and cultural roots of which go back to the Romantic reaction to the European Enlightenment. While expressive freedom or authenticity is hard to reconcile with the 'procedural' model of liberalism that tends to shape the self-understanding of liberalism today, it is not, according to Taylor's proposal, incompatible with basic liberal principles or with liberalism as such. On the contrary, it points forward to an enlarged, more radically pluralist model of liberalism which can itself give content to the legitimate emancipatory goals of the politics of recognition.

It is important, to avoid some widespread misapprehensions of Taylor's position, to consider briefly the expressivist understanding of freedom and authenticity. On the expressivist view, authenticity is a capacity that all human beings have irrespective of their social or cultural location. A society can rightfully be called free, in the expressivist sense, if it recognizes and respects this capacity in everyone, and in this sense expressivism has a radically egalitarian character. On the other hand, the standards of authentic self-expression vary enormously, both at the individual and the collective level; or in terms Taylor also uses, at the level of 'we-identity' as well as 'I-identity' (Taylor 1995: 192). An expressively free people, accordingly, is one that is able to pursue its own common purposes as expressed in its own distinctive languages and cultures. It cannot be authentic, or enjoy expressive freedom, if it has an alien language or set of cultural values imposed on it. For this reason, expressivism is radically particularized as well as egalitarian. Not only is there is no generalizable formula of authentic self-definition, but there can be no final, settled formulation of any one 'we-identity' (or 'I-identity'). According to the expressivist theory, self-definition is a constantly changing and unending process (Taylor 1975, 1991).

Something like this ideal of authenticity, Taylor suggests, is woven into the cultural backcloth against which a whole range of experiences of misrecognition and moral expectations of due recognition appear. Taylor then considers the scope available to liberal societies for meeting such expectations. He notes that a liberal society is defined, in the first instance, by the *equal status* enjoyed by its citizens under the law. This equality is widely understood to be based on the 'equal dignity' of its members, which is in turn widely understood to be grounded in the equal capacity individuals have rationally to choose their own way of life. A liberal society recognizes the equal dignity of its citizens – whether based on autonomy, authenticity, or some other feature – by granting them the same basic rights: the right to life, free association, freedom of speech, religious freedom, and so forth. Everyone is entitled to these rights simply in virtue of their common dignity as human beings. With regard to their fundamental liberties, the citizens of a liberal society are entitled to equal treatment, and if they are discriminated against on account of their particularity, they in turn suffer a damaging and unjust form of misrecognition. The misrecognition results not from 'difference-blindness', as Taylor puts it (Taylor 1992: 40), but from what we could call 'sameness-blindness'. In Taylor's view, difference-blindness with regard to fundamental liberties is an essential feature of a liberal society and it circumscribes the scope available for the recognition of particularity.

Taylor takes issue not with this liberal principle, but with the version of liberalism that defines the purpose served by the liberal democratic state *exclusively* in terms of impartial or difference-blind procedures for protecting the equal dignity of individuals. The main reason he opposes it is that this is not in fact how the citizens of certain societies conceive of the common good served by their particular liberal democracy. To the extent that they are forced into conceiving it or relating to it in that way, they are subject to a kind of misrecognition. The charge Taylor puts to 'procedural liberalism', as he calls it, is that while it is justly difference-blind at the level of basic liberties, it is unduly restrictive in its construction of the *expressive possibilities* consistent with the protection of those liberties, and this makes it difference-blind in an oppressive way.

Taylor backs up the charge by considering the predicament of liberalism in Canada. He notes how the proceduralist model has alienated Quebeckers who regard themselves as belonging to a 'distinct society' within Canada with their own particular 'we-identity'. 'It is axiomatic for Quebec governments', Taylor writes, 'that the survival and flourishing of French culture in Quebec is a good' (Taylor 1992: 58). And *in the circumstances Quebec finds itself in*, this good – the good of *survivance* – can only be secured by actively promoting it in public policy. To this end, a number of language laws were introduced which enforce French-language education on the children of immigrants and prohibit commercial signs in languages other than French. Now Taylor is by no means uncritical of the measures Quebec has taken to ensure *survivance* (Taylor 1993). But he does accept that *survivance* is a legitimate goal for the Quebec government to pursue.

There are inevitable costs: certain individual 'immunities and privileges', like the freedom to display commercial signs in English, have to be sacrificed for the common good. Moreover, in Taylor's view *survivance* requires more than policies that make the French language 'available for those who might choose it'; it cannot be left to individual choice. If the policies are to work, they must '*create* members of the community' by 'assuring that future generations continue to identify as French speakers' (Taylor 1992: 58–9). In both these respects, the promotion of *survivance* seems incompatible with procedural liberalism: they give precedence to a collective goal over individual freedoms and they favour the group whose conception of the good they serve. Yet if the Quebeckers were to follow the procedural path, they would be putting at risk the basis of their own distinctive identity, if not guaranteeing its demise. To the extent that the rest of Canada has sought to impose procedural liberalism upon them, they have been subject to an oppressive form of difference-blindness. A liberal society can avoid this kind of outcome, Taylor suggests, if it allows for the pursuit of collective goals, while 'respecting diversity, especially when dealing with those who do not share its common goals', and by providing safeguards for the fundamental liberties.

For Taylor, then, a liberal multicultural society at once protects basic freedoms and has mechanisms in place for ensuring the survival of minority cultures. But it does not base the good of cultural survival on the notion that different cultures are of *equal worth*. The idea that different cultures deserve equal recognition on account of possessing equal value, Taylor observes, underlies a popular stance in debates over multiculturalism in education. Advocates of multicultural curricula in the humanities, for instance, sometimes argue that the traditional Western 'canon' has been arbitrarily enforced. It owes its privileged place in the curriculum not to its superior worth, but to the parochialism and ethnocentrism of traditional educationalists. The challenge now is to discard this parochialism, the multiculturalists argue, and to give due recognition in the curriculum of other cultures which presumably have the same worth. Now Taylor has sympathy for the 'presumption of equal worth' as a point of departure or 'starting hypothesis' for the study of another culture. But the worth of a culture cannot be determined without actually engaging with it. To assert the equal worth of cultures independently of such engagement, to lay it down as a general principle of curriculum design, defeats the purpose of the reform. On the one hand, to collapse the distinction between cultures that deserve the recognition of serious study and those that do not homogenizes them as effectively as the traditional canon did. And on the other hand, if one reasons that all cultures have the same right to inclusion because there is really no such thing as a difference in worth, it makes comparative judgments a simple matter of taking sides. This in turn betrays a certain arrogance, as it implies we have nothing to learn from comparative study.

Taylor's critique of the well-intentioned but ultimately 'half-baked' relativism that can underlie multiculturalist programs of curriculum reform is tagged onto the end of his essay on recognition and stands independently of the expressivist critique of procedural liberalism that forms the core of the essay. We should bear in mind here the occasion for which the essay was written: as the inaugural lecture for Princeton University's Center for Human Values, it would have been expected to include some comment on the humanities wars then raging in the United States, and to reflect on the philosophical framework most suited for an avowedly pluralist educational institution. This provides the context for his brief discussion of the idea of the 'equal worth' of cultures. However, this stylized account of the reasons multiculturalists and others give for studying different cultures opened up an ambiguity in his overall argument that came to dominate the critical reception of 'The politics of recognition'. For Taylor's essay now invited a reading that took it to be claiming that only those cultures that either can be 'presumed' to have worth on account of being long-lasting or that prove their worth through some kind of cross-cultural comparison *deserve to survive* (and so *deserve recognition* and public support aimed at securing their survival). Habermas summed up the concern such a view would naturally provoke by noting that 'Taylor's politics of recognition would be on shaky ground if it had to depend on the "presumption of equal value" of cultures and their contribution to world civilization' (Habermas 1993: 141). Peter Jones has raised similar concerns about Taylor's approach to the politics of recognition, which rests, so he argues, on the possibility of 'our finding value in, or presuming the value of,' other people's cultures (Jones 2006: 35–6). While Habermas, Jones and others (Blum 1998) have mounted powerful arguments against such an approach, these arguments do not in fact address Taylor's basic thesis: that the collective good of cultural survival is something that liberal societies can and sometimes should socially endorse depending on its compatibility with the preservation of basic liberties – which, as I have remarked, has little to do with his anti-relativist reflections on multiculturalist educational reform.

Another issue that dominated the reception of Taylor's essay was its appeal to the notion of authenticity. This was seen as problematic both from a theoretical and practical point of view. Maeve Cooke, for example (Cooke 1997, 2009), has questioned whether judgments about authenticity, which Taylor presents as inwardly generated and as unique to singular individuals or groups, can ever be more than sheer subjective assertions. As there is no way of critically evaluating authenticity claims, Cooke continues, the theorist is left helpless in face of conflicting interpretations of what an authentic given identity consists in. As if reflecting this fact, the best Taylor can offer is 'uncritical affirmation of strong collective goals' (Cooke 1997: 260), such as the Québécois goal of *survivance*. Moreover, the politics or recognition powered by the ideal of authenticity seems to leave individuals at the mercy of aggressively self-assertive groups: it seems to subordinate individual autonomy to collective authenticity. For this reason, Taylor's model has been rejected for being fundamentally illiberal. Following Habermas and Cooke in this vein, Benhabib has argued that any 'right to authentic self-expression' must rest on the individual's right to autonomy, and not, as Taylor allegedly claims, vice versa (Benhabib 2002: 53). Taylor's problematic inversion of the moral priority of autonomy and authenticity, Benhabib continues, arises from his falsely essentialist conception of group identity. According to this objection, which crops up routinely in the literature (Emcke 2000; Markell 2000; Tully 2000; McNay 2008), authenticity is a misplaced goal because it rests upon the false and ultimately oppressive idea there is something natural, pre-given or fixed in advance for a group to be authentic to. This inevitably simplifies the process of identity formation, it overlooks the discrepancies and conflicts that are bound to arise between individual and group identities, and it is governed by an invidious logic of exclusion.

There is no space here to examine the complex relations between multiculturalism, essentialism and the ethics of authentic self-expression (Mason 2007), save to remind ourselves that the expressivist account of freedom Taylor uses to analyze the politics of recognition by no means *entails* commitment to a problematically homogeneous or totalitarian notion of authenticity. As we saw at the beginning of this section, the notion of expressive freedom or authenticity that Taylor draws on is not 'essentialist' in the sense of relying on some external, metaphysically given ground of identity; but then nor is it an arbitrary matter bereft of any standards of critical evaluation. As for the relation between authenticity and autonomy, it is not clear, even from within Taylor's own account, why they *must* be rival ideals or conflicting basic principles. In Taylor's view, procedural liberalism makes them *appear* incompatible by insisting on the uniform application of rights irrespective of cultural context and the historically indexed aspirations of specific groups, thus enforcing a false choice between individualism and collectivism. Tariq Modood has rightly drawn attention to the universalist thrust of *both* the principles of autonomy and authenticity, or as he puts it – departing somewhat from Taylor's own usage – 'equal dignity' and 'equal respect', both of which are 'essential to multiculturalism' in his persuasively argued conception (Modood 2007: 53).

The advantage of expressivism for Taylor is that it shows that, in cases such as Quebec, sacrifices of individual 'immunities and privileges' *may* be legitimately made for the sake of recognizing a collective good. The extent to which the Québécois have *actually* been motivated by an expressivist understanding of authenticity is, of course, another matter. Here it is important to distinguish between Taylor's use of the Quebec case to illustrate the limitations of procedural liberalism and his advocacy of a particular stance within the Quebec debate. Taylor is sympathetic to the grievance expressed by Quebeckers that procedural liberalism threatens their cultural identity by excluding the pursuit of collective goals. Given the *particular circumstances* of Quebec – a French-speaking culture bordering with an Anglophone cultural superpower – some collective action needs to be taken to ensure the continuity of its distinct identity. Proceduralism seems to prevent such measures and this generates the grievance. Taylor is sympathetic to it as a nationalist because he acknowledges the legitimacy of the aspiration to pursue common goals around a national identity. He is sympathetic to it as a liberal to the extent that the common goal pursued is consistent with the protection of basic freedoms. But that is not to say that the form of nationalism that prevails in Quebec is as liberal as it should be, or that the form of authenticity that is sought amongst Quebeckers is as expressivist as it should be. For Taylor, the backward-looking, ethnic orientation of traditional Quebec nationalism is in fact as much a danger to the continuation of Quebec as a distinct society as procedural liberalism is. By locking itself into the past, such a national identity is incapable of dealing with the challenges of the present, and in particular the challenge (and opportunity) posed by multiculturalism. To be sure, it is sometimes hard to tell when Taylor is simply describing the grievance the Quebec nationalists have with proceduralism and when he is advocating a certain response to the grievance. But to present Taylor as a spokesperson for the more reactionary wing of Quebec nationalism – or its philosophical equivalent, as a champion of discredited essentialism about individual or group identity – simply gets things wrong. In Taylor's view, contemporary Quebec provides a circumstance in which core liberal values are reconciled with the social endorsement of a particular conception of the good. It shows that a regime can pursue the collective goal of cultural survival while respecting basic liberties. To this extent it illustrates a general model that can serve as an alternative to procedural liberalism. Within the model, however, there is much room for manoeuvre.

It is this opening up of the possibilities of liberal politics that, in my view, constitutes the core and enduring insight of Taylor's essay on the politics of recognition. Taylor's argument is addressed first and foremost to those who consider there to be only one legitimate way of securing the basic individual freedoms that characterize modern liberal democracies. The doctrine that espouses this ideal is, in Taylor's mind, procedural liberalism, and the society that approximates most closely to it is the United States. The onus of Taylor's argument is to replace this picture with one in which there are many liberalisms giving expression to multiple, equally legitimate variations of the liberal ideal. Taylor wants us to countenance not just multiplicity by way of conceptions of good or cultural identity, within a liberal framework that enables their peaceful coexistence, but multiplicity of the framework itself – a kind of second order pluralism, a pluralism of accommodating pluralism. 'The politics of recognition' can thus rightfully be read as a multiculturalist manifesto only in the specific sense that it advocates multiculturalism *about* liberalism – a 'multi-liberalism', so to speak. In other writings (Taylor 2004, 2007), Taylor has sketched a sociological theory of 'multiple modernities' to complement this position. Rather than viewing modernity as the inevitable outcome of processes of rationalisation, secularisation, or 'enlightenment', he proposes a model of social change undergirded by culturally contingent realizations of increasingly universalistic norms. If the theory is right, the politics of recognition would be playing itself out throughout the modern world, and certainly not just in Canada and the US, in ways that western modernity has potentially much to learn from.

Fraser on Recognition and Redistribution

Taylor's 'multi-liberal' framing of the politics of recognition nevertheless suffers from two major drawbacks. The first is that it fails to appreciate the resources that are available from within the procedural liberal paradigm for dealing with the conflicts between individual freedoms and group-based identity-claims that Taylor is concerned with in his essay. The conception of procedural liberalism with which Taylor contrasts his own position is certainly rather narrow and it bears little resemblance to the sophisticated proceduralism elaborated by theorists such as Habermas. As Habermas has pointed out, the opposition between individual rights and sensitivity to cultural differences based on the recognition of collective rights is by no means unavoidable from a proceduralist liberal point of view – indeed, properly understood, they *cannot* be intrinsically opposed (Habermas 1993: 131). This is because, according to Habermas's theory, the responsibility to recognize and respect cultural difference in law has the same basis as the responsibility to recognize and respect individual rights: both are grounded in the procedure of uncoerced intersubjective will-formation. The recognition of cultural difference thus needs no special justification within a properly conceived procedural liberalism. The second drawback of Taylor's 'multi-liberal' model is that it only applies to a narrow band of recognition struggles. As Habermas also pointed out, there are many contexts in which struggles for recognition occur and only a small proportion of them follow the pattern exemplified in Quebec. If the 'politics of recognition' is to be grasped in its full range, we need a more comprehensive and differentiated model than the one advanced by Taylor.

These two flaws in Taylor's model of the politics of recognition provide the point of departure for Fraser's intervention in the debate. On the one hand she is convinced by Habermas's proceduralist account of the binding moral principles of liberal democracy, which in her view has the distinct advantage of not appealing to substantive conceptions of the good or particular cultural values, as Taylor's does. The defining mark of a just, democratic society, according to Fraser, is 'parity of participation' (Fraser 2003: 36). This principle prevents the kind of subordination of individual rights to collective interests that Taylor's model allegedly countenances, and it does so without reference to any metaphysical beliefs, or psychological attachments (and so 'needs for recognition'), that individuals may happen to have. On the other hand the moral force of this principle reaches well beyond those zones of conflict Taylor had in view when describing the politics of recognition. For it extends into all those spheres of struggle triggered by the subordinate 'status' socially ascribed to members of a particular group (Fraser 2003: 30). Women, gays, blacks, and other discriminated against groups are subject to this kind of misrecognition – not just ethno-national minorities such as the Québécois. Moreover, the ground of this misrecognition is not some withdrawal of esteem towards a culture, or subjective feelings of hurt on the part of individual members of groups, but objective inequalities in status that prevent individuals from some groups from being as autonomous – qua effective participants in the processes of self-rule – as members of others. Fraser maintains that this approach captures the objective *moral* basis of the struggles for recognition that characterize contemporary societies in *all* their forms.

There is much to reflect on here, but the main point for my current purposes is that Fraser's strategy leaves her in an even more ambivalent position in relation to multiculturalism than Taylor. It is true that Fraser embraces the emancipatory potential of the politics of recognition. She also considers the recognition of cultural difference as in certain circumstances a requirement of justice. Both these commitments are of course congenial to the multiculturalist. But in Fraser's case they come with two important provisos. First, the politics of recognition has a progressive character only insofar as it addresses status subordination as measured against the deontic norm of parity of participation. It does not extend to the affirmation of cultural identity. At times, Fraser suggests that cultural identity (as opposed to status) is not a moral matter at all, and so is not something that progressive politics should be concerned about (Fraser 2001). On other occasions though, and more typically, she suggests that we can be more or less progressive in the stance we take towards identity – and that we ought to be 'deconstructivist' rather than 'essentialist' on the matter (Fraser 1997, 2003). Fraser's second proviso is that the politics of recognition, restricted now to issues of status subordination, must be considered as but one of at least two distinct loci of struggle against injustice. For in addition to struggles aimed at the elimination of status subordination (the proper goal of 'identity politics', in Fraser's view) there are also 'class' conflicts aimed at a just redistribution of resources. In order to keep both kinds of conflict in view, Fraser advocates a 'dual perspective' approach that takes into account maldistribution injustices arising from the capitalist economic order as well as misrecognition injustices arising from the cultural order. By adopting the economic and cultural perspectives at once, Fraser argues, we will be able to see how maldistribution and misrecognition are intertwined in the contemporary world, how the cultural and economic orders we inhabit causally interact to bring these injustices about, and the best political strategies for remedying them.

These two provisos enable Fraser to take a critical stance in regard to what she calls 'mainstream multiculturalism' (Fraser 1997: 27–8, 2003: 75). Whereas Fraser detects in mainstream multiculturalism a tendency to 'reify' identity, to uncritically accept the value of actually existing identities and the cultural values they are based upon, her own 'transformative' approach would deconstruct 'the symbolic oppositions that underlie currently institutionalized patterns of cultural value' and thus 'change *everyone's* self-identity' (Fraser 2003: 75). And whereas multiculturalism, like all forms of 'culturalism', tends to 'displace' redistributive struggles by focusing narrowly on the politics of recognition (Fraser 2000: 108), her own approach would avoid this shortcoming by attending equally to the root causes of economic (as well as cultural) disadvantage. Occasionally, Fraser has pointed to the possibility of an alternative to mainstream multiculturalism – a so-called 'critical multiculturalism'- that would meet these two provisos (Fraser 1997: 36, 2003: 106). But she has not herself elaborated on what such a critical multiculturalism would look like and how it would be informed by a critical politics of recognition.

We can, however, anticipate some difficulties that a critical multiculturalism understood along Fraser's dual perspectival lines would face. Let us first briefly consider how the first proviso – that concerning identity – would be met. The first thing to note is that the deconstructive identity Fraser describes would on the face of it be a very demanding one to maintain, and surely no less demanding than the ideal of authenticity which Fraser herself criticises for the excessive burden it can place on members of culturally stigmatized groups (Fraser 2000: 112). While Fraser's point relates directly to the cultural–symbolic conditions of identity-formation, rather than the psychological mechanisms necessary for maintaining a healthy (or at least properly reflexive and self-critical) identity, the transformation she has in mind would clearly have to draw on psychological capacities that we all already possess. And on this point Fraser is in a bind. For while some account of the origin and development of these powers would seem to be an obvious desirable feature of a critical multiculturalism (given its goal of progressive self-transformation), Fraser does not want to mortgage her theory to questionable empirical claims and she does not want to tie her key critical norm of participative parity to any particular conception of the good (or even undamaged) life. But without some account of how we are able to develop, maintain, and indeed intensify the kind of reflexivity that the deconstructive stance requires, we are left with an apparently ungrounded hope that this is what progressive politics will make of us. Critical multiculturalism conceived along these lines would thus seem to involve an unlikely and far from stable coupling of avant-gardist ontology and deontic morality.

The manner in which Fraser proposes to meet the second proviso is just as problematic. Multiculturalists are routinely attacked, especially but not exclusively by leftists, for obsessing about culture, identity and recognition in the midst of appalling, and much more morally significant, economic inequalities (Barry 2001). As we have seen, Fraser shares this suspicion of mainstream multiculturalism, but rather than taking this as a reason to dismiss multiculturalist concerns, she seeks to expand the critical horizon of multiculturalism by providing it with a framework within which economic injustice and material deprivation can also be taken into account. This is the main motivation behind 'dual perspectivism', and it is hard to question it. What is more open to doubt is the specific means by which Fraser attempts to correct mainstream multiculturalism's culturalist one-sidedness. The key idea, as we have seen, is to supplement the cultural perspective with an economic one. But what justifies the adoption of a distinct 'economic' standpoint? Here again, Fraser is in a bind. For on the one hand, it could be justified by the real existence of a distinct economic realm, separate from culture, which perhaps can 'causally influence' the recognition order and the status positions of different groups within it. On the several occasions Fraser invokes the 'autonomous' nature of the market in capitalist society and the fact that it has a 'logic of its own' (Fraser 2003: 214), she seems to be endorsing this view. Certainly, she takes it as a major virtue of her theory that it can *explain* economic maldistributions, presumably on the basis of its conception of what the capitalist economy *is*. But this ambitious social-theoretical claim is more of an aspiration than an achievement: indeed, Fraser's conception of capitalism is so minimal and formal – limited as I have said to invocations of independent system-mechanisms and tendencies to accumulation – that it is hard to see where its explanatory power could come from. As if recoiling from such grand explanatory ambitions, Fraser claims that her theory is only committed to distinct economic and cultural *perspectives* on society, without presuming there is any ontological correlate to them. This is, after all, why she calls her theory 'perspectival' as opposed to 'substantive' dualism. But that just brings us back to the question: why *these* two perspectives?

The only credible answer, and one which Fraser herself offers, is that it is *pragmatic* for those engaged in progressive politics and social criticism to adopt them. It serves the purposes of progressives such as critical multiculturalists, Fraser would say, to keep a critical perspective on both cultural and economic sources of injustice, and to engage in a common fight against misrecognition and maldistribution. Fraser's theory provides a framework within which these struggles can be seen as complementary rather than antagonistic and this is perhaps its greatest strength. But the distinction between recognition and redistribution has problematic implications even from the point of view of its usefulness for social criticism. Recall, for example, that for Fraser the underlying moral norm breached by misrecogntion and well as maldistribution is parity of participation: those with a subordinate status on account of their cultural identity suffer the same fundamental wrong as those with a lowly class position because they both lack the resources to interact as equals. This is no doubt true. But is the full – or even the most salient – moral content of contemporary modes of social suffering captured by this norm? Is the norm of parity of participation really rich enough to encompass the gamut of moral injuries social critics have a responsibility to address? Surely the experiences of those who are subject to humiliation, disrespect, and alienation on a daily basis – say in the household or workplace – are typically only remotely informed by disappointed expectations of participatory parity, which suggests that from the point of view of sufferer at least, other normative breaches are also in play.

Experiences such as these provide the central phenomena for Honneth's theory of recognition. They are so important because, according to his theory, they can at once *reveal* the moral state of the world and *motivate* progressive social change. For Fraser, however, they are contingent responses to states of affairs whose moral measure is given independently by the norm of parity of participation. Experiences of misrecognition or the withdrawal of recognition have neither social-theoretical nor normative significance in Fraser's account; nothing of explanatory or normative weight turns on them. And for this reason, it is questionable whether we should call Fraser's theory a 'recognition theory' at all. It is not just, as Owen and Tully have pointed out, that Fraser has a 'restricted' concept of recognition that contrasts with Honneth's 'general' notion (Owen and Tully 2007: 268). It is more that, for Fraser, recognition lacks *constitutive* significance: we don't need it to explain social change or to evaluate societies normatively. And we can see, returning to Fraser's critique of mainstream multiculturalism, that neither of Fraser's proposals for meeting the conditions of a genuinely critical multiculturalism – the deconstructive stance to identity and the adoption of a redistributive perspective on the economy – has much to do with recognition. If in the end these proposals are hard to justify on anything other than pragmatic grounds, this should not lead us to conclude that recognition theory itself has reached its limit in this area.

Honneth's Recognition Paradigm

We saw in the previous section that Fraser's rethinking of recognition is motivated by the thought that the established theories of recognition – by which she means Taylor's and Honneth's – suffer from a 'culturalist' bias. By this she means that they exaggerate the moral significance of cultural identity to the extent even of 'reifying' it, and that they ignore – and more problematically encourage a 'displacement' of – struggles over the distribution of economic resources. If it turns out that these other theories are not in fact 'culturalist' in this pejorative sense, that they do not reify culture or ignore 'class' politics, then clearly the 'rethinking' Fraser proposes loses much of its rationale. So let us turn now to Honneth's theory, its alleged culturalism, and its implications for multiculturalism.

First, what is the core idea of Honneth's theory of recognition? The central task Honneth sets himself in *The Struggle for Recognition* (Honneth 1995a) is to make plausible an ambitious historical claim: that modern society emerged from, and develops in a manner shaped by, social conflicts which have a moral content in virtue of being aimed at relations of mutual recognition. It is important to bear in mind the very broad sweep of this hypothesis, and the matching sweep of the theories it opposes. Thus, at the most general level, Honneth's 'theory of recognition' contrasts with social theories that reject the explanatory purport of human intentionality, such as those that solely invoke 'laws of nature', or the law-like adaptations of a system to its environment. At the next level down, the theory contrasts with explanations of social conflict that invoke only one kind of intentionality – self-interest – as if social conflicts were always a matter of 'amoral' competition between individuals or groups over scarce resources. Bringing these two levels together, Honneth's hypothesis entails that social change admits of 'action-theoretic' explanation where the *explanans* includes not only the interest in self-preservation and competitive advantage, but action-motivating experiences with a moral or 'normative' content.

But it is only at the next level down from here, where the structure of the moral grievances that drive the conflicts characteristic of modern society is at issue, that the hypothesis at the heart of the theory of recognition really kicks in. The theory construes the moral content of experience not in terms of matter of fact pleasure or pain, but as *social* suffering – epitomised in experiences of humiliation and disrespect – which all human beings are vulnerable to on account of their dependence on the recognition of others for the 'practical self-relations' (such as self-respect and self-esteem) minimally necessary for a good life. But this general anthropological structure takes different social forms. And in its modern form, Honneth's historical hypothesis runs, the radicalization of the *individuating* process characteristic of modern societies involves a *differentiation* of the sources of these practical self-relations, which in turn provides the context for moral expectations of *mutual* recognition. The crucial development here is the separation of the basic social means by which the 'respect' an individual is due merely on account of being a 'person' is secured – namely, fundamental legal rights and equality under the law – and the social mechanisms by which 'esteem' is allocated to individuals in recognition of their particular achievements and contribution to society. Social conflicts could then be generated around expectations of inclusion under the legal category of the person, or more concretely, around possession of basic legal entitlements which recognize the equal dignity of persons belonging to the excluded group. Such struggles are aimed at the mutual recognition that binds equals under the law and co-authors of law. On the other hand, social conflicts could also emerge over the social status accorded to members of particular groups. What these struggles aim at is recognition in the sense of social esteem, or due recognition of the worth of particular achievements or ways of life. The 'individualization of achievement' in modern society means that esteem has to be earned; it is not given in advance, on the basis say of the family one was born into, or as in previous times, one's 'estate' (Honneth 1995a: 125). This gives rise to cultural conflicts over what it means to make a worthwhile contribution to society, that is, over the interpretation of the 'achievement principle'. As Honneth put it:

> In modern societies, relations of social esteem are subject to a permanent struggle, in which different groups attempt, by means of symbolic force and with reference to generals goals, to raise the value of the abilities associated with their way of life (Honneth 1995a: 127).

But this leads to a problem which, on Honneth's own account, represents the most serious conceptual difficulty facing the theory of recognition, one which the pioneers of the theory (Hegel and Mead) both failed to solve (Honneth 1995a: 91). For whereas the sense in which co-possessors of basic rights and co-authors of the law mutually recognize each other is relatively clear (as persons with equal dignity), it is harder to see how relations of *mutual* recognition are involved when social esteem is based on individualized achievement. That would seem to require a situation in which everyone enjoyed social esteem (or social standing) on the basis of their individual contribution to the collective goals of the society. If the mutuality of the recognition relationship is to extend to all, it must be on account of achievements that are generally acknowledged, or contributions to goals that are shared. Given the entwinement of individuation and socialisation posited by the theory of recognition, this would simultaneously have to provide each individual with the basis of self-esteem, and bind people together in a more robust way than is possible merely on account of membership of the category of persons (that is, subjects with equal dignity). As Hegel and Mead saw, without social bonds that extend beyond the familial sphere, and which have greater binding power than those generated by the mutual recognition of persons under law, the social cohesion of highly individuated, modern societies is at risk. Social esteem through mutual recognition could in principle provide such cohesion, thus helping to secure the integrity of the society and individual identities in one stroke.

The problem, however, is that with the individualization of achievement, agreement about the ways of life that are worthy of social esteem gradually breaks up. In a context of value-pluralism, itself the 'inevitable consequence' of the individualization of achievement (Honneth 1995a: 125), a crucial condition for social integration through mutual recognition seems to be lacking: namely a general consensus on what counts as 'achievement', a 'valuable contribution' to society, and so forth. Honneth's way around this difficulty is to suggest that the potentially disintegrative effects of value-pluralism and the individualisation of achievement are mitigated by a form of 'societal integration' in which individuals see themselves as having the *opportunity* to contribute meaningfully to society through the expression of their distinctive traits and abilities. Mutual recognition between such individuals does not require them to esteem each other's contribution to society to the same degree – the individualisation of achievement means that the degree of social esteem one receives depends on how successful one manages to be – but it does require that they all recognize each other as *potential* contributors, as having some *chance* of success. Although esteem is not given in advance to members of any particular group, no one is excluded from the means of social esteem merely on account of their membership of a group. So long as 'every subject is free from being collectively denigrated so that one is given the chance to experience oneself to be recognized in light one's own accomplishments and abilities, as valuable for society', relations of mutual esteem can be said to obtain (Honneth 1995a: 130). This provides Honneth with a solution to the problem that threatened to nip the Hegel–Mead theory of recognition in the bud, namely a way of reconciling the demands of individualization (as expressed in the achievement principle) with those of social integration.

Honneth's theory of recognition thus provides a critical perspective on the exclusion of individuals from the legal protections to which they are entitled as persons (whatever their group membership or cultural background) on the one hand, and on the moral injury suffered by individuals who are not able to have their talents and abilities recognized on account of belonging to a stigmatized or denigrated group on the other. It also explains how such experiences of moral injury can give rise to conflicts with the potential for bringing about progressive social change. Struggles aimed at the proper appreciation of the 'value' of certain traits and abilities – such as those traditionally associated with women – have this role. The theory also puts us in a position to criticise arbitrary exclusions from the process of the social interpretation of worth, as well as one-sided or distorted prevailing interpretations of the achievement principle. It locates the *progressive* character of such struggles in the contribution they make to widening the 'inclusion of subjects into the circle of full members of society', and to increasing the possibilities individuals have to express all aspects of their personality without fear of denigration (Honneth 2003: 184–5).

If this is an accurate reconstruction of the central tenets of Honneth's theory of recognition, it is hard to see why it is 'culturalist' in the sense Fraser finds so objectionable. Of course, if we begin by *stipulating* a distinction between 'identity politics' aimed at cultural recognition and 'class politics' aimed at economic redistribution, then a recognition 'monism' of the kind advocated by Honneth will indeed look problematically reductive. But for Honneth it is just this initial move that puts us on the wrong foot. It should also be clear from the foregoing that the struggles for recognition that lie at the heart of the theory hardly give expression to overblown, narcissistic conceptions of self-identity bent on obliterating self-other distinctions. Something like this idea lies behind the charge that the recognition paradigm exaggerates human powers of political agency by positing an impossible notion of sovereignty (Markell 2003), though it has also been used to reach the opposite conclusion, that Honneth's theory of recognition excludes political agency altogether (McNay 2008). Such objections would be hard to make any sense of if it were not for the role that culture and cultural identity allegedly plays in Honneth's theory. But from what we have just seen, the motivation for the struggles for recognition Honneth is concerned with arise out of experiences of disrespect for individuals or forms of life as measured against expectations of *equality* or due recognition of achievement. Nothing in Honneth's account hinges on the notion of inter-cultural recognition or recognition between cultures, and there is no place in it for recognition of cultural identity *simpliciter*. Thus, while Honneth's recognition paradigm has been seen as culturally one-sided, as naively unaware of the real motivation behind many progressive political conflicts, and as dangerously uncritical of the kind of politics motivated by the desire for recognition of one group by another, it is difficult to see what would warrant these criticisms if it were not for the hasty manner in which the problems of multiculturalism are read into the theory from the start.

Indeed, if anything it is the very *absence* of any sustained reflection on culture and the problems of multiculturalism that is striking about Honneth's writings on recognition. It is clear from the brief discussion of multiculturalism in Honneth's exchange with Fraser that Honneth considers the normative core of multiculturalism to be encompassed by the principle of equal respect (Honneth 2003: 161–70). When he writes that 'the moral grammar of the conflicts now being conducted around "identity-political" questions in liberal-democratic states is essentially determined by the recognition principle of legal equality' (Honneth 2003: 169), he is no more than endorsing Habermas's original critique of Taylor's claim that the norm of autonomy is insufficient for grounding the politics of recognition. Whether a conflict is triggered by discrimination based on group or cultural membership, or if it is aimed at defending an endangered way of life or promoting the well-being of some group, the *moral* content of the motivation can be explicated in terms of the equal respect due to each person under the law. In Honneth's view, only those demands for cultural recognition that are backed up by either the principle of equal respect or the merit principle have a genuine moral claim on us. For Honneth, then, it is the new semantic reach of these old principles, rather than a new principle of cultural recognition, that is really at issue in the debate about multiculturalism.

In addition to these explicit but brief remarks on cultural identity, Honneth's recognition paradigm has other resources for coming to grips with the problems of multiculturalism. Perhaps the most fundamental advantage Honneth claims for his recognition paradigm relative to other attempts at reviving critical social theory is that it does not pin itself to the objectives of particular social movements, including the multicultural movement. As he points out, the self-understanding of the new social movements, and the claims they present in the public sphere, are far from reliable indicators of the nature and scope of social suffering (Honneth 2003: 115). A better way for the critical theorist to proceed is to attend to the actual experiences of disrespect and humiliation endured by people in everyday life contexts. Such experiences of injustice at the same time reveal counterfactual expectations of what *would* amount to proper recognition. It is the disappointment of these expectations – the lack of recognition or withdrawal of it – that is experienced as a moral injury. The primary 'multicultural' problematic from a recognition-theoretic perspective, accordingly, is how the co-existence of people from many cultures provides a context in which such withdrawals of recognition and denied recognition can occur. On the basis of empirical investigation of such contexts, normative models may open up regarding how *fulfilled* expectations of recognition are mediated through experiences of cultural difference. In this way the recognition paradigm can embrace the 'everyday multiculturalism' model being explored by some contemporary sociologists (Velayutham and Wise 2009).

But the differentiation of respect and esteem recognition posited by the historical hypothesis at the core of Honneth's theory of recognition, together with the increasingly individuated basis on which achievement is recognized, suggests that one context in particular will provide the test for this kind of multicultural recognition: the sphere of work. For it is above all in work that one's worth as a social being, and our contribution to the larger life that defines us, is made concrete. It is in part for this reason that work is such a potent source of experiences of denied or withdrawn recognition, and consequently, such a vigorous source of experimentation in the struggle for recognition. Although Honneth's earlier writings are more attuned to the emancipatory potential of work-based struggles for recognition than his more recent texts, his theory never loses sight of the crucial identity-shaping function of work and its significance for maintaining healthy practical self-relations, on the one hand, and healthy social bonds on the other (Honneth 1995b, Smith 2009). Honneth follows Dewey in arguing that in the latter case, the experience of cooperation that can be engendered at work prepares the worker for the demands of democratic self-rule (Honneth 1998). It does this by *bracketing* notions of individual or group self-identity that are external to the purposes of the common work project. It may not be far-fetched to suppose that the bracketing of identity that is part of the experience of solidarity and cooperation at work provides the necessary background for multicultural democracy too.

Work provides one important context in which people suffer daily from the lack or withdrawal of recognition, from humiliation and disrespect. Neither Taylor's multi-liberal model of the politics of recognition, nor Fraser's dual perspectivism of recognition and redistribution grounded in a norm of participative parity, is conceptually well-equipped to deal with these phenomena. Honneth's recognition paradigm, with its differentiated notion of recognition and its wide focus on the normative expectations we bring to all contexts of action, fares much better in this regard. On the other hand, the impact that multiculturalism could have beyond the legal sphere has not yet been explored by Honneth or others associated with his recognition paradigm. Furthermore, these researchers are generally sceptical of Taylor's conviction about the intrinsic worth of cultures and the intrinsic good of multiplicity in the way of cultural identity. If, as I suggested in the first section of this essay, there is an enduring insight in Taylor's expressivist critique of procedural liberalism, we would then need to find a way of combining Taylor's multi-liberalism with the recognition-theoretic approach to everyday multiculturalism hinted at by Honneth. We may need such a synthesis to take our still sketchy understanding of the relation between recognition and multiculturalism further.

Postcolonial Multiculturalism[1]

Monica Mookherjee

Introduction: The Idea of Postcolonial Multiculturalism

At first glance, there appears to be so intimate a connection between the terms 'postcolonialism' and 'multiculturalism' that integrating the two theoretically seems almost inevitable. If multiculturalism is understood as a normative account of justice for cultures across and within nations, it would seem clearly concerned with the legacy of imperial practices. A more specific reason for assuming the connection is that the pluralist character of most societies today has been markedly intensified by global migration patterns following the last century's movements for decolonization. Moreover, the continued poverty of and discrimination against indigenous peoples raises pressing questions concerning how governments might adequately confront the legacy of the domination of their forms of life. Yet, in spite of these clear points of connection, in *Haunted Nations*, Sneja Gunew (2004) complains of the lack of engagement between postcolonial and multicultural theorists. Liberal defenders of cultural diversity generally disregard the complex theoretical innovations of postcolonial writers, she claims; and the latter, located within cultural and literary studies, often dismiss mainstream arguments for group-differentiated rights and other concrete forms of political inclusion within nation-states today. If Gunew is correct, postcolonial multiculturalism is not inevitable, but elusive and hard to define.

This chapter explores this tension in order to articulate the features of an appropriately 'postcolonial' account of multiculturalism. Accordingly, the following two sections focus on the specific claims advanced by postcolonial and multicultural writers, explaining how each body of thought supplies the other with resources for an account of the legacy of imperialism for cultural minorities today. Ultimately, a problem that plagues both postcolonialism and liberal multiculturalism is also identified, attention to which is proposed in order

---

1   I would like thank Duncan Ivison for extremely helpful advice on and perceptive criticisms of an earlier draft of this chapter, and for his kind invitation to contribute to this volume.

to strengthen the proposed approach. Specifically, by examining the debate about 'recognition' and 'redistribution' in critical social theory, I contend that postcolonial multiculturalism must theorize the interlocking nature of the cultural and economic realms of liberal civil society when assessing the inclusiveness of the political deliberation that it centrally recommends. In sum, postcolonial multiculturalism involves not just synthesizing liberal multiculturalist and postcolonial insights, but also going beyond both accounts. The approach proposed here recommends: (a) recognizing the paradoxical nature of minorities' struggles for group-specific rights; (b) defending an ideal of 'deliberative political inclusion'; and (c) an awareness of the need to transform cultural and economic spheres of civil society to address exclusion from political deliberation. The final issue of political exclusion might be considered the most intractable legacy of past imperial practices, as I attempt to demonstrate in the following discussion.

Postcolonial Theory: Hybridity Against Multiculturalism?

The task of defining the key terms of this debate poses difficulties not least because scholars from a variety of disciplines increasingly use the word 'postcolonial' in confusing ways (see Bhabha 1994, Spivak 1988, Parry 1987, Mongia 1996, Williams and Chrisman 1993). While it might seem that the word connotes the period following European empires between the seventeenth and twentieth centuries, Homi Bhabha maintains that it 'describe[s] ... criticism that bears witness to the unequal ... processes of representation by which the historical experience of the once-colonized Third World comes to be framed in the West' (1991: 63). Thus, although the term appears to suggest an examination of power-relations different than those under colonialism, in fact it directs attention to the persistence of the latter. The term therefore signals the complex ways that colonial power continues to manifest itself through a variety of media such as art, literature and political theory; and in its more positive form it proposes, as another writer observes, 'a methodological revisionism, enabling ... a critique of Western structures of knowledge and power ... of the post-Enlightenment period' (Mongia 1996: 2).

These formulations indicate immediately that the objectives of postcolonial theory are complicated; and it appears that clarifying the meaning of multiculturalism presents a no less challenging task. While Gunew (2003) explains that the idea might be taken to imply a factual divergence from a notional monoculturalism, often wrongly identified with 'the West', the word now has a wide variety of descriptive and normative connotations. As surveying all definitions here would involve reprising too sketchily the accounts of other chapters in this volume, I shall narrow my focus from the outset to a liberal understanding of 'multiculturalism' which entails a normative defence of rights for minority cultures and an exploration of their relation to modern ideals such as the state, citizenship, human rights, equality, liberty and dignity (e.g. Kymlicka 1989a, 1995b; Taylor 1992; Parekh 2000). As I shall argue here, postcolonial writers have taken aim at the tendency of this form of multiculturalism to rely on theoretical concepts derived from the European Enlightenment in its response to current geopolitical diversity. Equating multiculturalism with its liberal variety, postcolonial critics often consider the idea embarrassing on account of its being, so they claim, 'automatically aligned with and hopelessly co-opted by the state in its role in certain conscious kinds of nation-building' (Gunew 2003). In this section, I shall suggest that postcolonial theorists' challenge to liberal multiculturalism centres on three risks which threaten to undermine its socially progressive potential. These are: (i) its tendency to rely on falsely universal ideals; (ii) the risk of 'tokenism', or a failure to defend cultural diversity in a way that responds to the real disadvantages confronting minority groups;[2] and (iii) the problem of 'essentialising', or attributing immutable features to, cultures. In elaborating on these points, I contend that postcolonial critics, far from wishing rejecting multiculturalism *tout court*, provide important if under-developed resources for a more transformative conception which theorizes the power-relations that endure in many postcolonial nations of the world today.

As an introduction to these claims, consider how a critique of multiculturalism derived from Enlightenment concepts is implied by the best known voice in postcolonial studies. Edward Said famously reveals the dangers of false universalism and cultural essentialism in European thought, by arguing that prevalent ways of referring to cultural differences in this tradition need to be understood in terms of 'a discourse ... by which European culture was able to ... produce the Orient politically ... militarily, ideologically, scientifically, and imaginatively' (1979: 3). He invoked Foucault's (1984) notion of a discourse in order to define 'Orientalism' as a specific mode of representing cultural differences which said more about the West than the East (1979: 15). Its key representations branded non-Europeans with such clichéd characteristics as hierarchy, infantilism, untrustworthiness, inaccuracy and mendacity (1979: 33), which, pertinently, enabled a double manoeuvre. First, these representations served to deny colonial subjects' claims to self-government: the Oriental was understood to require 'development', even though they were deemed never to progress sufficiently but was eternally conceived as 'static, frozen, fixed' (1979: 27). Second, whilst these ideas testified to the struggle of Enlightenment thinkers to reconcile the tension between their emergent claims of universal enfranchisement with the political denial of the autonomy of approximately 80 per cent of the world at the time, the assertion of universal ideals of freedom and citizenship was also supported by the identification of an ethnic 'other' as a means to emphasize what these ideals were not (Norton 2011). Said's account thus implies that theories of multiculturalism committed to rights that protect 'authentic' cultural differences are liable to universalize political ideals in contentious ways and to sustain the problematic

---

2   The term 'subaltern' is taken from Gramsci (1971) who used it to refer any groups that lay outside the prevailing hegemonic structure of power. It is now used by many postcolonial writers to connote a group marginalized or excluded through the operation of neo-colonial relations of power specifically.

classifications that imperialism created by assuming the timeless fixity of cultural differences. Such forms of multiculturalism would seem to constitute a hollow victory for contemporary 'subaltern' of minority peoples.

I shall return to this point, but merely emphasize for now that the question arising from this interpretation of Said's thought is whether postcolonial criticism could propose an alternative account of multiculturalism that is not marred by such problems as false universalization and essentialism. As drawing attention to Orientalism is not to overcome it (Chakrabarty 1992: 2), the interventions of scholars writing 'subaltern' historiographies in the 1980s may be thought more fertile from a normative perspective. By presenting a critical history of South Asian society that draws upon a modified Marxist perspective, these scholars question, like Said, the way in which concepts of privacy, nationhood and global relations are understood in Enlightenment thought. But they go further by insisting on the capacity of the subaltern for agency and resistance in spite of the apparent pervasiveness of their social and political subjection (Prakash 1990, Das 1986, Spivak 1988). By rejecting what they understand as the Eurocentrism of standard Marxist or Leninist narratives of progress, they urge a rethinking of stable Enlightenment concepts by recognizing, on the one hand, the potential to theorize outside those narratives, and, on the other, their residual power to constrain our understanding of the meaning of key normative ideas. Attention to this tension creates a space in which the formerly colonized can be conceived as capable of resisting prevalent structures of power. Through their focus on little-documented peasant insurgencies during colonial times, their insights promise important resources for a critical multiculturalism not based in an uncontested universalization of Enlightenment ideals; and which also stands to free the debate about cultural diversity from 'Orientalist' habits of thought.

Yet the prospects for a more critical postcolonial multiculturalism appear highly unstable when we consider Homi Bhabha's incisive critique of theories of multiculturalism located within the institutions of liberal nation-states today. While Bhabha claims to support 'multiculturalism' if and to the extent that it genuinely promotes the agency of the formerly colonized (2003: 166), his challenge to Charles Taylor's (1992) liberal politics of recognition evinces deep concerns about all three issues of false universalism, 'tokenism' and essentialism, as outlined earlier. His underlying contention is that the cultural protection bestowed on subaltern peoples by the neo-colonial state would entice the latter to accept asymmetrical relations and undermine the emergence of the equitable relations in late-modern conditions through which cultural differences could be creatively articulated. As we shall see, the most convincing aspects of his critique raise the question of how an alternative multiculturalism can be formulated in a way that is not undesirably apocalyptic or utopian to an unproductive degree.

Bhabha's own perspective on this debate arises from his insistence on the complex standpoints from which claims for justice are raised today. Rather than replace established emphases on 'class' and 'gender' with assertions of 'culture', he introduces the idea of 'cultural hybridity' (1994: Introduction), which refers to the admixture of different ethnic, religious, economic or other differences in producing a person's identity. Any theory that fails to accommodate such a fluid understanding of cultural identities in postcolonial states will simply fail to see that its defence of multiculturalism amounts to a 'portmanteau term' (1996: 55), a 'floating signifier', which gains its positive and negative connotations from its institutional location (2003: 165). On this account, while thinkers like Taylor rightly focus on the recognition of minority groups, their emphasis on the state's bestowment of rights, as will be explained shortly, risks reinstating the old colonial binary opposition between 'Europe' and its 'others'. This is because multiculturalism can only respond to the messy reality of cultural diversity if it appreciates explicitly that assertions of cultural difference in a liberal state 'may *be no more than a stalking horse*' (2003: 169, my emphasis). In other words, these differences will be supported when doing so is cohesive with the institution, but are abandoned soon enough if they challenge prevailing regimes of power.

This problem seems indeed to risk affecting Taylor's theory. In his famous essay 'The politics of recognition' (1992), he defends a scheme of individual civil rights alongside rights for minorities in a manner that endorses recent Canadian governments' devolution of self-determination over land and resources to its linguistic and indigenous groups. Such a politics of recognition, which Bhabha finds appropriate in a very abstract sense (2003: 156), depends on two claims. Taylor's first point is that the marginalization of a person's cultural identity can inflict psychological harm (1992: 76) in the sense of leading the person to internalize a deeply negative self-conception. Since our identities are always formed through a quasi-Hegelian dialectical interaction between oneself and others, persistent social misrecognition of a culture with which one identifies can lead one to a deficient sense of personal worth. Moreover, and again schematically put, Taylor's second argument for cultural rights holds that, from a 'merely human' perspective, it must be assumed that the marginalized person's way of life has value because it has sustained large numbers of people over time (Taylor 1992: 90). The historical durability of the marginalized culture suggests its value from the perspective of universal humanity; and, thus, justifies a presumption to accord it respect in the form of rights (1992: 90).

Bhabha is unconvinced. For one thing, he claims, behind Taylor's language of the universally human lurks a very specific idea of a national culture which forms the inevitable basis for the relevant judgements about cultural difference (2003: 170). In spite of Taylor's efforts to emphasize the Gadamerian process of 'fusing horizons' of different ethical systems in drawing sensitive cross-cultural judgements, Bhabha insists that the allegedly universal standpoint from which the state considers a group worthy of respect is a particular nation-state in which groups are asymmetrically situated, such that the only recognition that it is likely to offer would consolidate those disparities. Thus, group rights do not represent real inclusion but a tokenistic concession to subaltern minorities within the prevailing order. In contrast, what needs to be acknowledged is the 'partial milieux', or the impure context from which cultural claims emanate today, and the 'productive but anxious representation' of the differences that postcolonial citizens assert in the public sphere (2003: 182). The basis for evaluating these representations must be recognized as culturally constructed too; it cannot simply claim universality in the sense that Taylor suggests.

Moreover, in response to Taylor's first point concerning the psychological consequences of cultural misrecognition, Bhabha questions Taylor's limited analysis of the thought of Frantz Fanon, the psychiatrist who classically theorized the psychopathology associated with decolonization movements in Algeria.[3] Whereas Taylor draws attention to Fanon's depiction of the colonized's internalization of an inferior self-image to explain the harm perpetrated by the Canadian state's historical failure to recognize its minorities (Taylor 1992: 71), Bhabha insists that, for Fanon, it is precisely the status of a person's cultural difference that must be questioned if liberation and independence are to be achieved (2003: 177). In *Black Skin, White Masks*, Fanon did indeed argue that, while at the moment of decolonization the colonial subject desires recognition in their own right, not for any attribute deemed essential to them such as their ethnicity, the residual effects of colonial power impel them to express this desire in terms of a claim for 'cultural authenticity', which confirms their continued psychological dependency on the colonial relationship (Fanon 1986: 218). Here Fanon famously identifies what he sees as the deplorable stagnation of the middle classes of newly decolonized states, who are only too content with their roles as 'Western bourgeois business agents'. Bhabha himself focuses on a central idea developed in *The Wretched of the Earth,* namely that real equal respect between cultures can only lie in our efforts to relate to one another in full awareness of the difficulties of overcoming the complexities of colonial dependency (Fanon 1967, Bhabha 2003: 177). He also highlights Fanon's later claim that liberation that transcends this psychic dependency could only emerge from violent struggle rather than from a declaration of recognition or a grant of freedom from colonial authority (Fanon 1986: 140–2; Bhabha 2003: 177). In light of these points, Bhabha seems right that Taylor misunderstands the dynamics of cultural recognition and thus puts forward an unsurprising but problematic state-centred defence of multiculturalism.

The question is what kind of multiculturalism could survive such heavy criticism, especially given that Bhabha repudiates Fanon's specific call to revolutionary violence as outmoded or, in his words, 'lost in a time-warp' (2003: 178). The problem is that this criticism leaves unclear how any struggle for recognition within a liberal state can be deemed valuable, if, according to Bhabha's fluid account of diversity, each assertion of identity would produce a new set of oppressions. Also, it is far from obvious how minorities would assert their 'hybrid' cultural identities successfully, as he insists that the neo-colonial state's conception of value threatens to regulate all judgements of human diversity (2003:

---

3   Fanon classically argued that: 'If psychiatry is the medical technique that aims to enable man no longer to be a stranger to his environment, I owe it to myself to affirm that the Arab, permanently alien to his own country, lives in a state of absolute depersonalization' (1967: 63). Later, as I suggest in this chapter, he would claim that such 'depersonalization' could be overcome through violent struggle.

178). Yet evidence of Bhabha's desire for an alternative form of multiculturalism seems implicit in his defence of postcolonial citizens' acts of mimicry and 'sly subversion' (1994: Chapter 4), which he views as effective ways of resisting neo-colonial power. One possibility here is that Bhabha's perspective would support liberal recognition, if it were taken up by subaltern peoples *strategically*. As he observes, minorities who use terms such as 'blackness' and 'minority' typically do so not in order to draw attention to their authentic identities but as a conscious means of gaining a political voice in order to transform social inequalities more broadly (1994: 111). Yet while this possibility offers a means of evading Terry Eagleton's (1988) criticism of what he sees as the 'vacuously apocalyptic' nature of postcolonial theory, the problem with construing Bhabha's account in these terms is that the mere intention to assert one's identity strategically does not entail that one has sufficient social power to challenge prevailing structures of power.

The upshot of this discussion is that, in order to articulate a multicultural theory that addresses the real risks contained in liberal approaches, we need to think further about the predicament that postcolonial theorists identify. The dilemma is that, while the subaltern may struggle for recognition in an institutional context which appears to confirm their subordination, the point of their struggle is always to transcend that social positioning. Although postcolonial writers suggest the importance of subversion and resistance as responses to this dilemma, they do not ultimately show how subaltern struggles could be socially transformative without resorting to revolution or violent protest. And whilst a postcolonial multiculturalism might indeed question the rights-based emphasis of liberal multiculturalism, it would also have to show how doing so would take a socially progressive form.

Before proposing a partial solution in the following section, let me suggest briefly why Bhabha's concept of 'hybridity' seems to fall short. One problem is that the condition seems to entail the amalgamation of two or more entities and therefore seems to presuppose exactly what the postcolonial critic denies, namely the existence of discrete cultures (Modood 2007). Moreover, by analysing disparate localities around the world, the idea of hybridity risks homogenizing diverse postcolonial experiences to a point of defending yet another 'grand narrative' (Mongia 1996). Finally, while the point of the 'hybrid' conception of cultural difference lies in suggesting the possibility of a position through which the subaltern can resist restrictive structures of power that cast her identity in terms of eternal, unchanging and pervasively negative features, celebrating this condition might risk foregrounding the perspectives of privileged constituents of minority groups (Loomba and Kaul 1994: 13, Parry 1987: 13, Dirlik 1994) without theorizing the lives of those whose agency is undermined on account of the deepened material inequalities that have accompanied major movements for decolonization. The final issue is not clearly addressed by colourful articulations of cultural mixity alone.

To summarize: the 'audacious steps back into history' (Gilroy 2004) and creative insights into neo-colonial power supplied by postcolonial critics draw attention to three risks contained in liberal theories of rights-based multiculturalism. The brief examination of Taylor's account provided here highlights the urgency of these risks and, thus, the pressing nature of postcolonial concerns. However, it remains unclear how, on this account, an alternative normative theory of multiculturalism would be articulated, especially when postcolonial critic Gayatri Spivak (1993) questions the very plausibility of 'postcolonialism' as a normative theory. Rather, in her view, the postcolonial describes the predicament of having to speak from a space that one inevitably inhabits (the authoritative sentence) and yet which one must criticize (from the perspective of what the sentence fails to say). On this basis, moreover, Spivak wearily concludes that in modernity liberalism represents a 'violating enablement', or a discourse which creates injuries whilst also representing the path through which the injured must effect a limited recovery. Liberal rights, she argues, should thus be understood as that which the oppressed 'cannot not want' (Spivak 1993: 101). While you cannot celebrate your wounds neither can you refuse to mitigate them. As this point seems all-important but under-explanatory, I turn next to ask how the supposed 'paradoxes' of liberal group rights might be invoked by a postcolonial theory of multiculturalism in a socially progressive sense.

Liberal Multiculturalism: Rights, Deliberation and a Pragmatic Politics of Paradox

Assuming that it would be misconceived to dismiss liberal theories of multiculturalism without further analysis, I propose to go deeper now, inquiring whether these accounts can accommodate postcolonial insights concerning the pervasiveness of neo-colonial relations of power. This strategy might be considered contentious, given that many early liberals supported the unfettered free markets that justified colonial expansion.[4] Yet while there is an empirically obvious relationship between liberalism and colonialism, a number of liberals today focus on the impact of past imperial relations in entrenching global inequalities (e.g. Pogge 1997); and there are also long-standing concerns in this tradition to protect diversity on account of the plurality of human values (Berlin 1969). Liberals, then, base their protection of diversity on the claim that beliefs about the good life should not be coerced; and although more would ideally be specified here about the limits of cultural diversity envisaged by liberals of the past (Arneil 1992; Squadrito 1996; Habibi 1999), the key point is that liberals typically seek to structure society to accommodate diverse perspectives through a common set

---

4   It should be recognized, however, that Adam Smith opposed imperialism, on grounds that relations of dependence between the metropolis and the periphery distorted self-regulating market mechanisms. For a broader discussion of this point, see Pitts (2005).

of rights. As the best life is one that is lived 'from the inside' (Dworkin 2000), cultural differences should be tolerated in principle.[5]

Against this theoretical background, minority rights have been defended by key proponents of liberal multiculturalism such as Taylor and Kymlicka (also Carens 2000; Parekh 2000), as a logical extension of the defence of toleration. Notably, these thinkers build on Rawls' (1971) concern to rectify disadvantages which individuals cannot be assumed to be responsible, by characterizing membership in a minority culture as a source of 'bad luck' which might lead their members to lack dignity or autonomy for which compensation should be granted by means of these rights.[6] My suggestion will be that these accounts can be rendered more receptive to the structural inequalities that persist in postcolonial states if they acknowledge the paradox which holds that the struggle to achieve group rights both reiterates and challenges unequal social structures. Moreover, I shall submit that recognizing this paradox openly encourages liberals to shift their attention from rights to political deliberation through which their content might be negotiated in transformative ways. This synthesis of postcolonial and liberal insights suggests resources for a postcolonial theory of multiculturalism which avoids the risks affecting the defence of liberal rights discussed earlier.

In order to reach this conclusion, consider briefly Kymlicka's recognition that, if a person's inherited culture is threatened by persistent marginalization or even extinction, their capacities to make meaningful life-choices can be undermined (1989a: 60, 1995b: 34–60). While such a claim, like Taylor's, risks falling prey to the risks of which postcolonial critics warn, Kymlicka's approach does seem to acknowledge the structural inequalities that pervade liberal states today. For instance, it recognizes that, while it could be fair to hold, say, indigenous groups accountable for gross violations of human rights, such groups might legitimately contest any further paternalistic interference from a state that has historically defrauded and abused them (1995b: 100; Spinner-Halev 2001). In contrast, Kymlicka advocates weaker rights for immigrants, on grounds that they consent to their host societies' norms. Thus, their claims to preserve their cultural distinctiveness would be limited to 'polyethnic' rights, which provide more limited opportunities to negotiate the terms of their political integration (1995b: 120).

Now whilst it might seem that Kymlicka fails acutely here to recognize the imperialist power-relations that undergird global migration patterns,[7] and although he is thus open to the charge of being 'yet another pragmatic liberal eager to be insulated from the chill of globalization by the warm glow of cosmopolitan

---

5   For contemporary explorations of the idea of toleration, see Horton (1993).

6   The literature on group-differentiated rights is enormous and I shall not attempt to present even a partial survey of it here. Key literature in the area includes Kymlicka (1995b), Jones (1999a, b).

7   'Imperialism' is usually thought to have wider application than the term 'colonialism'. While the latter connotes military, cultural and jurisdictional control over a particular territory, the former term is used to describe a broader and more indirect control over subaltern peoples.

imperialism' (Gilroy 2004: 156), that both he and Taylor are well aware of the deep inequalities that pervade postcolonial societies suggests hope for a reformulated, more progressive defence of group rights. For consider: Kymlicka explicitly rejects the idea that cultural groups constitute hermetically sealed collectives with authentic voices (1995b: 156), and emphasizes that to conceive cultural differences in terms of a 'clash of civilizations' (Huntington 1996) obviously recreates the essentialist thought characteristic of colonial relations.[8] Moreover, Taylor (2003) responds vigorously to Bhabha's charges of essentialism by insisting that he had always assumed that the internal contestability of all cultures was the 'given background' of his theory; and that it is an idea which, as an inhabitant of a francophone region of Canada, he could hardly reject. Moreover, while fully accepting Bhabha's complaint that the language of group rights constitutes an impoverished means through which to address cultural misrecognition (and even that 'part of what we are as human beings is crushed' by that poverty), he insists that there is little virtue in denying the political importance of ideas such as the 'state' and 'rights' to the campaigns of minority groups, as these concepts are 'still the major loci of what fragile democratic control [people] have' (2003: 186).

This pragmatic point is significant, in that it suggests that the liberal multiculturalist focus on group rights might be reconciled with the postcolonial concern about their 'disciplinary' or exclusionary effects. This reconciliation might be achieved through the conscious acknowledgement that group rights instantiate a paradox. Recalling Spivak's formulation of liberalism as a 'violating enablement', we might recognize that, on the one hand, the language of group rights is likely to be the inescapable medium through which minorities express their claims institutionally; but, on the other, that their campaigns represent struggles against the dominant conceptions of value and unequal social structures in which these very rights threaten to re-inscribe them. This is an important possibility, because, while difference-blind laws clearly fail to respond to the social diversity characteristic of current postcolonial states (Kymlicka and Norman 2000: 4), the achievement of 'rights to be different' is also not an end in itself for many oppressed groups (Patrick 2000). The point of pursuing these rights more often lies in the promise that they contain for transforming the cultural valuations and social hierarchies that construct subaltern groups as deviant (Young 2007: 61). Wendy Brown usefully explains the paradox of liberal group rights in relation to feminist struggles as follows:

> [T]he more highly specified rights are as rights for women, the more likely they are to build that fence insofar as they are more likely to encode a definition of women premised on our subordination ... Yet the opposite is also

---

8   This criticism may be directed against the distinction that Kymlicka (1995b) draws between 'good' cultural rights (which are designed to limit the assimilative pressure that liberal societies can legitimately impose on minority communities) and 'bad' cultural rights, or 'internal restrictions' which serve to enable groups to violate the civil liberties or welfare needs of members of minority cultures.

true – the more gender-neutral ... a right, the more likely it is that rights are liable to enhance male privilege ... **The paradox, then, is that rights that entail some specification of our suffering, injury or inequality lock us into the identity defined by our subordination and potentially even enhance it** *(2002: 422–3, my emphasis).*

While Brown presents this situation as paradoxical in order to suggest that group rights have both positive and negative features (i.e. 'on the one hand, X; but on the other, Y'), the implication is that the pursuit of rights is ultimately self-defeating. Putting faith in rights is a zero-sum game for subaltern groups for three reasons that emerge in her essay. First, group rights mitigate oppression without enabling group members to escape it; second, such rights inscribe into law the specific experience of some members, presenting them as though they were true for all and thus ignoring the variability of interests within in the group; and, third, if the content of the group right is defined abstractly so as to try to include all members, the experiences of individual members then always appear too idiosyncratic to qualify as examples of the harm against which the right protects (Brown 2002: 437–8; Lever 2000: 245). Now, against Brown, one could conclude that group rights do have these features but that, if the issue is that rights do not redress substantive inequalities, this is not paradoxical but a straightforward fact about liberal law or a predictable result of the forms of inequality in our society (MacKinnon 1989: Chapter 11; Lever 2000: 246). For Annabelle Lever, the *conceptual* formulation of rights as paradoxes thus reifies and mystifies the subject under discussion, by assuming a definitive conception of the form of rights and the interests and capacities that they are supposed to protect (i.e. it is only by assuming a determinate idea of what rights are, or which interests they protect, that one could assume that they are conceptually paradoxical). Thus, understanding Brown to mean that rights involve a deep philosophical paradox further sidelines the more productive issue of 'our effort to create a politics that uses these paradoxes in efficacious ways' (Lever 2000: 242). This is an important observation, as it suggests that the real issue that Brown's account raises is the pragmatic one of what subaltern groups stand to gain by viewing rights as paradoxes. On this point, Brown is rather more illuminating: she recommends that rights be viewed consciously by their holders as transitional measures (an imperfect means of proceeding while justice remains to be achieved); *and* as potentially transformative (that is, as assisting social change). Minority groups are prompted to ask:

How might attention to paradox help formulate a political struggle for rights in which they are conceived neither as instruments nor ends but as articulating ... what equality and freedom might consist in that exceeds [those rights]? How might the paradoxical elements of the struggle for rights in an emancipatory context **articulate a field of justice beyond that which we 'cannot not want'?** *(2002: 432, my emphasis).*

By endorsing this aspect of Brown's account I am not suggesting that group rights be viewed as the unique response to cultural diversity in postcolonial multiculturalism, and I do not deny that the injustices following colonialism might require a more supple range of policies such as apologies or other forms of symbolic reconciliation. However, as rights are likely to be the predominant basis on which struggles for cultural recognition proceed, once the paradox that surrounds them is confronted, postcolonial multiculturalism can then ask how minorities might deploy struggles over their form, content and justification to achieve in social change than the theoretical defence of rights enables (see also Rorty 2000). Such pragmatism and irony in the liberal understanding of rights addresses Povinelli's (1999) concern that liberal recognition constitutively entraps minorities in the futile task of proving their authenticity over time. Moreover, Ivison (2003) defends a version of this approach by suggesting that postcolonial citizens explicitly acknowledge, on the one hand, that group rights may be the inescapable object of their campaigns as well as, on the other, that such rights are categories that they must redefine according to their own self-understandings.

But, as I observed earlier, the self-conscious intention to take up a liberal politics with an awareness of its risks and possibilities does not entail that one has real opportunities to challenge existing relations of power. Instructively here, Coulthard (2007) recently suggests that the negative social meanings in which liberal recognition re-inscribes subaltern identities might be challenged through a shift of emphasis from the state-based apparatus of rights to the deliberative practices of minority groups. If he is right, a postcolonial theory of multiculturalism could build productively on its explicit awareness of the 'paradox' of group rights by shifting its focus on to the negotiations leading up to their formulation and implementation. Significantly, the transformative potential of such a shift has not gone unrecognized in liberal theory. A key dimension of the theories of James Tully (1995) and Antony Laden (2001), whose writings are in many ways consistent with liberal multiculturalism, involves defending the ideal what I shall call 'deliberative political inclusion'. The aim of their accounts is to re-present public deliberation in post-imperial settings in terms freed of deliberative democracy's standard emphasis on the achievement of rationally motivated consensus (Cohen 1989, Nino 1996). These more innovative accounts recognize that unanimity can seldom be found on most contentious issues in a diverse polity (Tully 1995: 144); and that settlements achieved through communicative activity often represent 'good enough' compromises or modus vivendi accommodations rather than unanimous and reasoned assent. Their defence of deliberative inclusion also challenges deliberative democrats' suspicion of identity-related discourses (see Kelly 2005). While deliberative democrats typically concede that the self-representation of particular groups such as ethnic minorities may be necessary, they believe that unconstrained deliberation will inevitably lead these groups to *modify* their 'thick' identity-related interests and values in the course of the debate (Deveaux 2006: 67). While this expectation is not always unreasonable in relation to matters that clearly affect the common good, theorists of postcolonial deliberative inclusion recognize that to focus always on the transformation of all citizens' views towards common problems and the common good would sometimes ignore the justice of asserting one's cultural particularity. For it might be recognized that the point of some postcolonial minorities' struggles for rights in political contexts involves contesting or disputing the priority of supposedly 'common' values such as autonomy (Tully 1995: 41).

Two conditions of deliberative inclusion seem crucial for postcolonial multiculturalism. The first is *reciprocity*: conversations that prefigure the implementation of group rights must involve not only increasing the capacity of minorities to speak, but the willingness of the state and majority citizens to *listen*. *Audi alteram partem*, the injunction to hear the other side of the case (Tully 1995: 72), challenges the Enlightenment-derived assumption that the meaning of ideals such as equality and freedom can be defined a priori. Second, and connected to the issue discussed above, is the idea of *public reasons as social constructions*. To the degree that theories of deliberative democracy have been accused of presupposing as preconditions of political debate the norms and principles that they would like to believe emerge through communicative activity, they may not in fact meet their own aspiration to escape the difficulties with liberal theories of public reasoning derived from Rawls (see Deveaux 2006: 112). Here Laden (2001: 120–3) helpfully explains that such accounts of public reasoning have wrongly insisted on all parties' compliance with previously defined notions of the 'reasonable', which have long stifled legitimate demands by women and ethno-cultural minorities. In contrast, Laden's approach to deliberative inclusion involves jettisoning the view of public reason as a philosophical truth and understanding it instead as a contingent, socially constructed ideal (2001: 124). Thus, instead of banishing all identity claims – by precluding, say, aboriginal communities from introducing considerations regarding the importance of their traditional lands to their cultural lives – the task would be to listen to the arguments that such groups consider relevant, and to work together to understand which reasons might support their claims (2001: 125).

This shift of emphasis from rights to deliberation is further conceptualized in terms of a distinction between 'theoretical' and 'political' approaches to multiculturalism. The former approach holds that the task of governments lies in working out a scheme of principles and rights, on account of which judgements concerning the degree of justice exhibited by institutions, policies and so forth can be articulated. In contrast, a 'political' approach focuses on struggles *over* 'rights' and 'recognition', in the context of which normative attention focuses on the *field of interaction* (Owen and Tully 2007: 267) in which 'norms' (laws, rules, conventions and customs) under which members of any society recognize each other as members are debated. While questions undoubtedly arise here concerning how mutually acceptable procedures for the conduct of such deliberation would be specified (that is, if these accounts are not to be prey to the very same objections to more standard theories of deliberative democracy), the advantage of a political approach is that the normative objectives of minorities' struggles are not assumed in advance, but are the subject of articulation and renegotiation in a process that manages to avoid the three criticisms that postcolonial critics direct at liberal theories of group rights, as outlined earlier. Specifically, the approach escapes the charge of cultural essentialism by insisting that the object of minorities' struggles, or that which they seek to affirm through the medium of group rights, does not pre-exist the process of negotiation 'in some unmediated or ascriptive pre-dialogue realm' (Owen and Tully 2007: 282). Moreover, the process escapes the charge of 'tokenism' by precluding a state from arrogating to itself the task of defining the form and content of rights without engaging with its members interactively. Finally, it resists the universalization of thick conceptions of terms such as 'humanity' or 'dignity', by recognizing the cultural contingency of all settlements and, thus, by affirming the universality of the norm of deliberative inclusion only.

I concede that a fuller account of postcolonial deliberative inclusion would need to confront the problems that plague most deliberative democratic accounts under conditions of deep diversity. These difficulties include intercultural misunderstanding; the mistrust of minorities which often render them unwilling to deliberate (Deveaux 2006); and the possibility that deliberation will not yield a workable settlement owing to the ambiguities surrounding the economic, cultural and psychological consequences of imperial rule.[9] At the same time, the defence of institutional fora for struggles over the form, content and justification for group rights promises greater transformation of relations between minorities and majorities, or between states and communities, than could be effected by the theoretical defence of group rights as such. Moreover, and perhaps most pressingly today, it would allow citizens to dispel the forms of disaffection and resentment that might otherwise be discharged in violent forms of protest or terrorism (Owen and Tully 2007: 290).

While this account confronts a final problem which I address in a moment, at this stage it is worth summarizing my claims. I have argued that key to postcolonial multiculturalism is a self-conscious awareness of the paradox of group rights. The social possibilities that come to light once minority groups self-consciously acknowledge this paradox encourages liberalism to shift its focus from the theoretical defence of group rights to a political conception of multiculturalism that focuses on the ideal of 'deliberative inclusion' and the negotiation of settlements that struggles over group rights anticipate. This commitment represents, I argued, an avenue through which liberal multiculturalists might accommodate postcolonial writers' criticisms of their accounts. Yet, in the final analysis, postcolonial multiculturalism must also confront the residual problem of how to guard against the social exclusion that undoubtedly undermines effective political participation in the real world. If social exclusion grounded in both cultural marginalization and economic deprivation afflict the account of postcolonial multiculturalism proposed here, then it may not truly escape one

---

9   Recognizing this point seems to entail that postcolonial multiculturalism should engage with a wider set of concepts such as apology, forgiveness and reconciliation, an engagement which I cannot be undertake in this chapter. For key literature in this area, see Digeser (2001), Schaap (2005) and Kymlicka and Bashir (2008).

key postcolonial criticism of liberal multiculturalism, namely that its merely 'tokenistic' accommodation of cultural diversity fails to address the real roots of subaltern peoples' subordination. I therefore ask next whether an awareness of this problem undermines or strengthens a postcolonial account of multiculturalism.

Postcolonial Multiculturalism: On the Cultural and Economic Base of Everyday Life

It could be argued that it is not the task of normative political theory to guarantee inclusion of all citizens in political deliberation, and, in any case, that the settlement reached on any issue in conditions of deep diversity is always, as noted earlier, a contingent and partially exclusionary achievement, one that is ultimately 'a thing of the world' (Owen and Tully 2007). However, still relevant from a normative perspective is the objection that the deliberative practices proposed under any liberal form of public reasoning, however reformulated to accommodate cultural differences, will remain exclusionary in a structural sense. This objection appears plausible in so far as liberals are frequently accused of playing down the economic disadvantages experienced by subaltern groups within a 'racially stratified capitalist economy', and even of complicity with those structures (Coulthard 2007, see also Gilroy 2004: 12). On this issue, it also seems problematic that much of the attention bestowed on postcolonial theory focuses on cultural, symbolic, discursive or representational aspects of colonial legacies rather than on economic issues affecting citizens of post-imperial societies broadly. In this concluding section, I acknowledge the possibility that the deliberation recommended in the previous section may harbour exclusions that are problematic from the perspective of postcolonial multiculturalism. In view of the global economic disparities that have set the pattern for migration and the movement of capital within former settler colonies after the demise of empire, postcolonial multiculturalism should, I finally contend, endorse a model of deliberative inclusion that considers the interlocking nature of cultural and economic realms in order to free itself of the risk of 'tokenism' which it aims to avoid.

To grasp the problem fully, consider that, while a general opposition to global capitalism might be implicit in postcolonial accounts, the bulk of literary and cultural theory in this area seems to emanate from 'metropolitan' centres; and the often apparently self-conscious failure of writers in this field to consider the relation of material inequality to the representation of contemporary cultural identities renders it only too easy in their accounts to disconnect the celebration of, say, 'cultural hybridity' from problems such as deepening poverty and the escalation of migration through human trafficking (Bales 1999; Kyle and Koslowski 2001). A different but connected problem is that it also becomes somewhat too straightforward to ignore the commodification of cultural identity which fragments many groups today in terms of those for whom cultural identity represents a financially viable asset and those for whom it does not. This is a complex point; and the failure to theorize the issue explicitly in liberal multiculturalist or postcolonial writing should not be seen as synonymous with a failure to consider the link between cultural and material inequality as such. Nonetheless, the failure to elaborate on this specific issue might be seen as symptomatic of the larger matter of how symbolic and economic inequalities intertwine. If this is a plausible point, postcolonial multiculturalists should be intrinsically concerned that the mass of indigenous peoples, minus those who find a 'home' in the capitalist market economy, are 'consistently amongst the most disadvantaged people on earth according any number of socioeconomic indicators' (Ivison 2002: 15; Wilkinson, Ryan and Hiller 2001). Put briefly, then, postcolonial multiculturalism cannot avoid theorizing the relation between culture and economy, but should resist prioritizing one realm over the other in ensuring the inclusiveness of the political deliberation that it advocates.

One useful avenue for theorizing this problem appears to lie in Nancy Fraser's 'dual systems' account (Fraser 1997, 2003). Although in this concluding stage of my discussion I contend that her proposed remedy for deliberative exclusion is not entirely apt for post-colonial multiculturalism, she nonetheless diagnoses the bases of political exclusion in an instructive way. To be sure, where Fraser writes of the link between 'cultural' and 'economic' disadvantage, she intends the former term to refer to a wider range of social identities than ethno-cultural groups, and generally favours emphasizing not culture but race, sexual orientation and gender (1997: 12). For this reason, it has been claimed that the protection of cultural diversity is not her objective (Blum 1998: 91). However, this is not obviously the case, if the symbolic disadvantages that she identifies with 'misrecognition' involve the depreciation of the characteristics that groups view as central to their 'mode of being' (Modood 2005). Modood uses this term to refer to the features on account of which a group develops a sense of its difference from the wider society and, possibly, a common consciousness of its historical oppression. If Fraser intends the term 'misrecognition' to apply to the denigration of a group's 'mode of being' so conceived, then her account pertains as much to the ethno-cultural groups on which multiculturalists focus as to other identity-related groups.

With this clarification in mind, it is worth highlighting the relevance of Fraser's claims to postcolonial multiculturalism. Her central and highly apt point is that demands for equality today increasingly take the form not only of campaigns for economic redistribution but also of struggles to resist assimilation to dominant cultural norms. She rightly views the proliferation of identity-claims in modernity as connected to the demise of colonialism and the surge of free market ideology, in the context of which treating cultural and economic struggles as distinct is a 'false antithesis' (2003: 8). Justice today requires both economic redistribution and cultural recognition, because each provides a distinct perspective on social justice which can be applied to any movement. Conceding that her claim might appear counter-intuitive, as the two paradigms advance different conceptions of injustice (in that economic deprivation is thought to be rooted in waged labour whereas cultural domination is seen as a matter of subjection to a hegemonic value system), Fraser correctly insists that these two forms of inequality reinforce one other, and, thus, that the bases on which postcolonial citizens might be excluded from political participation are complex.

Moreover, she observes instructively that maldistribution and misrecognition pertain to contemporary inequalities 'in forms where neither of these injustices is an indirect effect of the other, but where both are primary and co-original' (2003: 19). For instance, the disadvantages that women experience on account of the sexual division of labour co-exist with, but are not reducible to, their cultural marginalization in an androcentric society. This claim, if true, enables postcolonial multiculturalism to acknowledge that securing justice for postcolonial minorities cannot only involve granting special rights or even a greater voice in political deliberation, as material deprivation might undermine the capacities of certain sections of these groups to use these rights effectively or to have their points readily understood in debate. As Fraser expresses the point, cultural and economic inequalities undermine the 'bourgeois public's claim to full accessibility' (1997: 77). Yet while her diagnosis is sound, the remedies that she proposes sidestep Fanon's much earlier but influential observation that attacking colonial power at the level of material relations does not guarantee a reciprocal transformation in the cultural or psychological realms (Fanon 1967: 11, see also Coulthard 2007: 446). As we shall see, Fraser curiously evades Fanon's insistence that direct opposition to the cultural hegemony of colonial power is often experienced as necessary for liberation; the formerly colonized feels that they *must* turn back consciously 'to their unknown roots', the 'sari becom[ing] sacred, the shoes from Paris … left off' (Fanon 1986: 126, Bulhan 1985: 149).

Exposing Fraser's evasion of this issue will enable me to articulate what could either be seen as a productive challenge or a deep dilemma confronting postcolonial multiculturalism. Whilst Fraser claims to be committed to remedying 'bivalent' (that is, cultural *and* economic) inequalities through both 'transformative redistribution' *and* 'transformative recognition', the order through which she envisages change in civil society is through the reordering of market relations first. But this is contentious because, if Fanon is right, that alone would not necessarily guarantee the capacity of postcolonial minorities to participate in the public sphere. The problem is a curious one, given Fraser's trenchant critique of her interlocutor Axel Honneth's (2003) disregard for the economic realm, in the context of which she rightly suggests that Honneth's complete 'psychologization' of social inequality fails to challenge the double-edged nature of most contemporary disadvantages.[10] Yet a hint of her commitment to the fundamental nature of economic inequality (and, thus, of the fundamental need to bring about socialist transformation in civil society before other forms of social justice) becomes apparent in her claim that no group at all, even sexual minorities, could be thought to suffer from cultural disadvantages exclusively (1997: 15). Moreover, it then emerges explicitly that in her view economic transformation is

---

10   For a more detailed discussion of the points of departure between Frazer and Honneth, see Chapter 9 in this volume.

the precondition for a non-oppressive conception of multiculturalism. Whilst she critically observes that the 'bourgeois' liberal public sphere historically ignored ethnic and racial differences and erroneously bracketed of all forms of social diversity, her defence of an anti-essentialist multiculturalism explicitly favours a prior socialist reordering of political economy, which she states would serve as the crucial democratic standard against which claims concerning cultural difference could be assessed. For Fraser, a non-oppressive form of multiculturalism must involve asking:

> *how a given identity or difference is related to social structures of domination and social relations of inequality ... what sort of political economy would be required to sustain non-exclusionary identities and anti-essentialist understandings of difference ... which identity claims are rooted in the defence of social relations of inequality and domination? (Fraser 1997: 183–84).*

From the perspective of postcolonial multiculturalism, the claim that 'cultural differences can only be freely elaborated and democratically mediated on the basis of social equality' (Fraser 1997: 186) may seem fair enough, if social equality is not defined in exclusively economic terms and if we recognize that cultural inequalities are not merely super-structural – a point that Fraser recognizes herself (1997: 189). However, ultimately Fraser's prescriptions for redressing the 'underlying generative framework' (1997: 23) of contemporary inequalities is not adequately supple for postcolonial multiculturalism, because it assumes that, while enabling subaltern peoples to challenge dominant cultural meanings will 'avoid fanning the flames of resentment', the fundamental issue, to reiterate, is 'transformative socialist redistribution' (1997: 31). This formulation fails to consider that some postcolonial minorities are excluded from the 'participatory parity' that Fraser prizes owing to the hegemony of values associated with economic rationalism, productivity and marketability, at the expense of their ecologically or communally oriented modes of living. Now, perhaps Fraser would concede that capitalism sustains itself as much through the hegemony of market-driven ideas as through disparities of wealth, and would not ignore Althusser's (1977) insistence on ideology as an instrument in capitalist social reproduction. But if this is so, it is then hard to deny that subordinating either culture to economy, or vice versa, in the everyday life of liberal civil society risks obscuring the depth of the social exclusion that a postcolonial approach to multiculturalism must confront.

If this point is persuasive, postcolonial multiculturalism then seems to confront either a productive (though enormous) challenge, on the one hand, or, on the other, problems of irrelevance or even impossibility. On the negative side, an awareness of this predicament would seem to entail that cultural dominance and relations of inequality might only be challenged politically (i.e. through the struggle over the content of group rights) if they are first deconstructed at the more complex level of civil society.[11] One *might* argue here that doing that would put the cart before the horse, because political and legal change can produce change in civil society. But one might claim that the problem of cultural devaluation is so deep that it suggests the irrelevance of the political recommendations of postcolonial multiculturalism. For, after radical transformation of the social structuring of society, political deliberation about group rights would be unnecessary. Even more seriously, the account might be thought impossible, if the radical changes needed to rectify informal structural inequalities would require violent forms of opposition, which postcolonial multiculturalism, with its faith in dialogue and discussion, does not defend.

I do not believe that postcolonial multiculturalism is likely to be irrelevant or impossible; but must defer a full response to these charges to another occasion. For now, suffice it to say that postcolonial multiculturalism's recognition of the depth of structural inequality helps the account at least to remain wary of the problem of 'tokenism', one of the three charges against multicultural theory with which we began this chapter, by striving to ensure the empowerment of the most marginalized in society through social reform. Central here is a recognition that although 'subordinated social groups usually lack equal access to the material means of participation' (Fraser 1997: 79), the key to political inclusion entails more than increasing access to commodities. By retaining an awareness of their interlocking nature, an increasingly *less* tokenistic, and more representative, debate might ensue about the content of rights in a context that could claim, in one sense at least, to be genuinely *post*colonial.

Conclusion

By exploring the key claims of postcolonial writers, liberal multiculturalists and critical social theorists, this chapter has specified three issues that should inform an account of 'postcolonial multiculturalism.' Appropriating postcolonial writers' insights concerning the persistence of neo-colonial power-relations, I first recommended an acknowledgement of the paradoxical nature of group rights, by conceiving these legal devices as means of reconstituting minority groups in former relations of inequality as well as a measure through which such relations could be challenged and potentially overturned. I then argued that a self-conscious understanding of this paradox enables a shift of attention to political deliberation in order to resolve struggles over the content, form and justification of subaltern minorities' rights. Finally, I claimed that postcolonial multiculturalism should

---

11   Here I understand 'civil society' (or the informal social institutions through which society is organized) to be related to, but analytically distinct from, the state-backed institutions of the public sphere.

be attuned critically to the intermeshing of cultural and economic inequalities that exclude certain citizens from participating in political debate. Owing to the interlocking nature of cultural and economic spheres in liberal civil society, it is not possible, I argued, to prioritize one sphere over another in addressing social exclusion in civil society. Of course, as I have said, this proposal will inevitably fall short for those who contend that, without heeding the call for violent struggle, the accommodation of diversity simply represents the tokenistic inclusion of minorities within what some label 'cosmopolitan liberal imperialism' (Gilroy 2004). Yet, in striving to avoid adversarial political conclusions, postcolonial multiculturalism must engage in the difficult task of specifying how justice can be achieved in currently imperfect conditions, without, in that endeavour, also reiterating and entrenching all the imperfections of the past.

Conditional Multiculturalism:
Islam in Liberal Democratic States

Michael Humphrey

Introduction

The post-September 11 scrutiny of Islam and Muslims in the West over their alleged resistance to 'integration' is in fact a particular instance of the historical tension between immigration policy and the national project. Immigration has always represented a problem for the ideology of the nation-state as culturally standardizing and assimilating. While immigration policy is instrumental it is at the same time deeply culturally ambivalent. After all immigrants came both as workers and bearers of other national, ethnic and religious identities. The so-called 'problem of Muslim integration' in Western secular national societies amounts to a post-multicultural revisionism re-imagining of the nation-state as culturally singular in the age of globalization, global cities and transnational citizens. The international politicization of Islam as culture has made it

> less social than political, tied less to realities of particular countries than to global political events like the tearing down of the Berlin Wall or 9/11. Unlike the culture studied by anthropologists – face-to-face, intimate, local and lived – the talk of culture is highly politicised and comes in large geo-packages (Mamdani 2004: 17).

Muslims have been turned into nationally shared objects for transnational governance, a focus for national and international coordination of security, cultural critique and population management.

This chapter examines the position of Islam and Muslims in the West post-September 11 and the growing conditionality of their presence in multicultural Western societies. A critical element in the process of their social and cultural marginalization is the politicization of Islam as a source of danger, political extremism and violence. Islam and Muslims have come to symbolize the challenge of globalizing cultural identities to the Western national project and the global risks associated with transnational identities and citizenships. The response of Western states to the presence of Islam and Muslims as global risks has been their domestication and securitization through the adoption of policies designed to help produce a national (moderate) Islam on the one hand and a transnationally policed extremist Islam on the other.

The contemporary political and cultural predicament of Muslims in Western societies reveals the complex dimensions of contemporary multiculturalism as social imaginary, as identity politics and as policy. The concept of multiculturalism and its articulation as public policy was originally a response to growing cultural difference produced by large-scale immigration to the north. But, as Wieviorka (1998) argues, the persistence of cultural difference produced originally through immigration is not only an expression of reproduction (heritage) but is also increasingly an expression of production (invention). Cultural fragmentation prevails over homogenization and

> cultural difference is the outcome of permanent invention, in which identities are transformed and recomposed, and in which there is no principle of definitive stability, even if the newest identities are sometimes shaped in very old moulds, as can be seen in the tendencies which reinvent Islam in Western societies (Wieviorka 1998: 891).

The debate about Muslim difference in multicultural societies has seen a shift from a critique of cultural compatibility to political loyalty as a result of September 11 and the threat of jihadist terrorism. This amounts to the construction of culture not as practice but as politicized collective identity. It is not just 'Othering' Muslims but constructing them as opponents, if not the enemy, whose presence in the West is made conditional on their 'moderate' status and rejection of violence. From the Muslim perspective it raises questions about multiculturalism as a national versus transnational social imaginary and as a discourse of inclusion/exclusion.

A key issue in the state's political management of Islam and Muslims is the transformation of the construction of cultural difference in multicultural societies engendered by international Islamist terrorism. Islam and Muslim cultural difference have been essentialized and constructed as embodied through the defensive politics of domestication and securitization of Muslims in the West. Domestication seeks to redefine the cultural parameters of citizenship, especially through symbolic inclusion and exclusion, while securitization polices them as transnational objects of risk. Securitization and domestication are governance strategies based on the logic of spatial exclusion and inclusion through disciplining cultural bodies (see Chapter 13 in this volume). While national sovereignty and territoriality have long been the focus of securitization what is new is the national/transnational dimension of governmentality and the impact of transnational securitization on culturally differentiated citizenship as conditional and degradable. Thus while securitization and domestication are state-managed strategies they are at the same time expressions of transnational governmentality, the re-scaling of sovereignty up and down as one outcome of globalization (Gupta and Ferguson 2002). As Foucault defines it, governmentality entails 'the ensemble formed by the institutions, procedures, analyses and reflections, the calculations and tactics that allow the exercise of this very specific albeit complex form of power, which has as its target population' (Foucault 1991: 102). Transnational governmentality refers to processes which occur both within and beyond national boundaries in which the laws, procedures, discourses and practices emanate from forms of governmentality reaching across national boundaries. These emanate from the disciplining projects of states but also the counter transnational disciplining projects of Islamic movements. Securitization and domestication are policy responses to 'states of emergency' in which a central concern is the re/linking of people to the state and the production of the state 'as a social subject in everyday life' (Aretxaga 2003: 395). And behind the intensification of policing and linking bodies is state anxiety about sovereignty and legitimacy in the era of globalization. The potentiality of exclusion becomes the embodiment of the law and the state, and the means of legibility of power (Aretxaga 2003).

Securitization is 'a political technique of framing policy questions in logics of survival with a capacity to mobilize politics of fear in which social relations are structured on the basis of distrust' (Huysmans 2006: xi). The effect of securitizing Muslim immigrants and Islam is to displace them as a social category within a particular multicultural national space to a transnational 'western' space. Securitization constitutes 'Muslim immigrants' as a transnational social category for policing increasingly detached from specific national social and political contexts while at the same time it provides a common language to connect diverse Muslim communities as threats (Risley 2006). Securitization as a transnational process is articulated within a 'transnational security field' in which Muslims have emerged as an integrating focus (Risley 2006). Securitization is a policy of social defence defining political community at the national level and a project of transnational governmentality constituted by inter-state cooperation, the harmonizing of policies and laws and the forging of a transnational western public sphere focused by threats.

Domestication refers to state management of social and cultural difference with the purpose of defining limits with respect to national values and culture (Bowen 2004). The project of the domestication of Islam and Muslims in Western societies has sought to promote a moderate Islam by creating national Islams – in President Sarkozy's phrase 'to be Muslims of France practicing an Islam of France' (Bowen 2004: 43) – and to address the social causes of Islamic radicalization understood as social exclusion. A major focus of policy promoting 'moderate Islam' has been state intervention in the organization of Muslim immigrant religious life. The term 'moderate Islam' is problematic and has divergent meanings for non-Muslims and Muslims, however as a cultural classification by Western governments it primarily involves a political judgement about loyalty and values (Modood and Ahmad 2007; Aly 2005). The focus of intervention in religious life has been the attempt to create more representative and authoritative national Islamic organizations to counteract the historical absence of a church like structure in Islam and the ethnic fragmentation of religious organizations and structures of diaspora Islam. This has made Islam the target of governmental techniques, the state reaching into civil society in order to discipline Muslims by reconfiguring and legitimating domesticated religious institutions and leaders as well as producing a public discourse on moderate Islam (Bowen 2003, 2004).

Securitization and domestication describe forms of political management and disciplining directed at Muslims and Islam as threats understood to be globalized through international migration, the formation of a Muslim diaspora, the emergence of a politicized global Islam, the circulation of itinerant radical clerics in the diaspora, and Internet witnessing of Muslim suffering by the globalized *Umma*. Securitization and domestication represent the dual strategies of exclusion and inclusion on the basis of cultural essentialization and the construction of Muslim as a transnational category. The securitization of radical Islam as a non-state threat also locates it in a systemic conflict between 'vertebrate' (vertically integrated) and 'cellular' (horizontally networked) global systems (Appadurai 2006). The mediatization of risk and formation of Western transnational public opinion about the Muslim threat reinforces the process of cultural essentialization. Securitization and domestication of Muslims and Islam are expressions of transnational governmentality, the disciplining and management of a social category beyond state borders. They have been increasingly constituted as a homogenized transnational object through the harmonizing of public policy and law and through the creation of a Western public sphere produced by spectator-citizens witnessing mediated risk events (Feldman 2004). Bigo (2002) describes the securitizing of the 'suspect other' as the 'government of unease' managed through the interventionist state and no longer the protective state. Everyday Muslim life in the West is now set against a backdrop of national and international events in which local–global mediation is an integral part of producing meaning and identity. But at the same time that Muslims in the West are being positioned at the margins of the Western multicultural public sphere a counter Muslim 'transnational public sphere' is shaping their ideas about membership and identity. Muslim immigrants in the West have not only experienced a changed relationship to the state: they are confronted also with divisions within Islam over visions of the future, including millenarian ones.

Islam and Muslims in the West

The cultural marginalization of Islam and Muslims has been an integral part of the experience of post-1945 Muslim immigration to the West. Many Pakistani Muslims in Britain, North African Muslims in France and Spain, Turkish Muslims in Germany and Lebanese and Turkish Muslims in Australia have shared the experience of being an unskilled immigrant working class. The paradigm of Muslim 'cultural backwardness' has positioned Muslims on the margins of Western secular societies trapped in tradition. But cultural marginalization of Islam is only a particular instance of the more general relationship between immigration, cultural difference and the national project. In Australia, for example, immigration policy has historically been an important vehicle to define national identity through immigrant selection. The current widespread criticism of multiculturalism is directly connected to the revival of the national project as culturally singular. The destabilization of sovereignty under globalization leaves the 'fiction of ethnos as the last cultural resource over which it has full dominion' (Appadurai 2006: 23). Cultural difference in this revived nationalist project becomes a measure of distance from integration and full citizenship (Rosaldo 1989). Integration means cultural invisibility, being culturally indistinguishable from the dominant culture. In fact implicit in the emigration from the south to the north has been the idea of progress; leaving behind the traditional world for the modern world. From this perspective Islam and Muslims simply become the limit case in determining the margins of citizenship.

As Islam and Muslims in the West have become securitized the policing of internal and external borders have converged, the former through the penal state focused on identifying and controlling deviant bodies and the latter through immigration policy auditing and evaluating migrant 'performance' (level of integration) on the basis of cultural difference. The convergence of policing internal and external borders arises from the challenge faced by the state in managing the dangerous global circulation of largely invisible threats – terrorists, transnational crime, illegal immigration, epidemics. Essentializing cultural difference becomes a way of making visible threats otherwise invisible.

The illegibility of terrorist threats for all states is juxtaposed with the impact of terrorist 'events' globally. These 'events' are used to mediate a relationship between potential global threats and local understanding and action. Thus the September 11 terrorist attacks have helped forge a new transnational (Western) public sphere subsequently reinforced by a series of violent incidents in Europe – Holland, Spain and the UK – which served to intensify the sense of shared threat and heightened danger from the 'transnational' Muslim immigrant. In Australia one 'event', the 7 July 2005 terrorist bombings of the London transport system, really brought home the transnationality of Muslim immigrants and their potential threat. The fact that the London bombers were second generation (home-grown) British Pakistani Muslims radicalized in Britain was interpreted as a failure of UK immigration policy to promote effective integration. The bureaucratic response was to try to manage the terrorist threat by establishing 'terrorist' profiles to help make more transparent the previously undetected threat. The bombers were constructed as second-generation alienated Muslim youth. However, the foiled UK 'Muslim doctors terrorist plot' in 2 July 2007, very close to the second anniversary of the London transport bombings, showed that the terrorism threat could not be quarantined within the category 'alienated second-generation Muslim youth'. To this profile had to be added the internationally mobile and morally outraged Muslim professionals recruited by Western governments for their needed skills as medical doctors.

The role of global 'events' in securitizing Muslims as transnationals highlights the local and global dimensions of all contemporary discussion of Islamic difference and Muslim experience in the West. It is not just that these events point to shared terrorist threats (we are at risk here too!) but that 'events' themselves have come to mediate the local and global helping to transnationalize a 'Western' public sphere, homogenize a transnational public policy towards Islam and Muslims in the West, and reiterate the role of violence, both terrorism itself and counter-terrorism responses to it, as a regulating principle in the era of globalization. The local–global nexus shapes the cultural construction of Islam and Muslims, the formation of Muslim community and religious networks, the modes of politicization of Islam, the global recruitment of jihadists for terrorist violence and martyrdom, and Muslim feelings of moral outrage and victimhood.

The attempt to make legible terrorist threats by representing them as culturally embodied is a bureaucratic response by the state seeking to re-stabilize sovereignty and legitimacy already destabilized under globalization. States are caught between defending and opening their borders and find they have to 'perform dramas of national sovereignty' and 'simultaneous feats of openness' designed to attract investments (Appadurai 2006: 22). International terrorism reveals a systemic challenge to national sovereignty arising from the confrontation between two quite different global systems of organization and circulation, the vertebrate and cellular systems. The nation-state is part of the vertebrate system based on their singularity and difference but at the same time coordinated by regulative norms and signals in an international system. The cellular system is global, independent yet still connected. International terrorism is organized as a cellular system:

> connected yet not vertically managed, coordinated yet remarkably independent, capable of replication without central messaging structures, hazy in their central organizational features yet crystal clear in their cellular strategies and effects, these organizations clearly rely on the crucial tools of money transfer, hidden organization, offshore havens, and nonofficial means of training and mobilization, which also characterize the working of many levels of the capitalist world (Appadurai 2006: 28).

Hence the state's confrontation with international terrorism is in fact a confrontation with a different form of global circulation and organization.

Terrorism and counter-terrorism are not just in opposition but also expressions of the clash between the vertebrate and cellular global systems. The nexus between Islam and international terrorism is therefore not simply extremism (ideology) but a product of the dual globalization of Islam and violence as cellular systems of organization. In other words, the internationally decentralized character of Islam has permitted the transformation of religious authority, organization and communication as a cellular system, just as the political aspirations of non-state actors have been able to deploy violence in the form of international terrorism. What international terrorism articulates are the risks inherent in the global cellular system as revealed in the political convergence of the insecurity of everyday life with the insecurity of states.

Securitizing Islam and Muslims in the West

A critical aspect of the present securitizing of Islam and Muslims is the way 'culture' is being constructed under globalization. The nation-state is seeking to manage Islam as a transnational cultural system within a national imaginary which is re-emphasizing cultural singularity to reassert sovereignty. Securitizing Islam is a state bureaucratic response of classification to try to manage potential threats to disorder. This only reinforces the essentialization of cultural difference as a strategy to make threats legible. Muslim resistance to this bureaucratic project of cultural essentialization has provoked its counter essentialization in the defence of authenticity and re-authorizing of tradition. This includes the revivalist and neo-fundamentalist projects of the recovery of 'pristine' Islam (Werbner 2004).

The dual strategy of securitizing and domesticating Muslims in the West emerges from the clash between vertebrate and cellular systems; the dual processes of immigrants being incorporated into nation-states across generations and, at the same time, their growing consciousness of belonging to a transnational culture, the global *umma*. The latter is a specific instance of general emergence of new forms of global consciousness (e.g. environmentalism, human rights, global justice). These dual processes have seen Islam in the West gradually become transformed from 'diaspora' to 'globalized' Islam (Humphrey 2007). Diaspora Islam refers to the immigrant origins and ethnic diversity of Muslims in Australia whose social worlds have been shaped by immigration policy and their continuing social ties to family and community. Globalized Islam, a term borrowed from Roy (2004), refers to second-generation, de-ethnicized, individualized, *umma*-conscious Muslims but is also characterized by a return to 'pristine' Islam (authentic traditions) described as neo-fundamentalism.

Globalized Islam, Roy (2004: 103) argues, is the product of a 'growing discrepancy between the forms taken by Islam in the West and in the cultures of origin'. This expression of Islam is culturally (ethnically) detached and individualist rather than collective in orientation and has emerged in the transition between first and second-generation presence in the West. Roy (2004: 21–2) sees

> the need to formulate what it means to be Muslim, to define objectively what
> Islam is – in short, to 'objectify' Islam – is a logical consequence of the end of
> the social authority of religion, due to westernization and globalization.

Re-Islamization is a response to de-culturalization, the loss of context of social and cultural reproduction. De-culturalization creates the context for the cultural imaginary of recovering 'pristine' ahistorical Islam, uncontaminated by cultural/ethnic influences. Globalization also reinforces neo-fundamentalism by creating the opportunity to build 'a universal religious identity' by presenting itself as a defence against the cultural products of globalization – i.e. corrupt and decadent Westernization (Roy 2004: 25).

Globalized Islam is no longer based on social authority or conformity but on personal belief and choice. It is about the self and the realization of the self through faith. However, subjectivity and self-esteem remain connected to collective identity, the new collective identity of the global *umma*. The globalization of Islam is leading to its secularization but across a wide spectrum from the individualization and privatization of faith on one side to the re-anchoring of faith in the moral individual 'in the name of fundamentalism' on the other (Roy 2004: 41). From the neo-fundamentalist perspective the reconstruction of a true Muslim community begins with the individual and is based on 'an individual reappropriation of Islamic symbols, arguments, rhetoric and norms' (Roy 2004: 99).

Neo-fundamentalism's project seeks to reconstruct 'pure' religion outside culture. Because their community is no longer based in actual social relations it has to be reconstructed and experienced as an act of faith. Their global community is a virtual *umma* (community of believers) whose existence relies on their behaviour and deeds. With the de-territorialization of Islam there is no longer a distinguishable religious geography of *dar al-harb* and *dar al-islam.* The obsession about blasphemy and apostasy goes hand in hand with the vanishing of the social authority of Islam. Boundaries become embodied and both sides – the neo-fundamentalists and the host state – become obsessed with assessing loyalty and transgression from very different perspectives. The boundaries of Islam have to be daily recreated. 'They work in minds, attitudes, and discourses. They are more vocal than territorial, but also so much more eagerly endorsed and defended because they have to be invented, and because they remain fragile and transitory' (Roy 2005: 7).

A key issue underlying the changing social contexts of Muslim belonging and identification is the process of mediation. As Mazzarella (2004: 345) points out, mediation is a 'constitutive process in social life' and not just the product of new technologies and mediums so closely associated with globalization. All mediums of representation involve mediation. Mediums make 'society imaginable and intelligible to itself in the form of external representations' (Mazzarella 2004: 346). But mediation depends on the apparent separation of form and content for its efficacy. The media, for example, claims neutrality on the basis of this apparent separation. Through the distancing between form and content mediation tends to promote cultural reification and essentialization. If the mediation process is integral to the re/production of all culture then it is not so much the emergence of new mediums of mediation but how different mediums impact on the ongoing processes of representation/reflection.

In the shift from 'diaspora' to 'globalized' Islam the space and distance of mediation has changed. Diaspora Islam refers to the formation of immigrant Islam reproduced through the ties and networks of local face-to-face relationships within a national context. While diaspora Islam is also transnational, social memory is largely anchored in locality and biography and conveyed through intimate personal networks, even long-distance ones. The disciplining of diaspora Islam consisted of an unofficial auditing process of migrant performance scrutinizing unemployment, criminality, segregation and gender relations.

The shift to globalized Islam brought a change in the spatial dimensions of local–global mediation. Islam was no longer anchored in the social memory and biographies of first generation Muslim migrants. Instead Islam was increasingly de-ethnicized and made a question of belief and values distinct from their communities of origin. In Wieviorka's (1998) terms, while diaspora Islam is based on reproduction, globalized Islam is based on production.

The cultural articulation of globalized Islam is expressed in local social idioms. Pnina Werbner's ethnography of the Pakistani Manchester Muslim diaspora reveals the different uses of the idiom of 'community' in Muslim and ethnic diasporic discourses connecting the local and global.

> The allegory of community was repeatedly invoked. From an analytical perspective, 'community', like Pakistani 'family' or 'lineage', is a relational concept, it is invoked situationally by the same subjects to refer to quite different collectivities, on a rising social scale. Even global diasporas are communities ... the exemplary communities of the transnational moment (Werbner 2002: 102).

Community was invoked by Manchester Muslims to situate themselves in different collectivities and discourses, from the city to the nation and the transnation. The diaspora has multiple imaginings with different connections; there is the transnational diaspora sustained through kinship obligations expressed in chain migration of family members, arranged marriage, and remittances but also more cosmopolitan diasporas articulated through different imaginaries – the cultural aesthetics of South Asian consumption and the idea of 'a compelling sense of *moral co-responsibility* and *embodied performance*' (Werbner 2002: 11). Hence Manchester Muslims redefined themselves as a Muslim diaspora and, reflecting their own experience as a marginal minority, refocused 'on the Islamic peripheries – on minority Muslim communities, often persecuted and displaced, beyond the Islamic heartland. Hence Pakistanis in Britain have rediscovered their connection to Palestine, Bosnia, Chechneya, Kashmir' (Werbner 2002: 12).

The spatial re-imagining of the Muslim diaspora has been accompanied by the emergence of a 'diasporic public sphere' (Werbner 2002). This diasporic Muslim imaginary should be understood as continuous with the historical emergence of a Muslim public sphere in the late nineteenth century as a result of Islamic religious debate moving beyond the confines of elite Islamic religious scholars, especially through the politicisation of religion as a source of resistance to colonial rule. The new popular Islamic discourse was 'marked by a reification of keywords such as *Shari'a, umma* or *Islam...*' (Werbner 2002: 257). The Muslim diasporic public sphere is a largely hidden world to non-members in which different 'subjectivities and subject positions' are worked out. These Muslim diasporic spaces on the ethnic margins of Western societies are not simply encapsulated worlds.

> In their public oratory Pakistanis consciously attack the cultural imperialism of the west, but they do so in order to reject its effects upon themselves – true

> *Muslims, members of the working classes. They address the affairs of nations and states, world affairs, in a rhetoric that easily combines discourses of socialism, democracy, nationalism and human rights with a vision of Islamic utopias, a perfect moral order, the coming of the millennium (Werbner 2002: 256).*

Because the diasporic public sphere is porous and complex 'neither access to it or agendas for debate can be predefined by criteria of moral or political homogeneity' (Werbner 2002: 253).

While the Muslim public sphere provides a discourse in which to situate self and community within the global, Manchester Muslims also confront the impact of globally mediated events on Muslim identity and Islam. Islamic jihadist terrorism as a global event has highlighted the vulnerability of Muslims in the West to their location and standing being radically destabilized. These are further reinforced by 'moral panics, expressed in the speeches of politicians, in newspaper columns and global news reports' (Werbner 2004: 1). The events of September 11, 2001 and the subsequent London bombings in July 2005 by Pakistan British citizens brought home the sense of estrangement and the fact that life in the 'diaspora is a matter of continually negotiating the parameters of minority citizenship' (Werbner 2004: 15). Community is the locus of a narrative about the 'local' in which individuals situate themselves in a larger social and political topography both in relation to the state and beyond. The metaphor of community is invoked to ground and make meaningful social life in the context of global social transformation. No longer a local matter of multicultural difference, Islam positions diaspora Muslims at the centre of world struggles and global imaginaries.

Werbner (2004) notes the appeal of millennial or utopian visions of Islamic hegemony in the diaspora. She describes these millennial visions as

> *a story that Muslims tell themselves in the confines of their own arenas, far from the gaze of other publics. It is an empowering millennial discourse that starts from a sense of the cataclysmic failure of the present-day Islamic community (Werbner 2004: 456).*

The Muslim diaspora appears vulnerable to global events precipitating 'radical diasporic estrangement' which in turn leads to 'self-estrangement' reinforced by moral panics expressed by politicians and the media. What is distinctive about these millennial discourses is that they may be widely 'held without organization or effective mobilization' (Werbner 2004: 451). The millennial vision embraces the return to 'pristine' Islam but the paths to reach it vary from personal moral reform, to political coercion and revolutionary violence. However, the millennial and redemptive character of the narrative means it does not necessarily demand action. Rather it is an apocalyptic vision of history and how things will unfold. Holding millenarian visions does not mean believers will seek to enact it. In Muslim diasporas the relationship between holding millennial visions and being mobilized politically is shaped by just where their 'identification, the centres of their subjective universe, lie' (Werbner 2004: 466). The personal project of becoming an exemplary Muslim is therefore a righteous path which contributes to recovering an ideal Islamic society.

The securitizing of Islam attempts to culturally construct an Islamic identity of a Muslim population co-existing in two different kinds of social worlds, diaspora Islam and globalized Islam. The moral and subjective centre of these worlds is shifting with the growing the conditionality of citizenship in the West displaced to the global *umma*.

Domestication of Islam and Muslims in the West

While securitization has seen the policing of Muslims as potentially dangerous encultured bodies, domestication has intervened in Muslim culture in order to promote acceptable expressions of Muslim difference, a 'moderate Muslim'. Determining the acceptable parameters of 'Muslim assertiveness' in the context of a 'deeply embedded secularism' have constituted the 'crisis of multiculturalism' in most Western states (Modood and Ahmad 2007: 189). The thrust of domestication strategies has been to promote 'moderate' individuals as exemplars of 'good' Muslims and to reform religious institutions and leadership by making local mosque communities and Muslim clerics accountable to national Islamic bodies.

The term 'moderate' as a classification of acceptable Islamic religiosity and identity by Western states has been particularly problematic. Firstly, it is a relational term coined in opposition to the 'Muslim' extremists who conceived and carried out the 11 September attacks – the international jihadists. A 'moderate Muslim' is therefore anti-terrorism and against the use of Islam as a militant political rhetoric. Secondly, the 'moderate Muslim' is one who holds modern and progressive views on the religious interpretation of 'the *Qur'an* and *Hadith* as read primarily enunciating and illustrating principles for correct action not as concrete and fixed sets of actions' (Modood and Ahmad 2007: 192). The idea of a Euro-Islam, a secularized Islam informed by human rights, would be viewed as the most progressive position (Alsayyad and Castells 2002). Modood and Ahmad (2007: 190) summarize this position:

> (the) excavation of the Qur'an as a charter of human rights, which, for example, abolished slavery and gave property rights to women more than a millennium before either of these was achieved in the West; a restoration of the thirst for knowledge and rational inquiry that characterized medieval Muslim societies; a re-centring of Islam around piety and spirituality, not political ideology; a 'reformation' that would make Islam compatible with individual conscience, science and secularism.

Thirdly, while it may appear to mark out a middle ground the term is seen pejoratively by Muslims to mean a Muslim who has been co-opted and represents no-one, or worse, is so secular that more religious members of the Muslim diaspora would regard them as lapsed 'Muslims'.

While domestication takes place nationally it does so within a securitized transnational space constituted through the harmonization of policies towards Islam and Muslims and a Western-mediated public sphere. The harmonization of these policies and laws regulating cultural difference and risk are expressions of the reassertion of sovereignty. They also represent transnational strategies of Western nation-states, as part of the global vertebrate system, seeking to contain the risks of international terrorism as an expression of the global cellular system. The scalar character of this transnational sovereignty, its hierarchy, is evident in the way the harmonization of policies and laws are being borrowed on the basis of a transnationalized and homogenized understanding of Islam and Muslims in the West.

The main areas of transnational social policy and law harmonization have been counter-terrorism, immigration and integration. Counter-terrorism is concerned with enhancing state power through the courts to prevent terrorist actions. For the individuals affected by anti-terrorist laws this means curtailing their legal rights through the possibility of prolonged detention without charge and delayed legal accountability before the courts. Immigration policy has focused on greater scrutiny of visa applicants and restricting the rights to citizenship based on tests of character as well as social knowledge and language skills. Integration policies have targeted Muslim communities by seeking to domesticate Islam and Muslims by supporting advocates of moderate Islam and marginalizing extremists.

Counter-terrorism strategy has strongly focused on the strengthening of legal powers to regulate the threat of terrorism. In Australia George Williams (2007) has identified 37 new anti-terror laws since September 11 2001 covering 'everything from banning speech through to new sedition laws to detention without charge or trial to control orders that permit house arrest to closing down courts from public view'. The political effect of this reactive legislative activism focused on anti-terrorism has been to create the climate of a perpetual state of emergency (national terrorist alert status) and to justify the extraordinary powers of detention on the basis of suspicion rather than crimes committed, to extend the threshold of coercive interrogation and to permit the rapid deportation of non-citizen residents considered security risks. These laws have not only been reactive but in many cases mirror anti-terrorist legislation in the US and the EU. 'Homeland security' has become a widely used term to refer to national security, counter-terrorism and border protection. Counter-terrorism is shaped by the 'precautionary principle' which highlights the immanent risk of terrorism which is then made real, actualized, with every terrorism event in the West. Hence the local-global mediation of terrorism events constantly reaffirms 'us' as potential targets even when attacks have happened to someone else. This has led to a reciprocal cultural reductionism and identification, breathing life into Huntington's 'clash of civilizations' thesis, as Westerners (they don't like our values) and Muslims (we are being victimized). The transnational harmonization of counter-terrorism policy seeks to manage disorder arising from the international jihadist use of violence as an organizing principle. However, the transnational management of invisible terrorist threats through the intensification of policing by profiling and targeting is likely to exacerbate the essentialization of Islam, and the resentment and alienation of Muslims in the West, not least because their local efforts to demonstrate their good citizenship can be so quickly overwhelmed by over-determining global events.

Immigration policy has been an area of policy harmonization for some time between Australian and the EU (Humphrey 2002). The two areas immigration policy has been used to further counter-terrorism are in the assessment of visa applications and in granting citizenship. Being tough on migration applicants from the Middle East for example is in line with public opinion polls which reveal that more than 50 per cent of Australians would prefer to see fewer migrants from the Middle East (Kerbaj 2006). Citizenship has become politicized around the issue of integration and national security. For some time Muslims have been judged to be a problem immigrant community in Australia on the basis of their 'performance' in becoming citizens. According to the discourses on 'good migrant'/'bad migrant' Muslims have been judged as unwilling to work, too bound by tradition, too controlling of their women, too slow to learn English and, most recently, too unwilling to integrate and become Australian (Kerbaj 2006). The moral panic around terrorism however has led to the situation where any expression of Islamic religious identity is readily suspected as a sign of fundamentalism or radicalism and therefore a potential national security threat. Australian Muslim immigrants, as a consequence, are made to symbolize the margins of citizenship. The conditionality of citizenship has been emphasized by policy harmonization over new 'citizenship tests' in the US, UK and Australia which scrutinize the extent to which immigrants have integrated on the basis of language skills and cultural, social and political knowledge of their adopted country.

In Europe the harmonization of policy managing Islam and Muslims has been served as a vehicle for greater EU political integration. Securitization extended the framework established in the Tampere Summit (1999) on EU immigration and asylum policies focused on border security and integration. September 11 turned 'social relations into security relations' (Huysmans 1998: 232). Social problems such as immigration have increasingly been framed so as to 'dramatize the threat they pose to Europe's citizens' (Loader 2002: 134–5). However, despite efforts to harmonize securitization through a common EU counter-terrorism policy, continuing disagreement over the role of Islam and Muslims as the source of terrorism has so far prevented it (Burke 2008). Instead each EU state has legislated their own national counter-terrorism measures which have consistently eroded citizenship and residence rights – e.g. detention without charge, invasion of privacy on the basis of perceived threat, banned organizations, criminalizing intentions over acts, and expulsion. Many of these laws police Muslims and Islam through administrative exclusion directed at individuals and organizations identified as suspicious – e.g. rejection of naturalization applications, refusing visas to visiting imams, expelling activists, proscribing organizations as terrorist.

The role of 'home-grown' British Pakistanis in the 7/7 London terrorism attacks made integration a priority issue for the political management of Muslim communities. Muslim cultural difference is now constructed as cultural resistance and 'extremist' views a risk of radicalization and political violence. In 2006 the former Australian Prime Minister John Howard explicitly identified Muslims for their unwillingness to integrate by allegedly failing to learn English and to adopt Australian values, especially in regard to treating women equally (Duffy 2006). The 'No *Shari'a* in Australia' comment by Mr Peter Costello, the former Treasurer and Deputy Leader of the Liberal Party, also reinforced a very essentialized view of Islam as culturally backward, intolerant and separatist. He appeared to be quite unaware of what *Shari'a* actually meant in practice for Australian Muslims – i.e. primarily concerned with family law and inheritance (ABC News Online 2006).

A major focus of Muslim domestication has been the focus on Muslim women as evidence of Muslim 'cultural backwardness'. Intervention in Muslim communities targeting women as a vehicle for cultural change is a policy that has a long colonial history (Massell 1974, Abu-Lughod 2002). In Europe the controversy over the hijab has been particularly intense with the strongest rejection occurring in France where hijab as a religious symbol is forbidden in state institutions – especially schools (Bowen 2004). While wearing the hijab has not been the focus of legislative action in Australia some politicians have expressed their opposition to its use (Yaxley 2005). Nevertheless in Australia legislation prohibiting female circumcision (Crimes Act 1900 Sect. 45) and arranged/forced marriage (Mercer 2005) have been understood as Muslim practices in need of regulation – even though these laws are culturally neutral. These policies symbolically use Muslim women as a measure of Muslim integration.

The most prominent symbol of global Islam in the politics of embodiment is the headscarf (Motha 2007; Werbner 2007). However, its over-determined symbolic meaning can vary significantly with local context. In Britain

> [the] hijab ... expresses a 'new' identity, part of a deterritorialized global movement ... (which) is not necessarily, however, 'fundamentalist', 'Islamist' or radical, since its meaning and the politics of embodiment it represents may differ widely in different contexts and even from individual to individual (Werbner 2007: 163).

By contrast in France,

> girls who wear the headscarf are seen as the vanguard of a potential and dangerous French Muslim attack on the secular institutions of the state. The scarf is grasped as the precursor of further and more extreme demands for separate institutions and special treatment, and for the predatory expansion and colonization of public spaces (Werbner 2007: 174).

The principle thrust of the domestication of Islam in the West has been intervention in Islamic religious leadership and organization with the aim of promoting moderate over extremist influences. Characteristically Islamic religious leadership and organization has remained quite autonomous at the level of the local mosque community. In Australia, for example, the national body, the Australian Federation of Islamic Councils (AFIC), never supplanted the local authority of ethnically differentiated mosque communities, even though AFIC tried to remove the ethnic identification of its member organizations. In Germany by contrast, the dominant Turkish Muslim immigrant community was administered by a branch of the Turkish state, the *Diyanet*. In effect Germany saw both Islam and Muslims as a foreign and temporary presence which could be supervised by their home government (ICG 2007).

Another common strategy has been state sponsorship of the formation of national Muslim representative groups. In Australia, for example, a Muslim Advisory Council was given the task of reviewing the suitability of the continued leadership of the Mufti Taj ad-din al Hilali, a controversial Muslim leader based in the influential Lebanese Muslim community (McGrath 2006). A familiar Muslim criticism of such state-sponsored bodies is their lack of representativeness with respect to ethnic origin and religious outlook. The state has also supported the formation of national religious councils to establish bureaucratic hierarchies of religious authority and to support the establishment of forums for the education of Imams about the multicultural societies in which the Muslim diaspora lives to replace overseas Imams who tend to reproduce the world they have come from. The comment by Nicolas Sarkozy when he was French Minister of the Interior April 19, 2003 captures this sentiment. 'We should not depend on other countries for finding imams who speak not a word of French' (Bowen 2004: 43).

However, the domestication of Islam through state sponsorship of moderate leaders and national representative Muslim institutions has not always had the desired effect of nationalizing Islam. In Australia, for example, the government's support for an the Australian National Imams Council (ANIC) to register imams to make them more accountable to the ANIC than their mosque communities has also had the effect of creating institutions with greater Islamic legal authority which in turn has made them the focus of international religious and political patronage from overseas Muslim states. In Australia this has led to the accusation that the ANIC has accepted funding to promote conservative forms of Islam (Kerbaj 2008). The decision by the ANIC to create Boards of Imams at the national and state levels has been criticized for trying to establish a new source of Shari'a legal authority, plural law, in Australia (Perpetch 2007). In a study undertaken by the Islamic Women's Welfare Council of Victoria funded by the Australian government the Victorian Board of Imams was accused of condoning rape within marriage, domestic violence, polygamy, welfare fraud and exploitation of women (Zwartz 2008). These conflicts reveal the limitations of state sponsorship of nationalized moderate diaspora Islam. One response has been a shift away from the focus on 'moderate' religious to promote more 'secular' Muslims (Humphrey 2009). For example, in Germany the German Islam Conference (DIK) initiated under Chancellor Merkel moved away from its former reliance on Turkish state religious organizations (*Diyanet*) to represent Turkish Muslims in Germany to recruit a broader spectrum of secular and a Turkish Germans (ICG 2007: 27).

Conclusion

The post-September 11 challenge of the presence of Islam and Muslims in the West has questioned the meaning and role of multicultural policies and discourse in the West. The securitization and domestication of Muslims and Islam has essentialized cultural difference and displaced the Muslim from a national to transnational category for management. Islam is no longer seen through a multicultural lens where difference has been shaped less by diaspora Islam and more by globalized Islam. Muslim cultural difference is no longer seen as an expression of diversity and different origins but of cultural resistance.

The strategies of securitization and domestication represent the extension of neo-liberal urban policy using disciplining and penalisation, especially spatial separation, to manage poverty as a potential source of disorder. Instead of poverty now cultural difference has been made the object for disciplining or exclusion targeting zones and Muslim populations in the West and globally through the 'War on Terror'. Demands for national integration of Muslim immigrants are aimed at limiting expression of cultural difference as a strategy for producing moderate or domesticated Islam as 'moderate' on the one hand and the reduction of anxiety of Western citizen-spectators through the policing of social surfaces on the other.

The attempt to manage international jihadist terrorism as a culturalized threat conceals the systemic nature of the confrontation between the nation-state vertebrate system and international terrorism as a cellular system. Transnational governmentality as the harmonization of policy and law is the re-scaling of sovereignty upwards and downwards. Laws and policies are no longer expressions of democratic decision-making but transnational administrative borrowings and institutional integration, whether or not they are appropriate (Wacquant 2005). The attempt to reshape Islam in the West by reforming Islamic religious organizations and leadership along 'moderate' lines and emphasizing the need for a home-grown religious leadership ironically re-authorizes religion while claiming to promote a secular vision of modernity and the nation-state.

Securitizing Islam and Muslims in the West reveals the complexity of our contemporary world where sovereignty, social identity, belief and belonging are all being dislodged under globalization. The nation-state is resorting to spatializing strategies which seek to re-establish order within the nation-state reinforced by transnational forms of governmentality. The securitization and domestication of Islam and Muslims have revealed the parameters of multiculturalism as a space of only tolerated cultural difference. Securitization makes citizenship conditional on the basis of risk and threat and domestication policies delineate the cultural boundaries of inclusion/exclusion. The 'precautionary principle' underlying securitization and domestication has led to the re-essentializing of culture. In these policies Islam and Muslims are viewed as trapped and determined by tradition from which they need to be liberated. Diaspora Islam is a multilayered and multisited phenomenon and not something that can be institutionalized and domesticated through national Islamic institutions.

Multiculturalism and Cosmopolitanism

Charles Jones

Consider two recent currents of thinking in political theory. First, in the many modern societies characterized by cultural pluralism and liberal democratic political institutions, one of the most striking developments of the last several decades has been the extent to which some liberal democracies have embraced multiculturalism as a requirement of their basic moral commitment to the freedom and equality of their citizens. This development has led some theorists to embrace 'liberal culturalism', a label for the incorporating of group-differentiated cultural rights into the self-understanding of modern citizenship on liberal grounds. Second, at the same time much recent thinking about the scope of egalitarian liberal political morality, which assigns priority to equal freedoms for all individuals, has questioned the prevailing view that obligations of justice should apply first and foremost – and perhaps solely – to fellow citizens. Some liberal thinkers, that is, have embraced moral cosmopolitanism as a basic practical starting point and have concluded that the scope of justice includes all persons on an equal footing regardless of their citizenship. This second line of thinking has led to the claim that consistent liberal egalitarians should be cosmopolitans who conceive of citizenship as itself global. The upshot is that these developments have generated two important theoretical positions whose plausibility is still in dispute: liberal multiculturalism on the one hand, and cosmopolitanism on the other.

My goal is to try to understand the relationship between these two developments. On the one hand, multiculturalism can be given a plausible, though not uncontroversial, defense on liberal foundations. On the other, liberalism itself can be reconceived so that its basic principles apply with equal moral force to everyone in the world. We have, therefore, three powerful movements of thought in a series of complex relationships: multiculturalism, liberalism, and cosmopolitanism. The middle term of this relation is liberalism, the most influential ideology of the past several centuries. I sympathize with specific versions of all three sets of ideas, and I hope in this chapter to do three things: first, describe how they are related to one another; secondly, explain why they are acceptable only when interpreted in a certain way; and thirdly, ask whether there is a future for a hybrid theoretical position we might call 'multicultural cosmopolitanism'.

Liberal Multiculturalism

Let us consider what multiculturalism is and how it might be defended. I will argue that, to the extent that group-differentiated cultural rights are legitimate, their moral support will come from liberal premises. But given the resulting 'liberal culturalism' (Kymlicka 2001: 42), there will be significant limits on the kinds of group rights we should support. Of course there are other conceptions of multiculturalism, both liberal (e.g. Kukathas 1997) and non-liberal (e.g. Young 1990), but my present purpose is to set out what I take to be the requirements of – and grounds for – the most plausible form of liberal multiculturalism.

The background to recent discussions of multiculturalism is an earlier debate about the requirements of citizenship in modern liberal democratic states. In a lecture given in 1949, T. H. Marshall famously outlined a model of citizenship framed in terms of civil, political, social, and economic rights and duties. The goal of this model is to ensure that each citizen possesses, in a meaningful sense, the same rights and duties, ranging from civil rights to (for example) freedom of speech and the person, through political rights to vote and run for elected office, to social and economic rights to education and provision for protections from failures of the employment market (Marshall 1965). There are two expansionary tendencies in this argument, first for the recognition of more kinds of rights and corresponding duties than had been the norm in the practice of liberal democracies, and secondly for the inclusion of the economically disadvantaged as full members of society with the very same entitlements as their more well-off compatriots. If the first tendency calls for more protections, the second demands that these protections not be denied on grounds of class.

The thrust of Marshall's argument is to ensure that every citizen should be included as an equal in the benefits of citizenship, and that those benefits should themselves include more substance than had been usual in liberal political argument. The result is a kind of social democratic commitment to substantive equal citizenship for all: if citizens are the equals of one another, then their rights and duties should be both equal and substantial.

But modern societies are multicultural in that they contain various sorts of ethnocultural diversity, including immigrant groups, national minorities, and aboriginal peoples. This gives rise to the suggestion that equal rights for all citizens are a necessary but not sufficient condition for meeting the demands of modern citizenship. If justice demands the individual citizen rights mentioned above, it arguably also requires group-specific rights designed to respond to the unfairness left unaddressed by Marshall-style protections. The argument here begins by pointing out the blind spot at the root of the idea that citizenship rights include all and only equal individual entitlements. The problem with the traditional ideal is its promotion of a homogeneous citizen body sharing white, English, male, Christian, heterosexual features, and its consequent failure to notice differences in national and ethnic identity within the class of citizens (and religious and sexual differences as well).

Consider the following. In mid-twentieth century Britain, one could aim to satisfy all of Marshall's demands for modern citizenship rights while failing to address the disadvantages endured by Scots or Welsh citizens of Britain. Similarly, the distinctive plight of women and racial or ethnic minorities need not figure in those demands for protection. The key feature of state development in Western societies is *nation-building*, the conscious and necessary creation by states of a majority 'societal culture' and identity in a shared language, with common institutions of education, employment, and welfare (Kymlicka 2001: 23–32). This nation-building process privileges the majority culture, thereby ensuring that members of the cultural majority possess significant advantages over minorities in their life opportunities and their general access to many of the components from which they might make a flourishing life for themselves. In short, it seems unfair to individual members of cultural minority groups that nation-building privileges the cultural majority, therefore fairness demands minority protections in the form of group-specific cultural rights designed to ensure equal life prospects for everyone.

On the uniform citizenship model, where each citizen has exactly the same rights as every other, citizens can possess the full range of individual citizens' civil, political, and socioeconomic rights while continuing to suffer from exclusion, discrimination, or forced assimilation to one or more aspects of the majority culture. If citizenship really means that everyone is entitled to equal consideration on fair terms, then the very real progress embodied in the push for securing of the three (Marshall) types of individual citizenship rights remains inadequate to ensure satisfactory citizenship protections for all. What is demanded is that members of minority ethnocultural groups have the same chances of leading a life as members of the cultural majority. In order to meet this demand, the minority groups themselves need to be protected by group-specific rights from what would otherwise be an overwhelming majority cultural domination. Will Kymlicka summarizes this requirement in the phrase 'equality between groups' (Kymlicka 2001: 42).

So fairness requires group-specific rights, but what kind of rights do we have in mind here? Here are three main kinds of minority groups, along with the sorts of claims they make. First, national minorities have demanded rights to some degree of self-government in their home territory, including public institutions of law and education in their native language. Secondly, indigenous peoples have claimed self-government rights and secure claims on their land. And thirdly, ethnic, religious, and other minorities have sought public recognition, accommodation, and respect for cultural practices different from the majority norm: this includes recognizing minority religious holidays, allowing exemptions from certain laws, educating all children in the society to know and respect the main cultures and, crucially, heavily emphasizing general education and skills-development for ethnic minorities, both for its own sake and as a means to lift them out of the poverty that too often correlates with their ethnic group membership (Raz 1998: 198).

Jacob Levy has provided a useful classification of cultural rights-claims (Levy 1997: 25). These rights, some of which we have just mentioned, include exemptions, assistance, self-government, external and internal rules, recognition/enforcement, representation, and symbolic claims. Here we may emphasize two points: first, that some so-called group rights are in fact held by individuals insofar as they are members of minorities, and secondly, that even rights predicated directly of groups do not override the basic claims of individual members. This is because, for liberals, group-differentiated rights aim to promote the interests of individuals by protecting the groups to which they belong from majority dominance and by protecting the individuals themselves from any predictable and illegitimate constraints, whether those constraints stem from the state, the majority culture, or their own cultural minority group.

But why should minority cultural rights be assigned such value in the first place? Several answers might be provided. First, given the role of cultural identity in the lives of citizens, individuals' self-respect in part depends on recognition of that identity by their fellow citizens and their society more generally. Members of the cultural majority can easily gain this social basis for self-respect, since the main social and political institutions affirm their cultural identity. But for minorities the securing of group-specific rights formalizes the message of equal consideration for all: respect for identity is thus achieved by recognizing cultural minority rights. Secondly, cultural rights might be understood to embody one or another sort of intrinsic value. One might think, for instance, that cultural diversity is itself valuable, so if minority rights can promote diversity by protecting vulnerable groups, an intrinsic value is thereby promoted. Or, instead of diversity, culture could be seen as having value in itself, quite apart from any effects it might have on individual persons; so cultural rights protect something that needs no deeper justification in terms of anything else.

I will not evaluate these arguments here. The main point to notice is that these defenses of minority rights do not strictly count as *liberal* arguments. If we ask the question, 'why cultural minority rights?', the most influential – and promising – liberal answer is Kymlicka's appeal to the fundamental value of individual autonomy or freedom (the liberal value par excellence), 'the importance of allowing individuals to make free and informed choices about how to lead their lives' (Kymlicka 2001: 53). Briefly put, the reasoning moves from the value of individual freedom, through the claim that cultures enable the exercise of freedom by providing a context of choice, to the conclusion that vulnerable cultural contexts need protecting so that individual members of minority cultures can be as meaningfully free as their cultural majority co-citizens.

The process of nation-building has generated a majority 'societal culture' – a territorially based set of institutions of law, state, and education, operating in the dominant national language – that provides the means for choosing good lives for those sufficiently fortunate to be members of the national majority. But since fairness requires that every citizen should have such means, cultural and national minorities need protections designed to promote their own legitimate life projects. For immigrants, this means integration into the societal culture to ensure equal opportunity, an integration that nonetheless accommodates their ethnocultural practices and thereby recognizes their distinctive identities. For members of minority nations, it means freedom 'to live and work in their own societal culture,' because their own distinct society offers the best chance for them to lead autonomous lives. Consequently, national minorities that now form a distinct society should be enabled to maintain themselves as such, in the name of their members' claims to freedom on equal terms with members of the national majority (Kymlicka 2001: 54–55, 152–76).

There is an important implication for proponents of ethnocultural, group-specific rights who appeal to autonomy as the core underlying value that these rights are designed to protect: if autonomy matters, then it needs protection from any source that might threaten it and it needs promotion on fair terms for every citizen. So far we have outlined the need for members of minority cultural groups to be enabled to choose good lives for themselves, and this led to an argument for minority groups to be protected from the majority culture, especially as this culture is inevitably imposed on all citizens through the main social, legal, and political institutions. But now we need to point out that minority cultures themselves can be oppressive to their own members, so that promoting autonomy on equal terms for everyone requires not only the basic uniform citizenship rights but also provision for citizens in cultural minorities to reflect on, learn about, and (where necessary) reject received practices where they obstruct individual autonomy. So, on the one hand, minority cultures need protecting from majority cultural dominance and, on the other hand, those minority cultures themselves need limiting when they threaten to unjustly impose on their own members. But notice that, in both cases, the rationale for taking action is a basic concern for the autonomy of individuals, who need a secure cultural structure for making life choices but who should be protected in making those choices from their own cultural group when it poses a threat to their independence of mind and action.

This liberal argument for multiculturalism is straightforwardly universalist in its affirming of autonomy as a value for every individual. The main premise of this argument is susceptible to the objection that autonomy is not a universal value, or is a value only for members of some cultural groups, or is too controversial to form a reliable basis on which to rest a policy meant to include people with a wide range of views about what should be included in living a good human life. Individuals deserve respect as individuals, one might say; therefore, no one should assume that what they take to be good for themselves is thereby good for others (Raz 1998: 194).

If autonomy is often thought to be a questionable basis for multiculturalism, perhaps a more reliable and appealing liberal argument can be framed in terms of 'concern for the dignity and well-being of all human beings' (Raz 1998: 197). Liberals emphasize the equal moral worth of all individual persons, and it is this valuing that generates – in the context of modern culturally plural societies – concern for the well-being of the cultural groups to which those individuals belong. What makes the argument a liberal one is not an appeal to autonomy but an unwavering commitment to equal concern for each individual. It is this commitment that also provides the rationale for every individual's right to exit their cultural group and for placing limits on cultural practices that do not tolerate non-members, or constrain their own members' basic freedoms or their opportunities to participate in the wider economy and society (Raz 1998: 199). Kymlicka makes this point by saying that we must not only (as mentioned above) ensure equality between cultural groups; we must also guarantee freedom within groups, so that individuals are not oppressed by the leaders of their minority group or by the group as a whole: external protections are necessary, but internal restrictions are prohibited (Kymlicka 2001: 22).

The predominant way to think about multiculturalism and nationalism, then, is what Kymlicka calls 'liberal culturalism', an umbrella term designed to encompass 'both liberal nationalism and liberal multiculturalism' (Kymlicka 2001: 42). Liberal culturalism cites two necessary conditions for liberal-democratic justice: first, equal citizenship rights to ensure civil, political, and socioeconomic protections for every citizen; and secondly, group-specific rights to accommodate minority ethnocultural groups, including immigrants, national minorities, and aboriginal peoples. Both conditions are liberal in their equal concern for every citizen's interest in leading a good life, but only the second condition generates the 'culturalist' component in which that interest is acknowledged to be tied to cultural membership. It is worth noting, too, that liberal culturalism is liberal in another respect, namely, its support for 'policies which make it possible for members of ethnic and national groups to express and promote their culture and identity, but reject any policies which impose a *duty* on people to do so' (Kymlicka 2001: 42, emphasis in original). Individuals should be free to reject any or all aspects of their own culture, or to develop a mixed identity derived from cultural cross-fertilization. In short, liberal culturalism affirms the value of culture to individual lives, but it does not demand that citizens promote their distinctive ethnocultural identities since this would violate the core liberal commitment to equal freedom.

Culture itself is a slippery notion. For our purposes we can confine ourselves to the idea of a societal culture, i.e., the legal, political, and educational institutions in a territory that provide the main conditions – within a common language – for citizens to pursue their various interests and projects. Even if we can achieve a clear idea of culture, we may get stuck when trying to identify clear cultural boundaries. But in response to these worries, perhaps it is not necessary to draw clear borders between groups that overlap each other; we only need reliable evidence that individual members identify themselves as such. Moreover, as Amartya Sen has explained, individuals belong to a wide range of groups, including in many cases more than one cultural group (Sen 2006). The goal of multicultural group protections is not to cast cultures in stone forever, thereby confining members to one and only one unchanging cultural structure. Rather, the goal is to protect those whose memberships include vulnerable minority identity groups from being unable to achieve meaningful freedoms on account of their minority status.

Common citizenship fosters a sense of shared commitment to democratic politics and social justice, since both democracy and justice are values implicit in citizenship itself. It is therefore a noble goal. But shared citizens' rights have the added benefit of focusing those commitments on every other co-citizen and promoting a discussion about duties of democratic participation and institutional guarantees of justice for all. We might say that shared citizenship identifies those who count and makes it possible to discuss political goals with them, including the crucial goal of achieving just outcomes. To the extent that minority rights can temper or qualify common citizenship, social unity – with its many desirable consequences – can seem threatened. Can we have both unity and diversity at the same time? Multicultural policies accommodate differences between fellow citizens; but societies still need some social cement to ensure loyalty amongst compatriots. Can multiculturalists explain how difference and commonality go together, or whether perhaps there is a way to combine multicultural group identities with national shared commitment? Is it possible for a person to be both a member of a distinct ethnocultural minority group and a loyal co-national dedicated to larger shared causes? We will return to these questions later.

In recent years, while minority nationalism has stood firm there has been a backlash against immigrant multiculturalism in some countries. Kymlicka suggests that this adverse reaction is correlated with three factors: high levels of illegal immigration, the perception that many immigrants embrace illiberal cultural practices (such as coercive arranged marriages for young girls, female genital mutilation, and honour killing), and the predominance of low-skilled immigrants presumed likely to pose an economic burden. By contrast, in countries such as Canada, where illegal immigration is not a large problem, where most immigrants accept liberal norms, and where immigrants are traditionally net economic contributors, public support for immigrant multiculturalism remains strong. But since many countries will continue to struggle with problems of illegal immigration, illiberal practices, and immigrant economic burdens, the future of liberal culturalism as a whole is uncertain (Kymlicka 2007a: 51–9). This is a worry for practical politics, to add to the theoretical concern mentioned in the previous paragraph, namely, the problem of social unity in societies characterized by many forms of diversity. To address both types of issue, the best way forward may be to continue emphasizing the equal value of all individuals, with claims to dignity and respect that in turn generate cultural minority rights whose recognition provides the only just basis for national integration and a shared sense of purpose across the society.

Cosmopolitanism and Culture

Having outlined liberal multiculturalism, let us now describe some of the main varieties of cosmopolitanism and then consider the link between cosmopolitanism and culture.

Cosmopolitanism originated in fourth century BC Athens when the Cynic philosopher Diogenes of Sinope declared himself to be a citizen of the world. This assertion of the equal moral membership of each person in the community of all human beings aimed to reject the received view that the world is a community of communities. For cosmopolitans the human race is, morally speaking, a unified community of individuals. The cosmopolitan tradition may be traced from these beginnings through ancient Stoicism to eighteenth-century Enlightenment ideas about the law of nations and Immanuel Kant's defense of human rights and rejection of colonialism and imperialism. From there the tradition leads to more recent claims about the moral community of persons, the possibility of a law-governed planet, and the relation between cultural membership and the good human life (Jones 2005). Cosmopolitans today frequently support a range of value commitments, including freedom, equality, democracy, 'human rights, tolerance, cultural interchange, and international peace and cooperation' (Kymlicka 2001: 220).

Cosmopolitanism may be distinguished into moral, political, and cultural varieties, although there are significant overlaps between each of these. *Moral* cosmopolitans believe that individual human beings are the basic units of ethical concern, that each person counts equally, and that this concern applies impartially to everyone regardless of their particular subspecies identities of sex, race, nation, ethnicity, culture, or religion. In short, moral cosmopolitans are egalitarian, universalist, and morally individualist. This moral stance gives rise to puzzles about the possibility of combining, on the one hand, special concern for associates such as family members, friends, and fellow citizens with, on the other hand, universal and equal concern for all persons in virtue of their humanity.

Much recent philosophical debate concerns a kind of test case for moral cosmopolitanism: how, if at all, do duties of *distributive justice* apply globally? Some, such as David Miller, suggest that these duties presuppose a more local community, such as a nation, capable of providing people with the motivation to care about each other and thereby to meet the demands of justice (Miller 2007). Others, such as John Rawls, limit distributive questions to particular societies governed by their own basic institutional structure, leaving international justice to be concerned mainly with rules for international peace and toleration (Rawls 1999a). Cosmopolitans are suspicious of claims to limit the demands of justice to nations or peoples when so many individuals lack protections for their basic material and social interests. Perhaps there is a moderate view that combines cosmopolitan concern with national commitment: Miller and Rawls, for instance, both reject a strong impartialist approach to justice yet affirm minimal human rights claims for all persons.

Even if there is a legitimate role for national sentiments, moral cosmopolitans nonetheless have tended to sympathize with some form of *political* cosmopolitanism, where this is understood as the view that institutional authority should be shifted – to some significant degree – from the national to the supranational level. While a world state would possess unprecedented powers and therefore pose obvious dangers, there still seems to be a case for some suitably constrained global institutional framework as a means to protect basic human rights and to distribute fairly the obligations necessary to guarantee those rights against predictable threats. This leads to a controversy about the best way to understand the relation between liberal citizenship at the state level and cosmopolitan citizenship – or citizenship of the world.

Liberals and cosmopolitans share a commitment to equal concern for persons. Every individual is entitled to be treated with respect and dignity regardless of race, class, religion, sex, or sexual orientation. But this core moral egalitarianism might seem to imply a split between liberals and cosmopolitans on the status of nationalism. Liberalism has in fact been nationalist in its main assumptions (Tamir 1993; Kymlicka 2001: 39–41). Liberalizing the nation-building process has meant ensuring individual citizens' rights and – according to liberal multiculturalists – providing ethnocultural rights. Both sorts of rights aim to secure equal life prospects for every citizen in modern, culturally diverse, multinational societies. Cosmopolitans want to know why we should stop there: why should moral egalitarians not seek equal life prospects for everyone, in any society or nation or cultural group? G. A. Cohen famously asked a core question for some proponents of egalitarian economic justice: If you're an egalitarian, how come you're so rich? (Cohen 2000). Cosmopolitans might ask liberal nationalists the following question: If you're an egalitarian, how come you're so focused on the rights of your fellow citizens? In both cases, one worries that unjust privilege coexists with powerful moral arguments exposing that injustice. Kymlicka suggests a trajectory 'from Enlightenment cosmopolitanism to liberal nationalism' (Kymlicka 2001: 203–20), but I believe we should continue to ask, in the spirit of Enlightenment cosmopolitanism, whether we cannot go beyond liberal nationalism in the name of securing significant human rights protections for non-nationals.

Cultural cosmopolitans argue that a person can live a good life by mixing elements of different cultural traditions rather than relying solely on one cultural context to which one must feel a deep attachment (Waldron 1995). Cultures themselves constantly grow and change through interaction with each other; individuals can make their way in the world by interacting with others who themselves are informed by plural identities. Good human lives can take many forms, inspired by the many cultural sources of individual identity. Cultural cosmopolitans reject the view that for each person there is one cultural context – their own – which provides the materials from which persons develop their conceptions of the good and seek to put that conception into practice in their lives.

It is helpful to distinguish moral from cultural cosmopolitanism. Morally, all human beings possess equal moral worth and each is entitled to equal moral concern. Culturally, good lives generally depend on – or generally benefit from – cultural variety. But these two strains of thought are related to each other more closely than one might think. In fact, Anthony Appiah's recent articulation of cosmopolitanism affirms moral commitments to both universal scope of concern and particular recognition of individuals' cultural attachments (Appiah 2006: xv, 4–8). On this view a cosmopolitan is someone who affirms both (1) concern and responsibility for every other human being and (2) an obligation to respect legitimate differences between persons. This second idea is 'that we take seriously the value not just of human life but of particular human lives, which means taking an interest in the practices and beliefs that lend them significance' (Appiah 2006: xv). The challenge of cosmopolitanism is precisely to learn to live with difference in a world where responsibilities are global. There is no algorithm to solve conflicts of value, but the cosmopolitan insists that we take others' interests seriously and try to imagine what it is like to live very different sorts of lives: the result might be not agreement but simply getting used to each other and being able to live together. But, in the end, '[a] tenable cosmopolitanism tempers a respect for difference with a respect for actual human beings' (Appiah 2006: 63, 78, 113). People have a right to live their own lives. In practice this will result in many different ways of life often coexisting side by side, with the guarantees provided by individual human rights to be free from oppressive threats posed by states and non-state cultural groups to which one is linked.

We now have, therefore, a conception of human beings 'as *both* culture-bearers and rights-bearers' (Shachar 2009: 152). We possess cultural identities and we possess basic human rights. This raises the question of what to do when promoting identities violates rights. Susan Moller Okin's liberal feminist critique of multiculturalism says that cultures do not deserve respect if they do not themselves recognize the autonomy and gender rights of their members. Patriarchal cultures should get no support from liberal multiculturalism (Okin 1999). This view has its attractions, but it is important to point out that *all* cultures – including the dominant liberal culture – contain elements of sexism, intolerance, and moral blindness. One implication is that outright rejection of a culture is rarely, if ever, desirable. Instead we should cast a critical eye on all cultural practices – those of our own and of others – while seeking at the same time to understand the social values they nonetheless embody. The message is that cultural reform is a continuous process while unqualified cultural support or rejection are both non-starters. Morally questionable cultural practices should be discussed and debated openly with the aim of achieving policies that respect what is valuable in the practice while ensuring protections for the basic individual rights and freedoms of those vulnerable to those practices.

We might see both multiculturalism and cosmopolitanism as responses to the dominance of liberal nationalism in the contemporary world. Nation-building raises the spectre of unfair treatment of national and ethnocultural minorities, so multicultural policies can function as protections for these minorities against the national majority, either by promoting fair terms of integration (for immigrants) or by entrenching self-government rights (for minority nations or indigenous peoples). And liberal nationalism's commitment to basic liberal civil, political, and socioeconomic rights for citizens of a nation-state threatens to leave non-citizens – both within and without the state – in the lurch, unprotected because untouched and abandoned by the patchwork arrangements of international politics. So cosmopolitanism functions as a means to ensure that liberal nationalist policies do not unfairly neglect the basic rights of those not fortunate enough to be included within the official purview of the nation-state.

We must acknowledge the influential role of *liberal nationalism* in conceptualizing citizenship by emphasizing a non-aggressive, inclusive national public culture that recognizes its citizens' equal claims to freedom (Kymlicka 2001: 39–41). Nationalism of the liberal variety certainly is an improvement on illiberal forms in which non-nationals are vilified, mistreated, and relegated to second-class status. But multiculturalism itself can be seen as a response to the inadequacies of nationalism, especially in versions that have called for one nation, one state. Since nationalism provides a clear and persuasive basis for the political bond between persons, however, defenders of multiculturalism need to provide an alternative, persuasive understanding of that bond (Raz 1998: 195–6). Joseph Raz interprets liberal multiculturalism not as a new normative theory of political life but as a way of reconceiving society as 'a plurality of cultural groups.' In line with this new societal self-image we must recognize that universal values may be instantiated in various cultural practices and that common nationality is not the proper cement for ensuring reliable and ethically acceptable political bonds between citizens (Raz 1998: 197, 200–2).

Multiculturalism is not only compatible with the idea that a common culture is necessary to solidify social unity and a commitment to sacrifice for the public good; it is arguably itself a necessary condition for citizens to identify with their political society (Raz 1998: 203–4). The reason is that this identification follows only when society's members are respected, but this respect works through respect for the minority identity groups to which people belong: respect for citizens demands respect for citizens' cultures. In this way multiculturalism succeeds where nationalism fails as a key part of the political bond uniting many-sided individuals in the common project that is the modern liberal-democratic welfare state (Raz 1998: 195, 204). On one reading, then, both multiculturalism and cosmopolitanism face the same question of accounting for the bond that nationalism has provided for the development of both democratic politics and social justice since the mid-nineteenth century.

Multicultural Cosmopolitanism

Multicultural cosmopolitanism combines universal cosmopolitan concern with multicultural conversation across cultural divisions. To be concerned for all individuals regardless of national or cultural affiliation is not to reject those affiliations outright. Instead cosmopolitanism demands that individuals should seek to understand both themselves and each other, to recognize the strengths of specific cultural practices as distinctive expressions of a common humanity while pointing out mistaken or otherwise objectionable cultural practices. Raz is especially concerned to emphasize this need for understanding of others and of ourselves: we properly criticize the sexist or homophobic cultural traditions of others, but we must seek also to point out analogous problems within mainstream liberal-democratic Western culture (Raz 1998: 205). The need to understand stems from the focus on the well-being of individuals that constitutes the core of both liberal and cosmopolitan thinking.

If multiculturalism is 'a response to majority nation-building' (Kymlicka 2007a: 49), the question for multicultural cosmopolitans becomes not whether nationalism will figure centrally in an overall account of individuals' self-conceptions, including their conception of duties to others. National membership, suitably restrained and liberalized, has proven to be a realistic basis for ensuring reliable support for a framework of institutions designed to promote the interests of individuals. Liberal multiculturalists bid us to ensure that the main institutions of law, state, and economy do not disadvantage members of ethnic and national minorities; but they do not deny the centrality of nationalism as provider of the framework for promoting basic rights, freedoms, and opportunities. The question for multicultural cosmopolitans centres, instead, on the role of national and ethnocultural identities in determining *both* (i) an individual's proper self-conception (as a member of an ethnic group, nation, religion, and the entire human race, with countless other identity groups in between) *and* (ii) the duties of justice themselves.

The ongoing process of attempting to understand ourselves can benefit from looking at the recent evolution of the multiculturalism debate. One great lesson taught us by multiculturalism, or at least its new variant on an old lesson, is that *our identities are plural*: we are not irrevocably tied to a single identity group, nor is there an obvious way to set priorities amongst these groups to decide on our normative commitments. Sen has argued that every culture is internally complex and affirms a range of often-conflicting values. Individual identities are too complicated to be captured by the idea of singular affiliation to one cultural group (Sen 2006). Recognizing these facts of internal complexity protects against the danger of misconceiving culture.

Moreover, if recent evidence is reliable (see Banting and Kymlicka 2006), it is possible to be strongly committed *both* to an ethnic minority group *and* to an overarching national community. It is possible because it is actual: members of minority communities tend to identify more strongly with national institutions when those institutions themselves affirm minority identities as valuable and important. But for cosmopolitans this suggests an important implication: pointing out and defending the equal claims to dignity and respect of every person on earth – the moral basis of human rights – can be part of realizing a combined commitment to *many* identity groups, with special emphasis (and priority with respect to justice) on the group of all human beings. Multicultural cosmopolitanism embodies both plurality of identity and justice-focused emphasis on humanity as the identity group that is the most inclusive and basic of all.

Described in one way, the point of multicultural policies in Western liberal democracies has been to promote fairness in the integration process for minority ethnic and national groups. If citizens are to be treated as moral equals, they must meet the state's demands to contribute to, and participate in, the life of the nation; but at the same time they must have realistic equality of opportunity in competition for jobs and for positions with significant social status, and they must be enabled to participate in the national democratic debate over policy and social life more generally. Members of ethnic and national minorities must not only be included and integrated, they must be included and integrated on fair terms that take full account of their equal status as persons deserving respect and having lives to lead just like anyone else. In this way, we may say that liberal multiculturalism is fundamentally about fairness.

Now consider cosmopolitanism about justice. It is reasonable to describe it as basically a movement of thinking aimed at ensuring that all persons – regardless of citizenship or nationality – are treated fairly from the standpoint of distributive justice. If multiculturalists demand fair terms of integration into the national community, cosmopolitans demand fair terms of integration into the international community, with specific reference to basic human rights protections. Cultural communities who have been badly treated, such as aboriginal peoples, have a special claim to priority when identifying who merits group-specific rights. But even here the cosmopolitan will insist that individuals are the main concern, so that proposed group rights themselves should be judged on their ability to promote individual interests, and groups or their leaders may not restrict their own members in the pursuit of their life projects on equal terms with everyone else in the wider society. Beyond this, of course, group-based solutions are never sufficient to address injustice: we need as well the secure basic rights to equal freedoms for individuals if we are to enable members of disadvantaged groups equal opportunities and freedom from discrimination.

There is a tension between the centripetal tendency of group protections, where ethnocultural rights may solidify the group itself against encroachment by outside forces, and the centrifugal force of individuals seeking their own way in life, where rights to freedom and equality for persons are likely to put in question cultural boundaries and traditional practices. Multicultural cosmopolitans might be characterized as suggesting that we live with this tension because group claims can secure equal life prospects for members of cultural minorities but individual members of those minorities should never be constrained by any demands to retain a received cultural practice, to identify with their cultural group, or to reject ideas and activities discovered in the wider cultural world.

Some might object that there is a motivation problem involved in going beyond liberal culturalism to a liberal-culturalist or multicultural cosmopolitanism. What, they might ask, motivates persons to pursue the global aspirations of the cosmopolitan project? In reply, we could consider again the analogy with worries about the possibility of thinking beyond the confines of a narrow nationalism.

We know that it is possible to get beyond aggressive, exclusionary nationalist sentiments: this is one lesson of Kymlicka's multiculturalist narrative in which (i) nationalism itself becomes liberalized and then (ii) ethnocultural group rights are introduced in response to the process of nation-building. The prevailing view in the literature now is a form of liberal nationalism, but it is possible – and, I would argue necessary (though not easy) – to get beyond the liberal nationalist perspective in order to enable us to embody in our institutions a realistic commitment to equal effective concern for *all* individuals, regardless of class, race, sex, sexual orientation, ethnicity, religion, and national or state membership.

Multiculturalism can be understood as part of the 'logic of civil rights liberalism' (Kymlicka 2007b: 106). Liberal egalitarians, on this interpretation, support women's equality, gay rights, and ethnocultural group rights – for immigrants, indigenous peoples, and minority nations – as requirements for ensuring equal freedoms for all citizens. Cosmopolitanism, too, can be described as the next stage in the working out of basic liberal rights and duties: as citizens of the world we owe to each other the conditions of equal freedom for all persons.

Both liberal multiculturalism and cosmopolitanism, then, focus on the question of rights and justice. For liberal multiculturalists, the question is whether minority cultural rights are needed to ensure that cultural minorities are treated fairly by the nation-building projects of the national majority. For cosmopolitans, the question is whether the rights of persons as persons – human rights – are adequately protected in a world of nation-states in which basic protections for citizens vary between jurisdictions. Liberal multiculturalists defend ethnocultural group rights as part of a theory of social justice and national citizenship, while cosmopolitans defend basic human rights as part of a theory of global justice and world citizenship. There seems to be no principled barrier to combining these two concerns: an overall account of rights, justice, and citizenship can find a place for culturally differentiated citizens, suitably restrained nation-states, and global duties of justice for all.

Robert Goodin (2006) has identified two models of liberal multiculturalism that, in my view, help to clarify some key features of multicultural cosmopolitanism. The first type, 'protective multiculturalism,' defends ethnocultural rights as protections for cultural minorities against oppression, assimilation, and homogenization by the cultural majority community. Protectivists argue that the dominant position of the majority generates an obligation on their part to recognize minority claims as vital to promoting the well-being of individual minority group members. The second type, 'polyglot multiculturalism,' defends cultural variety as a means to 'expanding the choice set of autonomous agents' (Goodin 2006: 290). Polyglots argue that the presence of many cultural tongues enables individuals to choose from more potential options than would be the case in a less varied cultural framework. Goodin rightly emphasizes that this benefits the majority, but there is no reason to deny that it can benefit cultural minorities as well, given that minority cultures themselves change and grow in constant interaction with other cultures.

Goodin defends polyglot multiculturalism by reframing a famous debate between the liberal multiculturalist Will Kymlicka on the one hand, and Jeremy Waldron, a prominent cultural cosmopolitan, on the other. Kymlicka argues that individual autonomy requires secure access to one's own culture as the main context of choice, but Waldron denies two core aspects of this requirement, namely, that the culture must be one's own and that members must belong to it in some deep way (Waldron 2000: 228, cited in Goodin 2006: 293). Instead of deep immersion in the ocean of one's own culture, Waldron defends a (shallow) dipping of one's toes in the various bodies of cultural water created and maintained by others. Goodin nicely summarizes this debate and reaches the following conclusions: first, Kymlicka is correct that English-speaking Americans have a secure societal culture to which they belong; secondly, that culture is itself internally diverse; and finally, it is possible to borrow from a minority culture without fully living in that culture.

For cosmopolitans there is an underlying reason for taking seriously both protective and polyglot arguments. This can be explained by distinguishing three claims: (a) every individual, whether a member of a cultural minority or majority, possesses a vital interest in having secure means to finding their own way in life. Consequently, (b) everyone has a good reason to recognize that cultures, as contexts of choice, should be supported where vulnerable (excluding features that do not promote that vital interest). Claims (a) and (b) together constitute a 'protective' argument for multiculturalism. But consider, as well, the claim that (c) everyone has a good reason to seek new ideas for living that are offered by extensive cultural variety. This is a polyglot sort of claim, and when we combine it with (a) – the vital interest claim – we get a polyglot argument. While cosmopolitans should not privilege either approach, it is likely that the value of cross-cultural learning, experimentation, and appropriation will benefit everyone, whether they are members of the minority or the majority. Cultural minorities need their own culture protected, but everyone's lives are improved when the overarching societal culture is itself internally diverse. Since cosmopolitans are naturally attracted to policies that benefit everyone, they should be especially supportive of the polyglot approach.

Conclusion

Some of the central questions of political philosophy, dating back to ancient Greece, include the basis of political obligation (what, if anything, justifies citizens' obedience to political authorities?), the rationale for democracy (why should the masses have the right to rule?), and the issue of justice (how should society's goods be distributed?). Until relatively recently, these questions were asked and answered without much critical awareness of ethnic and national differences between people. But once we recognize these differences we are led to address their relevance for those central questions themselves, both within states and beyond. Within states, new issues become relevant: for political obligation (how does legitimate political authority require sensitivity to differences among citizens?), for democracy (how should political debate include differentiated yet integrated citizens?), and for justice (how should citizens' rights be reinterpreted to meet the demands of fairness and equality for ethnocultural and national minorities?). Beyond states, we also see new questions: for political obligation (are there legitimate political authorities beyond the nation-state?), for democracy (should those authorities be democratic and, if so, in what ways?), and for justice (what entitlements can persons claim simply by virtue of their status as human beings?). Multiculturalism and cosmopolitanism can be understood as two sides of a coin that together challenge the legitimacy of the undifferentiated citizen and the homogeneous nation-state. The challenge has been made, but the outcome – both in theory and practice – remains to be seen.

PART III
ALTERNATIVE PERSPECTIVES

Intercultural Relations at the Limits of Multicultural Governmentality

Ghassan Hage

Introduction

Multiculturalism has always been a multifaceted reality that has meant different things to different people. It exists as an academic theory of what social justice entails when aiming to balance demands for equality with demands for cultural recognition. It exists as a general conception of how a culturally plural nation-state can conceive of its identity. It operates as a cosmopolitan principle of cultural production in the arts and the culinary sector. It also circulates among individuals and groups belonging to ethnic minorities as a mode of making a claim on some state resources in the name of cultural preservation. Finally, it exists as a mode of governing cultural minorities and intercultural relations. These are perhaps the more common and dominant ways, but by no means the only ways, in which multicultural principles and dispositions have left their mark on the ideas, practices, social relations and institutions that constitute various societies. In their totality, and in the different ways they end up being interrelated in various contexts, they constitute varieties of national-specific forms of multicultural governmentality. That is, they work alongside other governmental discourses to create and interpellate cultural subjects and regulate their interaction within a more general framework of intercultural relations. In my previous work, I have shown how this governmentality produces a spectrum of colonial White/ Third-World-looking subjects of unequal power and unequal sense of centrality and entitlement within the multicultural nation-state (Hage 2000, 2003). In this chapter, I am concerned with the limits of this governmentality. I want to investigate the spaces where it fails: the spaces where it comes face-to-face with what I will call the 'ungovernable'. In particular, I want to examine how this 'ungovernable' has become embodied in the figure of the Muslim immigrant.

In general, the ungovernable is that which is produced from within and yet cannot be defined, encompassed and regulated by an existing governmentality. The encounter with this ungovernable is akin to what Alain Badiou would call an event (Badiou 2006). It heralds a dead end for an existing form of governmentality. It acts as a point of condensation of its limitations and contradictions. At the same time, however, it is also a site of potentiality: it opens up the sociopolitical space for a multiplicity of new, though not always or necessarily rosy, possibilities. In the chapter, I will look at the dramatic Cronulla riots in Australia as a practical expression of this relation of un-governability as it has come to exist within Australian multiculturalism and will show how it condensed both the crisis of multiculturalism and what can come after it.

Assimilationist Governmentality and its Ungovernable

Given my intended focus on the questions of the ungovernable within multiculturalism, I will begin by examining the latter's rise at the point where the assimilationist governmentality that preceded it was faced with its own ungovernable, the ungovernable that ended up ushering in the multicultural era.

The move from assimilationist to multicultural forms of government is often debated in the media, particularly in the Anglo-Saxon world, as if it is the mere result of a change of policy. Within this logic of 'policy determinism' those on the right of the political spectrum make statements such as 'the policy of assimilation gave us the cohesive and well-integrated society and the policy of multiculturalism gave us the fragmented society of ethnic communities', those on the left reply 'the policy of assimilation gave us racism while the policy of multiculturalism gave us the ethnically plural and cosmopolitan society'. While many are willing to argue with the particular details of these statements, it is surprising how very few venture into a critique of their overall logic and the way they fetishize cultural policy and give it such unrealistic powers in shaping society. Apparently, and regardless of what is happening on the ground, society is magically transformed almost immediately after a change in government policy.

That 'things' do not happen this way is not very hard to prove if any proof is needed. For instance, even a cursory historical investigation of the 1970s period, with an eye on actual social developments on the ground and not just policy, can show that far from 'creating' ethnic communities, multiculturalism evolved as a reaction to their growth. However, the obvious and well-documented fact that ethnic communities began emerging under the policy of assimilation is not something that those who are today arguing for a 'return to assimilation', and who blame multiculturalism for fragmenting society by supposedly introducing ethnic communities, like to contemplate. Certainly, multiculturalism later facilitated the growth and institutionalization of such communities, but it is important to say that multiculturalism came about because ethnic communities emerged rather than the opposite.

Policy being an instrument of government, the pressure to change it begins when governments feel it is not performing its governing role. This is when it faces, or even becomes complicit in producing, what I am calling the 'ungovernable': that which cannot be conceived, let alone governed from within given institutions responsible for defining social 'issues' or 'problems' and designing and implementing policy to deal with them. From this perspective we can restate the preceding paragraph: far from being 'the product' of multiculturalism, ethnic communities were in fact the 'ungovernable' of the cultural policy of immigrant assimilation.

Assimilationist governmentality operated with the explicit assumption that immigrants were culturally assimilable and as such worked towards achieving that goal with the expectation that this is what immigrants do. It appeared to work while migrants were newly arrived, isolated, small in number and happy to conform and keep the non-assimilable part of themselves locked in cupboards. However, as migration increased, and migrants found themselves amongst their own, the desire and the capacity to publicly 'retain' aspects of one's culture became easier to express and 'ethnic communities' started taking shape. From the outside there was an increasing public visibility of ethnic concentrations in certain streets or parts of streets which helped create this 'communal effect'. From the inside, there was the rise of an increasing number of people with relatively high cultural and educational capital who were willing and able to formulate 'ethnic demands' and in the process give shape to the varieties of ways in which 'ethnic communities' became a practical symbolic presence on the national social scene. They slowly became 'the ungovernable' of assimilation policy in that the tools, techniques and the expected cultural outcomes available within assimilationist governmentality could not even define the 'problem' of 'ethnic communities' conceptually, let alone deploy its apparatus on it to govern it.

'Ungovernability', then, is not an essential quality of the ungovernable. It is a quality that emerges when something 'escapes' the relation between a governmental apparatus and what it is aiming to govern. When a process or a social group is deemed ungovernable it might be a reflection of certain qualities and features that the process or the group possesses and that makes it hard to govern, but it is also a reflection of the capacity and the limitations of the governmental apparatus to deploy itself on it, capture it both conceptually and institutionally, and govern it. Furthermore, there is nothing in the ungovernable that makes necessary the emergence of a new form of governmentality to deal with it. The ungovernable can give rise to a multiplicity of possible governmental forms, but it can also lead to the collapse of all forms of governmentality and give rise to revolutionary upheavals.

That ethnic communities – and other cultural minority formations – in the West gave rise to a general trend towards multiculturalism had more to do with conjunctural global conditions which allowed for the rise of what we can call a multicultural sensibility across many Western countries. Such generalization is possible despite the local conditions which gave each multiculturalism its national and sometimes regional specificity.

The Multicultural Sensibility

The key elements that make up the generalized multicultural sensibility are first, the dominance in the post-World War Two era of a 'relaxed' form of nationalism, second, the rise of cosmopolitanism as a popular aspiration and third, the popularization of 'sociological' modes of thinking. Each of these has its own historical roots.

In his famous work on the 'mirror stage', Jacques Lacan (1977) argues the existence of a period in life when a child begins to experience a disparity between their internal sense of themselves as fragmented and the ideal image of a cohesive non-fragmented self that is given to them from the outside (the mirror image). Lacan's work builds on various elements of the psychoanalytic tradition to offer a concept of the self that is constructed through the fragmented self's constant attempt to almost literally 'pull itself together', to live up to the non-fragmented ideal of itself. It also invites a conception of identification which sees the formation of identity as a 'trying to be I' rather than as a simple process of 'being I'.

For psychoanalysts working within this tradition, what differentiates people is not only that some feel more fragmented than others, but also, and more importantly, the degree of anxiety that people experience as they engage in their never-ending attempt to overcome this sense of fragmentation. Some frantically and anxiously try to 'pull themselves together', dreading the experience of fragmentation. Others are more relaxed about their fragmented 'I', and even though they also 'try to be I', and try to 'pull themselves together', they do so in a more relaxed way.

What is true about the subject's imagination of their individual 'I' is also true of their imagination of their 'we', such as the 'we' of national identity. Indeed it could be argued that this 'trying to be' in the face of fragmentation is even more readily perceivable when we are dealing with the 'we' that is structured around the nation-state. Nationalists, even of the mildest variety, always experience their nation-state as fragmented when compared with an ideal of total cohesion and non-fragmentation. Nationalist rhetoric is replete with the desire for unity, togetherness, the people as one, etc. And it is this desire to attain an ideal of a cohesive nation that often drives all national theorizing and national institutions.

In much the same way as individuals differ according to the degree of anxiety they experience in their trying to be I, nationalists differ in the degree of anxiety they experience as they are 'trying to be we'. Some suffer a great deal of anxiety in the face of national fragmentation and work feverishly for ideological cohesion. Others are more relaxed in the face of a similar image of fragmentation: though they also work towards national cohesion, they do so in a more relaxed manner. They are capable of conceiving of cohesion in a less strict fashion than do the more anxious nationalists, which has led throughout history to continuing conflicts between the two.

Of course, relaxed and anxious nationalism are not simply the result of individual psychological variations. They are also social facts or trends related to social and historical variables such as level of education and economic well-being within the nation. It is in this sense that they are important for an understanding of the rise of a multicultural sensibility. The post-World War Two economic boom in the West was favourable to a more relaxed type of nationalism, particularly among the economically and culturally 'comfortable' social classes. The latter could afford to feel less threatened by a looser conception of national cohesion that was less dependent on a strict homogenization of whatever is considered national values and customs and whereby cultural diversity was no longer constructed as a disintegrating force.

The above disposition became an important component in the rise of a multicultural sensibility, particularly when it fused with another disposition which not only saw cultural diversity as 'less threatening', but perceived it as a positive gain. This disposition has its direct roots in the twentieth century rise of a cosmopolitan sensibility which strived on valorizing and accumulating the experiences of cultural difference (Vertovec and Cohen 2002: 12–14). As Hannerz has described it, cosmopolitanism is

> *first of all an orientation, a willingness to engage with the Other. It entails an intellectual and aesthetic openness towards divergent cultural experiences, a search for contrasts rather than uniformity. To become acquainted with more cultures is to turn into an aficionado, to view them as artworks (Hannerz 1996: 103).*

Sociologically, this sensibility was also becoming widespread mainly among the well-to-do classes mentioned earlier. The change in the nature of international tourism which made it more financially and practically accessible to a greater number of people led to the rise and popularization of the cosmopolitan orientation beyond a select group of adventurers as it had been in the past. This was crucial for the generalization of a more detached, transcendent and less 'primordial' identification with one's own national culture, as well as a relativist anti-Eurocentric tendency that saw value in most previously devalorized (because underdeveloped) cultures. Both of these cosmopolitan tendencies became an integral part of the multicultural disposition, even when cosmopolitanism was merely experienced as a mode of capitalist consumerism (Calhoun, in Vertovec and Cohen 2002). The cosmopolitan disposition was the core ideological source of multiculturalism's anti-assimilationist tendency, particularly its valorization of the maintenance and promotion of cultural otherness as something beneficial to the development of a national culture. Coupled with relaxed forms of nationalism, it transformed the inability of the state to nationalize cultures into something positive, rather than as a loss of power as it was experienced by the assimilationists.

The final important sociocultural tendency which contributed to the emergence of the multicultural disposition, as well as becoming an integral component of it, is a sociologically and communally informed sense of social justice that we shall call an intercommunal egalitarianism. This was a combination of a number of key ideas. The first was the sociological idea that individual life chances are determined by larger socio-economic conditions: they are not just a matter of individual will. The second is the idea that certain identity-based communities or groups such as 'black Americans', 'Greek Australians' or 'women' can share similar structural conditions despite the existence of other differences between them. Finally, such structural conditions shared by the group or community are the product of relations of power between groups, not individuals: blacks and whites, men and women, heterosexuals and homosexuals, non-indigenous and indigenous, locals and migrants, etc.

While a version of this sociological and communal conception of justice existed in the forms of 'collectivist justice' and 'communitarian' political philosophy taught in the universities, what is important to us here is that this sociological and intercommunal egalitarianism was now circulating at a wider popular level. Even though it never became a general national orthodoxy anywhere in the world, it was finding support among many politicians and media commentators and becoming an everyday belief of important sections of the national population. The general economic well-being of the post-war era and the rise of a form of 'social literacy' ensured that this mode of conceiving society was propagated well beyond the tertiary educated classes where it has usually flourished. This popularization was also partly due to the impact of communal/identity politics such as class, anti-racist and feminist struggles, which invited a conception of justice and egalitarianism that emphasized reversing relations of power between groups, not just between individuals. It was also due to the propagation in schools and in the media of a basic sociologically derived causal thinking which encouraged people to see personal conditions as part of, and determined by, wider social realities: a kind of popularizing of Durkheim's causal 'social facts'. It was this perception of social justice as beyond individual factors that allowed for the rise of varieties of notions of 'positive discrimination' and 'affirmative action' and the acceptance that group justice should sometimes override justice towards specific individuals despite its potential unfairness to the individuals concerned.

It was these various conceptions of intercommunal justice that fused with the relaxed experience of national unity, the cosmopolitan detachment from one's own culture and the valorization of cultural difference, to create the core of what became the multicultural disposition. Multicultural governmentality is the cluster of discourses, policies and practices that were born from the interaction of these dispositions with the rising ethnic and sometimes local indigenous forms of communal cultural affirmation that accompanied them.

Part of the existing crisis of multiculturalism is linked to the decline in the sensibility and disposition described above. Changing historical conditions, often associated with the rise of neo-liberalism and the intensification of the processes of globalization, have undermined the conditions that generated forms of relaxed nationalism and encouraged more individualistic conceptions of justice. Only forms of cosmopolitanism are thriving though they are arguably recovering a certain elite character.

However, by itself this does not explain why it is the figure of Muslim immigrants more than any others that increasingly became 'the ungovernable' of the multicultural apparatus. As I have argued above, ungovernability is a relation. In what follows, I will show how Muslims reflect certain specific social qualities and features that can only be understood as 'ungovernable' from within multicultural governmentality.

The Faith of the Other: The Profoundly Religious Muslim and the Crisis of the Multicultural Politics of Encompassment

The first element that contributed to a conception of 'the Muslim' as outside the multicultural realm is the existence among them of a substantial and increasing number of profoundly religious people. To be profoundly religious here does not simply mean going frequently to the Mosque or holding intense religious beliefs, nor does it denote a high degree of enthusiasm. It means considering *all aspects* of one's everyday life as ruled by the laws of one's God (Brague 2005). It is this kind of religiosity, particularly when it is the religiosity of the Other, that constitutes a serious negation of the logic of multiculturalism. Multiculturalism has always found a way, and indeed can be defined by an ability, to find room for minor elements of 'the law of the Other' to exist within the dominant national law. Here I don't necessarily mean 'law' in a formal sense, though that could apply, but more an anthropological conception of law as 'the order of things' or 'the way of life'. In this sense, we can say that multicultural governmentality is primarily defined by a relation of encompassment. The dominant national law opens a space, a space of exception if you will, where the law of the Other can exist for as long as it is encompassed by the national law. The space where the law of the Other exists can vary in content and in magnitude: what cannot possibly change is that the dominant culture has to be the encompassing culture and the law of the other the encompassed culture.

The difficulty that arises with profoundly religious Muslims is that they see their laws as the laws of God – these are not equivalent to minor laws such as the rules of a specific national cuisine or even the ethno-specific laws of marriage and kinship. The idea that you can have a space where you can speak your language, eat your food and follow your rituals as long as you understand that this is a space offered to you, so to speak, by the dominant language and modes of conduct etc. is relatively unproblematic. That the laws of a nation should offer little space for the laws of God to be exercised is sacrilegious: those who take their religion seriously experience the reverse of this position. The laws of God are all-encompassing and the national laws of the host nation, or any other nation for that matter, are the minor ones. For a profoundly religious Muslim migrant integrating with the host nation is a matter of finding a space for these national laws within the all-encompassing laws of God. The relationship of encompassing–encompassed cultures on which multicultural governmentality is based is here inverted and intimations of ungovernability start to arise. If those laws of God were only concerned with ruling over one's spiritual needs, this would not be so much of a problem. The difficulty arises because for many profoundly religious Muslims the laws of God are also the laws that rule a politicized transnational community or *Umma*. This gives a more earthly flavour to this mode of living under the law of God, transforming it into a kind of politicized metaphysical transnationalism.

International political developments which articulated themselves to both Islamic transnationalism and to local patterns of Islamic disadvantage have also made a difference. The starting point of these developments and perhaps the most important one is the rise of Iran as an 'Islamic nation'.

The Iranian revolution instituted for the first time a rule of law that openly portrays itself as a kind of transcendent Muslim political will which was perceived to exercise itself for the first time transnationally with the Salman Rushdie affair. It was as if suddenly Muslims were in a position to openly 'sentence' a person living in and subject to the protection of the law of a Western nation state. Even more threatening to the Western national will, numerous Muslims who were supposed to be subjects to it show themselves to be the willing agents of the transnational Muslim will by calling for the *fatwa* to be carryied out, or volunteering to carry out the sentence themselves. Since then there have been many occasions on which some Muslims have shown themselves to be the subjects of a transnational will that is Other to the West: the 9/11 attacks and the London bombings led to a perception of the Islamic will not just as the will of the Other, but as the will of the enemy. It is this more than anything else that has put Muslims outside the realm of multicultural governmentality, because multiculturalism was always about finding a space for the culture of the Other in so far as this culture does not claim a sovereignty over itself that clashes with the laws of the nation. Multicultural governmentality has always remained grounded in a colonial logic of 'political necrophilia' towards the other: a kind of 'we'll love your art and dancing but only after we've made sure that we've broken your spears'. In a Hobbesian sense, Others are seen, and see themselves, as politically alive in so far as they retain a potential, but not necessarily the desire, to hurt. To kill someone politically is to remove from them this potential and make them predictable and safe. It is in this sense that multicultural governmentality is a continuation of a colonial logic: there is no space within it for recognizing or valorizing an Other who retains the potential to hurt you. The Other who retains such a capacity becomes by definition ungovernable.

On Mis-interpellation: Assimilation Fatigue and the Islamic Space of Self-constitution

Perhaps because it has carved itself a space outside the multicultural logic of encompassment, Islam has also created a space of subjective self-constitution outside the multicultural logic of recognition which is often experienced, particularly by second and even third-generation immigrants who embark on the voyage of 'trying to be recognized by the dominant culture', as a dead-end.

Some of the most frequent comments that circulated following the London terrorist bombing of 7 July 2005 had to do with the fact that the London bombers were 'second-generation' immigrants, 'home-grown', as everyone was claiming in disbelief. This was taken to demonstrate how 'unassimilated' London's South Asians are given that 'not even' the second generation is assimilated. The relationship between not being assimilated and hatred is not clear, however. Lack of assimilation produces lack of interest and emotions toward the culture one has not assimilated to, and to express such strong and destructive feelings towards a place comes from intense and even intimate interaction with it. That is, hatred does not come from lack of assimilation – if anything it comes from a frustrated and unrecognized sense of *over-assimilation*. It comes from an experience of rejection. This is not to say that there is a necessary link between terrorism and second generation immigrants: rather, if one has to choose between a first-generation and a second-generation candidate for being a terrorist full of hatred towards the host country, it is far more likely that the person will be second generation.

It is worth noting here that everywhere the dominant multicultural or liberal Western culture is having problems with 'Muslims' whether in France, Denmark, England or Australia, and the problem is primarily linked to youth. This is because, as much work done with immigrants has shown (see Phoenix 2005), the second generation is likely to experience a different and more intense sense of injury from racism than the first generation. Here lies one of the problems with multiculturalism as an anti-racist ideology limited to a form of ideological anti-Eurocentrism. As I have argued in detail in *White Nation* (Hage 2000) multiculturalism is generally very limited as an anti-racist policy. It never stops reproducing the centrality of white Europeans' entitlement to the nation. Nevertheless, multicultural recognition as a form of anti-Eurocentrism and valorization of the other's culture can be seen as a form of anti-racism. The issue I want to deal with here is that this form of multicultural anti-racism is far more geared to dealing with migrants who are relatively new to their host country. The pain of 'not being recognized' or 'being recognized negatively' is a predominantly first-generation experience. Furthermore, there is a sense in which the first generation 'expects' the racism directed towards them. Indeed, in my own fieldwork, I often hear migrants engaging in discourses aiming to even legitimate the racism towards them. They say things like: 'I would have done the same, if they had come to my country' and 'well, it is their country … you know, we have to accept that'. The second generation, on the other hand, becomes if anything over-sensitive to any kind of exclusionary behaviour directed towards them. This is partly because they always get a whiff of the racism experienced by their parents before them, but more importantly because, unlike their parents, they experience racism from an early age, and because this racism is directed at them with a language and culture that is their own, they develop an excessive and even a reactive idealized sense of entitlement to non-discriminatory treatment. This is what I meant above by overassimilated: they develop an idealized sense of non-discriminatory belonging that even non-racialized citizens have no access to. Through a long history of being on the receiving end of everyday modes of being demeaned, ostracized and excluded, they develop a kind of *habitus*, a well-attuned capacity to recognize or detect all those small insignificant modes of mostly petty, subtle and unsubtle, direct and indirect, implicit and explicit, voluntary and involuntary, exclusionary behaviour that become part of their everyday life. It is this everyday petty racism coupled with the exaggerated sense of entitlement that can swell up into a sometimes formidable state of resentment very different in intensity from the sentiment felt by first-generation immigrants when faced with racism.

A slightly transformed notion of ideological interpellation that Althusser (1971) developed is useful in helping us theorize and get a better analytical grasp on the difference between the two experiences. For Althusser, the notion of interpellation helps explain the social formation of subjects within society. Althusser was inspired by a Lacanian tale that roughly went as follows: when parents talk about their forthcoming baby, prepare his or her room, and start planning their lives as if the baby is already present, a symbolic space is created that actually awaits the baby to simply come and occupy it. In Althusser's conception of subject formation, society operates in the same way: it has already allocated symbolic structural locations, such as 'worker', which simply 'hail' or 'interpellate' a person to fill the already existing space. The moment a person is hailed and comes to occupy a certain position is the moment that gives meaning to their lives.

From this perspective, racism is a failure in the interpollation system, whereby society falls short of allocating the racialized person a space that makes their life meaningful. But this failure varies. It can be said that first-generation immigrants experience a racism that takes either the form of non-interpellation or the form of a negative interpellation. To be nationally non-interpellated is to find no space for yourself in the ideological plane which constitutes people as subjects of a particular nation. This is the drama of non-recognition: you do not feel you are being hailed from anywhere. Non-recognition produces invisibility and a yearning to be noticed and acknowledged. Negative interpellation is different. It does not lead to invisibility, rather it is the visibility produced by classical modes of racist inferiorization. This is where migrants say of their racist experience 'I was treated like an animal', indicating a form of recognition, but recognition of someone as less than human. While the second generation can experience the above forms of racism, its primary experience is one of mis-interpellation. To be mis-interpellated is far more dramatic and emotionally complex than being negatively interpellated for here, the person recognizes themselves as being interpellated only to find out that they are not. When the nation hails you as 'hey you citizen' everything in you leads you to recognize that it is you who are being hailed: but you reply 'yes it is me' you experience the shock of the rejection where the very ideological grid that is inviting you in the nation expels you through the petty and not so petty acts of exclusion that racists engage in in their everyday life. You say 'it is me' and the ideological structure of society replies with cruelty: 'No. Piss off. It is not you I am calling.' Mis-interpellation is a far more traumatizing experience of racism than negative or non-interpellation. Subjection to racism always involves an experience of fragmentation. When this subjection is intense as in the case of mis-interpellation it can become an experience of shattering, and while a fragmented subject can always manage to pull themselves together to be operational in the world, the shattered racialized person needs a space immune from the effect of racism in order to 'pick up the pieces' as it were. It is here that Islamic religion plays an important role among Muslim youth in the West that multiculturalism does not and cannot play.

Because it is directed at promoting both the recognition of the culture of the other and the valorization of this culture, multiculturalism has always been geared to deal with the forms of exclusion and lack of recognition that emanate from non-interpellation and negative interpellation. It has not been conceived to handle the drama of mis-interpellation. As such it often leaves the second generation outside its operative sphere as it were and as such positions them, yet again, as 'ungovernable'. This is not surprising: the mis-interpellated is not someone yearning to have their culture recognized, paradoxically they are someone who was yearning to assimilate, who has offered the nation their assimilation and found it was rejected by the nation through the medium of a variety of racist subjects. Many such subjects suffer from what I have called 'assimilation or recognition fatigue'. They become sick of trying to assimilate as a mode of defining themselves in viable terms. Instead, they start looking outside official ideologies, to each other (gangs), to music (rap) or as is the case among many Muslim youth, to religion, to find a space where they can develop a viable sense of themselves and immunize themselves against the constant threat of psychological disintegration that racism constitutes for them.

For those youth with a Muslim background who turn to religion in this way, Islam becomes the anti-racist ideology par excellence. It offers the youth a space where they can develop a healthy conception of themselves as opposed to the negatively racialized one that is constantly thrown at them by some sections of society. This works to reinforce the process of non-encompassment described above. Islam begins to appear vis-à-vis multiculturalism as a competing governmentality rather than as a culture that can be governed by it.

In the remainder of this chapter I want to move to a more empirical register and examine the dramatic Cronulla events in Australia as a condensation of the crisis of multicultural governability in the face of the ungovernable Muslim.

Cronulla and the Crisis of the Multicultural-assimilationist Apparatus

Historically speaking, Muslims have not been considered Australia's most threatening Other. Even as late as the 1990s, and while the Muslim Other became increasingly important following the first Gulf war, Australia's core threatening Other remained what it has always been: 'Asians', which in Australia meant primarily South East Asian. While in terms of international threats Muslim Indonesia has always loomed large, it was more the fact that Indonesia was an underdeveloped and populous rather than an Islamic nation which mattered most. When the racist movement of Pauline Hanson emerged in the mid-1990s, there was hardly a mention of Muslims, and Asians were still its primary target.

It was only at the turn of the century that Muslims became by far the primary threat, in a period which saw a globalization of the Islamic Other around the world. Like all processes of cultural globalization, it involves contradictory processes of homogenization and heterogenization of a cultural trend (Hannerz 1996). Thus while 'Islam' was becoming homogenized as the global threatening other, the category that embodied the Islamic threat differed from one country to another: Asians in Britain (there meaning Indians and Pakistanis), Turks in Germany and North Africans in France. In Australia the category 'Lebanese' came to embody this threat. Although in the early nineteenth century and until the middle of the twentieth century Lebanese migration to Australia was primarily Christian, the number of Muslim Lebanese began to rise considerably from the 1960s onward. More importantly, the Lebanese migrants of the 1960s, 1970s and 1980s were unskilled and with very low level of education. They were initially recruited into an industrial sector (particularly the automobile industry) that was soon to be decimated and they soon suffered massive unemployment. Because of their lack of educational and cultural resources (relative to the Australian context) this unemployment became of a chronic nature: it was inherited across generations. Muslim Lebanese today have the highest rate of unemployment in the country. This also meant that an underclass culture structured around various black economies flourished among them and featured highly mediatized gang formations dubbed Middle Eastern or Lebanese gangs.

In December 2005, a crowd of around 5,000 white, largely male, Australians were mobilized to descend on one of Sydney's most popular beaches, Cronulla beach, and 'reclaim it' from 'Muslims', 'Lebanese' and 'wogs'. The crowd chased and violently attacked a number of lone individuals deemed to be of Middle Eastern descent (this apparently included a Greek and a Bangladeshi).

The immediate trigger of the events was an altercation a week before between a couple of Lebanese Muslim youth and two lifeguards in which the latter ended up being severely beaten. This event itself followed a history of tensions between the largely white locals and non-local Muslim Lebanese men who were increasingly perceived to have 'taken over' imposing their forms of masculinity (modes of playing football and modes of harassing girls) on the beach. Given the lifeguards' iconic status in Australian society this was construed as crossing a line beyond what can be tolerated, and as another example of the Muslims' arrogant disregard of and disrespect towards Australian values. This is a theme that has been constantly expressed by various public commentators over the last few years. Thus, what followed the beating was public outrage expressed in, and fomented by, parts of the populist media (tabloids and talkback radio). This same media gave high exposure to the various calls to reclaim the beach that circulated through SMS messaging. Well-known racist right-wing fringe groups also mobilized and exploited the situation.

Unlike other global 'racial' events such as the LA or Paris riots, this was not rioting by yet another racialized, socially disadvantaged, and marginalized group. Here, the rioters were whites from the dominant Anglo-Celtic culture chasing people belonging to a minority. As one commentator has put it, this was in the tradition of pogroms not the tradition of riots (Moses 2006), and pogroms are indicators of a specific kind of governmental tension. They are performed by individuals from a cultural grouping within society that sees themselves as dominant enough to feel capable of 'legitimately' taking the law in their own hands as an expression of what they see as the failure of the state to act in their name. In Cronulla, the white crowd had a strong sense of entitlement that the beach was theirs, that they knew what the right way to behave on the beach was, and that they were entitled to judge who was behaving properly and who was not. At one level, the white crowd deployed itself to perform what they felt the government should have performed but failed to do so: preserve a specific Australian way of life. What is interesting is that not all the crowd saw this specific way of life that needs to be protected as a 'monocultural' one, some spoken to by various reporters saw themselves defending a 'multicultural' way of life that they believed the Muslims were ruining. This was also confirmed in a number of academic works on the event (Lattas 2007). It was as if the exterminatory impulse that moved the crowd, and that was there for all to see in the way it surrounded and pounced on its Lebanese/Muslim prey, was itself the result of an impasse generated not by the 'crisis of multiculturalism' eagerly declared by some, nor by the crisis of monocultural assimilationism, but the crisis of the very governmentality that was based on a supposed choice between the two.

Here we come to an important point. In many parts of the world, but particularly in Australia, multiculturalism is portrayed as an alternative and a transcendence of monocultural assimilation. This to a certain extent is obviously true, but it also obscures a very important fact. Assimilation was never buried by multiculturalism – it continued to co-exist with it. In some ways, for the white subject, it was always comforting to know that if multiculturalism doesn't work 'we' can always return to assimilation. More importantly, it can be said that multicultural governance has always relied on the continued existence of an assimilationist tendency at the very heart of multiculturalism in order to achieve its aims. All government documents on multiculturalism in Australia from the foundational Galbally report of 1978 onward celebrate diversity, but they ensure with a 'but' or an 'as long as' or 'in so far as' that no one forgets that this diversity should not happen at the cost of

Australia's cohesion, core values, etc. This co-existence of a multicultural and assmilationist imperative is also present in Canadian and British multiculturalism. Assimilationism, therefore, always existed as a disciplinary technique which was deployed specifically to ensure that the diverse cultures that were integrated into the multicultural fold were 'good to integrate and be multicultural about' in the first place. If multiculturalism was deployed to teach multicultural horses how to be mounted by those who wanted to enjoy their culture, assimilation was the technique deployed to 'break them' before such a training. It is in this sense that we can realistically speak of a multicultural–assimilationist apparatus. It is an apparatus in which multiculturalism and assimilation were positioned respectively in the guise of carrots and sticks: even at the very height of multiculturalism, assimilation was continuously deployed, either through a government report, a politician's statement or even sometimes through popular mobilization, as a way of domesticating 'the wild side' of certain communities, and as the very precondition of them entering the multicultural realm: 'You are welcome but leave your conflicts behind', 'We are enriched by this aspect of your culture but not that', etc. Those who are polemically inclined should note here that I am not saying that this was necessarily a bad governmental policy because of this. Perhaps this combination of multiculturalism and assimilation was the most appropriate policy that the government could take at the time. Nonetheless, it remains worthwhile to note analytically that the very condition of multicultural governmentality worked through fostering an ideological polarity between assimilation and multiculturalism while, practically speaking, both policies were intimately related in the same governmental apparatus.

This is why those who see the Cronulla events as a crisis of multiculturalism and offer the need for more assimilation instead fail to see how dramatic a governmental crisis Cronulla represented. After all, it is important to remember that Cronulla emerged not at the height of multicultural fervour but following ten years of fostering anti-multicultural assimilationist rhetoric by the highly conservative government of John Howard, the bulk of which was directed at Muslims whether as immigrants with a settlement problem, or as 'illegal refugees' who are barbarians enough to 'throw their children overboard' or uncivilised enough to 'jump the queue'.

A Lebanese background youth I interviewed after the Cronulla event, Marwan, had a story about what happened to one of the Lebanese men who got bashed on the beach: 'after punching him to the ground, this bloke got on top of him and shoved the Australian flag in his face and said: "kiss the flag". The (Lebanese) guy said: 'but that's my flag'. The bloke on top of him said: 'No it's not. Kiss the flag'.

Given the number of mythical stories that have circulated about Cronulla, I have no way of verifying that this happened. Nor has Marwan, though he firmly believes that it has, but like all mythical stories it denotes a structure of experience well beyond the immediate event. And this story reveals how the Lebanese-background young men on the beach experience the dead-end of the forced assimilationism exhibited by some of the crowd who fantasized themselves doing the job of taming the Muslims that multiculturalism was supposedly not doing. The assimilationists tell their other: 'Assimilate'. If the other says: 'but I am assimilated', the assimilationist simply ignores this and says: 'no you're not. Assimilate!' It is well known that monocultural assimilationists are never interested in the assimilation of the Other. Rather, they are interested in portraying them to be 'in need of assimilation'. This shows itself in assimilationist politics again and again, but at Cronulla the assimilationist demand reaches another degree of absurdity and it takes us close to how the Cronulla 'Leb boys' saw themselves and how they were seen by both the multiculturalists and the monoculturalists.

The cultural forms exhibited by some of the Lebanese boys on the beach, which became generalized as 'Lebanese behaviour' and irked so many people, were clearly a hybrid formation: the forms of working/under class masculinity that were put on show were a touch Lebanese, but nothing that you can find exhibited in this way in Lebanon, except perhaps among Lebanese Australians living in Lebanon(!). They also contained a touch of the Black and Latino American cultural subaltern hype that has been globalized by the mass media through the propagation of particular type of music, clothing, walking, etc. And they were in other ways quintessentially Australian: working class Australian perhaps, but Australian nonetheless.

However, what is striking about the boys was not so much the fact that they lived in a marginal working/under class hybrid culture but how *at ease* they were with their working/under class hybridity: they shamelessly exhibited it. They were totally comfortable on the beach being sexist, being macho, being vulgar and being aggressive. They were really very much at home. It is in this that they placed themselves outside the multicultural–monocultural field of governmentality. They rubbed the multiculturalists the wrong way because they did not represent a 'valuable' culture that one can be multicultural about: no Anglo-cosmopolitan-multiculturalist looked at them and thought: 'I am enriched by your presence in my country.' But then, they couldn't care less, they were looking neither for recognition nor for valorization, and they were certainly not looking for toleration. They just assumed that they could merely 'be' Australian in the way they have grown to be. Paradoxically, this is where they rubbed the monocultural assimilationists the wrong way. For on the one hand they seemed like obvious candidates for the 'assimilationist stick', a stick that can tame them and make them ready to enter multiculturalism and start cooking some Lebanese food rather than desiring and harassing 'Aussie' girls in a vulgar way. But, on the other hand, those boys had no sense of needing to assimilate to anything. It is at this point that the absurdity, and also the hypocrisy, of deploying assimilation on them emerges. For beneath the complaint that the boys were not well-assimilated and well-integrated was really the fear that the boys acted as if they were completely assimilated and integrated *despite* their cultural marginality and difference. They were assimilated on their own terms. They were not Australians in the way others wanted them to be, but they nonetheless felt themselves fully and *unproblematically* Australian. And this is exactly what triggers the monocultural assimilationist fear inherent in the 'no that's not your flag. Kiss the flag' myth and its successive apparently contradictory injunctions: 'how dare you say you are Australian. No you're not Australian. Become Australian.' What is behind the claims that the Leb boys were un-integrated was the fear that they seemed *over-integrated*: for people who are so different they were too integrated for their own good: no sense of their assumed marginality – arrogant. 'We don't expect you to act like this on the beach' the assimilationists and the multiculturalist were really screaming in unison. 'Can't you be a bit shy for God's sake! You should feel like hiding your feelings when you are desiring an Aussie chick on the beach in *this* way.' Here was a lament that is an established and ongoing feature of all forms of racialized relations of power, already well-known to slave owners when addressing their slaves who looked a touch too long at 'the lady': How dare you exhibit your desire from your position of difference and marginality! It is in this that they exhibited their 'ungovernability' in the face of the multicultural–assimilationist duo that were often deployed *in tandem* to ensure the integration of people in Australian culture.

The problem with these boys was that, born in Australia, in an Australian-grown (albeit hybrid and racialized) culture, they seem to have lost sense of the marginality of that culture. Or, more correctly, they felt totally Australian in their very marginality. That is, *they felt marginal* within *Australia not* from *Australia*, and many are often genuinely surprised to hear their Australian-ness being questioned. This is something that often comes up in ethnographic and interview material. And it was the case in the interviews I conducted after Cronulla as well.

'So how did you feel when the riots happened?' I asked Marwan. 'In all honesty, many of my mates were shocked … we grew up having all kind of confrontations with many of these blokes … there's one of them I still see on the beach. I punched him when he was ten or eleven', he says.

Marwan speaks as if the little periodical confrontations they had with the 'Australians' on the beach over many years were part of his Australian culture. So, to have a confrontation that brings all confrontations to an end was kind of un-Australian. 'I was shocked' he kept repeating. To get stuck into each other ritually was fine: 'we knew it will happen again on the next-weekend', he said. It was as if somehow people like Marwan being hated by 'the Aussies' was how he saw himself and his friends being interpellated on the beach and as Australians. Strangely, it was a position he felt comfortable with. What he couldn't cope with was that the riots were not part of the game: they were aiming to end the game and end his position within it. That took him and his friends by surprise and hurt him in ways that losing a fight on one of the routine days on the beach did not. The riots were not aiming at portraying him negatively. They were aiming at terminating his very physical presence and symbolic existence on the beach.

'So what did you feel like when you saw the riots on the TV?' I asked. 'I wanted to bash an Aussie', Marwan said, without any hesitation. 'But, you just told me that many of your friends from school and on the building site are Aussies' I replied. 'Did you feel like bashing them?' 'No, not those Aussies', he replied and then repeated: 'I wanted to bash an Aussie'. 'What do you mean?' I insisted. But

I must have sounded unconvincing. Marwan gave me a pretty threatening look. 'Don't fuck around with me mate. You know very well what I mean.' And he repeated for the third time: 'I wanted to bash Aussies!'

I want to finish with this section of the interview because it gives a good sense of what it must have felt like for the Lebanese boys who went out on the rampage after the Cronulla pogrom. They were out to bash and destroy, and the 'Aussie Other' moves from being a kid one has punched in the past but that one can still recognize to a non-recognizable abstracted *enemy*: not *those* Aussies, but 'Aussies'. The sense of intimacy is gone and there is no attempt at voicing grievances, no attempt at positing a political goal or being part of a political process. There is just a numb and dumb desire for, and an acting out of, senseless violence.

For obvious reasons, there is a similarity between this violent disposition exhibited by Marwan and the violence that was exhibited by the Lebanese boys in their 'revenge attack' following the Cronulla pogrom when they returned the day after, destroying cars and property and bashing people. There is also a similarity between this and the nature of the violence exhibited in the attacks by the racialized Parisian youth in the suburbs during the so-called Paris riots. There is even a similarity between both and the violence that is part of Islamicist suicide bombing. Needless to say, I am certainly not saying that there is an ideological continuity between the rioters and Islamic terrorism. Rather, I am positing that all these reactions seem to share something which is akin to an ideological void: no politicized demand or programme, just the will to hurt, and not even hurt the other that is perceived to have hurt you.

Slavoj Zizek (2008) argues that this kind of violence is 'meaningless' in a radical sense. He claims that it is a violence that takes one from the realm of the Symbolic into the Real as it aims to go beyond 'meaning' and constitutes what Lacan calls *'passage a l'acte'* (literally: the move to action). I am not convinced about the meaninglessness of this violence. This kind of violence seems to me a rejection of the most fundamental but also the most colonial tenet of multicultural governmentality, what I have termed above as political necrophilia. It is a refusal to take on the role of the tame, safe and predictable Other. Coming often from the position of people facing the threat of symbolic annihilation, acting is often meant to convey just that: the very capacity to act. Far from being an action that is beyond the realm of communication, it is trying to communicate something. It is trying to say to those who are aiming to neutralize you: 'I can still make a difference'. It is trying to say to those who want to annihilate you: 'I am still alive.' This is the politics of bare life (Agamben 1998). Far from being a given static state of being, as some claim, bare life is actually a field of struggle. Big battles are waged within that field and the subjects participating in those battles can still claim their subjecthood. They say: 'I can still create damage therefore I am.' In this sphere, the will to power is reduced to its absolute minimum, the will to hurt, but it persists nonetheless as a will to power in its continual struggle to assert itself. It is in this sense that it points to a realm of life that is outside the existing symbolic order: in our case, outside what is increasingly becoming the platitudes and dead-ends of the monocultural and the multicultural alternatives. Violence becomes something waiting for a new symbolic effort that aims to capture it, domesticate it, and make it part of another governmentality.

At the Limits of Multiculturalism: Extermination or Negotiation?

As I began by pointing out, what makes an object 'ungovernable' is not only the qualities it possesses but the capacities of the governing subject as well: ungovernability is the relation between the two. Consequently, while the nature of the Muslims' current radical difference in their encounter with multiculturalism should not be underestimated, this difference by itself does not explain how they have become ungovernable. Nor does it explain the intensity of the reaction and the fears that their ungovernability arouses. What explains this intensity is the fact that the white Australian culture that is facing this Islamic difference is marred by a sense of insecurity that has emerged independently of the Islamic question. This sense of insecurity is rooted in the way the process of globalization has rendered fragile people's structural integration into their nation-states.

When multiculturalism emerged, it aimed at helping integrate people from cultural minorities into the nation-state. The integration of people from the dominant culture was never considered an issue. It was taken for granted. This was a time when a nation meant primarily a national economy. By having a job people were already integrated in the nation, when they didn't have a job the welfare state gave them that sense of integration. Globalization and neo-liberal policies have meant that in many instances the economy has detached itself from the nation. To be located within the economy does not locate you within the nation. This has meant that one's position within the nation is increasingly predicated on the domain of identity and culture. It has also meant that for many whites their sense of belonging to the nation has become exceptionally brittle. Their need to reaffirm the nations' identity in terms of the culture of the majority rather than in relativist terms became increasingly important. White European culture was increasingly experienced as besieged, as maligned, relativized and devalued in the face of Third World cultures that were, in the eyes of white nationalists, very obviously inferior despite the views of the multiculturalists who are considered as too polite and politically correct to say so. It is in this context that the sentiment 'we've had enough of silently copping the behaviour of this third world Muslim minority imposing its uncivilised standards of behaviour on us when we know that our standards of behaviour are so much better' becomes prevalent.

In that sense, the actions of the white Australians of Cronulla beach echoes many other forms of white reactions to Muslims across the globe, including the infamous 'Muhammad cartoons' debacle. These incidents and many others are manifestations of a growing need among sections of the white populations of the West to reassert and reaffirm both their majoritarian status as cultural group and the superiority of their European values in the face of what they see as an Islamic, but also more generally a multicultural relativist, threat.

The problem is that because this reassertion is in a sense imprisoned by the 'multiculturalism–assimilation polarity' it can only lead to the kind of dead-ends that the Cronulla events have led to. It has become crucial to find ways of moving beyond such a polarity. Unfortunately, Cronulla carried within it the seeds of one very unpleasant possible way out of the polarity which clearly needs to be avoided, and that is the path of extermination. If this is to be avoided, it seems clear to me that we must find forms of cultural governmentality that are no longer grounded in colonial political necrophilia and the politics of recognition that has been shaped by it. We need to move to forms of intercultural relations where we can live with the sovereignty of the other, and their potential capacity to hurt us. Derrida likens the sovereign Other that sneaks in and lives among us to the figure of the wolf. In that sense what is at stake today is our capacity to negotiate with wolves.

Security Warning:
Multiculturalism Alert!

Rita Kaur Dhamoon

In the summer of 2006, Canadian law enforcement agencies arrested and charged 17 Muslim men living in Toronto, including five youths, on the basis of various terrorism offences. This group of Muslim men – dubbed the 'Toronto 17' – was accused of taking steps to obtain three tons of ammonium nitrate (a commonly used fertilizer) to use for a terrorist attack. The arrests made national and international news with such headlines as 'Raids prove that Canada not soft on terror, Days says' (Chase 2006), 'Generation Jihad: angry, young, born-again believers' (Wente 2006), 'You think they would be more grateful to be Canadians' (Taylor 2006), 'What could anyone have against Canada? The view from Washington' (May 2006), and 'Multiculturalism has its limits' (Turley-Ewart 2006). Multiculturalism was, and continues to be, scripted as a tool of terrorism, one that breeds 'home-grown terrorists' and threatens the security of the nation, specifically the nation's identity, property, economic prosperity, and its citizens. Interestingly, after the arrests of the Toronto 17, this view was advanced not only by conservative-oriented agents such as the Canadian Security Intelligence Service, Conservative government officials, and conservative media reporters, but also by what might be characterized as soft liberals, namely citizens who supported diversity but require strong limits to diversity in the name of national security. In short, the conservative and soft liberal charge against multiculturalism has been that it has gone too far in its accommodation of diversity.

In the context of these charges, defenders of multiculturalism have argued that illiberal practices (which would include acts of terrorism) exist in all western democracies, regardless of whether or not multicultural policies are in place. The philosophy underlying the policy of multiculturalism, defenders contend, 'is a philosophy of human rights and civil rights liberalism, and the policy is only intended to support organizations and activities that will advance that agenda' (Kymlicka 2007b: 163). As such, supporters argue that multiculturalism does not condone or breed terrorism. Indeed, among others, leading philosopher Will Kymlicka suggests that a deeper commitment to *liberal* multiculturalism can counter security concerns. This emphasis on a liberal version of multiculturalism (as opposed to, say, critical or radical multiculturalism or anti-racism or decolonization) has dominated the field of contemporary political theory and political practice in those western nations that have adopted multicultural policies. Kymlicka recognizes that there has been the 'resecuritization' of state–Muslim relations since the events of September 11, 2001 and the subsequent Madrid and London bombings, and he also notes that 'the public acceptance of multiculturalism in the West has depended on the perception that it is consistent with both the geo-political security of the state and the personal security of individual citizens' (Kymlicka 2007b: 125, 127). But he concludes that overall, in liberal democracies, 'the securitization of ethnic relations erodes both the democratic spaces to voice minority demands, and the likelihood that those demands will be accepted' (2007b: 120).

These two perspectives – the conservative/soft liberal position and the liberal multicultural one – tend to present security and multiculturalism as oppositional. The conservative/soft liberal position requires that security trumps multiculturalism, and the liberal multicultural position requires that multiculturalism, or what Kymlicka frames as 'the democratic box' (2004: 144–6, 2007b: 125), should balance security concerns so as to promote human rights. In the first instance it is argued that multiculturalism goes too far, and in the second it is argued that the ideals of liberal multiculturalism have not been adequately applied.

While liberal multicultural theory has indeed not been fully applied, I want to suggest that even if it were, the script of multiculturalism versus security mischaracterizes the relationship between these two discourses. Rather than being oppositional to one another, I contend that liberal multiculturalism is a mechanism of security, one that regulates various modalities and degrees of difference. Certainly, on both a domestic and transnational level, liberal multicultural discourses have been successful in opening up avenues to pursue human rights agendas, including in situations that are otherwise hostile to ethno-cultural difference. But these very transformative instruments are more than often folded back into nation-building projects. Certainly nation-building projects are important in providing different kinds of assurances to the people within a nation, including legal rights, economic opportunities, education and so on; this is true in the case of new and renewed nations (e.g. former colonies) as well as established ones. But at the same time, even in defining the terms of citizenship and belonging nation-building inevitably involves social relations of difference. In particular, I will contend that in spite of, and indeed even through the commitment to human rights issues and justice, liberal multiculturalism performs to *secure* hegemonic nation-building endeavors in ways that re-entrench unequal relations of power. I will term this process 'multicultural securitization'.

Multicultural securitization refers to the ways in which liberal multiculturalism is intrinsically a theory and policy that is constitutive of security mechanisms. According to Michel Foucault (2007: 56), security mechanisms operate in tandem with and through legal–juridical mechanisms and disciplinary ones, but they are distinct in how they deal with normalization. Rather than starting with a norm and subsequently establishing what is normal and abnormal, security mechanisms perform by giving shape to what is deemed normal and abnormal and then bringing unfavorable norms in line with more favorable ones (Foucault 2007: 63). Accordingly, not unlike juridical–legal and disciplinary mechanisms, *technologies of security operate as processes of subject formation – creating, recreating, and delimiting corporeal and national difference.* Based on this definition, I approach security not primarily as danger, threat or an assault, but as a discourse of meaning-making. In particular, I consider the ways in which multiculturalism secures meanings about the nation and belonging.

My critique of the intertwined relationship between security and liberal multiculturalism might be understood from another angle. Philosophically, the idea of security as a first freedom or right is a fundamental component of the liberal tradition, which is, of course, the basis of liberal multiculturalism. This understanding of security as a right, as Wendy Brown notes, emerges through social contract ideas, 'in which we largely surrender to the state the power to protect our lives and our property ... [On this premise] the state [is] is founded on the promise to secure its members *against each other*' (1995: 111, emphasis added). In other words, the idea of security as a right and freedom is historically ingrained in liberal political theory as the need to be protected from each other – protected from internal enemies as well as external ones. In this understanding, the role of the state is to secure both the nation and the individuals' right to security. It is this link between security, liberal multiculturalism, the nation, and individual citizens that I explore through the concept of multicultural securitization.

In this chapter, I draw on the Canadian context to examine four interrelated ways in which multicultural securitization functions to secure dominant nation-building projects: those related to territory, identity, whiteness, and economic development. Canada is an interesting case not only because of its demographic diversity (which consists of dominant settlers, national minorities, and immigrants), but also because it is often cited as the ideal multicultural model. While it should not be assumed that security or multiculturalism (as a demographic fact, policy, ideology or process) operate in the same way across geopolitical contexts, my arguments may be applicable elsewhere. Ultimately I conclude that there are reasons to be suspicious of both multicultural discourses and security ones because, despite some of the political openings that arise from multiculturalism and the sense of safety that emerges from national security policies, these discourses are co-implicated in reiterating processes of normalization and Otherness that consolidate unequal relations of power. In light of my argument that multiculturalism cannot in fact go far enough in addressing issues of difference and social inequities because it is shaped by discourses of security, I conclude by briefly considering how issues of identity/difference politics might be approached beyond the scope of liberal multiculturalism.

Multiculturalism as Mechanism to Secure Nation-building

Securing Territory

Even before the events of September 11, 2001, liberal multiculturalism functioned to secure and legitimize the already-established colonially defined territorial borders of the Canadian nation in two key ways. First, liberal multiculturalism fostered the idea that the Canadian nation was legitimately co-founded by two European nations composed of the French and English. The 1971 policy on multiculturalism introduced by then Prime Minister Pierre Trudeau, was specifically deployed to diffuse Francophone nationalist aspirations because of anxieties that the nation would be split, a concern that continues to shape Canadian politics today. This concern was salient in the late 1960s and early 1970s because Quebec nationalists became increasingly organized at the provincial level under the leadership of René Lévesque. Fearing Quebec secession and the division of Canada's territory and people, Trudeau hoped to secure Quebec's place in the nation by recognizing the importance of *all* cultural differences, but without dismissing the privileges associated with being of French or English origin.

This recognition of all cultural differences, as articulated in the 1971 policy, had the effect of muting Quebec's distinctive cultural claims, at least temporarily and in some measure. The policy stated that there was a need to 'support all of Canada's cultures', 'assist all cultural groups to overcome the cultural barriers to full participation in Canadian society', 'promote creative encounters and interchange among all Canadian cultural groups in the interest of national unity', and 'assist immigrants in acquiring at least one of Canada's two official languages in order that they would become full participants in Canadian society.' The policy thus positioned multiculturalism within a bilingual framework as a way to lock Quebec's place in the Canadian nation. As such, the 1971 policy secured and further legitimated the colonially defined borders of the nation and the continued assumed superiority of the English and French, an assumption also reflected in the 1969 Official Languages Act which had formalized linguistic duality at the federal level. Himani Bannerji (2000: 92–7) describes this birth of multiculturalism as a continuation of the wars between the two colonial powers seeking to consolidate territorial and political control over Indigenous land.

Importantly, as Kymlicka (2007c: 70) has noted, as well as being driven by a national unity impulse, the 1971 multiculturalism policy was also informed by a human rights impulse, which was led by marginalized ethnic groups, especially Ukrainian Canadians. It is also the case that the policy was consistent with other liberation movements of the 1970s, such as the movement to legalize abortion and decriminalize homosexuality. Yet, the move towards liberal multiculturalism was also somewhat of a bribe to ethnic minorities who were making more demands on the state; the 1971 policy was a way to appease these ethnic minorities about the emphasis on bilingualism in Canada while also averting a national crisis about the security of Canadian boundaries, with the by-product of also securing

Canada's image as a more immigrant-friendly nation. Here then, the national unity and human rights impulse were co-produced.

The second way in which liberal multiculturalism discourse in Canada has been operationalized to secure the Canadian nation territorially is by sidelining and, paradoxically, simultaneously encompassing Indigenous claims. While the initial 1971 multiculturalism policy reduced Indigenous issues of sovereignty, nationhood, inherent rights, and land to cultural issues, the 1982 Canadian Charter of Rights and Freedoms recognized aboriginal rights and the multicultural heritage of Canada in two separate sections (section 25 and 27 respectively), and the 1988 Multiculturalism Act opened with a statement that Canada recognizes the rights of aboriginal peoples. The idea that Indigenous issues fall under the umbrella of multiculturalism is often reproduced in liberal multicultural theory, even though many Indigenous scholars have repeatedly made the argument that their claims about culture are about power, nation, and history rather than multicultural diversity (Alfred 1999, 2005; Coulthard 2007; Green 2000; Monture-Angus 1995, 2002). But liberal multiculturalism provides a way for the Canadian nation to further legitimate a nation premised on the expropriation of Indigenous land and the attempted eradication of Indigenous bodies and knowledge. In particular, the disjuncture between Indigenous ways of connecting to the *land* and state-interests in consolidating *territory* has established exclusive boundaries that are defined by dominant Eurocentric interests (Alfred 2005: 206).

Liberal multiculturalists (and others trying to secure the authority of the state) are not unaware of this colonial history. But since the very historical and contemporary (re)production of Canada as a nation that is based on European notions of 'territorial consolidation and rationalism' (Alfred 1995: 11) is a reminder of its shameful past, an alternate narrative is needed to redeem the nation; liberal multiculturalism serves as this alternative narrative. Groups marked as multicultural minorities are repeatedly positioned as symbols of redemption. One recent manifestation of this re-formed national narrative in Canada is the slew of apologies made to various historically marginalized groups. In 2005, the Canadian government formally apologized to Chinese Canadians who had been legally discriminated against in the late 1800s/early 1900s through a prohibitive head tax, to Italian Canadians who had been labeled as 'enemy aliens' and imprisoned during World War II, and to Ukrainian Canadians who suffered internment. In May 2008, an apology was made for the 1914 Komagata Maru incident in which 376 would-be migrants of mostly Indian origin were denied entry to Canada, and in June 2008 an apology was made to former students of 'Indian' residential schools who had been subject to sexual abuse and colonial tactics of forced assimilation. This shameful history is muted by the national claim that Canada is now multicultural and thus (supposedly) fair to minorities, effectively masking the ways in which the nation-state has gained legitimacy on terms set by settlers. As William Connolly (1995: xii) notes, 'the contemporary pluralist imagination, proclaimed as the guardian of diversity and generosity in social relations, remains haunted by ghosts it seeks to exorcise.'

The statement of apology made by Prime Minister Stephen Harper (Canada, 2008) to residential school survivors is especially telling. The apology was deeply meaningful to some Indigenous people, and indeed it is an important national symbolic gesture of recognition. But the apology also did not include an acknowledgment of the practices that have secured Crown land at the expense of Indigenous ways of living; rather, the apology was a way to narrate a supposed shift from the terrible past (forced assimilation) to the more ideal present (multiculturalism). Indeed, even while making the apology, the Conservative Canadian government (alongside New Zealand, Australia, and the US) refused to sign the UN Declaration on the Rights of Indigenous People because sections of it were deemed to be incompatible with, and potentially threatening to, Canada's constitutional framework. The double-speak of apology/multiculturalism and the denial of Indigenous land and rights operated on terms that did not threaten the sovereignty of the Canadian state.

Nation-building discourses like liberal multiculturalism operate to secure the idea that the Canadian state has a natural and legitimate legal right to define the borders of the nation, even though land was neither surrendered nor ceded by Indigenous peoples. Indeed various land and resource disputes between the Canadian state and Indigenous peoples continue today. This includes disputes involving the people of Tyendinaga (who blockaded the CN rail line and a major highway in April and June 2007 in protest of the lack of adequate drinking water, and because lands which comprise of the Culbertson Tract and Simcoe Deed have not been returned), the Tahltan First Nation (who blockaded Royal Dutch Shell's coal bed methane project in 2007), and the Secwepemc First Nation (who have had to set up road blocks since 2001 after a ski hill development was planned on traditional Indigenous land that has been used for hunting and medicinal plant gathering). Even as the Canadian government and various corporations seek to secure their claim to the land on the basis of liberal–capitalist principles of property and the free market, liberal multicultural discourses – whether deliberately or inadvertently – work to counter the vision of a racist nation.

Elizabeth Povinelli (1998: 581), who examines multiculturalism in the Australian context, rightly notes that upon such occasions 'Multiculturalism is represented as the externalized political testament both to the nation's aversion to its past misdeeds, and to it recovered good intentions.' In particular, she continues, the public purging of the past requires a new abstracted national imaginary; while the law and the state do not now require all citizens to go through the same type of corporeal cleansing that characterized the earlier relationship of colonizers to the Indigenous people, the imaginary of a nation defined by its welcoming borders – welcoming to the right sort of multicultural subjects – operates to solidify national identities and allegiances (Povinelli 1998: 581). Rather than displacing classic disciplinary liberal models of the state and citizenship, multiculturalism sanctions cultural difference, giving the state 'the right to discern when a social or cultural difference has ceased to function as a difference as such' (Povinelli 1998: 582).

The capacity of the state to regulate and decertify cultural difference through the discourse of multiculturalism specifically secures the legitimacy of the colonially defined borders of the nation, for while the state claims to be an open and just society it also continues to claim sovereignty over the land. This claim to state sovereignty is so normalized now for most Canadians that it seems to them absurd to question it. And new generations of 'multicultural' immigrants are invited by the state to be part of this nation-building project, fostering the idea of an open society, even while Indigenous issues get appropriated or ignored. Yet, justice is not possible until decolonization processes genuinely address Indigenous freedoms; until such time, multiculturalism will continue to be a tool to secure relations of power rooted in colonialism.

Securing National Identity

Related to the processes of securing the nation's territory are the processes of securing particular notions of national identity. In particular, two constructs of national identity dominate: first, that Canada is highly tolerant of diversity, and second, that it is a nation that benevolently gifts culturally different subjects (i.e. uncivilized, backward, and nonwhite Others) freedoms through the principle of diversity-within-unity. These constructs of national identity are sustained by and sustaining of the idea that Canada is sociologically multicultural, committed to the principle of multiculturalism, and even already ideally multicultural (Day 2000: 6). Despite the fact that governments have repeatedly attempted to corporeally and symbolically exterminate Indigenous and other modes of nonwhite difference, the identity that has been promoted of the Canadian nation is that of a naturally and objectively diverse nation (Day 2000: 4). But the myths of tolerance and diversity-within-unity are vehicles for securing existing historically established relations of power. Indeed, tolerance and diversity-within-unity both limit forms of difference, allowing only those that are permissible until such time as they too are deemed to be threatening to the nation, and keeping those as acceptable in line with national norms. The character of these norms has varied depending on whether the country is ideologically led by the Liberal Party or the Conservative Party of Canada, as well as other sociopolitical factors, but on the whole liberal multiculturalism has been deployed to present a particular national identity to those living in Canada and to the external international community.

In particular, while the identity of a tolerant nation is often repeated, the *scope* of toleration is more than often qualified. Following the arrests of the Toronto 17, for example, Prime Minister Stephen Harper stated that 'Canada's diversity, *properly nurtured*, is our greatest strength' (Mickleburgh 2006, emphasis added). Diversity is acceptable but has to be regulated, appropriate for whatever standards are deemed to be tolerable for the state – an agenda that is that crosses party lines. Harper goes on to say, 'They [the terrorists] hate open, diverse, democratic societies like ours, because they want the exact opposite ... [They want] societies that are closed, homogenous and dogmatic' (Mickleburgh 2006).

Canadian national identity is presented here as universally open, diverse and democratic, with the effect of erasing the human rights abuses of the Canadian state *within* the nation, such as those that have led to the indefinite detainment of five Muslim and Arab men who have been held under the Security Certificate Program and subjected to secret trials; and the effect of erasing human rights abuses of the Canadian state *outside* of the nation, such as the complicit and active role of Canadian officials in the detention and torture of prisoners in Afghanistan. Canada, it is regularly declared, is not racist, but tolerant.

But while multiculturalism is often equated with tolerance, tolerance is not an unproblematic value (Brown 2006). This not simply because there is in fact much *in*tolerance towards all sorts of gendered, class-based, sexual, religious, and bodily differences that deviate from the norms, but also because where an agent is empowered to be tolerant, he is also empowered to be intolerant (Hage 1998: 85). As Ghassan Hage argues, multicultural tolerance 'is a form of symbolic violence in which a mode of domination is presented as a form of egalitarianism' (1998: 87). It is a strategy aimed at reproducing and disguising relations of power, reinforcing the objectification and Otherness of that which is tolerated by the tolerator, and clouding elements of coercion by presenting tolerance as a generous gift.

Importantly, because the lines of toleration are constantly redrawn, representations of national identity are not static. On the contrary, meanings of national identity are always in movement. There are continued attempts to master meanings of national identity and fix them for sure, but the shifting circulation of meanings is also an important part of nation-building because such movement enables dominant members of the Canadian nation to claim that it has historically transitioned from a monocultural society to a multicultural one. As Foucault (2007: 65) reminds us, while the circulation of meanings takes place, the internal dangers of this circulation (in this case, danger posed by those who threaten dominant conceptions of Canadian identity) are canceled out through security mechanisms.

Liberal multiculturalism serves as one of these security mechanisms. This may not be the intent for some theorists and practioneers, but liberal multiculturalism provides a legitimated discourse to draw and redraw the lines of tolerance and also the relationship between unity and diversity. The relationship between unity and diversity is specifically determined by terms that seek to secure the authority of the state and liberal-defined individual rights. The role of the state in 'managing' (i.e. disciplining) diversity on terms that are deemed to be appropriate for securing a unified national identity is thereby a crucial feature of liberal multiculturalism. Indeed, liberal multiculturalism seeks to secure what Day refers to as 'a hegemonic articulation between a single nation and the state' (2000: 222). Even a commitment to diversity is bound with:

> [*a prevailing*] *set of presumptions about the terms of national security, the basis of gender difference, the normality of heterosexuality, the source and scope of rights, the monotheistic or monosecularist basis of morality, the*

> *shape of the economy, and the generic nature of justice, reason, identity, and nature (Connolly 1995: xiii–xiv).*

In other words, diversity itself is not free of power. But it is often presented as such by defenders of liberal multiculturalism, even though it is a value that gets molded into a liberal form – one that is grounded in the authority of the state – as if this liberal formation was natural.

The idea that liberalism entails an attempt to master difference is not only confusing because rights discourse can sometimes be generative of legal change, but it also makes liberal multiculturalists uncomfortable; consequently, the processes of normalization that are necessary to secure the social contract (between civil society and the state) tend to be couched in terms of choice or freedom. Though liberal multiculturalists contend that 'there is an important difference between coercively imposing liberalism and offering various incentives for liberal reforms' (Kymlicka 1995b: 168), there is no doubt that immigrants *should* integrate into the dominant (liberal) societal culture so as to secure national unity. As a committed liberal, Kymlicka (1995b: 78), for instance, cannot argue that strangers have to be kept out; rather he appeals to the strangers within the borders of the nation-state to take note of multicultural tolerance and accommodation, all the while defining the limits of multiculturalism by requiring a commitment to national unity.

The normative commitment to national unity is echoed in practice. Well before September 11, 2001, multicultural policy was positioned and re-positioned within the federal government structure according to the shifting terms of national identity. Under a Liberal government, the Department of Multiculturalism, which had been created under the 1988 Act, closed in 1993 and then was shifted to a new Department of Canadian Heritage. This new department amalgamated the Department of Multiculturalism, the Secretary of State, the Department of Fitness and Amateur Sport, the parks section of Environment Canada, and the cultural components of the Department of Communication (Abu-Laban and Gabriel 2002: 112). The significance of multiculturalism was effectively downgraded as the crisis of national disunity seemed to lessen.

Then again, under a Conservative government, in December 2008, the Multiculturalism Program (which includes Canada's Action Plan against Racism, Asian Heritage Month, Black History Month, Canadian Multiculturalism Day, and the Human Rights Program) was moved outside of Canadian Heritage to Citizenship and Immigration Canada (CIC). In the meantime, programs such as the Canadian Studies Program, A Roadmap for Canada's Linguistic Duality, Games of La Francophonie, Discovering Aboriginal Cultures, and a national creative and writing artwork contest remained under the domain of Canadian Heritage. This latest shift is especially noteworthy because rather than falling under the rubric of Canadian history and national identity, the multiculturalism program now falls under the domain of a department that is responsible for determining and securing the national character of its diverse citizenry by regulating who is welcomed into the borders of the nation. Among its responsibilities of helping Canadians and newcomers adapt to Canadian society, CIC (2008a) 'manages access to Canada to protect the security and health of Canadians and the integrity of Canadian laws.' Immigrants, foreign students, visitors, temporary workers, and newcomers are all identified as diverse groups who are encouraged to economically, socially and culturally 'integrate' into a set of pre-established norms, whereby integration is a condition through which the nation and its identity can be better secured. Articulated through the imperative to build 'a stronger Canada', multiculturalism is thereby officially linked to national security.

The notions of tolerance and diversity-within-unity are also central to Canada's first comprehensive national security policy, which is outlined in a 2004 document entitled, 'Securing an Open Society: Canada's National Security Policy' (SAOS). Alongside the creation of the An Integrated Threat Assessment Centre, National Security Advisory Council, and new Department of Public Safety and Emergency Preparedness, the national security policy entailed the creation of a Cross-Cultural Roundtable on Security (CCRS). The SAOS document specifies that the CCRS, which is to be comprised of members of ethno-cultural and religious communities from across Canada, 'will engage in a long-term dialogue to improve understanding on how to *manage security interests in a diverse society* and will provide advice to promote the protection of civil order, mutual respect and *common understanding* (Canada 2004: 13, emphasis added). Here, the philosophical commitment to diversity within unity is put into policy. Moreover, this document repeatedly makes specific reference to the relationship between national security and cultural diversity. For example, in the opening pages, it is stated that:

> [This document] articulates **core national security interests** and proposes a framework for addressing threats to Canadians. It does so in a way that fully reflects and supports **key Canadian values of democracy, human rights, respect for the rule of law, and pluralism** (Canada 2004: 4, **emphasis added**).

The creation of the CCRS, according to the Chair, Dr. Zaheer Lakhani, is specifically based on an inclusive multicultural model. In a presentation in May 2006, Dr. Lakhani states,

> It [the Roundtable] bought us together, 15 individuals, all volunteers, from diverse ethno-cultural and religious communities from across the country. While we may come from different backgrounds and different cultures, it is our commitment to human rights, to strong and safe communities, and to protecting Canada and Canadians from harm, that unites as a Roundtable. The diversity within our membership and the spectrum of opinions reflects the diversity and concerns of Canada's citizens. The Roundtable is part of a pluralistic process of consultation, collaboration, and learning (Lakhani 2006: 1).

The CCRS thereby not only seeks to secure the nation's identity by pointing to Canada's commitment to human rights, diversity, unity, and collaboration *and security*, but it also presents itself as a symbol of (diverse and unified) national identity.

The CCRS is also striking because it symbolizes an official link between security and liberal multicultural discourses. Indeed, attending the first meeting of the CCRS, and the several that followed, were not only those government officials that one would expect at a national security meeting – namely the Minister of Public Safety, the Minister of Justice and Attorney General, the National Security Advisor to the Prime Minister, Agency Heads for CSIS and the RCMP, the Vice-President of Canada Border Services Agency, but also the Minister of State for Multiculturalism and Deputy Ministers of Canadian Heritage. As a *formalized* agent of multicultural securitization, the CCRS is a symbol of the extent to which multiculturalism can openly be deployed for the purpose of securing state-led national interests. Echoing the explicit management role assigned to the state in liberal multicultural political theory, the CCRS is deployed to manage the supposed unruliness that arises from ethno-cultural Otherness. Through the CCRS the government can better regulate diversity on the basis of national security commitments, not simply by forcing a security agenda onto cultural Others but by inviting those marked as different to discipline other Others who question the value assigned to a cohesive Canadian national identity.

In sum, through the imaginings of toleration and diversity-within-unity, multicultural securitization functions so as to produce, discipline, and secure nationalist fantasies of an ideal unified multicultural and liberal-democratic identity. This process ultimately requires that diversity be performed, acknowledged, and displayed, and that it also remains contained in its 'proper' place.

Securing the White Nation

In the process of securing the identity of Canada as a tolerant nation which is committed to diversity-within-unity, nation-building practices have relied on historically generated distinctions between white and nonwhite bodies. Initially such distinctions were operationalized to secure an open colonial project, but now they are operationalized so as to represent and secure Canada's formal identity shift from monoculturalism to multiculturalism while simultaneously maintaining a set of Western Eurocentric norms rooted in colonial ideas. As such, rather than explicit racist policies of immigration and assimilation, multiculturalism is deployed to secure the dominance of whiteness, whether intentionally or not. By fulfilling the function of providing a relational difference between the Norm and Other, liberal multiculturalism provides a discourse to keep in check those subjects marked as (racially and ideologically) too different and potentially threatening to the nation. Since cultural Others (read: nonwhite Others) are blamed for national disunity, but overt racial exclusion is not consistent with the values of the 'new' nation, other mechanisms are needed to secure the limits of difference. One such mechanism is liberal multiculturalism.

The work of liberal multiculturalism as a security mechanism is often difficult to gage because it is masked over by a specific version of culture-talk. Unlike anthropological employments of culture in which the 'western' anthropologist studies 'non-western' places, liberal multiculturalists utilize culture in reference to non-western people who make claims within the boundaries of the 'west'. Culture is specifically deployed as a code for speaking of particular ethnic groups, historical nations and linguistic minorities outside the context of racialization (Dhamoon 2006, 2007). While a racial designation is consistently presupposed, the focus is on cultural lineage, heritage, and tradition without contextualizing the meanings given to these within various racialized orders, and without addressing how meanings of culture are produced by and productive of other modes of difference, such as those related to gendering, class, and disability. As David Scott (2003: 104) notes, culture has become 'the grid and horizon of difference. It becomes, so to speak, the commanding natural language of difference.' Indeed, as *the* horizon of difference in liberal multicultural politics, culture is a way to regulate nonwhite immigrants who deviate from nationally defined liberal norms, without adequate reference to the different global racialized histories of white supremacy that mark difference within Canada, and without a sufficient understanding of the interactive relationship between signifiers of culture, race, religion, gender, class, dis/ability, and sexuality.

The status of culture is specifically linked to liberalism by converting the communal dimension of culture to universalistic principles of rights and recognition. In other words, by claiming the concept of culture (in the form of the Othered who needs liberalizing or recognizing) liberal multiculturalists are able to regulate it. This regulation of culture functions in ways that reiterate white privilege, especially in a time when cultures are depicted as civilizations that are clashing. Even anti-racist versions of multiculturalism tend to essentialize differences between groups, over-emphasize the contact thesis (whereby nonwhites are expected to share their stories while whites listen and express their horror and guilt), and individualize racism as a problem of knowledge rather than a problem about systemic white privilege (Srivastava 2007). Certainly those marked as non-western subjects may well find multiculturalism a positive venue for articulating social and political inequities, but for many mainstream white westerners multiculturalism is a way to experience palatable forms of Otherness.

Meanings and degrees of Otherness have of course varied. Donald Avery's (1979) study of Eastern, Central and Southern European immigrants in Canada during 1896 and 1931 demonstrates that while initially groups such as the Germans, Ukrainians, Italians, Hungarians, and Bulgarians were 'candidates for Canadianization' (in contrast to Blacks and Asians), they were also marked as foreigners because they were 'persons thought to lie outside the country's Anglo-Saxon Protestant and French Canadian Roman Catholic communities' (Avery 1979: 14). When WWI broke out, national fear of the *dangerous* foreigner was fuelled by international fears of Bolshevik-type activity and the 'Red Scare' (i.e. communism) which threatened Canadian norms of industry, the family, and ownership of personal property. To deal with these dangerous foreigners, the Dominion (federal) government adopted guidelines and the 1914 War Measures Act to deal with 'enemy alien residents'. This act enabled the federal government to legally suspend individuals rights such that 'the suspension of rights appears not as violence but as the law itself' (Razack 2007: 8).

Representations of Central, Eastern and Southern European ethnic groups have changed over time: through dominant lenses they have been constructed as manipulating foreigners, dangerous foreigners, deprived working class migrants, and they are not now viewed as a threat to national identity but contributors to the nation's national history (although they may well still face marginalization depending on such factors as accent or length of time in Canada). Despite these shifts, what is striking is a historical pattern that emerges about national identity in which there is a constant preference for whiteness, however historically defined. By whiteness I do not mean simply white bodies, although clearly white men and women perform and constitute relations of domination. Rather, in the Canadian context whiteness operates as a national fantasy that materializes in some of the following ways: an express privilege for certain European languages, in this case English and French whereby accent and race matter as much as linguistic fluency; a specific set of liberal ideological values, as opposed, say, to socialist values; a system of free enterprise, in which the ideal worker is an able-bodied male worker who contributes to the growth of the national economy and its infrastructure; and the political status quo, namely the existing structures, policies and laws of industry and the state.

Liberal multiculturalism is operationalized in such a way as to secure these kinds of technologies of whiteness. Recall that even before the events of September 11, Canadian multiculturalism was framed in the context of bilingualism and biculturalism, both in theory and policy, hence maintaining the privilege of the English and French. This focus on language and culture rather than racialization and racism or the relationship between these signifiers of difference effectively masks over and indeed legitimizes what Hage (1998) calls the fantasies of white supremacy in a multicultural society.

While Hage's (1998: 28) analysis focuses on Australia, it is pertinent to the Canadian context because Canadian nationalist practices also assume an image of a white national space, an image of the nationalist as master of this space, and an image of the ethnic Other as mere object within this space. This is regardless of whether nationalist practices are advanced by neo-Nazi groups or multiculturalists, for nationalism has many degrees. The role of the white nationalist, Hage argues, is to spatially manage the white nation and act as guardian of diversity and the dominant national white order. The role of manager and guardian is especially important in securing 'the national home', a home that is structured around 'themes of familiarity, security, and community' (Hage 1998: 40), because various forms of Otherness are deemed to be behind the potential loss of the national fantasy of a white home. While this threat is clearly evident in the case of explicit racist practices of nationalism, Hage demonstrates that nationalism is also central to what he refers to as white multiculturalism, in that in both instances 'Aboriginal people and non-white "ethnics" are merely national objects to be moved or removed according to a White national will.' Even though liberal multiculturalism is scripted as a gift from white Europeans to nonwhite subjects, it is in fact a tool to 'infuse a sense of security among White[s]' (Hage 1998: 235).

Indeed, the discourse of liberal multiculturalism adds to the nationalist pride of some Canadians, including Kymlicka. In an article published entitled 'Being Canadian' (2003), Kymlicka contends that as a secular, constitutional liberal democracy (with a market economy and a welfare state), Canada is an exceptional country. The distinctiveness of Canada, he claims, lies in the symbolic and constitutional accommodation of diversity. He states: '[that] this model of economics and politics should be adopted is completely undisputed in Canada. Few Canadians doubt that this model is the recipe for a successful country, and most would applaud the adoption of this model elsewhere' (2003: 361). Kymlicka (2003: 380) continues by acknowledging that there is not always a strong sense of one unified Canadian identity, but despite this, be continues to assert that '[e]ven people who lack a feeling of Canadian identity can see the international benefits that flow from being recognized as Canadian.' While I am sensitive to Kymlicka's nationalist pride, his characterization of Canada masks over histories of racism and resistance against assimilation and discrimination, as well as the continuing practices of nation-building that secure white privilege by presenting cultural diversity as a generous gift to nonwhite Others.

The narrative of the white nation gifting its culturally diverse subjects is further troubling because it suggests that multicultural policies and theories are *responsible* for creating cultural diversity! Yet, with or without multiculturalism (of whatever breed), cultural, ethnic, religious, linguistic, and national differences would exist in Canada – not just demographically but also in terms of how government would secure the nation, and how people live, work, socialize, and enter personal and familial relationships. 'There would still be an irremovable cultural diversity,' says Hage, '[and] there would still be the need to recognize and govern this cultural diversity' (1998: 238). But Canadian nation-building works in part through the idea that white people can *give* cultural diversity to the already culturally diverse. This 'giving', and the simultaneous demand for regulated integration, indicates that in fact it may be those who are invested in securing the white national fantasy, rather than those marked as being culturally too different, who may need multiculturalism. Indeed, the Canadian government quite openly notes that multiculturalism is not only for those ethnic and cultural minorities who are 'different', but also for 'true Canadians':

> *Multiculturalism ensures that all citizens can keep their identities, can take pride in their ancestry and have a sense of belonging. Acceptance gives Canadians a feeling of security and self-confidence, making them open to, and accepting of, diverse cultures (CIC 2008c).*

Thus multiculturalism is not just a tool to secure the management of unruly Others, but also a tool to secure those 'real Canadians', namely mainstream white Canadians.

These racialized distinctions have the effect of more firmly securing some modalities of belonging and citizenship while defining others as contrary to the white nation. Liberal multiculturalism can specifically have the effect of erecting distinctions between the undesirable and desirable cultural (i.e. nonwhite) Other. The undesirable nonwhite subject is one who substantively deviates from the construct of the ideal white, heterosexual, male able-bodied worker-citizen, and who questions and therefore supposedly threatens the pre-existing terms of integration. The more desirable nonwhite Other is one who can mostly conform/integrate to the existing national norms in ways that do not fundamentally change the status quo, which includes the privilege of whiteness and its associated values. While recent Conservative government (and also past and current Liberal Party) statements explicitly indicate that immigrants are required to quickly conform to 'our' values, and liberal multiculturalists in political theory argue that the process of 'integration' may take some time and cannot be imposed, in both instances conformity is ultimately expected. In the meantime, some deviancy from the norm is deemed to be acceptable and indeed even necessary when it is in the interests of the nation (e.g. to define the nation as tolerant).

Yet subjects marked as multicultural Others must explicitly prove their loyalty to the white nation in order to be worthy of belonging; this is especially the case if the nonwhite subject is a refugee or temporary worker. The same proof of loyalty to the nation is not required of mainstream white Canadians. Indeed, after September 11, 2001 there were repeated warnings about a common enemy who could be lurking among our midst, and who should be condemned unconditionally, regardless of the human rights violations this might entail. Condemnation-without-conditions meant that the imperialistic impulses of Canada and other western nations could not be criticized – you were either with 'us' or against 'us'. This kind of nationalist pride not only exhibited itself with the 2007 birth of white supremacist groups like the Alberta-based Aryan Guard who has campaigned against immigration and multiculturalism, but is also evident in mainstream media with the likes of Margaret Wente, a writer for the 'Opinions' section of the *Globe and Mail* national newspaper, who regularly writes about the dangers of too much diversity

Even where there is support for multicultural policies, there are norms that constitute belonging in the white nation. Sedaf Arat-Koc has noted, for example, that anti-imperial Muslim feminists in Canada have been cast as bad subjects because they criticize Canada's and US foreign policy, because they do not fit the more suitable mould of liberal feminism (a brand of feminism that seeks moderate rather than fundamental social change), and because they do not conform to the essentialized image of a culturally oppressed woman. The exclusions of national belonging are evident specifically with the rise of Islamophobia, the assault on the basic civil liberties of many Muslims and Arabs, and the heightened state of surveillance (Arat-Koc 2005: 203).

What is striking to note is that even while there is sometimes movement between constructs of the good and bad multicultural subject, the privilege of whiteness remains centred – always determining the conditions of belonging and citizenship. All the while, the insecurities that Muslims, Arabs and other vulnerable groups experience are judged according to how well they coincide with a national security agenda. And the state of *in*security about white norms – an insecurity framed as the unruliness of nonwhite subjects – merely gives credibility to the notion that multiculturalism can be deployed to secure the requirement of 'more integration'. The events of September 11 have served to give credence to this demand for more integration, especially because the existing boundaries of a white national identity and the associated terms of belonging have been confirmed along civilizational lines (Arat-Koc 2005). While this reconfiguration of national identity could be understood as a retreat from multiculturalism, Sedaf Arat-Koc (2005: 32) rightly argues that it in fact represents 'a crystallization of certain inequalities, as well as inherent ambiguities and tensions, present in liberal multiculturalism even in the best of times.' The renewal of Canadian nationalism has been particularly fuelled by the idea that Canada needs to be more patriotic rather than ambivalent and tolerant. On this basis, those of Arab and Muslim descent (and others deemed to be potentially dangerous nonwhite Others) are constantly reminded that the gift of belonging to the nation can be taken away, for 'their' kind have demonstrated that they cannot be fully trusted (a sentiment that replayed itself again and again after the arrests of the Toronto 17). In short, September 11, 2001 provided a catalyst for solidifying the pre-existing idea that there were real Canadians (i.e. those marked as white, western, Europeans), and then those Other-Canadians (i.e. nonwhites of non-western, non-European origin).

It is important to note that this fantasy of the white nation which benevolently extends tolerance to Others is not just a post-9/11 desire. The mechanisms of multicultural securitization have been deployed to secure versions of belonging and citizenship in ways that have historically privileged a conception of the white nation. For instance, since the bombing of Air India Flight 182 in 1985 by suspected and confirmed Sikh nationalists who wanted a separate homeland for Sikhs in India, there has been a racist backlash against Sikhs. This has been particularly the case with Sikh men who wear turbans, and who have, in the post September 11 context, also been scripted as Muslim terrorists. Simultaneously, some Sikhs, such as Member of Parliament Ujjal Dosanjh (who does not wear a turban) are mounted as model multicultural minorities when they participate in the norms of the white nation. In particular, the model minority is the nonwhite Other who unquestioningly accepts the benevolence the state, and who is also well-educated, fluently English-speaking, upwardly mobile, and a contributor to the economy. Yet the model multicultural minority remains 'the minority', always defined as the Other in relation to those standards of whiteness that secure Eurocentric liberal values of economic exceptionalism, industry, and reason (Arneil 2004).

Securing the National Economy

Whereas political theorists tend to approach liberal multiculturalism either as an instrumental resource for individual development and self-realization (Kymlicka 1995b: 83) or as a resource that foregrounds the intrinsic value of cultural recognition (Taylor 1985: 136, 1992: 34), in political practice liberal multiculturalism is treated as a resource that can be and is owned by individuals, groups, and the state. While maintaining some social justice aspects, liberal multicultural policies have entered the business of what Yasmeen Abu-Laban and Christina Gabriel (2002) call 'selling diversity', and George Yúdice (2003) calls 'cultural economy'. As such, liberal multiculturalism not only helps to the secure the nation's cultural and social capital but it also helps to secure economic capital – it is a national property, to be produced, exchanged, bartered, and reproduced. In short, liberal multiculturalism works to secure the nation's place in the global economy. This is not, in my view, just an effect of the imperfect practice of multiculturalism, but an intrinsic feature of liberal multiculturalism because of the ways in which liberal principles of freedom and individualism are operationalized in terms of free market enterprise and competition. Certainly some liberal multicultural theorists are concerned with redistributive justice, but even these theories tend to assume that the social and economic success of immigrants depends on how well they integrate into the existing economic structure.

While the policy of multiculturalism in Canada did not initially emphasize the business value of diversity, even before September 11, 2001 there was a shift towards this direction (Abu-Laban and Gabriel 2002: 105–24). Large banks and corporations (such as airlines) operationalized the discourse of multiculturalism for marketing reasons, hiring front-line staff who spoke Hindi, Punjabi, Cantonese, Mandarin, and Japanese so as to secure a customer-base. Abu-Laban and Gabriel (2002: 116) note that the emphasis on selling diversity has explicitly run through government policies since the 1980s, with repeated notions of 'multiculturalism means business', 'the competitive advantage of a multiculturalism', and the need to link 'diversity to corporate strategies'. For example, a major conference supported by the federal government was organized in 1986 on the theme of 'Multiculturalism means Business'; in 1995 the government initiated and, since then, has funded the Metropolis Canada Program which fosters an international network for comparative research and public policy development on migration, diversity and immigrant integration in Canada and around the world, including economic and labour market integration (as well as justice, policing and security); and in May 2007, the Canadian government launched the Foreign Credentials Referral Office, with funding of over $1.2 million (Canadian) so as to 'help individuals selected under the federal skilled worker category to understand the requirements of the labour marker in Canada' (CIC, 2008b). Again, these initiatives cut across party lines.

Moreover, while migration from diverse countries is a significant feature of Canadian immigration policy and repeatedly presented as proof of the nation's multicultural commitment, there is a preference for applicants who apply under the business/independent class rather than the family class (Abu-Laban 1998: 73–8). The point system of immigration specifically works in tandem with the idea that particular kinds of multicultural subjects are necessary for securing economic growth, namely those who are able-bodied workers. More specifically, in a neo-liberal climate that values market citizenship rather than social citizenship, immigration selection since the 1980s 'has increasingly focused on attracting self-sufficient immigrants who can pay the costs of their own integration and contribute to Canada's global competitiveness' (Abu-Laban 2004: 22). The consequence, as Abu-Laban notes, has been diminished rights for those already in Canada and diminished opportunities for would-be citizens to immigrate. This is especially the case because multicultural policy fosters a business model that seeks to secure international trade links and global competitiveness at the expense of dealing with gender and class inequities (Abu-Laban and Gabriel 2002: 124).

At times, the desire to have an open border for the purposes of market multiculturalism might appear contrary to national security concerns. There have been, for example, renewed calls for increased security at the Canada–US border, and a simultaneous desire for more flexible and open trading borders. Tighter security measures at the border have been pushed not only internally, but also by Americans who see Canada as a country with lax immigration laws and a safe haven for terrorists; and yet, as a result of the Free Trade Agreement and the North American Free Trade Agreement, Canada relies on an open border with its major trading partner, the US (Abu-Laban 2004: 25). Despite this seeming tension between the desire for heightened security and open borders, multicultural securitization operates to secure a state-led economic agenda. This is alongside other government market-driven policies, such as the Security and Prosperity Partnership Agreement, which allows for free corporate access across borders through economic integration of Mexico, the US and Canada, while establishing a security perimeter that tightens borders to the movement of people.

In the current era, this economic dimension of liberal multiculturalism is openly featured in government policy. In a November 13, 2008 speech to the Canadian Club, for example, Jason Kenny, the Minister of Citizenship, Immigration and Multiculturalism, not only promoted the fantasy that Canada's national identity has always been celebratory of its diversity, but he also signaled how multiculturalism secures the legitimacy of the two-founding nations narrative, the image of Canada as a universally tolerant and diverse nation, and the government's agenda for economic growth. It is worth quoting at length an excerpt of his speech:

> we all want a multiculturalism that builds bridges, not walls, between communities. We want a Canada where we can celebrate our different cultural traditions, but not at the expense of sharing common Canadian traditions. We don't want a country that is a hotel, where people come and go with no abiding connection to our past or to one another, where citizenship means only access of a convenient passport. We want a Canada where we are citizens loyal first and finally to this country and her historically grounded values.

The key to building such a Canada, to maintaining our model of unity-in-diversity, is the successful integration of newcomers. And that should be the focus of today's multiculturalism. Integration that empowers newcomers by ensuring that they can speak one or both of our languages. Integration that opens the doors of economic opportunity by properly recognizing the skills, experience, and education of new Canadians (Kenney 2008).

The themes of diversity-within-unity, integration into existing norms, and economic development are repeated. Kenney goes on to openly define multicultural minorities as commodities – whether they are already in Canada or potential migrants – necessary to secure the economic growth of the nation according to market demands. As such, the success of the multiculturalism is rooted in its capacity to secure political, sociocultural, and economic integration. Even while the federal government continues to drastically reduce funding to its multiculturalism program, liberal multiculturalism continues to be globally touted as a mechanism to secure business and trade.

Conclusion

Processes of multicultural securitization ultimately secure hegemonic nation-building projects by codifying and regulating modalities and degrees of difference. These processes do not, of course, work alone, but instead function through various productive and disciplinary forces of power. Nonetheless, as a distinctive set of processes that make meanings about the nation and subjectivity, multicultural securitization legitimates colonially defined borders, promotes national identity claims of tolerance and diversity without adequately scrutinizing the demand for unity and eventual conformity, fosters the fantasy of a white nation, and provides a venue for capitalism to expand its reach even further. In short, processes of multicultural securitization consolidate existing relations of power and create new hierarchies of difference. The problem with multiculturalism is therefore not that it breeds terrorism (the conservative perspective) or that it has not been adequately applied (the liberal multicultural perspective), but that it cannot go far enough in addressing issues of power.

To be sure, the theoretical and policy-oriented discourse of liberal multiculturalism has opened up ways to articulate claims of culture, but on its own this interpretation fails to account for the ways in which security mechanisms function. While there are openings that are created by liberal multiculturalism both for state agencies and marginalized populations, there are also always counter disciplinary and normalizing rationalities at play. These rationalities constantly modify the shape of nation-building, but the general principles and terms of nation-building continue to be structured by historically constituted relations of power, with the effect of consolidating and freezing particular configurations of difference. In different moments of history, particular kinds of Otherness are welcomed while others are rejected and/or disciplined, but differences are evaluated, re-evaluated, positioned and re-positioned according to how well they serve nation-building projects, projects that are constituted by asymmetrical relations of power. Coco Fusco (1989) sums up when he says:

> We welcome you, but first we must fingerprint you, interrogate you, probe you, scope you ... We exempt you, we absolve you, we exonerate you, but only if you qualify for our benevolence ... We forgive you, but first we must certify you, standardize you, normalize you, merge you, melt you, validate you, authenticate you, assimilate you.

In light of my critique of liberal multiculturalism, let me conclude with some brief remarks on how to then navigate the politics of identity/difference. Overall, I do not think that liberal multiculturalism is a policy, practice, ideology, or normative position that can be simply dismissed. In places like Canada, the discourse of multiculturalism can affect how people experience subjectivity and subjection – whether as a result of positive or negative encounters. No matter who we are, as Bannerji (2000: 120) notes, we get drawn into the 'belly of the beast'. This is because liberal multiculturalism is a living site of struggle, a mode of articulation of social relations and state authority, rather than an entity to be simply dismissed.

As a site of struggle, I suggest two interrelated directions for responding to issues of difference. First, alternative counter practices and discourses are necessary, ones that challenge the dominance of liberal multicultural interpretations of difference. Counter-hegemonic discourses are intrinsic to pluralistic visions of society, and yet, while proponents of liberal multicultural claim to be committed to pluralism there is a persistent refusal to see difference through any other lens. This is a sign of arrogance in my view, one that repeats the mantra that liberalism has a monopoly over difference, that defeats the possibilities that can arise from genuine pluralism, and that limits the possibilities of sociopolitical change. Accordingly, it is important to develop counter-hegemonic discourses and support those that already exist, namely those that exist in the work of anti-racist feminists, anti-colonialists, anarchists, anti-poverty activists, and so on. The focus for existing counter-hegemonic movements is not on the imperative of securing cultural recognition from the state, but on securing gender or disability or sexual rights, a life without violence, adequate and safe housing, equitable employment and wages, safe working conditions, mobility, access to education. Intellectual and practical support is needed for these concrete struggles that directly affect people's living conditions. While it may be the case that those committed to liberal multiculturalism may support such endeavors, the lens of this approach is overly determined by the agenda of state (i.e. the governance of difference) and therefore bound to hegemonic projects of nation-building. Accordingly, even when a liberal multicultural approach is adopted, a critical eye is needed about its disciplinary aspects.

The second way in which to respond to issues of difference is to disrupt those processes of subject formation that secure asymmetrical relations of power. This is necessary of not only dominant processes but also marginalized ones, for none are free of power. When scholars and practioneers centre power as the site of struggle and the site of transformation, rather than cultural diversity, they disrupt the boundaries of liberal multiculturalism and the associated power dynamics of state and nation-building. Moreover, disruption of these vehicles of power opens up the possibility of constituting difference in alternate ways (Dhamoon 2009). It is this disruption of the mechanisms of power that holds the potential to radically shift sociopolitical inequities.[1]

---

1   My thanks go to William Dyck, Emily Moore, Olena Hankivsky, and Duncan Ivison for their insightful comments and thoughts about the ideas in this chapter. Thanks also to two research assistants, Peter Gill and Tim Yessilbayev, for their careful work on Canadian government policies related to security and multiculturalism.

Master Kong *versus* Master Mo: Two Views of Cosmopolitanism and Multiculturalism in the Early Chinese Philosophical Tradition

Jeffrey Riegel

The purpose of this chapter is to explore and explain concepts of cultural difference found in two texts of a philosophical nature that survive from the early period of the Chinese philosophical tradition: Confucius's *Analects* (parts of which are as early as the *c.*fifth century BCE) and the *Mozi* (*c.*fourth century to third century BCE). Basic questions that this essay strives to answer are how the familiar and the foreign are defined in these two sources and what implications these definitions have for early theories of ethical responsibility, strategies for creating social cohesion, and taxonomies of local systems of values and practices.

The term 'cosmopolitanism' appears in the title because it will be shown that both the *Analects* and the *Mozi* are concerned with transcending narrow and particularistic affiliations in favor of concerns and loyalties that are broader and more comprehensive in scope. What is perhaps surprising is the conceptual gulf that separates them and leads them to argue over whose affiliations are narrow and what accounts for their narrowness, the techniques and policies required to overcome or transform parochialism, and the identity of those who must be embraced in order to demonstrate a genuinely broad understanding of others.

Of the two texts, the *Mozi*, perhaps because it is later in date than the *Analects*, reflects – admittedly somewhat dimly – an awareness that what we now know as China and its more immediate neighbors consisted of a multiplicity and diversity of cultural traditions. Though this diversity of customs is noted in the *Mozi* as part of an argument of primary relevance to the cultural context in which the text was written, because the text appears at the same time to be interested in cultural difference for its own sake, it is tempting to view the *Mozi* as an early advocate of 'multiculturalism.'[1] But rather than measure either ancient Chinese source against alien concepts and ideals, this essay is primarily concerned with exploring the language and discourse they employ for differentiating the foreign and the familiar.

The Teachings of Confucius (Traditional Dates 551–479 BCE)[2]

Perhaps the biggest intellectual challenge faced in the centuries before the founding of the first imperial dynasty in 221 BCE, was how to establish viable governance and a stable society in times so turbulent that the very fabric of life appeared to be coming apart. At one point in his *Analects* or 'selected teachings,' Master Kong – better known in the West by versions of his Latinized title and surname, Confucius – volunteers that the path he follows for bringing about good government and harmonious social relations does not involve 'inventing anything new' but relies instead on 'transmitting what he was taught' (*Lunyu* 7.1).[3] In another passage Confucius characterizes his way of transmitting what he has learned as one in which he 'reanimates the past' and he claims that he does so in order to 'gain knowledge of the new' (*Lunyu* 2.11).[4] For Confucius, breathing life into the inanimate past is essential groundwork for any understanding of how to face challenges yet to come.

But Master Kong had a particular past in mind when he made this claim about the origins of the path he would have others follow. Of foremost importance for him were the ceremonies, customs, and models of behavior handed down in his native state of Lu from the defunct royal Zhou dynasty. Commenting on how the Zhou had surveyed the two dynasties that preceded it – the Xia and the Shang

---

1   For a good summary of the relative differences between cosmopolitanism and multiculturalism, see Donald (2007).

2   There are several good translations of the *Lunyu* or *Analects of Confucius*, the canonical collection of the Master's sayings. Those by Arthur Waley (1989) and D.C. Lau (1992) are still regarded as standard and reliable interpretations. For an introductory overview of Confucius's life and thought, see Riegel (2006). The bibliography provided there is a starting point for exploring studies that are far more detailed and comprehensive. For readers of Chinese, the new annotated version of the *Analects* by Li Ling (2007) is highly recommended.

3   It can be argued that Confucius invented or at least significantly contributed to the prominence of the idea of the past as precedent and of 'the way of the Ancients' as worthy of careful study and emulation. Be that as it may, his invoking of the past in this *Lunyu* passage and other similar gestures he makes elsewhere are part of the reason Confucius came to be regarded by later generations of historians and historiographers as both their direct ancestor and an early master of their arts.

4   The sages of the early Chinese philosophical tradition were expected to be seers capable of predicting the future and advisers who could offer counsel on the proper preparations for the unknown that only they could glimpse.

– and had developed culture that far exceeded theirs in richness, Confucius proclaimed: 'I follow Zhou!' (*Lunyu* 3.14). It is arguable that the intellectual and political contexts in which Master Kong made this statement were ones in which not only the definition of the past but also its very relevance were being fiercely challenged and questioned by those who advocated a broader and more modern basis for creating good government and a peaceful and prosperous society.

It is not possible within the scope of the present chapter to mention all of the important concepts that figure in the Zhou pathway trod by Confucius and those who followed in his footsteps. For my present purposes I will highlight only one: the formulation of how ethical values are identified, learned, and practiced. Central to all ethical teachings found in the *Analects* is the notion that the social arena in which the tools for creating and maintaining harmonious relations are fashioned and employed is the extended family. Among the various ways in which social divisions could have been drawn, the most important were the vertical lines that bounded multigenerational lineages. And the most fundamental lessons to be learned by individuals within their lineages was what role their generational position had put them in and what obligations to those more senior or more junior than they flowed from those roles.

The system of moral obligations that derives from this way of dividing society can be called, for want of a better term, 'vertical ethics.' In the world of the *Analects*, such a system means that the dynamics of social exchange and obligation primarily involve movement up and down along familial roles that are defined in terms of how they relate to others within the same lineage. For example, in the *Analects*, the terms *xiao* and *di* refer, respectively, not only to positions of subordination to one's parents and one's older brothers, they also signify the obligation of those in such subordinated positions to treat their parents and older brothers with respect. If I occupy a position in the generation between my parents and my children, I am obliged to act with filial piety toward my parents and I am entitled to have my children treat me with similar piety and even greater piety toward my parents, i.e., their grandparents. My obligations towards my parents do not end when they die. Indeed my piety toward them should be even more manifestly intense after their deaths when I mourn and bury them.[5] A particularly controversial practice supported by Confucius and his followers was that children mourn their dead parents into the third year after their death, i.e. for at least twenty-five months (*Lunyu* 17.21).[6]

Needless to say, it was necessary for everyone to play roles within other social structures – a neighborhood, community, political bureaucracy, guild, or school of thought for example – that brought one into contact with a much larger network of acquaintances and created ethical issues that went beyond those that had an impact on one's family. But the extended family was, at the very least, regarded as a microcosm of those other social structures and the moral values that one learned within the family were thought of as essential foundations for

---

5   Book II of the *Analects* devotes several passages to the proper treatment of parents.
6   See also *Lunyu* 1.11, 4.20, and 14.40.

knowing the right way to act outside the family. Thus Master Yu, who figures as a prominent disciple in the opening book of the *Analects*, says that those who are *xiao* and *di*, i.e. behave respectfully toward parents and brothers, 'rarely show a liking for transgression against their superiors' and that those who are not disposed to transgression 'never start a rebellion' (*Lunyu* 1.2). In this account Mao Zedong would be judged as someone who must have behaved abominably toward his elders. And in antiquity it appears that guarding against those who might be rebellious was also a great problem. It was a commonplace in the age of Confucius for rulers to insist that their subjects and comrades-in-arms swear blood oaths to which the most powerful gods were called to witness in order to guarantee the faithful execution of their promises. Even within the narrow structure of the family there might be problems. Someone points out to Confucius that in his community an 'honest body' is someone who reports even the minor crimes of his father. Confucius rejects this and says that in his community honesty can encompass a son shielding his father and a father his son (*Lunyu* 13.18). The reciprocity involved seemed to justify such nepotism in Confucius's eyes; others have viewed it as a weakness in an ethical system so dependent on hierarchical relationships.[7]

But Master Yu is so inspired by what he regards as the untroubled movement from faithful son or younger brother to loyal subject he coins a metaphor that will serve well the conception of 'vertical ethics' being offered here: 'The gentleman devotes his efforts to the trunk. When the trunk is well-established the way sprouts. As for *xiao* and *di*, are they not the trunk of Goodness?' It is worth emphasizing that the extended family was at the center of other structures, that these structures were parallel to the family in that they too consisted of hierarchical layers organized along a vertical continuum of obligation and entitlement, and that the boundaries between them were permeable so that values practiced in one structure, e.g. the extended family, were transferable to another such as a state's bureaucratic apparatus. It would not be far wrong to imagine that the lineage was one of many nested into the community and the latter, along with others, was nested into the state. One who behaved morally in all possible parallel structures that extended outwards from the family probably approximated Confucius's conception of *ren* or 'Goodness,' an achievement granted to the very few in the teachings of Confucius. All of the forms of moral obligations mentioned in the *Analects* were thought to operate within these nested silos of vertical relations, though the base of each could be quite broad; the lower levels of the state encompassed its entire population.

It is instructive to pursue exactly how moral obligations were thought to operate for Confucius and his followers for this will help us understand their nature and scope. Here is a famous example from the *Analects*. The 'one thread' that Confucius says runs through his philosophy is identified by the prominent disciple Zengzi as the complementary pair: *zhongshu* 'loyalty and sympathy'

---

7   Li Ling (2007) complains that Confucius's putting family first accounts for China's legacy of corruption (241).

(*Lunyu* 4.15). Loyalty in this context refers to maintaining one's integrity by meeting the expectations of one's community. Elaboration is provided in another of Confucius's sayings: 'A ruler should be a ruler, a subject a subject, a father a father, and a son a son (*Lunyu* 12.11). Those who are loyal fully embrace their roles as those roles are defined by their communities; loyalty resides not in being true to people but to customary expectations. This requires a constant vigilance of the self, measuring one's acts and intentions against the benchmarks set by tradition and custom, no matter whether one is in a superior or a subordinate position.

'Sympathy,' on the other hand, focuses one's attention away from oneself and one's role toward the situation of others. Confucius defines the term in its other appearance in the *Analects*, when he is asked by another disciple Zigong whether there is one lesson that might last a lifetime: 'It is surely that of sympathy. What you yourself do not desire, do not impose on others.' This definition – recognizable of course as a version of 'the Golden Rule' – means that we should understand sympathy as the act of assessing the desires of others and not imposing on them what they do not want. The sympathy called for is clearly one that involves the acts of superior towards their subordinates. It is the sympathy of fathers for their sons and rulers for their subjects. In combination with such 'sympathy,' 'loyalty' seems to refer to the need of those in a superior role to ensure that they are adhering to the strict definition of that role without succumbing to feelings of pride with regard to their position and place. Indeed it is the exercise of sympathy that can remind those in power of the consequences of their acts for those they govern. By the same token, loyalty inhibits those in power from merely indulging their feelings of compassion without reference to the standards set by community and tradition.

Herbert Fingarette quite rightly observes of Confucius's formulation of *zhongshu* that it was designed to make human society not only possible but also humane (Fingarette 1979: 392). But it is worth remembering that Confucius was not speaking of all of human society. He did not mean *zhongshu* as a universal imperative but rather as an ethic that operated within a community that adhered to particular definitions of superior and subordinate. Confucius was speaking of the ruler of a state like his own state of Lu who should embrace the role of ruler in order to preserve the institution intact while at the same time responding compassionately to the needs of his population. But there is nothing in this program that suggests that the definition of a ruler involved obligations that embraced the populations of other states, let alone the people who were entirely outside the landscape of Confucius's experience. Indeed this conception of 'vertical ethics' appears to make little or no room for the problems of moral obligation affecting people of equal or similar rank within a single vertical structure or for the issues related to crossing the impermeable vertical boundaries that separate, for example, one extended family from another or one state from another. Perhaps Confucius and his followers regarded the boundaries as genuinely impermeable and so questions related to them of no practical concern. Others who came after Confucius would, however, challenge such a perspective.

Confucius's proclamation 'I follow Zhou!' was not only confirmation that Master Kong based his teachings on earlier precedents; it was also an affirmation of the superiority of the practices of his native Lu.[8] Other states might have been the repositories of different ritual legacies – the state of Song, for example, was popularly thought to have been heir to Shang dynasty traditions – but what they possessed and preserved were remnants rendered incomplete and fragmentary by their remoteness.[9] Zhou culture had been perfect and because the Lu was originally the fief of the Duke of Zhou – the virtuous paragon whom Confucius admired most among all the ancient sages – Confucius's native state was where the Zhou tradition survived complete and intact (*Lunyu* 7.5).[10] Because he was so emphatically wedded to this tradition, Confucius advocated the study of old books transmitted from antiquity – in particular, the collection of ancient poems known as the *Book of Songs* – because he believed they contained relevant lessons for his students. Long after his death, the *Book of Songs*, the *Book of Documents*, and other early works traditionally associated with Confucius's name would form the 'Confucian Canon,' a body of texts the memorization of which was necessary for securing a position in government.

Yet it should also be noted that other passages in the *Analects* portray Confucius as equally enamored of sages closer to his time who flourished in neighboring states. For example, he praised Guan Zhong (d. 645 BCE'), a prime minister in the large state of Qi with which Lu shared the great Shandong peninsula: 'Were it not for Guan Zhong we might all wear our hair untied and flat against the back and fasten our lapels on the left' (*Lunyu* 14.17).[11] The cultural contributions attributed by Confucius to Guan Zhong are not ad hoc or miscellaneous in nature. Clothing and hairstyles are regularly mentioned in early discussions of the familiar and foreign. Confucius is just an early proponent in a tradition that regards wearing one's hair tied up and fastening the left lapel over the right as characteristic of the truly civilized (only barbarians and demons did otherwise). We should understand them, along with mourning and burial practices, as part of the body of rituals that defined culture for Confucius and hence should be kept alive and transmitted to later generations. Places that did not enjoy this legacy were not

---

8   Such emphasis on the traditions and practices of Lu and her neighbors in Confucius's teachings as well as in the tales of his life can be seen as a purposeful reaction to other early schools of thought that were not only de-centering the landscape through which Confucius moved but also questioning the privileged place bestowed on Zhou customs by Confucius and his followers and, moreover, claiming relevance for customs Confucius and his followers would have regarded as unknown or alien.

9   In *Lunyu* 3.9 Confucius complains about the lack of documents and learned men in the states of Qi and Song that makes it impossible to know the rites of Xia and Shang. He is clearly implying that this is not the case in Lu and that the rites of Zhou can thus be studied and practiced.

10   Confucius bemoans the fact that things have become so bad for him that he no longer sees the Duke of Zhou in his dreams.

11   Confucius holds a contradictory opinion of Guan Zhong in *Lunyu* 3.22.

only foreign but also unrefined, for they were deprived of the essentials of a cultured life.

For Confucius and his immediate followers, those who had mastered the ways of the ancients lived lives fully informed by the ethical values they held dear, and thus fully embodied the ritual customs and practices of the Zhou were *junzi* or 'Gentlemen.' The term in Chinese suggests that it originated in ideas having to do with nobility or aristocracy. But for Confucius's school of thought, the title was not to be bestowed on a superiority based on blood and privilege but rather on an excellence based on learning and accomplishment.

Beyond Lu and Qi how much of the world and its ways did the Master know? Confucius probably shared with many of his contemporaries the view that Lu, Qi, and their neighbors, known variously by such collective terms as the Central States or the Xia Union, were distributed among the 'Nine Provinces' laid out by the legendary Yu the Great and thus occupied a position at the center of the world.[12] According to this conception, there were, beyond the Central States, the peoples of the four cardinal directions whose names in Chinese suggest that they were viewed as uncultured and unruly.[13] Master Kong observes, 'The tribes of the East and the North may retain their princes, but still they do not equal the Collected Xia States who have lost theirs' (*Lunyu* 3.5).[14]

Though Master Kong is said, in some accounts, to have been forced to travel to other states during a long exile from his native Lu, not only do these travels confirm in his mind the superiority of his homeland, they do not seem to have inspired in Confucius a desire to know more of the lives and mores of other peoples and cultures that lay beyond the Central States.[15] Of course he was not a tourist let alone a cultural anthropologist. On a few occasions apparently late in his life, out of frustration over his lack of success at home, he expressed yearning to go someplace exotic: 'My way makes no progress. I'll get on a raft and float on the seas' (*Lunyu* 5.7).[16] (Presumably he meant the Four Seas that were believed to surround the Nine Provinces.) But Confucius was being ironic. He knew the limitations of his situation and that he lacked the necessary 'materials' to truly

---

12   The Central States are the *Zhongguo* in Chinese and the Xia Union is *Zhu Xia*. *Zhongguo* is understood today as one of the names for the modern nation-state of China but, in antiquity, it like *Zhu Xia* referred to an area that shared common customs and traditions rather than to a political entity with fixed boundaries. Yu the Great was the legendary controller of the floods. His exploits, including laying out the divisions among the Nine Provinces, are recounted in numerous early sources.

13   Hisayuki Miyakawa (1960) discusses the views of 'the Chinese people' toward their neighbors.

14   There are at least three ways to interpret this controversial passage. I follow the lead of Li Ling (2007: 89–91). The states that have lost their rulers is probably a reference to the many instances of usurpation that had occurred in Confucius's day.

15   For the stories of Confucius's exile from Lu, see Riegel (1986).

16   Li Ling (2007: 116) dates this passage to sometime after 497 BCE , when Confucius was in his fifties.

break free.[17] It was no doubt still another ironic expression of frustration when the *Analects* reports that the Master wished to live among the 'Nine Yi,' perhaps a reference to people who lived in lands in what are now southern Henan province and Anhui province, just beyond the pale of the old Xia Union. But no matter which exact people Confucius meant, they were obviously regarded as lacking the refinement of his homeland. 'Someone asked, "How would you cope with their backwardness and rudeness?" The Master replied, "Wherever a Gentleman dwells how could there be backwardness and rudeness?"' (*Lunyu* 9.14).

In his reply, Confucius makes clear that the learning and accomplishments of the superior man both help him succeed in alien lands and serve to transform the foreignness of those he encounters there. Significant in all this is the assumption that, for Confucius and those of like mind, one dealt with foreignness by adhering to what was familiar. Travel was thus not for the unschooled or weak-minded who are easily overwhelmed or beguiled by the exotic. Rather it was for those who could keep their values and practices intact even in strange and hostile environments. Indeed it was an obligation that those who traveled into such surroundings transform them so that they became familiar. This would have to mean that the Nine Yi would be taught how to wear their hair and how to fasten their clothes and, beyond those practices, how to eat, speak, and, most importantly, mourn and bury their dead. All of these changes would have to take place in a larger context of social transformation in which extended family structures are introduced along with the 'vertical ethics' that inform their workings. To do so was intended not only for the personal convenience of the traveler but to benefit those thus transformed.

There is a paucity of evidence to consider the situation of someone from a foreign land approaching Confucius for instruction. The passage in the *Analects* that appears to relate most directly to this question suggests that, while it might not matter where a student came from or how poor that student was, it was essential that he know and observe the proper rituals involved in making a request of a teacher: 'I have never refused to instruct anyone who brings me at the very least a small bundle of preserved meat' (*Lunyu* 7.7).[18] The preserved meat is not a tuition payment but rather a symbol of respect for a teacher and so, at a minimum, a prospective student needed to know the ritual. Confucius could excuse those too poor to make the proper gift – he would accept a small bundle of preserved meat, consisting probably of ten strips, though it was by any measure a paltry amount – but would not have overlooked the slight of presenting nothing or the wrong thing. Ignorance would not have been an excuse but rather a reason for rejection.

The list of disciples preserved in later texts claims that Confucius's followers numbered in the thousands and reveals that while most were foreign to Lu they

---

17   Confucius's metaphor about lacking the material, i.e., the timber to build the raft, is meant to refer to the fact that he personally doesn't have what it takes to leave home.

18   Li Ling (2007: 142) points out that the techniques for preserving meat were the same as those used for preserving corpses in ancient Chinese burial practices.

all came from others of the Central States: none were truly foreign in the sense that they came from the tribes of the four directions or the lands beyond the Xia Union.[19] They were thus to some degree already familiar with the necessary rituals that would help win them a place. The gift of preserved meat – signaling respect for a teacher – was just the first rite of induction. The language that the Master uses to describe his followers suggests that their becoming his students was thought of as tantamount to entering a family in which he was the elder or a community in which he was the village chief. Throughout the *Analects*, Confucius's disciples are called *dizi*: 'younger brothers and sons.'[20] On two occasions Confucius refers to them as the 'little ones of my village' (*Lunyu* 5.22 and 13.18), using language that suggests that he saw himself in some sense as the ruler of a community or group of communities made up of populations subordinate to him. (The same list of thousands of followers is entitled 'The Hereditary House of Master Kong,' and shows that, at least in the eyes of later observers, the school of Confucius and his followers was comparable to the noble houses that governed the Central States.) Noteworthy in all this is the fact that Confucius's school was in effect another ladder of vertical relations – a surrogate family or village – success in which would not only result in knowledge of the past and the canonical texts but also in vital experience that would prepare one to move to the other ladders that needed to be climbed in a lifetime.

It is tempting, mostly for the sake of convenience, to refer to the teachings highlighted in the foregoing discussion as representative of the Ru or 'Confucian' school of thought. This is, however, problematic. First it must be acknowledged that we still know very little about the nature and workings of the early schools of thought, if indeed there were any. Moreover, the key concepts listed above, though well-attested in the *Analects*, were not necessarily the exclusive preserve of Master Kong and his disciples and followers. Many appear not only to be tightly woven into the fabric of early Chinese society but also to have remained among the chief characteristics of pre-modern social values and practices; so much so, in fact, that we might as well refer to them as 'Chinese.' But this label, too, is problematic. There was no 'China,' so to speak, in pre-modern times. (Terms like 'Central States' or 'Xia Union' referred to a cultural ideal occupying an imagined center rather than a land with fixed boundaries.) There was a series of dynasties and their domains were referred to, by rulers and subjects alike, using the names of the dynastic houses in power, for example, Qin, Han, Tang, Song, etc.[21] Another problem with referring to these concepts as 'Chinese' is that it diminishes the importance and relevance of the philosophies and traditions that

---

19   *Shiji*, 'Kongzi shijia.'
20   *Dizi* occurs frequently in the *Lunyu* and is usually loosely translated as 'disciples.'
21   It is testimony to the prestige and power of Qin, the first imperial dynasty, that its name was used by outsiders and gives us our word China. But within 'China,' Qin ceased to be used in 210 BC when the dynasty fell. Early Greek and Latin names for 'China' derive from the Chinese word for silk and reflect the importance of that product as an import into the ancient Mediterranean world.

challenged them. And so, fully aware of the difficulties and problems involved in doing so, the shorthand label of 'Confucian' will be adopted below in discussing Confucius's intellectual legacy and those who challenged it.[22]

The Reply by the School of Master Mo (Fifth Century BCE)

By the middle of the fifth century BCE, philosophers were formulating approaches to cultural difference and the related questions of moral obligation in ways radically different to those found in the *Analects* of Confucius. Arguably the most important of those who challenged Confucianism was Mozi or Master Mo (sometimes referred to by what is taken to be his surname and given name, Mo Di). We know Mozi's philosophy from an eclectic work entitled *Mozi* that contains core chapters concerned with social and political philosophy, writings on logic and military philosophy, as well as records of conversations between Master Mo and his disciples that resemble in format the *Analects* of Confucius.[23] The core chapters, consisting of teachings attributed to Master Mo interwoven with the explanations and elaborations offered by his followers, were probably written over a period of 200 years that followed Mozi's death.

Master Mo shared with Confucius and his followers the goal of bringing about effective governance and a stable society but was troubled by the assumption that duties and responsibilities should be defined in terms of the vertical silos of family, community, and state that Confucius took as the given arenas of social and political activity. The Mohist rejection of Confucian doctrine involved not only a critique of Confucian ethics but also encompassed caustic comments on Confucian fondness for elaborate rituals – especially the rites of mourning and burial – and their skepticism with regard to the existence of ghosts and spirits.

For the Confucians an effective ethical system had to be built on individual social 'roles' that operated in relation to other roles in a vertically structured framework. Mozi and his followers constructed their ethical system not on the basis of social 'roles' but rather on the self or, to be more precise, the physical self that has cravings, needs, and ambitions. For the Mohists, the fact that an individual 'loves' his physical self is simply a given that all moral propositions had to recognize and accommodate in order to devise strategies by which people could be lead and coaxed into behaviors that are responsible to others.

---

22   The question of whether there were schools of thought in antiquity is complicated. My own position is that there were and that many of the arguments offered against their existence have failed to take the evidence fully into account.

23   The core chapters consist of ten essays – many preserved in three versions – that contain the fundamental teachings of the Mohist school. Translations of many of these chapters are found in Watson (1963) *The Essential Works of Mo Tzu*. For the purposes of this chapter I adopt as a standard edition of the core chapters Wang Huanbiao (1984).

The *Mozi* treatise 'Jian'ai' or 'Impartial Love' – preserved in the text in three versions or recensions: 'Upper,' 'Middle', and 'Lower,' – thus takes 'love of the physical self' as the starting point of its arguments. The challenge is to formulate ethical prescriptions that will get individuals to 'love others as they love themselves.' The 'Upper' version of 'Impartial Love' states:

> *If we could induce everyone in the world to love others unselfishly, so that each person loved others just as he loved himself, would there be any person who failed to be obedient to superiors? If each person regarded his father, elder brothers as well as his lord just as he did himself, how could he do anything that was disobedient? And would there be any person who failed to be affectionate to inferiors? If each person regarded his younger brothers, sons as well as ministers just as he did his own bodies, how could he do anything that was unaffectionate? Thus disobedient and unaffectionate conduct would cease to exist (Huanbiao 1984: 106).*

Confucius and his followers had spoken of how respect and compassion follow from people properly fulfilling their roles as superiors or subordinates. The Mohists argue that in order for those values to be enacted it is necessary to address the issue of 'love for self.' This is meant to contrast with what might be characterized as a Confucian love of one's own role in society. For Mozi, the Confucian position amounts to an exaggerated emphasis on social status and position as well as an inflated view of one's own integrity and what might pose a threat to it. The Mohists regarded the emphasis on social or political roles as an excessive form of self-centeredness that needs to be eliminated.

It is therefore somewhat ironic that the Mohist starting point for a program of ethical change depends on exploiting another form of self-interest, for it is difficult to see 'love for self' as anything but excessive self-interest. The difference is that, unlike the Confucians, the Mohists regard self-love as a necessary means to an end, not the end in itself that Confucian pride of position and place appears to be. Mozi and his followers appear to assume that ethics are of necessity built upon self-interest and that any attempt to change behavior will need to appeal to such self-interest. This is the key to how Mozi expected his moral system to succeed.

Throughout the three versions of 'Impartial Love' it is pointed out that such unselfish concern for others would lead to an improved world untroubled by wars between states, conflict in communities, and strife within families. But such lofty promises would not get the Mohist ball rolling. That would happen when people had come to realize that it was in their own self-interest to respect and show compassion for others. For Mozi, such realization is most likely to occur in moments of danger or crisis:

> *Suppose that on a flat plain or a broad field there is a man with armor buckled and helmet donned in anticipation of the coming battle where the outcome, life or death, cannot be known. Or suppose there is a grand officer who, on*

the order of his lord, is going out on a diplomatic mission to a distant place like Ba, Yue, Qi, or Jing and cannot know whether or not he will be able to return home. That being so, let us make bold to ask a question. When they do not know whom to rely upon, to whom will they entrust the household responsibilities[10] of providing for the support of their parents and guiding their wife and children? When they do not know whether the altruistic friend or the selfish one is the right choice, what will they do? I think that under the circumstances, no matter whether they were the most foolish man or woman in the world, even if they opposed altruism, they would choose an altruistic friend as the right one to whom to entrust their household (Wang Huanbiao 1984: 120–21).

Here the Mohists are appealing to a sort of common-sense notion that, in a crisis, when the wellbeing of the one's self and family are in jeopardy, pride is jettisoned: one relies not on one's status and the respect or concern that such status is supposed to inspire but rather on the altruism of others. For Mozi it follows that concern for others is in one's own self-interest and is, as well, superior to the fulfillment of social and political roles as a means of a getting what one wants for one's self, one's family, and one's state.

The Mohists are sufficiently thoroughgoing in their practical reflections on what will induce people to adopt altruism in place of the privilege and security of their social roles that they recognize that some people will, no matter how grave the crisis, fail to grasp what will truly benefit them. Thus Master Mo and his followers argue for a program of government intervention in which a ruler – already well-versed in the personal benefits of loving others – makes his preferences known to the population. Since a ruler controls the mechanisms of reward and punishment, the population will bend to his will no matter the difficulties and obstacles they imagine might exist. And for the Mohists, once they 'volunteer' to follow the path of regarding others as equal to themselves they will see that the benefits far outweigh the harms and the difficulties and obstacles will vanish. The 'Middle' version of 'Impartial Love' provides an example: as difficult as it is popularly thought to be, knights will nonetheless sacrifice their lives in battle if their ruler glorifies such feats among his population. And if the ruler possesses such powers of persuasion in getting people to give up their lives – i.e. to relinquish what they cherish most – wherein lies the difficulty, the Mohists ask, in getting people to do things that will ultimately enrich their lives? (Wang Huanbiao 1984: 110).

The importance of the Mohist discourse on the self and altruism is that its argumentation both assumes and advocates the destruction of 'vertical ethics' and their replacement by a system of 'horizontal ethics.' Throughout all three versions of the 'Impartial Love' essay, the text argues that the barriers that separate individual from individual, family from family, and state from state must be penetrated so that an individual will recognize responsibility for other individuals, families, and states. In this argumentation, self-love is not only a fact that informs the cultivation of respect for elders and concern for subordinates within one's own silo, it is also the basis for interacting laterally with those with whom one is not related, the 'free agents' who are not taken into account in the Confucian scheme of ethical obligation.

The Mohists are thus greatly expanding the arena of social and political interaction – and hence the network of obligations and compassion – beyond what is envisioned in the *Analects* of Confucius. Indeed it can be argued that what is behind the Mohist program is a desire to reconfigure society so that the social divisions that pitted family against family and state against state are eliminated and replaced by a more inclusive structure. This is one of the reasons why, early in the twentieth century when Chinese intellectuals became fascinated with Western socialism, they found in the Mohist ideals what they thought was a Chinese precursor (Chow 1960: 305, 374 n62). We may also recognize in these ideals one of the intellectual pillars necessary for the establishment of empire at the end of the third century BCE: a common identity and shared ideology that cross boundaries of the relatively narrow interests of self, family, community, and state.

Reciprocal interactions between unrelated parties work because self-interest – the pursuit of profit and benefit for oneself and one's own 'in-group' – need not depend on connections of family, community, and state.[24] Rather the ideology of self-interest transcends affiliations within local hierarchies and thus serves to link together those who are otherwise unaffiliated except in their shared desires to enrich themselves and protect their interests. How broad was the pool of 'free agents' that the Mohist argument intended to include? It appears that it extended beyond the lineages and states that constituted the old Central States and Xia Union into territories that were becoming part of an expanded *oikoumene*. There is nothing in the principles set out in the *Mozi* that would preclude from a Mohist realm governed by the union of self-interest and altruistic love those who would have to be regarded as truly foreign by virtue of their language and customs. It is just that the *Mozi* makes no mention of including them in the ideal realm governed by altruistic love.

Because Master Kong and his followers had justified their views of morality in terms of the past practices that they claimed they had inherited from the Zhou, Master Mo and his disciples challenge both the Confucian definition of the past as well as the appropriateness of the Zhou ritual legacy the Confucians adopted as their model. They contest Confucian ownership of texts that have come to be regarded as central to the Confucian Canon – the *Book of Songs* and the *Book of Documents* – attributing to them an antiquity that stretched back to the Xia dynasty well before the founding of the Zhou. At one point in a treatise that is part of the so-called 'Mohist Analects,' Master Mo criticizes a follower of Confucius for his obsession with imitating the language and clothing of the ancients: 'You pattern

---

24   Later followers of the Confucian path who had felt the sting of the Mohist criticism complained bitterly about how the use of the word 'profit' had come to dominate the discourse of rulers seeking advice on how to govern and win the loyalty of their subjects.

yourself on the Zhou but have not learned to pattern yourself on the Xia. Your antiquity is not antiquity at all!' (Wang Huanbiao 1984: 366).

Here and elsewhere in the text, the Mohists criticize the Confucians for their parochialism in defining what it means to be civilized. We have seen how the Mohists exploited self-interest in promoting their program in favor of altruistic love. They also recognized that the roots of self-interest are so deep that unless they are brought under control they could undermine the foundations of society. For Mozi and his followers – and arguably for many others at the time – the most grievous examples of selfishness and inflated pride in one's own family and lineage were to be found in the rites of mourning and burial. Typically mourning rites dictated that one mourn the death of parents for at least twenty-five months and bury them in elaborate tombs replete with expensive furnishings. The Confucians were regarded as the staunchest defenders of these rites.

Nowhere is the Mohist resistance to Confucian practice more pronounced than in the treatise devoted to mourning and burial practice: 'Jiezang' or 'Moderation in Burial.'[25] The treatise opens by conceding that both those who favor and those who oppose the rites can rely on ancient precedents to support their arguments. Rather, it claims, considerations of humaneness rather than antiquity are most relevant in arguing against elaborate mourning and burial rites and the text recounts the disastrous financial consequences of ignoring this advice and adopting the Confucian doctrine.

As it pertains to the mourning rites for kings, dukes, and great men this doctrine specifies that the family must provide multiple inner and outer coffins, abundant burial goods, numerous grave clothes and shrouds, elaborate decorations on the coffins, and a grand burial mound. As it pertains to the death of a commoner it specifies that the family must completely exhaust their wealth. As it pertains to the death of a feudal lord, it specifies that the treasury should be emptied in order to provide the gold, jade, and pearls that cover the corpse, the silk cords that bind the body, and the chariots and teams of horses that are interred in the grave (Wang Huanbiao 1984: 191).

The text continues in this vain, complaining about the wastefulness of wealth involved in such burials. It follows this with an equally vitriolic condemnation of the practice of extended mourning as advocated by the Confucians.

What are the rules to be observed by the mourner? The doctrine says:

> *The mourner should cry erratically and when he speaks should sound as if he were choking; he should wear as mourning vestments a hempen breast cover, as well as hempen bands tied about his head and waist, and tears should cover his face; he should live in a mourning hut and sleep on a straw mat with a clod of earth for a pillow.*

---

25   Though one of the core chapters, 'Moderation in Burial' survives in only one version. It has been assumed from very ancient times that the other two versions of the chapter were lost but it is possible that there was ever only one.

In addition, a mourner should force himself not to eat so will feel hunger, he should wear thin clothing so he suffers from the cold, and he should cause his face to look thin and drawn, his eyes to look sunken, and his complexion to darken and become black. His ears should become so hard of hearing, his eyes so dull, his hands and feet so lacking strength and vigor that they become unresponsive. The doctrine also says: 'Senior officials in the exercise of mourning rites should be unable to rise without assistance or walk without a cane.' And all of this is to last into the third year (Wang Huanbiao 1984: 196).

Mozi counters Confucian doctrine by quoting the laws of the ancient sage kings that proscribed elaborate burials and overly long periods of mourning (Wang Huanbiao 1984: 200) as well as tales that suggest that when the sage kings died they were mourned and buried in the simplest and most expeditious ways possible (Wang Huanbiao 1984: 201). But the refutation does not stop there. The text also challenges Confucian convention by referring to other ritual traditions. In a marvelous gesture of broad epistemological sweep, Master Mo reveals that he knows much more of the foreign ways of the world than Confucius did and he is happy to allude to them in order to undermine the authority of the Zhou ritual tradition.

At roughly the same time that the compilers of the core chapters of the *Mozi* were engaged in formulating their arguments *contra* the Confucians, a philosopher named Zou Yan (c.350–c.270 BCE) offered an account of the world that boldly departed from the old vision of Nine Provinces at the centre of the world.[26]

Zou Yan surmised that what the Ru (i.e. Master Kong and his followers) call the Central States occupies a mere one part in eighty-one in the world. The name of the Central States is the Spiritual Province of the Vermilion Region. Within this Spiritual Province of the Vermilion Region there are Nine Provinces. These are the Nine Provinces laid out by Yu the Great and they are not to be counted as *the* Nine Provinces. The Central States is one of nine that resemble the Spiritual Cont of the Vermilion Region. These then are what we call *the* Nine Provinces. They are surrounded by an encircling sea that prevents people and animals from going beyond them. Thus being within a single area they form a Continent. There are Nine Continents surrounded by a gigantic encircling sea that stretches to the juncture of Heaven and Earth.[27]

It is probably in this context of a broader vision of a world in which the Central States were not at the centre and their cultural traditions could no longer claim a position of absolute and unchallenged authority that we should view the *Mozi*'s reference to competing mortuary practices.

In the past, to the east, beyond Yue, there was the country of Shaishu. When their first son was born, they would cut him up and eat him,[20] calling this practice

---

26   Needham (1956: 232–46) provides a good overview of Zou Yan and the naturalist school of thought he helped to found.

27   This apparent fragment of Zou Yan's thought is preserved within a biographical notice composed in the second century BCE. See Needham (1956: 232–6) for a discussion of the biographical notice and this fragment.

'making his younger brothers secure.' When their paternal grandfather died, they put their paternal grandmother on their backs and carried her away, saying

> *It is improper to live in the same house with the wife of a ghost . . . In the far south, beyond Chu, was the Country of the Cannibals. When their parents died, they scraped the rotting flesh from their bones and threw it away. Only then would they bury the bones, believing that they had fulfilled their duties as obedient sons. In the far west, beyond Qin, was the country of the Yiqu. When their parents died, they collected brushwood and burned the bodies, letting the smoke rise up. They referred to this as 'ascending to the rosy clouds.' Only then did [the people of Shaishu, the Country of the Cannibals, and Yiqu] consider that they had fulfilled their duties as obedient sons. Their rulers made these practices into rules and subjects regarded them as established custom. They practiced them rather than giving them up and held on to them rather than abandoning them. But was this actually to practice the way of humaneness and righteousness? Rather this was to find one's own habits convenient and regard one's own customs as right (Wang Huanbiao 1984: 204–5).*[28]

By questioning whether the burial practices of Shaishu, the Country of the Cannibals, and Yiqu can really be judged 'humane and righteous,' i.e. moral, Mozi is suggesting that we need not prefer their frugally neglectful treatment of the dead to the lavish mortuary customs of the Central States. Mozi and his followers do not claim superiority for the foreign and exotic customs the text reports on. The point is that both frugality and lavishness are extreme. But it is significant that Mozi juxtaposes the burial rites of all along a continuous scale from the munificent to the miserly and uses this to demonstrate the excessiveness of the rites of his homeland. Such a 'multicultural' approach to judging the relative value of customs is absent from Confucius's *Analects* and the tradition built upon its foundation.

Mozi makes an additional 'multicultural' argument that is perhaps even more interesting: he uses the evidence of other cultures to demonstrate that the reason practices – abroad and at home – go unquestioned and become authoritative is not because they are inherently right but because they have become customary and habitual. This observation is intended to exposes a flaw in the Confucian preference for Zhou ritual by suggesting that Confucius and his followers are willing to advocate a practice without reflection and without regard for the consequences but simply because such practice has always been done this way and is assumed to be right. There is truth to this Mohist critique. For our purposes what makes it important is not so much the accuracy of what Master Mo says

---

28   No explanation is given for how Mozi learned of the customs of these foreign lands. The fact that the text locates them 'in the past' can, however, be taken as a signal that we should regard the accounts as somewhat uncertain if not legendary.

about Master Kong but rather that the evidence for his arguments derives from a multicultural and comparative approach to ritual and tradition.

The teachings of Mozi and those of the other ancient philosophers were suppressed by the Qin when they created their empire in 221 BCE. The Qin wanted no challenges to the Legalist doctrines they made the ideological foundation of their politics and governance. Mohism seems nevertheless to have survived into the subsequent Han dynasty but, during its four centuries of rule, Confucianism was ascendant and absorbed other systems of thought into a grand synthesis designed to serve Han dynasty imperial purposes. This synthesis obscured Mohism's influence on later thinkers and the numerous social movements in Chinese history that involved mobilizing a mass of the population irrespective of their individual status or local affiliation. It was perhaps Mozi's fate to dwell in obscurity until, early in the twentieth century, when he was 'rediscovered' as the non-Confucian whose thought might best serve a 'new China' in responding to and doing battle with the European intellectual tradition.[29]

---

29 The rediscovery of Mozi is exemplified in the writings of Liang Qichao (1873–1929). 'Liang rejoices in "our Mo-tzu's" speculative achievement in anticipating by almost two thousand years Hobbes, Locke, and Rousseau' (Levenson 1959: 125 n100).

Bibliography

ABCNewsOnline.2006.CostellodefendsMuslimcitizenshipcomments.February24. Accessed 6 June 2009, http://www.abc.net.au/news/stories/2006/02/24/1577268. htm.

Abu-Laban, Y. 1998. Keeping 'em out: gender, race, and class biases in Canadian immigration policy, in *Painting the Maple: Essays on Race, Gender, and the Construction of Canada* edited by V. Strong-Boag and S. Grace and A. Eisenberg and J. Anderson. Vancouver: UBC Press, 69–84.

Abu-Laban, Y. 2004. The new North America and the segmentation of Canadian citizenship. *International Journal of Canadian Studies*, 29, 17–40.

Abu-Laban, Y. and Gabriel, C. 2002. *Selling Diversity: Immigration, Multiculturalism, Employment Equity, and Globalization*. Peterborough, Ontario: Broadview Press.

Abu-Lughod, L. 2002. Do Muslim women really need saving? Anthropological reflections on cultural relativism and its others. *American Anthropologist*, 104(3), 783–790.

Adams, M. 2007. *Unlikely Utopia: The Surprising Triumph of Canadian Pluralism*. Toronto: Viking.

Agamben, G. 1998. *Homo Sacer: Sovereign Power and Bare Life*. Stanford, CA: Stanford University Press.

Agarwal, B. 2001a. Conceptualizing environmental collective action: why gender matters. *Cambridge Journal of Economics* 24, 283–310.

Agarwal, B. 2001b. Participatory exclusions, community forestry, and gender: an analysis of South Asia and a conceptual framework. *World Development*, 29(10), 1623–1648.

Ahmad, A. 1995. The politics of literary postcoloniality. *Race and Class*, 36(3), 1–20.

Alfred, G. R. 1995. *Heeding the Voices of our Ancestors: Kahnawake Mohawk Politics and the Rise of Native Nationalism*. Toronto: Oxford University Press.

Alfred, T. 1999. *Peace, Power, Righteousness: An Indigenous Manifesto*. Oxford: Oxford University Press.

Alfred, T. 2005. *Wasáse: Indigenous Pathways of Action and Freedom*. Peterborough, Ontario: Broadview Press.

Al-Hibri, A. 1999. Is Western patriarchal feminism good for third world/minority women?, in *Is Multiculturalism Bad for Women?* edited by J. Cohen, M. Howard, and M. Nussbaum. Princeton, NJ: Princeton University Press, 41–6.

AlSayyad, N. and Castells, M. 2002. *Muslim Europe or Euro-Islam: Politics, Culture, and Citizenship in the Age of Globalization*. Lanham, MD: Lexington Books.

Althusser, L. 1971. *Lenin and Philosophy and Other Essays*. London: New Left Books.

Althusser, L. 1977. *Ideology and the Ideological State*. London: New Left Books.

Aly, W. 2005. The clash of ignorance. *The Age*, 6 August, http://www.theage.com.au/news/opinion/the-clash-of-ignorance/2005/08/06/1123125843879.html (accessed 02/07/09).

Appadurai, A. 2006. *Fear of Small Numbers: An Essay on the Geography of Fear*. Durham, NC: Duke University Press.

Appiah, K. A. 2005. *The Ethics of Identity*. Princeton, NJ: Princeton University Press.

Appiah, K. A. 2006. *Cosmopolitanism*. New York: Norton.

Arat-Koc, S. 2005. The disciplinary boundaries of Canadian identity after September 11: civilizational identity, multiculturalism and the challenge of Anti-Imperialist feminism. *Social Justice*, 32(4), 32–49.

Aretxaga, B. 2003. Maddening states. *Annual Review of Anthropology*, 32, 393–410.

Arneil, B. 1992. John Locke, natural law and colonialism. *History of Political Thought*, 23(4), 587–603.

Arneil, B. 1996. *John Locke and America: The Defense of English Colonialism*. Oxford: Clarendon Press.

Arneil, B. 1999. *Politics and Feminism*. Oxford: Blackwell.

Arneil, B. 2004. *The Constitutive Norms of Liberal Citizenship and the Legacy of Cultural Colonization*. Paper presented at the Conference for the Study of Political Thought, University of Chicago.

Arneil, B. 2006a. Cultural protections vs. cultural justice: post-colonialism, agonistic justice and the limitations of liberal theory, in *Sexual Justice, Cultural Justice: Critical Perspectives in Political Theory and Practise* edited by B. Arneil, M. Deveaux, R. Dhamoon and A. Eisenberg. London: Routledge, 50–68.

Arneil, B. 2006b. *Diverse Communities*. Cambridge: Cambridge University Press.

Arneil, B. 2006c. The meaning of social in social capital, in *Assessing Social Capital: Concept, Policy and Practice* edited by Rosalind Edwards. Cambridge: Cambridge Scholars Press, 29–52.

Arneil, B., M. Deveaux, R. Dhamoon, and A. Eisenberg, eds 2007. *Sexual Justice/Cultural Justice: Critical Perspectives in Political Theory and Practice*. London: Routledge.

Avery, D. 1979. *Dangerous Foreigners: European Immigrant Workers and Labour Radicalism in Canada, 1896–1932*. Toronto: McClelland and Stewart.

Bader, V. 2005. Dutch nightmare? The end of multiculturalism?, *Canadian Diversity*, 4(1), 9–11.

Bader, V. 2007. *Democracy or Secularism? Associational Governance of Religious Diversity*. Amsterdam: University of Amsterdam Press.

Badiou, A. 2006. *Being and Event*, translated by O. Feltham. London: Continuum.

Bales, K. 1999. *Disposable People: New Slavery in the Economy*. New Haven, CT: Yale University Press.

Bannerji, H. 2000. *The Dark Side of the Nation: Essays on Multiculturalism, Nationalism and Gender*. Toronto: Canadian Scholars' Press Inc.

Banting K., T. Courchene and L. Seidle. 2007. Conclusion, in *Belonging?: Diversity, Recognition and Shared Citizenship in Canada*. Montreal: Institute for Research on Public Policy, 647–687.

Banting, K. and W. Kymlicka, eds 2006. *Multiculturalism and the Welfare State: Recognition and Redistribution in Contemporary Democracies*. Oxford: Oxford University Press.

Banting, K. and W. Kymlicka. 2004. Do multiculturalism policies erode the welfare state? in *Cultural Diversity versus Economic Solidarity* edited by P. van Parijs. Brussels: Deboeck Université Press, 227–2284.

Banting, K., S. Soroka and R. Johnston. 2006. Ethnicity, trust and the welfare state, in *Social Capital, Diversity and the Welfare State* edited by F. Kay and R. Johnston. Vancouver: University of British Columbia Press, 279–303.

Banting, K., W. Kymlicka, S. Soroka, and R. Johnston. 2006. Do multiculturalism policies erode the welfare state? An empirical analysis, in *Multiculturalism and the Welfare State: Recognition and Redistribution in Advanced Democracies* edited by K. Banting and W. Kymlicka. Oxford: Oxford University Press, 49–91.

Barry, B. 2001. *Culture and Equality*. Cambridge: Polity Press.

Baubérot, J. 2009. 'Liberté, laïcité, diversité – La France multiculturelle', in *Appartenances religieuses, appartenance citoyenne. Un équilibre en tension* edited by P. Eid, P. Bosset, M. Milot, and S. Lebel-Grenier. Quebec: Presses de l'Université Laval, 13–28.

Bawer, B. 2009. *Surrender: Appeasing Islam, Sacrificing Freedom*. New York: Doubleday.

BBC News. 2006. 'Straw's veil comments spark anger', 5 October, http://news.bbc.co.uk/1/hi/uk_politics/5410472.stm.

Benhabib, S. 2001. *Transformations of Citizenship: Dilemmas of the Nation State in the Era of Globalization*. Amsterdam: Van Gorcum Ltd.

Benhabib, S. 2002. *The Claims of Culture: Equality and Diversity in the Global era*. Princeton, NJ: Princeton University Press.

Benhabib, S. 2004. *The Rights of Others*. Cambridge: Cambridge University Press.

Berlin, I. 1969, 'Two concepts of liberty', in *Four Essays on Liberty*. London: Oxford University Press.

Besch, T. M. 1998. *Über John Rawls' politischen Liberalismus*. Peter Lang, Frankfurt a. M.

Besch, T. M. 2008. Constructing practical reason: O'Neill on the grounds of Kantian constructivism. *Journal of Value Inquiry*, 42(1), 55–76.

Bhabha, H. 1996. Culture's in-between, in *Questions of Cultural Identity* edited by S. Hall and P. Du Gay. London: Sage Publications, 53–60.

Bhabha, H. K. 1991. Caliban speaks to Prospero, in *Critical Fictions* edited by P. Mariani. Seattle: Bay Press, 62–65.

Bhabha, H. K. 1994. *The Location of Culture*. London: Routledge.

Bhabha, H. K. 2003. On writing rights, in *Globalizing Rights* edited by M.J. Gibney. Oxford: Oxford University Press, 162–188.

Bigo, D. 2002. Security and immigration: toward a critique of the governmentality of unease. *Alternatives* 27, 63–92.

Blair, T. 2002. New Labour and community. *Renewal*, 10(2), 9–14.

Blair, T. 2006. *The Duty to Integrate: Shared British Values*, speech presented at Downing Street, London, United Kingdom, http://www.number10.gov.uk/Page10563.

Bloemraad, I. 2006. *Becoming a Citizen: Incorporating Immigrants and Refugees in the United States and Canada*. Berkeley, CA: University of California Press.

Blum, L. 1998. Recognition, value and equality: a critique of Charles Taylor's and Nancy Fraser's accounts of multiculturalism, in *Theorizing Multiculturalism* edited by C. Willett. Oxford: Blackwell, 73–99.

Bohman, J. 2000. *Public Deliberation: Pluralism, Complexity, and Democracy*. Cambridge, MA: MIT Press.

Bohman, J. 2002. Critical theory as practical knowledge, in *Blackwell Companion to the Philosophy of the Social Sciences* edited by P. Roth and S. Turner. London: Blackwell, 91–109.

Bohman, J. 2003. Deliberative toleration. *Political Theory*, 31(6), 757–779.

Bohman, J. 2008. Transnational democracy and nondomination, in *Republicanism and Political Theory* edited by C. Laborde and J. Maynor. London: Basil Blackwell, 190–216.

Bouchard, G. and C. Taylor. 2008. *Building the Future: A Time for Reconciliation*. Report of the Commission de consultation sur les practiques d'accommodement reliées aux differences culturelles. Québec, QC: Gouvernement du Québec, http://www.accommodements.qc.ca/documentation/rapports/rapport-final-integral-en.pdf.

Bourdieu, P. 1986. The forms of capital, in *Handbook of Theory and Research for the Sociology of Education* edited by John G. Richardson. Santa Barbara, CA: Greenwood Press, 241–258.

Bowen, J. 2003. Two approaches to rights and religion in contemporary France, in *Human Rights in Global Perspective: Anthropological Studies of Rights, Claims and Entitlements* edited by R. A. Wilson and J. P. Mitchell. London: Routledge, 33–53.

Bowen, J. 2004. Does French Islam have borders? Dilemmas of domestication in a global religion. *American Anthropologist*, 106(1), 43–55.

Bowen, J. R. 2007. *Why the French don't like Headscarves: Islam, the State and Public Space*. Princeton, NJ and Oxford: Princeton University Press.

Boyd, M. 2004. *Dispute Resolution in Family Law: Protecting Choice, Promoting Inclusion*. Toronto: Ministry of the Attorney General of Ontario, http://www.attorneygeneral.jus.gov.on.ca/english/about/pubs/boyd/.

Brague, R. 2005. *La loi de dieu: Histoire philosophique d'une alliance*. Paris: Gallimard.

Brandon, J. and Hafez, S. 2008. *Crimes of the Community – Honour-Based Violence in the UK*. London: Centre for Social Inclusion.

Brodie, J. 1995. *Politics on the Margins: Restructuring and the Canadian Women's Movement*. Halifax: Fernwood Publishing.

Brown, G. 2004. Speech by the Chancellor of the Exchequer at the British Council Annual Lecture. July 7, 2004, http://www.hm-treasury.gov.uk/newsroom_and_speeches/press/2004/press_63_04.cfm.

Brown, W. 1995. *States of Injury: Power and Freedom in Late Modernity*. Princeton, NJ: Princeton University Press.

Brown, W. 2001. Reflections on tolerance in the age of identity, in *Democracy and Vision* edited by A. Botwinick and W. E. Connolly. Princeton, NJ: Princeton University Press, 99–117.

Brown, W. 2002. Suffering the paradoxes of rights, in *Left Legalism/Left Critique* edited by W. Brown and J. Halley. Durham, NC: Duke University Press, 420–434.

Brown, W. 2006. *Regulating Aversion: Tolerance in the Age of Identity and Empire*. Princeton, NJ and Oxford: Princeton University Press.

Brubaker, R. 2001. The return of assimilation? Changing perspectives on immigration and its sequels in France, Germany, and the United States. *Ethnic and Racial Studies*, 24, 531–48.

Brubaker, R. and F. Cooper. 2000. Beyond 'identity'. *Theory and Society*, 29, 1–47.

Bulhan, H. A. 1985. *Frantz Fanon and the Psychology of Oppression*. New York: Plenum Press.

Burke, J. 2008. Honesty best policy when talking militancy, says EU counter-terrorism chief. *The Observer*, Sunday 28 September. Accessed 21 January 2009, www.guardian.co.uk/world/2008/sep/28/terrorism.eu.

Burtt, S. 1994. Religious parents, secular schools. *Review of Politics*, 56, 51–70.

Buruma, I. 2006. *Murder in Amsterdam: The Death of Theo van Gogh and the Limits of Tolerance*. New York: Penguin Press HC.

Calhoun, C. 2002. The class consciousness of frequent travellers: towards a critique of actually existing cosmopolitanism, in *Conceiving Cosmopolitanism: Theory, Context and Practice* edited by S. Vertovec and R. Cohen. Oxford: Oxford University Press, 86–109.

Callan, E. 1997. *Creating Citizens*. Oxford: Oxford University Press.

Canada, G. o. 2004. *Securing an Open Society: Canada's National Security Policy*. Ottawa: Privy Council Office.

Canada, G. o. 2008. *'Prime Minister Stephen Harper's statement of apology'*. Government of Canada. Accessed December 26, 2008, http://www.cbc.ca/canada/story/2008/06/11/pm-statement.html?ref=rssandloomia_si=t0:a16:g2:r1:c0.223139.

Carens, J. H. 2000. *Culture, Citizenship, and Community: A Contextual Exploration of Justice as Evenhandedness*. New York: Oxford University Press.

Chakrabarty, D. 1992. Postcoloniality and the artifice of history, *Representations*, 37, 1–26.

Chambers, C. 2008. *Sex, Culture, and Justice: The Limits of Choice*. University Park, PA: Pennsylvania State University Press.

Chase, S. 2006. Raids prove that Canada not soft on terror, Day says. *Globe and Mail*, 5 June.

Chow, T. 1960. Anti-Confucianism in early republican China, in *The Confucian Persuasion* edited by A. Wright. Stanford, CA: Stanford University Press, 288–312.

CIC. 2008a. *Citizenship and Immigration Canada: About Us.* Government of Canada. Retrieved 27 December, 2008, http://www.cic.gc.ca/english/department/index.asp.

CIC. 2008b. *News release: Minister Finley marks first anniversary of Foreign Credentials Referral Office.* Citizenship and Immigration Canada. Retrieved January 10, 2008, http://www.cic.gc.ca/english/department/media/releases/2008/2008-05-30.asp.

CIC. 2008c. *What is Multiculturalism?* Citizenship and Immigration Canada, Government of Canada. Retrieved 10 January, 2008, http://www.cic.gc.ca/multi/multi-eng.asp.

CIC. 2009. *Promoting Integration,* Annual Report on the Operation of the Canadian Multiculturalism Act 2007–2008. Ottawa: Citizenship and Immigration Canada, http://www.cic.gc.ca/english/resources/publications/multi-report2008/index.asp.

Cohen, G. A. 2000. *If You're an Egalitarian, How Come You're So Rich?* Cambridge, MA: Harvard University Press.

Cohen, J. 1989. Deliberative democracy and democratic legitimacy, in *The Good Polity* edited by A. Hamlin and P. Pettit. Oxford: Blackwell, 17–34.

Cohen, J., M. Howard, and C. Nussbaum, eds 1999. *Is Multiculturalism Bad for Women?* Princeton, NJ: Princeton University Press.

Connolly, W. 1995. *Ethos of Pluralization.* Minnesota, MN: University of Minnesota Press.

Connolly, W. 1999. *Why I Am Not A Secularist.* Minneapolis, MN and London: University of Minnesota Press.

Consultation Commission on Accommodation Practices Related to Cultural Differences. 2008. *Building the Future: A Time for Reconciliation.* Quebec: Government of Quebec, http://www.accommodements.qc.ca/index-en.html.

Cooke, M. 1997. Authenticity and autonomy: Taylor, Habermas, and the politics of recognition. *Political Theory,* 25(2), 258–288.

Cooke, M. 2009. Beyond dignity and difference: revisiting the politics of recognition. *European Journal of Political Theory,* 8(1), 76–95.

Cossman, B. and J. Fudge, eds 2002. *Privatization, Law and the Challenge to Feminism.* Toronto: University of Toronto Press.

Coulthard, G. 2007. Subjects of empire: indigenous peoples and the 'politics of recognition' in Canada. *Contemporary Political Theory,* 6(4), 437–460.

Crimes Act 1900 – Sect 45, Prohibition of female genital mutilation, New South Wales Consolidated Acts, accessed 6 June 2009, http://www.austlii.edu.au/au/legis/nsw/consol_act/ca190082/s45.html.

Crowder, G. 2002. *Liberalism and Value Pluralism.* New York: Continuum.

Crowder, G. 2007. Two concepts of liberal pluralism. *Political Theory,* 35, 121–146.

Danley, J. R. 1991. Liberalism, aboriginal rights, and cultural minorities. *Philosophy and Public Affairs,* 20, 168–185.

Das, V. 1986. Subaltern as perspective, in *Subaltern Studies VI.* Delhi: Oxford University Press, 310–324.

Daston, L. 1992. Objectivity and the escape from perspective. *Social Studies of Science*, 22, 597–618.

Day, R. 2000. *Multiculturalism and the History of Canadian Diversity*. Toronto: University of Toronto Press.

Day, R. and T. Sadik. 2002. The BC land question, liberal multiculturalism and the spectre of aboriginal nationhood. *BC Studies*, 134, 5–34.

Declaration on the Rights of Persons Belonging to National or Ethnic, Religious or Linguistic Minorities. 1993. G.A. res. 47/135, annex, 47 U.N. GAOR Supp. (No. 49) at 210, U.N. Doc. A/47/49.

Deleuze, G. 1994. *Difference and Repetition*, translated by Paul Patton, London: Athlone and New York: Columbia University Press.

Deleuze, G. and Guattari, F. 1987. *A Thousand Plateaus: Capitalism and Schizophrenia*, translated by Brian Massumi, Minneapolis, MN: University of Minnesota Press.

Department of Justice Canada. 1982. The Constitution Act, 1982, section 35. Ottawa: Department of Justice Canada, http://laws.justice.gc.ca/en/const/annex_e.html.

Deranty, J-P. 2009. *Beyond Communication*. Leiden and Boston: Brill.

Derrida, J. 1992. *The Other Heading: Reflections on Today's Europe*, translated by Pascale-Anne Brault and Michael Naas. Bloomington, IN and Indianapolis: Indiana University Press.

Derrida, J. 1998. *Monolingualism of the Other or The Prosthesis of Origin*, translated by Patrick Mensah. Stanford, CA: Stanford University Press.

Deveaux, M. 2000a. *Cultural Pluralism and Dilemmas of Justice*. Ithaca, NY and London: Cornell University Press.

Deveaux, M. 2000b. Conflicting equalities? Cultural group rights and sex equality. *Political Studies*, 48, 522–539.

Deveaux, M. 2005. A deliberative approach to conflicts of culture, in *Minorities within Minorities: Equality, Rights and Diversity* edited by A. Eisenberg and J. Spinner-Halev. Cambridge UK: Cambridge University Press, 340–362.

Deveaux, M. 2006. *Gender and Justice in Multicultural Liberal States*. Oxford: Oxford University Press.

Dewey, J. 1986. Logic: the theory of inquiry, in *The Later Works*, Volume 12. Carbondale, IL: Southern Illinois University Press.

Dewey, J. 1988. The public and its problems, in *The Later Works, 1925–1937*, Volume 2. Carbondale, IL: Southern Illinois University Press.

Dewey, J. 1991. Liberalism and social action, in *The Later Works, 1925–1937*, Volume 11. Carbondale, IL: Southern Illinois University Press.

Dhamoon, R. 2005. Beyond inclusion politics: reconstituting the political order. Paper presented at the Annual General Meeting of the Canadian Political Science Association, University of Western Ontario, 2–5 June 2005.

Dhamoon, R. 2006. Shifting from culture to cultural: critical theorizing of identity/difference politics. *Constellations: An International Journal of Critical and Democratic Theory*, 13(3), 354–373.

Dhamoon, R. 2007. The politics of cultural contestation, in *Sexual Justice/Cultural Justice: Critical Perspectives in Theory and Practice* edited by B. Arneil and M. Deveaux and R. Dhamoon and A. Eisenberg. London: Routledge, 30–49.

Dhamoon, R. 2009. Identity/*Difference Politics: How Difference is Produced and Why it Matters*. Vancouver: University of British Columbia Press.

Digeser, P. 2001. *Political Forgiveness*. London: Routledge.

Dirlik, A. 1994. Third World criticism in an age of global capitalism. *Critical Inquiry*, 20, 328–356.

Donald, J. 2007. Internationalisation, diversity and the humanities curriculum: cosmopolitanism and multiculturalism revisited. *Journal of Philosophy of Education*, 41(3), 289–308.

Duffy, C. 2006. PM stands by Muslim integration comments. *The World Today*, ABC *News Online*, 1 September. Accessed 5 June 2009, http://www.abc.net.au/news/newsitems/200609/s1730918.htm.

Dworkin, R. 1978. *Taking Rights Seriously*. Cambridge, MA: Harvard University Press.

Dworkin, R. 2000. *Sovereign Virtue*. Oxford: Oxford University Press.

Eagleton, T. 1988. The politics of subjectivity, in *Identity* ICA Documents 6 edited by Lisa Appignanesi. London: Institute for Contemporary Art.

Eisenberg, A. 2003. Diversity and equality: three approaches to cultural and sexual difference. *Journal of Political Philosophy*, 11(1), 41–64.

Eisenberg, A. 2007. Identity, multiculturalism, and religious arbitration: The debate over shari'a law in Canada, in *Sexual Justice/Cultural Justice: Critical Perspectives in Political Theory and Practice* edited by B. Arneil, M. Deveaux, R. Dhamoon and A. Eisenberg. London: Routledge, 211–230.

Eisenberg, A. and J. Spinner-Halev. 2005. *Minorities Within Minorities: Equality, Rights and Diversity*. Cambridge UK: Cambridge University Press.

Emcke, C. 2000. Between choice and coercion: identities, injuries and different forms of recognition. *Constellations*, 7(4), 484–495.

Entzinger, H. 2003. The rise and fall of multiculturalism in the Netherlands, in *Toward Assimilation and Citizenship: Immigrants in Liberal Nation-States* edited by C. Joppke and E. Morawska. London: Palgrave, 59–86.

Fanon, F. 1967. *The Wretched of the Earth*. Harmondsworth: Pelican.

Fanon, F. 1986. *Black Skins, White Masks*, translated by H. K. Bhabha. London: Pluto Press.

Feldman, A. 2004. Deterritorialised wars of public safety. *Social Analysis*, 48(1), 73–80.

Fingarette, H. 1979. Following the 'One Thread' of the *Analects*. *Journal of the American Academy of Religions*, 47(3), 373–405.

Finkielkraut, A. 1988. *The Undoing of Thought*, translated by Dennis O'Keefe. London: Claridge.

Forst, R. 1994. *Kontexte der Gerechtigkeit*. Suhrkamp, Frankfurt a. M.

Forst, R. 1999. The basic right to justification: toward a constructivist conception of human rights. *Constellations*, 6(1), 35–60.

Forst, R. 2002. *Contexts of Justice*. Berkeley/Los Angeles, CA: University of California Press.

Forst, R. 2003a. *Toleranz im Konflikt*. Suhrkamp, Frankfurt a. M.

Forst, R. 2003b. Toleration, justice and reason, in *The Culture of Toleration in Diverse Societies* edited by C. McKinnon and D. Castiglione. Manchester: Manchester University Press, 71–85.

Forst, R. 2004. The limits of toleration. *Constellations*, 11(3), 312–325.

Forst, R. 2007a. Das grundlegende Recht auf Rechtfertigung. Zu einer konstruktivitischen Konzeption von Menschenrechten, in R. Forst *Das Recht auf Rechtfertigung*. Suhrkamp, Frankfurt a. M.

Forst, R. 2007b. *Das Recht auf Rechtfertigung*. Suhrkamp, Frankfurt a. M.

Foucault, M. 1984. Afterward: the subject of power, in *Michel Foucault: Beyond Structuralism and Hermeneutics* edited by H. Dreyfus and P. Rabinow. Chicago, IL: University of Chicago Press, 208–228.

Foucault, M. 1991. Governmentality, in *The Foucault Effect: Studies in Governmentality* edited by G. Burchell, C. Gordon and P. Miller. Harvester Wheatsheaf, 87–104.

Foucault, M. 2007. *Security, Territory, Population: Lectures at the College de France 1977–1978* translated by G. Burchell. Basingstoke, Hampshire: Palgrave MacMillan.

Fraser, N. 1997. *Justice Interruptus*. London and New York: Routledge.

Fraser, N. 2000. Rethinking recognition. *New Left Review*, 3(May/June), 107–120.

Fraser, N. 2001. Recognition without ethics. *Theory, Culture and Society*, 18(2–3), 21–42.

Fraser, N. 2003. Social justice in an age of identity politics, in *Redistribution or Recognition? A Political–Philosophical Exchange* edited by N. Fraser and A. Honneth. London: Verso, 7–109.

Fraser, N. and A. Honneth. 2003. *Redistribution or Recognition? A Political–Philosophical Exchange*, translated by. J. Golb, J. Ingram and C. Wilke. London: Verso.

Freeman, S. 2002. Liberalism and the accommodation of group claims, in *Multiculturalism Reconsidered 'Culture and Equality' and its Critics* edited by P. Kelly. Cambridge: Polity, 18–30.

Friedman, M. 2003. *Autonomy, Gender, Politics*. New York: Oxford University Press.

Frug, G. 1999. *City Making*. Princeton, NJ: Princeton University Press.

Furlong, R. 2004. Germans argue over integration, BBC News, Tuesday November 30, 2004. http://news.bbc.co.uk/2/hi/4056109.stm, accessed 10 March 2010.

Fusco, C. 1989. Border art workshop/taller de arte fronterizo. *Nation*, 248(17), 602–604.

Galeotti, A. E. 2002. *Toleration as Recognition*. Cambridge: Cambridge University Press.

Galston, W. A. 1991. *Liberal Purposes: Goods, Virtues, and Diversity in the Liberal State*. New York: Cambridge University Press.

Galston, W. A. 2002. *Liberal Pluralism*. Cambridge: Cambridge University Press.

Gatens, M. 2008. Conflicting imaginaries in Australian multiculturalism: women's rights, group rights and aboriginal customary law, in *Political Theory and*

Australian Multiculturalism edited by G. B. Levey. New York and Oxford: Berghahn Books, 151–170.

Gaus, G. F. 2005. The place of autonomy within liberalism, in *Autonomy and the Challenges to Liberalism: New Essays* edited by J. Christman and J. Anderson. Cambridge: Cambridge University Press, 272–306.

Geertz, C. 1973. *The Interpretation of Cultures: Selected Essays*. New York: Basic Books.

Geertz, C. 2000. *Available Light: Anthropological Reflections on Philosophical Topics*. Princeton, NJ: Princeton University Press.

Giddens, A. 1998. *The Third Way: The Renewal of Social Democracy*. Malden, MA: Polity Press.

Gill, E. 2001. *Becoming Free: Autonomy and Diversity in the Liberal Polity*. Lawrence, KS: University Press of Kansas.

Gilligan, C. 1993. *In A Different Voice*. Cambridge, MA: Harvard University Press.

Gilroy, P. 2004. *After Empire: Postcolonial Melancholia or Convivial Culture?* London: Routledge.

Gitlin, T. 1995. *The Twilight of Common Dreams: Why America is Wracked by Culture Wars*. New York: Henry Holt and Co.

Glazer, N. 1997. *We Are All Multiculturalists Now*. Cambridge, MA: Harvard University Press.

Goodhart, D. 2004a. Too diverse. *Prospect*, 95, 30–37.

Goodhart, D. 2004b. Discomfort of strangers. *The Guardian*, 24 February. http://www.guardian.co.uk/comment/story/0,1154650,00.html.

Goodin, R. 2006. Liberal multiculturalism: protective and polyglot. *Political Theory*, 34(3), 289–303.

Government of Quebec. 1990. *Au Québec, pour bâtir ensemble: Énoncé de politique en matière d'immigration et d'intégration*. Quebec: Ministère des Communautés culturelles et de l'Immigration du Québec. http://www.micc.gouv.qc.ca/fr/ministere/vision-mission.html.

Gramsci, A. 1971. *Selections from the Prison Notebooks*. London: Lawrence and Usher.

Gray, J. 2000. *Two Faces of Liberalism*. Cambridge: Polity.

Green, J. 2000. The difference debate: reducing rights to cultural flavours. *Canadian Journal of Political Science*, 33(1), 133–144.

Greenawalt. K. 2006. *Religion and the Constitution. Vol. 1: Free Exercise and Fairness*. Princeton, NJ: Princeton University Press.

Gunew, S. 2003. Postcolonialism and multiculturalism: between race and ethnicity. Available at http://faculty.arts.ubc.ca/sgunew/RACE.htm

Gunew, S. 2004. *Haunted Nations: The Colonial Dimensions of Multiculturalisms*. London: Routledge.

Gupta, A. and Ferguson, J. 2002. Spatializing states: toward an ethnography of neo-liberal governmentality. *American Ethnologist*, 29(4), 981–1002.

Gutmann, A. 1987. *Democratic Education*. Princeton, NJ: Princeton University Press.

Gutmann, A. 1995. Civic education and social diversity. *Ethics*, 105, 557–579.

Gutmann, A. 2003. *Identity in Democracy*. Princeton, NJ: Princeton University Press.

Gutmann, A. ed. 1992. *Multiculturalism and the Politics of Recognition*. Princeton, NJ: Princeton University Press.

Habermas, J. 1984. *The Theory of Communicative Action, Volume 2*, translated by. T. McCarthy. Boston, MA: Beacon Press.

Habermas, J. 1987. *The Philosophical Discourse of Modernity*, translated by. F. Lawrence. Cambridge: Polity.

Habermas, J. 1993. Struggles for recognition in constitutional states. *European Journal of Philosophy*, 1(2), 128–155.

Habermas, J. 1994. Struggles for recognition in the democratic constitutional state, in *Multiculturalism: Examining the Politics of Recognition* edited by A. Gutmann. Princeton, NJ: Princeton University Press, 107–148.

Habermas, J. 1996. *Between Facts and Norms*. Cambridge, MA: MIT Press.

Habermas, J. 1998. *The Inclusion of the Other*, edited by C. Cronin and P. De Greiff. Cambridge, MA: MIT Press.

Habermas, J. 2001. *The Postnational Constellation*. Cambridge, MA: Harvard University Press.

Habermas, J. 2006. Religion in the public sphere. *European Journal of Philosophy*, 14(1), 1–25.

Habibi, D. 1999. The moral dimensions of J. S. Mill's colonialism. *Journal of Social Philosophy*, 30(1), 125–146.

Hage, G. 1998. *White Nation: Fantasies of White Supremacy in a Multicultural Society*. Sydney: Pluto Press.

Hage, G. 2000. *White Nation: Fantasies of White Supremacy in a Multicultural Society*. New York: Routledge.

Hage, G. 2003. *Against Paranoid Nationalism: Searching for Hope in a Shrinking Society*. Sydney: Pluto Press.

Hale, C. R. 2002. Does multiculturalism menace? Governance, cultural rights and the politics of identity in Guatemala. *Journal of Latin American Studies*, 34, 485–542.

Hall, S. 1996. *Modernity: An Introduction to Modern Societies*. Cambridge: Blackwell.

Hankivsky, O. 2006. Imagining ethical globalization: the contribution of an ethic of care. *Journal of Global Ethics*, 2(1), 91–110.

Hannerz, U. 1996. *Transnational Connections: Culture, People, Places*. London and New York: Routledge.

Held, D., A. McGrew, D Goldblatt and J. Perraton 2000. *Global Transformations*. Stanford: Stanford University Press.

Helliwell, J. 2003. Immigration and social capital: Issue Paper, Issues Paper for the OECD/PRI Conference on Immigration and Social Capital, Montreal, November 23–25.

Hesse, B., ed. 2000. *Un/settled Multiculturalisms: Diasporas, Entanglements, Transruptions*. London: Zed Books.

Hirschmann, N. J. 1998. Western feminism, Eastern veiling and the question of free agency. *Constellations*, 5(3), 345–368.

Hirschmann, N. J. 1992. *Rethinking Obligation: A Feminist Method for Political Theory*. Ithaca, NY: Cornell University Press.

Hobson, B. ed. 2003. *Recognition Struggles and Social Movements*. Cambridge: Cambridge University Press.

Honig, B. 1999. 'My culture made me do it', in *Is Multiculturalism Bad for Women?* edited by J. Cohen, M. Howard and M. Nussbaum. Princeton, NJ: Princeton University Press, 35–40.

Honig, B. 2003. *Democracy and the Foreigner*. Princeton, NJ: Princeton University Press.

Honneth, A. 1991. *The Critique of Power*, translated by K. Baynes. Cambridge, MA: MIT Press.

Honneth, A. 1995a. *The Struggle for Recognition*, translated by J. Anderson. Cambridge: Polity.

Honneth, A. 1995b. *The Fragmented World of the Social*, ed. C. W. Wright. Albany, NY: SUNY Press.

Honneth, A. 1998. Democracy as reflexive cooperation. *Political Theory*, 26(6), 763–783.

Honneth, A. 2002. Recognition or redistribution? Changing perspectives on the moral order of society, in *Recognition and Difference: Politics, Identity, Multiculture* edited by S. Lash and M. Featherstone. London: Sage Publications, 43–56.

Honneth, A. 2003. Redistribution as recognition, in *Redistribution or Recognition? A Political–Philosophical Exchange* edited by N. Fraser and A. Honneth, translated by. J. Golb, J. Ingram and C. Wilke. London: Verso, 110–197.

Honneth, A. 2007. *Disrespect*. Cambridge: Polity.

Hooghe, M., T. Reeskens, and D. Stolle. 2007. Diversity, multiculturalism and social cohesion: trust and ethnocentrism in European societies, in *Belonging? Diversity, Recognition and Shared Citizenship in Canada* edited by K. Banting, T. Courchene and L. Seidle. Montreal: Institute for Research on Public Policy, 387–410.

hooks, b. 1981. *Ain't I a Woman?: Black Women and Feminism*. Boston, MA: South End Press.

hooks, b. 2000. *Feminist Theory: From Margin to Centre*. Boston, MA: South End Press.

Horton, J., ed. 1993. *Liberalism, Multiculturalism and Toleration*. New York: St Martin's Press.

Huanbiao, W. 1984. *Mozi jiaoshi*. Zhejiang: Xinhua shudian.

Humphrey, M. 2002. Humanitarianism, terrorism and the transnational border. *Social Analysis*, 46(1), 117–122.

Humphrey, M. 2007. From diaspora Islam to globalised Islam: changing Islamic religiosity and identity in the West, in *Islam and Political Violence: Muslim Diaspora and Radicalism in the West* edited by S. Akbarzadeh and F. Mansouri. London: IB Tauris, 107–124.

Humphrey, M. 2009. The securitization and domestication of diaspora Muslims and Islam: Turkish immigrants in Germany and Australia. *International Journal of Multicultural Societies* 11(1), 1–19.

Hunter, I. 2008. The shallow legitimacy of secular liberal orders: the case of early modern Brandenburg-Prussia, in *Religion and Multicultural Citizenship* edited by G. B. Levey and T. Modood. Cambridge: Cambridge University Press, 27–55.

Hunter, J. D. 1991. *Culture Wars: The Struggle to Define America*. New York: Basic Books.

Huntington, S. 1996. *The Clash of Civilizations and the Remarking of World Order*. New York: Simon & Schuster, Inc.

Hurrell, A. and N. Woods, eds 1999. *Inequality, Globalization and World Politics*. Oxford: Oxford University Press.

Huysmans, J. 1998. Security! What do you mean? From concept to thick signifier. *European Journal of International Relations*, 4(2), 226–255.

Huysmans, J. 2006. *The Politics of Insecurity: Fear, Migration and Asylum in the EU*. London: Routledge.

ICG (International Crisis Group). 2007. *Islam and Identity in Germany*, Europe Report No. 181, 14 March 2007. Accessed 4 July 2007. http://www.flwi.ugent.be/cie/documenten/islam_in_germany.pdf.

Indian and Northern Affairs Canada. 1969. *Statement of the Government of Canada on Indian policy*. Ottawa: Indian and Northern Affairs Canada. http://www.ainc-inac.gc.ca/ai/arp/ls/pubs/cp1969/cp1969-eng.asp.

Indian and Northern Affairs Canada. 1996. *Report of the Royal Commission on Aboriginal Peoples. Volume 2: Restructuring the Relationship*. Ottawa: Indian and Northern Affairs Canada. http://www.ainc-inac.gc.ca/ap/rrc-eng.asp.

Inglehart, R. 1999. Trust, well-being and social capital, in *Democracy and Trust* edited by Mark Warren. Cambridge: Cambridge University Press, 88–120.

International Covenant on Civil and Political Rights, G.A. res. 2200A (XXI), 21 U.N. GAOR Supp. (No. 16) at 52, U.N. Doc. A/6316 (1966), 999 U.N.T.S. 171, entered into force Mar. 23, 1976.

Ivison, D. 2002. *Postcolonial Liberalism*. Cambridge: Cambridge University Press.

Ivison, D. 2003. The logic of aboriginal rights, *Ethnicities*, 3(3), 321–344.

Ivison, D. 2008. Multiculturalism and resentment, in *Political Theory and Australian Multiculturalism* edited by G. B. Levey. New York and Oxford: Berghahn Books, 129–148.

Ivison, D., P. Patton, and W. Sanders, eds 2000. *Political Theory and the Rights of Indigenous Peoples*. Cambridge: Cambridge University Press.

Jelen, T. 1982. Sources of political intolerance: the case of the American South, in *Contemporary Southern Political Attitudes and Behavior* edited by R. P. Steed, L. W. Moreland and T. A. Baker. New York: Praeger, 73–91.

Jenkins, L. D. 2003. *Identity and Identification in India: Defining the Disadvantaged*. London and New York: RoutledgeCurzon.

Jones, C. 2005. Cosmopolitanism, in *Encyclopedia of Philosophy*, 2nd edn, edited by W. Borchert. New York: Macmillan. Volume 2, 567–570.

Jones, P. 1999a. Human rights, group rights and peoples' rights. *Human Rights Quarterly*, 21(1), 80–107.

Jones, P. 1999b. Group rights and group oppression. *Journal of Political Philosophy*, 7(4), 353–377.

Jones, P. 2006. Equality, recognition and difference. *Critical Review of International Social and Political Philosophy*, 9(1), 23–46.

Joppke, C. 2004. The retreat of multiculturalism in the liberal state: theory and policy. *British Journal of Sociology* 55(2), 237–257.

Kelly, U. 2005. Discourse ethics and 'the right to speechlessness'. *Political Studies Review*, 4(1), 3–15.

Kenney, J. 2008. *Speaking notes for the Minister of Citizenship, Immigration and Multiculturalism at the Canadian Club*. Citizenship and Immigration Canada, Government of Canada. Accessed 10 January 2008, from the World Wide Web: http://www.cic.gc.ca/english/department/media/speeches/2008/2008-11-13.asp.

Kerbaj, R. 2006. Howard stands by Muslim integration. *The Australian*, September 1. Accessed 10 October 2006, http://www.theaustralian.news.com.au/ story/0,20867,20322022-601,00.html.

Kerbaj, R. 2008. University 'an agent of extreme Islam'. *The Australian*, April 23. Accessed 8 August 2009, http://www.theaustralian.news.com.au/ story/0,23584548-12332,00.html.

Kittay, E. 2005a. At the margins of moral personhood. *Ethics*, 116, 100–131.

Kittay, E. 2005b. Equality, dignity and disability, in *Perspectives on Equality: The Second Seamus Heaney Lectures* edited by M. Lyons and F. Waldron. Dublin: The Liffey Press, 95–122.

Kline, M. 1997. Blue meanies in Alberta: tory tactics and the privatization of child welfare, in *Challenging the Public/Private Divide: Feminism, Law and Public Policy* edited by S. B. Boyd. Toronto: University of Toronto Press, 330–359.

Kukathas, C. 1997. Cultural toleration, in *Ethnicity and Group Rights: NOMOS XXXIX* edited by W. Kymlicka and I. Shapiro. New York: New York University Press, 69–104.

Kukathas, C. 2001. Is feminism bad for multiculturalism?, *Public Affairs Quarterly*, 15(2), 83–98.

Kukathas, C. 2003. *The Liberal Archipelago: A Theory of Diversity and Freedom*. Oxford: Clarendon Press.

Kukathas, C. 2008. Anarcho-multiculturalism: the pure theory of liberalism, in *Political Theory and Australian Multiculturalism* edited by G. B. Levey. New York and Oxford: Berghahn Books, 29–43.

Kyle, D. and R. Koslowski, eds 2001. *Global Human Smuggling*. Baltimore, MD: Johns Hopkins University.

Kymlicka, W. 1989a. *Liberalism, Community, and Culture*. Oxford: Oxford University Press.

Kymlicka, W. 1989b. Liberal individualism and liberal neutrality. *Ethics*, 99, 883–905.

Kymlicka, W., ed. 1995a. *The Rights of Minority Cultures*. Oxford: Oxford University Press.

Kymlicka, W. 1995b. *Multicultural Citizenship*. Oxford: Oxford University Press.

Kymlicka, W. 1997. Do we need a liberal theory of minority rights?: Reply to Carens, Young, Parekh and Forst. *Constellations*, 4(1), 72–87.

Kymlicka, W. 1998. *Finding Our Way: Rethinking Ethnocultural Relations in Canada*. Toronto: Oxford University Press.

Kymlicka, W. 2001. *Politics in the Vernacular: Nationalism, Multiculturalism, and Citizenship*. Oxford: Oxford University Press.

Kymlicka, W. 2002. *Contemporary Political Philosophy*, 2nd edn. Oxford: Oxford University Press.

Kymlicka, W. 2003. Being Canadian. *Government and Opposition*, 38(3), 357–385.

Kymlicka, W. 2004. Justice and security in the accommodation of minority nationalism, in *Ethnicity, Nationalism and Minority Rights* edited by S. May, and T. Modood and J. Squires. Cambridge: Cambridge University Press, 144–175.

Kymlicka, W. 2007a. The new debate on minority rights (and postscript), in *Multiculturalism and Political Theory* edited by A. S. Laden and D. Owen. Cambridge: Cambridge University Press, 25–59.

Kymlicka, W. 2007b. *Multicultural Odysseys*. Oxford: Oxford University Press.

Kymlicka, W. 2007c. The Canadian model of multiculturalism in a comparative perspective, in *Multiculturalism and the Canadian Constitution* edited by S. Tierney. Vancouver: UBC Press, 61–90.

Kymlicka, W. 2008. The three lives of multiculturalism, *UBC-Laurier Institution Multiculturalism Lecture Series*, University of British Columbia, April 15, 2008.

Kymlicka, W. 2010. Cultural rights and social democratic principles: dialogue with Alfredo Gomez-Müller and Gabriel Rockhill, in *Culture and Critique* edited by A. Gomez-Müller and G. Rockhill. Minneapolis, MN and London: University of Minnesota Press.

Kymlicka, W. and A. Patten, eds 2003. *Language Rights and Political Theory*. Oxford; New York: Oxford University Press.

Kymlicka, W. and B. Bashir, eds. 2008. *The Politics of Reconciliation in Multicultural Societies*. Oxford: Oxford University Press.

Kymlicka, W. and W. Norman, eds 2000. *Citizenship in Diverse Societies*. Oxford: Oxford University Press.

Lacan, J. 1977. *Ecrits: A Selection*, translated by. A. Sheridan. London: Tavistock Publications.

Ladd, E. 1999. *The Ladd Report*. New York: The Free Press.

Laden, A. 2001. *Deliberative Liberalism and Politics of Identity*. Ithaca, NY: Cornell University Press.

Lakhani, Z. 2006. *The Cross-Cultural Aspects of Security*. CCRS. Retrieved from http://www.publicsafety.gc.ca/prg/ns/ccrs/_fl/2006-08-31-pres-e.pdf.

Larmore, C. 1990. Political liberalism. *Political Theory*, 18(3), 339–360.

Larmore, C. 1994. Pluralism and reasonable disagreement. *Social Philosophy and Policy*, 11(1), 61–79.

Lattas, A. 2007. 'They always seem to be angry': the Cronulla riot and the civilising process of the sun. *The Australian Journal of Anthropology*, 18(3), 300–319.

Lau, D. C., trans. 1992. *Confucius: The Analects*, 2nd edn. Hong Kong: The Chinese University Press.

Lazzeri, C. and Caillé, A. 2007. Recognition Today: the theoretical, ethical and political stakes of the concept, in *Recognition, Work, Politics: New Directions in*

French Critical Theory edited by J-P Deranty, D. Petherbridge, J. Rundell and R. Sinnerbrink. Leiden: Brill, 89–126.

Levenson, J. 1959. *Liang Ch'i-ch'ao and the Mind of Modern China*. Cambridge, MA: Harvard University Press.

Lever, A. 2000. The politics of paradox: a response to Wendy Brown. *Constellations*, 7(2), 242–254.

Levey, G. B. 1997. Equality, autonomy, and cultural rights. *Political Theory*, 25, 215–248.

Levey, G. B. 2001. Liberal nationalism and cultural rights. *Political Studies*, 49, 670–691.

Levey, G. B. 2006. Identity and rational revisability, in *Identity, Self-Determination, and Secession* edited by I. Primoratz and A. Pavkovic. Aldershot: Ashgate, 43–60.

Levey, G. B. 2008. Secularism and religion in a multicultural age, in *Secularism, Religion and Multicultural Citizenship* edited by G. B. Levey and T. Modood. Cambridge: Cambridge University Press, 1–24.

Levy, J. T. 1997. Classifying cultural rights, in *Ethnicity and Group Rights*, *NOMOS XXXIX* edited by W. Kymlicka and I. Shapiro. New York and London: New York University Press, 22–66.

Levy, J. T. 2000. *The Multiculturalism of Fear*. Oxford: Oxford University Press.

Levy, J. T. 2005. Sexual orientation, exit, and refuge, in *Minorities Within Minorities: Equality, Rights and Diversity* edited by A. Eisenberg and J. Spinner-Halev. Cambridge: Cambridge University Press, 172–188.

Ling, L., trans. 2007. *Sangjiagou: wo du Lunyu*. Shanxi: Renminchubanshe.

Loader, I. 2002. Policing, securitization and democratization in Europe. *Criminology and Criminal Justice*, 2(2), 125–153.

Locke, J. 1963. A letter concerning toleration, in *The Works of John Locke, Volume. 6*. Aalen: Scientia, 1–58.

Loomba, A. and S. Kaul. 1994. Introduction: location, culture, postcoloniality. *Oxford Literary Review*, 16(1/2), 3–30.

Lowndes, V. 2000. Women and social capital: A comment on Hall's 'Social Capital in Britain'. *British Journal of Political Science*, 30, 533–540.

Lowndes, V. and R. Chapman. 2006. Faith, hope and clarity: developing a model of faith group involvement in civil renewal, in *Re-energising Citizenship: Strategies for Civil Renewal* edited by T. Brannan, P. John, and G. Stoker. Basingstoke: Palgrave, 163–184.

MacDonald, F. 2008. The neoliberal state and multiculturalism: the need for democratic accountability. Ph.D. dissertation, University of British Columbia.

MacDonald, F. 2009. The Manitoba Government's shift to 'autonomous' first nations child welfare: empowerment or privatization? in *First Nations First Thoughts* edited by A. M. Timpson. Vancouver: UBC Press, 173–198.

Macedo, S. 1991. *Liberal Virtues*. Oxford: Oxford University Press.

Macedo, S. 1995. Liberal civic education: the case of God v. John Rawls?, *Ethics*, 105, 468–496.

Mackenzie, C. 2007. Relational autonomy, sexual justice and cultural pluralism, in *Sexual Justice, Cultural Justice: Critical Perspectives in Political Theory and Practise* edited by B. Arneil, M. Deveaux, R. Dhamoon and A. Eisenberg. London: Routledge, 103–121.

Mackenzie, C. and N. Stoljar, eds 2000. *Relational Autonomy: Feminist Perspectives on Autonomy, Agency, and the Social Self*. New York: Oxford University Press.

MacKinnon, C. A. 1989. *Towards a Feminist Theory of the State*. Cambridge, MA: Harvard University Press.

Maclure, J. 2007. La reconnaissance engage-t-elle à l'essentialisme? *Philosophiques*, 34(1), 77–96.

Maclure, J. 2010. Respect for reasonable cultural diversity as a principle of political morality, in *The Plural States of Recognition* edited by M. Seymour and M. Blanchard. New York: Palgrave Macmillan.

Maclure, J. and C. Taylor. 2010. *Laïcité et liberté de conscience*. Montreal: Boréal.

Mamdani, M. 2004. *Good Muslim, Bad Muslim*. New York: Pantheon Books.

Margalit, A., and M. Halbertal. 1994. Liberalism and the right to culture, *Social Research*, 61, 491–510

Markell, P. 2000. The recognition of politics: a comment on Emcke and Tully. *Constellations*, 7(4), 496–506

Markell, P. 2003. *Beyond Recognition*. Princeton, NJ: Princeton University Press.

Marshall, T.H. 1965. Citizenship and social class (1949), in *Class, Citizenship and Social Development*. Garden City, NJ: Doubleday, 71–134.

Mason, A. 2007. Multiculturalism and the critique of essentialism, in *Multiculturalism and Political Theory* edited by A. S. Laden and D. Owen. Cambridge: Cambridge University Press, 221–243.

Massell, G. 1974. *The Surrogate Proletariat: Moslem Women and Revolutionary Strategies in Soviet Central Asia, 1919–1929*. Princeton, NJ: Princeton University Press.

May, C. D. 2006. What could anyone have against Canada? The view from Washington. *National Post*, 8 June.

Mazzarella, W. 2004. Culture, globalization, mediation. *Annual Review of Anthropology*, 33, 345–367.

Mc Andrew, M. 2008. Quebec interculturalism policy: convergence and divergence with the Canadian model, in *Multiculturalism: Public Policy and Problem Areas in Canada and India* edited by C. Raj, A. Nafey, and M. Mc Andrew. Delhi: Manak Publishers, 204–221.

McGrath, C. 2006. Muslim Advisory Group, ABC Radio AM, February 25.

McKinnon, C. 2006. *Toleration*. Abingdon: Routledge.

McNay, L. 2008. *Against Recognition*. Cambridge: Polity.

Means, A. 2002. Narrative argumentation: arguing with natives. *Constellations*, 9(2), 221–245.

Mehta, U. 1999. *Liberalism and Empire*. Princeton, NJ: Princeton University Press.

Mengue, P. 2003. *Deleuze et la question de la démocratie*. Paris: L'Harmattan.

Mercer, P. 2005. Australia acts on forced marriage, BBC News. Accessed 6 June 2009, http://news.bbc.co.uk/2/hi/asia-pacific/4740871.stm.

Meyers, D. T. 2000. Feminism and women's autonomy: the challenge of female genital cutting. *Metaphilosophy*, 31(5), 469–491.

Mickleburgh, R. 2006. Harper defends Canadian diversity. *Globe and Mail*, 20 June.

Miller, D. 1995. *On Nationality*. Oxford: Clarendon Press.

Miller, D. 2004. Social justice in multicultural societies, in *Cultural Diversity versus Economic Solidarity* edited by P. van Parijs. Brussels: Editions de boeck University, 13–31.

Miller, D. 2007. *National Responsibility and Global Justice*. Oxford: Oxford University Press.

Mills, C. 1997. *The Racial Contract*. Ithaca, NY: Cornell University Press.

Minow, M. 1990. *Making all the Difference*. Ithaca, NY: Cornell University Press.

Miyakawa, H. 1960. The Confucianization of South China, in *The Confucian Persuasion* edited by Arthur Wright. Stanford, CA: Stanford University Press, 21–46.

Modood, T. 2005. *Multicultural Politics*. Edinburgh: Edinburgh University Press.

Modood, T. 2007. *Multiculturalism: A Civic Idea*. Cambridge: Polity Press.

Modood, T. 2008. Muslims, religious equality and secularism, in *Secularism, Religion and Multicultural Citizenship* edited by G. B. Levey and T. Modood. Cambridge: Cambridge University Press, 164–185.

Modood, T. and F. Ahmad. 2007. British Muslim perspectives on multiculturalism. *Theory, Culture and Society*, 24(2), 187–213.

Mohanty, C. 2003. *Feminism Without Borders: Decolonizing Theory, Practicing Solidarity*. Durham, NC: Duke University Press.

Mongia, P. 1996. *Contemporary Postcolonial Theory: A Reader*. New York: St. Martin's Press.

Monture-Angus, P. 1995. *Thunder in my Soul: A Mohawk Woman Speaks*. Halifax: Fernwood Publishing.

Monture-Angus, P. 2002. *Journeying Forward: Dreaming First Nations' Independence*. Halifax, Nova Scotia: Fernwood Publishing.

Moore, M. 1996. On reasonableness. *Journal of Applied Philosophy*, 13(2), 167–178.

Morris, J. 2001. Impairment and disability: constructing an ethics of care that promotes human rights. *Hypatia*, 16(4), 1–16.

Moses, D. 2006. Pogrom Talk, in *On line Opinion*, 11 January 2006. Accessed 15 May 2009, http://www.onlineopinion.com.au/view.asp?article=4038.

Motha, S. 2007. Veiled women and the affect of religion in democracy. *Journal of Law and Society*, 34(1), 139–162.

Mozert v Hawkins 827 F2d 1058 (6th Cir 1987).

Murphy, A. R. 1997. Tolerance, toleration, and the liberal tradition. *Polity*, 29(4), 593–623.

Nagel, T. 1991. *Equality and Partiality*. Oxford: Oxford University Press.

Narayan, U. 1997. Contesting cultures: 'Westernization,' respect for cultures, and third-world feminists, in *The Second Wave* edited by L. Nicholson. London: Routledge, 396–414.

Narayan, U. 1998. Essence of culture and a sense of history: a feminist critique of cultural essentialism. *Hypatia*, 13(2), 86–107.

Nasstrom, S. 2007. The legitimacy of the people. *Political Theory*, 35(2), 624–658.

National Commission for Minorities (India). N.D. Minority population. Accessed 9 Janunary 2009, http://ncm.nic.in/.

Needham, J. 1956. *Science and Civilisation in China, Volume 2*. Cambridge: Cambridge University Press, 232–246.

Neuhaus, R. 1984. *The Naked Public Square*. Grand Rapids, MI: Eerdman's.

Nino, C.S. 1996. *The Constitution of Deliberative Democracy*. New Haven, CT: Yale University Press.

Norton, A. 2011. On the Muslim question, in *Toleration and Recognition in an Age of Religious Pluralism* edited by M. Mookherjee. Berlin: Springer, forthcoming.

Nussbaum, M. 1999. *Sex and Social Justice*. Oxford: Oxford University Press.

Nussbaum, M. 2006. *Frontiers of Justice: Disability, Nationality, Species Membership*. Cambridge, MA: Harvard University Press.

Nussbaum, M. 2008. *Liberty of Conscience: In Defense of America's Tradition of Religious Equality*. New York: Basic Books.

O'Neill, B. 2005. Canadian Women's religious volunteerism, in *Gender and Social Capital* edited by B. O'Neill and E. Gilengil. London: Routledge, 185–212.

O'Neill, O. 1988. Abstraction, idealization and ideology, in *Moral Philosophy and Contemporary Problems* edited by J. D. G. Evans. Cambridge: Cambridge University Press, 55–70.

O'Neill, O. 1989. *Constructions of Reason*. Cambridge: Cambridge University Press.

O'Neill, O. 1996. *Toward Justice and Virtue*. Cambridge: Cambridge University Press.

O'Neill, O. 2003. Constructivism in Rawls and Kant, in *The Cambridge Companion to Rawls* edited by S. Freeman. Cambridge: Cambridge University Press, 347–367.

Office of Multicultural Affairs ([OMA)] (1989) *National Agenda for a Multicultural Australia*. (Canberra: AGPS).

Okin, S. M. 1998. Feminism and multiculturalism: some tensions. *Ethics*, 108, 661–684.

Okin, S. M. 1999. Reply, in *Is Multiculturalism Bad for Women? Susan Moller Okin with Respondents* edited by J. Cohen, M. Howard and M.C. Nussbaum. Princeton, NJ: Princeton University Press, 115–132.

Okin, S. M. 2002. 'Mistresses of their own destiny': group rights, gender, and realistic rights of exit. *Ethics*, 112, 205–30.

Okin, S. M. et al. 1999. *Is Multiculturalism Bad for Women?* Princeton, NJ: Princeton University Press.

Olson, J. 2004. *Abolition of White Democracy*. Minneappolis, MN: University of Minnesota Press.

Olson, J. 2008. The limits of colorblind and multicultural personhood, *Stanford Agora: An Online Journal of Legal Perspectives*, 2(1), http://agora.standford.edu/agora/sgi-bin/article2_race.cgi?library=olson.

Owen, D. and J. Tully. 2007. Redistribution and recognition: two approaches, in *Multiculturalism and Political Theory* edited by A. Laden and D. Owen. Cambridge: Cambridge University Press, 265–291.

Parekh, B. 2000. *Rethinking Multiculturalism: Cultural Diversity and Political Theory*. London: Macmillan.

Parekh, B. 2006. Europe, liberalism and the 'Muslim question', in *Multiculturalism, Muslims and Citizenship: A European Approach* edited by T. Modood, A. Triandafyllidou and R. Zapata-Barrero. London: Routledge, 179–203.

Parry, B. 1987. Current problems in the study of colonial discourse. *Oxford Literary Review*, 9(1–2), 27–58.

Patrick, M. 2000. Liberalism, rights and recognition. *Philosophy and Social Criticism*, 26(5), 26–46.

Patterson, O. 1999. Liberty against the democratic state: on the historical and contemporary source of American distrust, in *Democracy and Trust* edited by M. E. Warren. Cambridge: Cambridge University Press, 151–207.

Patton, P. 1995. Mabo, freedom and the politics of difference. *Australian Journal of Political Science*, 30, 108–119.

Patton, P. 2005a. Deleuze and democratic politics, in *On Radical Democracy: Politics Between Abundance and Lack* edited by Lars Tønder and Lasse Thomassen. Manchester: Manchester University Press, 50–67.

Patton, P. 2005b. Deleuze and democracy. *Contemporary Political Theory*, 4(4), 400–413.

Patton, P. 2007a. Derrida, politics and democracy to come. *Philosophy Compass*, 2(6), 766–780.

Patton, P. 2007b. Derrida's engagement with political philosophy, in *Histories of Postmodernism* edited by Mark Bevir, Jill Hargis and Sara Rushing. New York and London: Routledge, 149–169.

Patton, P. 2010. Philosophy, politics and political normativity, in *Deleuzian Concepts: Philosophy, Colonization, Politics* edited by P. Patton. Stanford, CA: Stanford University Press, 137–60.

Pearce, N. 2004. Diversity vs. solidarity: a new progressive dilemma. *Renewal: A Journal of Labour Politics*, 12(3).

Perpetch, N. 2007. Imams deny seeking full sharia law. *AAP*, February 14. Accessed 2 April 2009, URL http://www.news.com.au/story/0,23599,21225290-1245,00.html (accessed 2 April 2009).

Petherbridge, D. 2009. *The Critical Theory of Axel Honneth*. Leiden and Boston, MA: Brill.

Phelan, S. 2001. *Sexual Strangers: Gays, Lesbians, and Dilemmas of Citizenship*. Philadelphia, PA: Temple University Press.

Phillips, A. 2007a. What is 'culture'?, in *Sexual Justice, Cultural Justice: Critical Perspectives in Political Theory and Practise* edited by B. Arneil, M. Deveaux, R. Dhamoon and A. Eisenberg. London: Routledge, 15–29.

Phillips, A. 2007b. *Multiculturalism without Culture*. Princeton, NJ: Princeton University Press.

Phillips, A. and S. Saharso. 2008. The rights of women and the crisis of multiculturalism. *Ethnicities*, 8(3), 291–301.

Phillips, T. 2004. Multiculturalism's legacy is 'have a nice day' racism: the mere celebration of diversity does nothing to redress inequality. *The Guardian*, Friday 28 May, http://www.guardian.co.uk/comment/story/0,3604,1226527,00.html.

Phoenix, A. 2005. Remembered racialization: young people and positioning in differential understandings, in *Racialization: Studies in Theory and Practice* edited by K. Murji and J. Solomos. Oxford: Oxford University Press, 103–122.

Pitts, J. 2005. *A Turn Towards Empire: The Rise of Imperial Liberalism in Britain and in France*. Princeton, NJ: Princeton University Press.

Pogge, T. 1997. Migration and poverty, in *Citizenship and Exclusion* edited by V. Bader. Basingstoke: Macmillan, 12–27.

Povinelli, E. A. 1998. The state of shame: Australian multiculturalism and the crisis of indigenous citizenship. *Critical Inquiry*, 24(2), 575–610.

Povinelli, E. 1999. The cunning of recognition: a reply to John Frow and Meaghan Morris. *Critical Inquiry*, 25(3), 631–637.

Povinelli, E.A. 2002. *The Cunning of Recognition: Indigenous Alterities and the Making of Australian Multiculturalism*. Durham, NC: Duke University Press.

Prakash, G. 1990. Writing post-orientalist histories of the Third World, *Comparative Studies in Society and History*, 32(2), 383–408.

PRI. 2003. Policy Research Initiative, Privy Council Office, Government of Canada, Draft Discussion Paper: 'Social Capital: Building on a Network-based Analysis', October 2003.

PRI. 2004. Policy Research Initiative, Privy Council Office, Government of Canada, Synthesis Report *Expert Workshop on the Measurement of Social Capital for Public Policy*. 8 June 8, 2004.

Prins, B. and S. Saharso. 2008. In the spotlight: a blessing and a curse for immigrant women in the Netherlands. *Ethnicities*, 8(3), 365–384.

Putnam, R. 1995. Bowling alone: America's declining social capital. *Journal of Democracy*, 6(1), 65–78.

Putnam, R. 2000. *Bowling Alone: The Collapse and Revival of American Community*. New York: Touchstone.

Putnam, R. 2007. *E Pluribus Unum*: diversity and community in the twenty-first century: the 2006 Johan Skytte Prize Lecture. *Scandinavian Political Studies*, 30(2) 137–174.

Rawls, J. 1971. *A Theory of Justice*. Cambridge, MA: Harvard University Press.

Rawls, J. 1985. Justice as fairness: political not metaphysical. *Philosophy and Public Affairs*, 14(3), 223–51.

Rawls, J. 1993. *Political Liberalism*. New York: Columbia University Press.

Rawls, J. 1999a. *The Law of Peoples*. Cambridge, MA: Harvard University Press.

Rawls, J. 1999b. The idea of an overlapping consensus, in *Collected Papers* edited by S. Freeman. Cambridge, MA: Harvard University Press, 421–448.

Raz, J. 1986. *The Morality of Freedom*. Oxford: Clarendon Press.

Raz, J. 1994. *Ethics in the Public Domain: Essays in the Morality of Law and Politics*. Oxford: Clarendon Press.

Raz, J. 1998. Multiculturalism. *Ratio Juris*, 11(3), 193–205.

Razack, S. H. 2007. 'Your client has a profile:' race and national security in Canada after 9/11. *Studies in Law, Politics and Society*, 40, 3–40.

Reich, R. 2002. *Bridging Liberalism and Multiculturalism in American Education*. Chicago, IL: University of Chicago Press.

Renault, E. 2004. *L'Expérience de l'injustice. Reconnaissance et clinique de l'injustice*. Paris: La Découverte.

Renault, E. 2008. *Souffrances sociales. Sociologie, psychologie et politique*. Paris: La Découverte.

Richardson, H. 2002. *Democratic Autonomy: Public Reasoning and the Ends of Policy*. Oxford: Oxford University Press.

Ricoeur, P. 2005. *The Course of Recognition*. Cambridge MA : Harvard University Press.

Riegel, J. 1986. Poetry and the legend of Confucius's exile. *Journal of the American Oriental Society*, 106(1), 13–22.

Riegel, J. 2006. Confucius. *Stanford Encyclopedia of Philosophy*. http://plato.stanford.edu/entries/confucius/.

Risley, S. H. 2006. The sociology of security: sociological approaches to contemporary and historical securitization. Paper presented at the annual meeting of the American Sociological Association, Montreal Convention Center, Montreal, Quebec, Canada, 5 March 2006.

Rorty, R. 1999. *Achieving our Country*. Cambridge, MA: Harvard University Press.

Rorty, R. 2000. Is 'cultural recognition' a useful notion for leftist politics? *Critical Horizons*, 1(1), 7–20.

Rosaldo, R. 1989. *Culture and Truth*. Boston, MA: Beacon Press.

Roy, O. 2004. *Globalised Islam: The Search for a New Ummah*. London: Hurst and Company.

Roy, O. 2005. A clash of cultures or a debate on Europe's values? *ISIM Review*, 15, 67. Accessed 8 August 2009, http://www.isim.nl/content/content_page.asp?n1=4andn2=21andn3=3.

Ruggie, G. 2000. *Constructing the World Polity*. London: Routledge.

Saharso, S. 2000. Female autonomy and cultural imperative: two hearts beating together, in *Citizenship in Diverse Societies* edited by W. Kymlicka and W. Norman. Oxford UK: Oxford University Press, 224–244.

Saharso, S. 2003. Feminist ethics, autonomy and the politics of multiculturalism. *Feminist Theory*, 4(2), 199–215.

Said, E. 1979. *Orientalism*. New York: Vintage.

Sartori, G. 2002. *Pluralismo, Multiculturalismo e Estranei*. Milan: Rizzoli.

Schaap, A. 2005. *Political Reconciliation*. London: Routledge.

Scheffler, S. 1994. *Human Morality*. New York: Oxford University Press.

Scheffler, S. 2007. Immigration and the significance of culture, *Philosophy and Public Affairs*, 35(2), 93–125.

Schmidt-am-Busch, H-C. and C. Zurn. 2010. *The Philosophy of Recognition: Historical and Contemporary Perspectives*. Lanham, MD: Lexington Books.

Schmitter, P. 1998. Is it possible to democratize the Europolity?, in *Democracy and the European Union* edited by A. Follesdal and P. Koslowski. Berlin: Springer Verlag, 13–36.

Scott, D. 2003. Culture in political theory. *Political Theory*, 31(1), 92–115.

Sen, A. 2006. *Identity and Violence: The Illusion of Destiny*. New York: Norton.

Shachar, A. 2001. *Multicultural Jurisdictions: Cultural Differences and Women's Rights*. Cambridge: Cambridge University Press.

Shachar, A. 2009. What we owe women: the view from multicultural feminism, in *Towards a Humanist Justice* edited by D. Satz and R. Reich. Oxford: Oxford University Press, 143–165.

Shaw, K. 2008. *Indigeneity and Political Theory: Sovereignty and the Limits of the Political*. Hoboken, NJ: Taylor and Francis.

Shklar, J. N. 1989. The liberalism of fear, in *Liberalism and the Moral Life* edited by N.L. Rosenblum. Cambridge, MA: Harvard University Press, 21–39.

Sibertin-Blanc, G. 2008. Peuple et territoire: Deleuze lecteur de la *Revue d'Études Palestiniennes*. To appear in Catherine Mayaux (ed.) *Ecrivains et intellectuels français face au monde arabe*, Actes du Colloque de l'Université de Cergy-Pontoise, January 31–February 2. Available online at : www. europhilosophie. eu/recherche/IMG/pdf/Deleuze_et_Palestine.pdf.

Skocpol, T. 2000. *The Missing Middle: Working Families and the Future of American Social Policy*. New York: Norton.

Smidt, C. 2003. *Religion as Social Capital*. Waco, TX: Baylor University Press.

Smith, N. H. 2009. Work and the struggle for recognition. *European Journal of Political Theory*, 8(1), 46–60.

Smith, R.M. 1993. Beyond Tocqueville, Myrdal and Hartz: the multiple traditions in America. *American Political Science Review*, 87(3), 549–567.

Song, S. 2007. *Justice, Gender and the Politics of Multiculturalism*. Cambridge: Cambridge University Press.

Spinner, J. 1994. *The Boundaries of Citizenship: Race, Ethnicity and Nationality in the Liberal State*. Baltimore, MD: Johns Hopkins University Press.

Spinner-Halev, J. 2000. *Surviving Diversity: Religion and Democratic Citizenship*. Baltimore, MD: Johns Hopkins University Press.

Spinner-Halev, J. 2001. Feminism, multiculturalism, oppression and the state. *Ethics*, 112, 84–113.

Spinner-Halev, J. 2005. Autonomy, association and pluralism, in *Minorities within Minorities: Equality, Rights and Diversity* edited by A. Eisenberg and J. Spinner-Halev. Cambridge: Cambridge University Press, 157–171.

Spivak, G. C. 1988. Deconstructing subaltern historiography, in *Subaltern Studies VI*. Delhi: Oxford University Press, 3–32.

Spivak, G. C. 1990. Postcoloniality and value, in *Literary Theory Today* edited by P. Collier and H. Gaya-Ryan. Cambridge: Polity Press, 219–234.

Spivak, G. C. 1993. *Outside in the Teaching Machine*. London: Routledge.

Squadrito, K. S. 1996. Locke and the dispossession of the American Indian, *American Indian Culture and Research Journal*, 20(4), 141–181.

Srivastava, S. 2007. Troubles with 'anti-racist multiculturalism': the challenges of anti-racist and feminist activism, in *Race and Racism in the 21st Century Canada: Continuity, Complexity and Change* edited by S. Hier and S. Bolaria. Peterborough: Broadview Press, 291–311.

Swaine, L. 2006. *The Liberal Conscience: Politics and Principle in a World of Religious Pluralism*. New York: Columbia University Press.

Tamir, Y. 1993. *Liberal Nationalism*. Princeton, NJ: Princeton University Press.

Tamir, Y. 1995. Two concepts of multiculturalism, *Journal of Philosophy of Education*, 29, 161–179.

Tamir, Y. 1996. Hands off clitoridectomy, *Boston Review*, 21, 3. Accessed 28 January 2009, http://bostonreview.net/BR21.3/Tamir.html.

Taylor, C. 1975. *Hegel*. Cambridge: Cambridge University Press.

Taylor, C. 1985. *Philosophy and the Human Sciences: Philosophical Papers 2*. Cambridge: Cambridge University Press.

Taylor, C. 1991. *The Ethics of Authenticity*. Cambridge, MA: Harvard University Press.

Taylor, C. 1992. The politics of recognition, in *Multiculturalism and 'The Politics of Recognition': An Essay*, edited by A. Gutmann. Princeton, NJ: Princeton University Press, 25–74.

Taylor, C. 1993. *Reconciling the Solitudes: Essays on Canadian Federalism and Nationalism*. Montreal: McGill-Queen's University Press.

Taylor, C. 1995. *Philosophical Arguments*. Cambridge: Cambridge University Press.

Taylor, C. 1999. Democratic exclusion (and its remedies?), in *Citizenship, Diversity and Pluralism* edited by A. Cairns, J. Courtney and P. Mackinnon. Montreal: McGill-Queen's University Press, 265–287.

Taylor, C. 2003. Response to Bhabha, in *Globalizing Rights* edited by M.J. Gibney. Oxford: Oxford University Press, 184–188.

Taylor, C. 2004. *Modern Social Imaginaries*. Durham, NC: Duke University Press.

Taylor, C. 2007. *A Secular Age*. Cambridge, MA: Harvard University Press.

Taylor, K. 2006. You think they would be more grateful to be Canadians. *Globe and Mail*, 10 June.

Tomasi, J. 1995. Kymlicka, liberalism and respect for cultural minorities., *Ethics*, 105, 580–603.

Tronto, J. 1993. *Moral Boundaries: A Political Argument for an Ethic of Care*. New York: Routledge.

Tully, C. 2000. Struggles over recognition and distribution. *Constellations*, 7(4), 469–482.

Tully, J. 1995. *Strange Multiplicity: Constitutionalism in an Age of Diversity*. Cambridge: Cambridge University Press.

Tully, J. 2000. The challenge of reimagining citizenship and belonging in multicultural and multinational societies, in *The Demands of Citizenship* edited by C. MacKinnon and I. Hamsphir-Monk. London: Continuum, 212–234.

Tully, J. 2009a. Recognition, distribution and civic freedom: the emergence of a new field, in *Public Philosophy in a New Key. Vol. 1: Democracy and Civic Freedom*. Cambridge, New York: Cambridge University Press, 291–316.

Tully, J. 2009b. Reimagining belonging in diverse societies, in *Public Philosophy in a New Key. Volume 1: Democracy and Civic Freedom*. Cambridge, New York: Cambridge University Press, 160–184.

Turley-Ewart, J. 2006. Multiculturalism has its limits. *National Post*, 8 June.

Turner, D. 2006. *This is Not a Peace Pipe: Towards a Critical Indigenous Philosophy*. Toronto: University of Toronto Press.

Turpel-Lafond, M. 1997. Patriarchy and paternalism: the legacy of the Canadian state for first nations women, in *Women and the Canadian State* edited by C. Andrew and S. Rodgers. Kingston and Montreal: McGill-Queen's University Press, 64–78.

United Nations Development Programme. 2004. *The Human Development Report 2004: Cultural Liberty in Today's Diverse World*. New York: United Nations Development Programme.

Van den Brink, B. and D. Owen. 2007. *Recognition and Power*. Cambridge: Cambridge University Press.

Van Dyke, V. 1982. Collective entities and moral rights: problems in liberal democratic thought. *Journal of Politics*, 44, 21–40.

van Gusteren, H. 1998. *A Theory of Citizenship*. Boulder, CO: Westview Press.

van Parijs, P., ed. 2004. *Cultural Diversity versus Economic Solidarity*. Brussels: Editions de boeck Univesity.

Velayutham, S. and A. Wise, eds 2009. *Everyday Multiculturalism*. Basingstoke: Palgrave Macmillan.

Verba, S., K. L. Schlozman, and H. E. Brady. 1995. *Voice and Equality: Civic Voluntarism in American Politics*. Cambridge, MA: Harvard University Press.

Vertovec, S. and R. Cohen (eds). 2002. *Conceiving Cosmopolitanism: Theory, Context and Practice*. Oxford: Oxford University Press.

Vertovec, S. and S. Wessendorf. 2005. Migration and cultural, religious and linguistic diversity in Europe: an overview of issues and trends. Working Paper, COMPAS, Oxford.

Wacquant, L. 2005. Penalization, depoliticization, racialization: on the over-incarceration of immigrants in the European Union, in *Perspectives On Punishment: The Contours Of Control* edited by S. Armstrong. Oxford: Oxford University Press, 83–100.

Wald, K. 1997. *Religion and Politics in America*. Lanham, MD: Rowman and Littlefield Publishers.

Wald, K., D. Owen, and S. Hill Jr. 1990. Political cohesion in churches. *Journal of Politics*, 52(1), 197–216.

Waldron, J. 1992. Minority cultures and the cosmopolitan alternative, *University of Michigan Journal of Law Reform*, 25(3–4), 751–93.

Waldron, J. 1995. Minority Cultures and the Cosmopolitan Alternative, in *The Rights of Minority Cultures* edited by W. Kymlicka. Oxford: Oxford University Press, 93–121.

Waldron, J. 1999. *Law and Disagreement*. Oxford: Oxford University Press.

Waldron, J. 2000. What is cosmopolitan? *Journal of Political Philosophy* 8, 227–44.

Waldron, J. 2003. Toleration and reasonableness, in *The Culture of Toleration in Diverse Societies* edited by C. McKinnon and D. Castiglione. Manchester: Manchester University Press, 13–37.

Waley, A., trans. 1989. *The Analects of Confucius*. New York: Vintage Books.

Walker, R. 1995. *To Be Real: Telling the Truth and Changing the Face of Feminism*. New York: Anchor Books.

Walzer, M. 1984. *Spheres of Justice*. New York: Basic Books.

Warren, M. 2007. Citizen representatives, in *Designing Deliberative Democracy* edited by M. Warren and H. Pearse. Oxford: Oxford University Press, 29–49.

Watson, B., translator 1963. *Mo Tzu: Basic Writings*. Cambridge: Cambridge University Press.

Weale, A. 1999. *Democracy*. London: St. Martin's.

Weinstock, D. 2006. Is 'identity' a danger to democracy?, in *Identity, Self-Determination, and Secession* edited by I. Primoratz and A. Pavkovic. Aldershot: Ashgate, 15–26.

Wendell, S. 1996. *The Rejected Body: Feminist Philosophical Reflections on Disability*. New York: Routledge.

Wente, M. 2006. Generation Jihad: angry, young, born-again believers. *Globe and Mail*, 6 June.

Werbner, P. 2002. *Imagined Diasporas among Manchester Muslims: The Public Performance of Pakistani Transnational Identity Politics*. Oxford and Santa Fe, CA: James Currey/School of American Research Press.

Werbner, P. 2004. The predicament of the diaspora and millennial Islam: reflections in the Aftermath of September 11. *Ethnicities*, 4(4), 451–476.

Werbner, P. 2007. Veiled interventions in pure space: honour, shame and embodied struggles among Muslims in Britain and France. *Theory, Culture and Society*, 24(2), 161–186.

Whelen, F. 1983. Democracy and the boundary problem, in *Liberal Democracy* edited by J. Pennock and J. Chapman. New York: New York University Press, 13–47.

Wieviorka, M. 1998. Is multiculturalism the solution? *Ethnic and Racial Studies*, 21(5), 881–910.

Wilcox, C. and T. Jelen. 1990. Evangelicals and political tolerance. *American Political Quarterly*, 18(1), 25–46.

Wilkinson, D., P. Ryan, and J. Hiller. 2001. Variation in morality rates in Australia: correlation with indigenous status, remoteness and socio-economic deprivation. *Journal of Public Health Medicine*, 23, 74–77.

Wilkinson, D., P. Ryan and J. Hiller, eds 2001. Short report; variation in mortality rates in Australia: correlation with indigenous status, remoteness and socio-economic deprivation, *Journal of Health and Medicine*, 23, 74–77.

Williams, G. 2007. Anti-terror laws. *Perspective*, ABC Radio National, transcript at URL http://www.abc.net.au/rn/perspective/stories/2007/1857402.htm.

Williams, M. 1995. Justice towards groups: political not juridical. *Political Theory*, 23(1), 67–91.

Williams, M. 1998. *Voice, Trust and Memory. Marginalized Groups and the Failings of Liberal Representation*. Princeton, NJ: Princeton University Press.

Williams M. 2000. The uneasy alliance of group representation and deliberative democracy, in *Citizenship in Diverse Societies* edited by W. Kymlicka and W. Norman. Oxford: Oxford University Press, 124–154.

Williams, M. 2005. Tolerable liberalism, in *Minorities within Minorities: Equality, Rights and Diversity* edited by A. Eisenberg and J. Spinner-Halev. Cambridge: Cambridge University Press, 19–40.

Williams, P. and L. Chrisman, eds 1993. *Colonial Discourse and Postcolonial Theory*. Hemel Hempstead: Harvester Wheatsheaf.

Wimsatt, W. 1974. Complexity and organization, in *PSA 1972: Proceedings of the 1972 Biennial Meeting of the Philosophy of Science Association* edited by K. F. Schaffner and R. S. Cohen. Dordrecht: Riedel, 67–86.

Wolfe, A. 1998. *One Nation After All*. New York: Viking.

Wolfe, A. and J. Klausen. 1997. Identity politics and the welfare state. *Social Philosophy and Policy*, 14(2), 231–255.

Wuthnow, R. 2002. Bridging the privileged and the marginalized?, in *Democracies in Flux: The Evolution of Social Capital in Contemporary Society* edited by R. Putnam and K. Goss. Oxford: Oxford University Press, 59–102.

Yaxley, L. 2005. Bronwyn Bishop calls for hijab ban in schools. *The World Today*, August 29. Accessed 6 June 2009, http://www.abc.net.au/worldtoday/content/2005/s1448343.htm.

Young, I. M. 2007. Structural injustice and the politics of difference, in *Multiculturalism and Political Theory* edited by A. S. Laden and D. Owen. Cambridge: Cambridge University Press, 60–88.

Young, I. M. 1990. *Justice and the Politics of Difference*. Princeton: NJ: Princeton University Press.

Young, I. M. 1996. Communication and the other: beyond deliberative democracy, in *Democracy and Difference: Contesting the Boundaries of the Political* edited by S. Benhabib. Princeton: NJ: Princeton University Press, 120–136.

Young, I. M. 2000. *Inclusion and Democracy*. Oxford: Oxford University Press.

Yúdice, G. 2003. *The Expediency of Culture: Uses of Culture in the Global Era*. Durham, NC and London: Duke University Press.

Zagorin, P. 2003. *How the Idea of Religious Toleration Came to the West*. Princeton, NJ: Princeton University Press.

Zizek, S. 2008. *Violence*. London: Picador.

Zwartz, B. 2008. Local Muslim clerics accused. *The Age*, 21 November 21. Accessed 8 April 2009, http://www.theage.com.au/national/local-muslim-clerics-accused-200811206ctp.html?page=-1.

Index